America's
TEST KITCHEN

ALSO BY THE EDITORS AT AMERICA'S TEST KITCHEN

The America's Test Kitchen Family Baking Book
The America's Test Kitchen Family Cookbook
The Best of America's Test Kitchen 2007, 2008, 2009, 2010
Cooking for Two 2009, 2010
The Best Simple Recipes

THE COOK'S COUNTRY SERIES:
Cook's Country Best Potluck Recipes
Cook's Country Best Lost Suppers
Cook's Country Best Grilling Recipes
The Cook's Country Cookbook
America's Best Lost Recipes

THE BEST RECIPE SERIES:
More Best Recipes
The Best Skillet Recipes
The Best Slow & Easy Recipes
The Best Chicken Recipes
The Best International Recipe
The Best Make-Ahead Recipe
The Best 30-Minute Recipe
The Best Light Recipe
The Cook's Illustrated Guide to Grilling & Barbecue
Best American Side Dishes
The New Best Recipe
The Best Cover & Bake Recipes
The Best Meat Recipes
Baking Illustrated
Restaurant Favorites at Home
The Best Vegetable Recipes
The Best Italian Classics
The Best American Classics
The Best Soups & Stews

THE TV COMPANION SERIES:
The Complete America's Test Kitchen TV Show Cookbook
America's Test Kitchen TV Companion Book 2009
Behind the Scenes with America's Test Kitchen
Test Kitchen Favorites
Cooking at Home with America's Test Kitchen
America's Test Kitchen Live!
Inside America's Test Kitchen
Here in America's Test Kitchen
The America's Test Kitchen Cookbook

834 Kitchen Quick Tips

For a full listing of all our books or to order titles:
http://www.cooksillustrated.com
http://www.americastestkitchen.com
or call 800-611-0759

America's
TEST KITCHEN

Light &
Healthy

2010

THE YEAR'S BEST RECIPES LIGHTENED UP

BY THE EDITORS OF
AMERICA'S TEST KITCHEN

PHOTOGRAPHY BY
CARL TREMBLAY, KELLER + KELLER, AND DANIEL J. VAN ACKERE

AMERICA'S TEST KITCHEN
17 Station Street, Brookline, MA 02445

Library of Congress Cataloging-in-Publication Data
The Editors at America's Test Kitchen

AMERICA'S TEST KITCHEN LIGHT & HEALTHY 2010:
The Year's Best Recipes Lightened Up

1st Edition

Hardcover: $35 US
ISBN-13: 978-1-933615-57-8   ISBN-10: 1-933615-57-5
1. Cooking. 1. Title
2010

Manufactured in Canada

10 9 8 7 6 5 4 3 2 1

Distributed by America's Test Kitchen
17 Station Street, Brookline, MA 02445

EDITORIAL DIRECTOR: Jack Bishop
EXECUTIVE EDITOR: Elizabeth Carduff
FOOD EDITOR: Julia Collin Davison
SENIOR EDITOR: Rachel Toomey
ASSOCIATE EDITORS: Louise Flaig and Suzannah McFerran
TEST COOKS: Erika Bruce, Jennifer Lalime, Chris O'Conner, Adelaide Parker, Dan Souza, and Dan Zuccarello
DESIGN DIRECTOR: Amy Klee
ART DIRECTOR: Greg Galvan
DESIGNER: Erica Lee
FRONT COVER PHOTOGRAPH: Carl Tremblay
STAFF PHOTOGRAPHER: Daniel J. van Ackere
ADDITIONAL PHOTOGRAPHER: Keller + Keller
FOOD STYLING: Marie Piraino and Mary Jane Sawyer
PRODUCTION DIRECTOR: Guy Rochford
SENIOR PRODUCTION MANAGER: Jessica Quirk
SENIOR PROJECT MANAGER: Alice Carpenter
PRODUCTION AND TRAFFIC COORDINATOR: Laura Collins
COLOR AND IMAGING SPECIALIST: Andrew Mannone
PRODUCTION AND IMAGING SPECIALISTS: Judy Blomquist and Lauren Pettapiece
COPYEDITOR: Barbara Wood
PROOFREADER: Kathryn Blatt
INDEXER: Elizabeth Parson

PICTURED ON THE FRONT COVER: Spaghetti Carbonara (page 121)
PICTURED OPPOSITE TITLE PAGE: Oven-Fried Fish (page 109)
PICTURED ON BACK OF JACKET: Spinach Lasagna (page 131), Roasted Vegetable Pizza with Broccoli and Feta (page 135), Philly Cheesesteak (page 95), Marble Cheesecake (page 277)

Contents

Introduction

AS MY FOUR CHILDREN AND LONG-SUFFERING WIFE will attest, I should have been born in the mid-18th century and have been long buried before the Civil War and the Industrial Revolution. This was a time in America in which we had few choices in the kitchen. Nobody was counting calories or worrying about cholesterol, whatever that was. You ate what was put in front of you and probably burned off 4,000 calories or more a day. Life was good. Life was simple.

Today, however, the success of American capitalism means that every need is filled almost instantly and with a vast, confusing array of choices. This is particularly true when it comes to "lite" food, healthy eating, natural foods—whatever you want to call it. My response has always been, "Eat an apple!" or "Have a salad!" You can imagine just how popular I have been with folks in our kitchen who are trying to live healthier lives, lose weight, or reduce their cholesterol. The problem is, and I have finally realized this, that people want to eat the food they are used to, not just an apple, a consommé, or a salad. They also want a cookie from time to time, a pasta dish, a stew, a curry.

For the home cook, it is nearly impossible to take a recipe and strip it of half its calories and fat while retaining any semblance of good flavor and texture. And when you want to use lower-fat ingredients, how do you know which brands and types to buy? (Our blind tastings have found that nonfat products are usually awful, whereas many low-fat brands are actually quite good.) What this points to, then, is that a test kitchen with 35 cooks is a pretty good place to sort through "light and healthy" recipes, figuring out how to make really first-rate makeovers of dishes such as Fudgy Brownies and Carrot Cake, or simply fine-tuning a recipe for Pesto Pasta Salad or Hearty Chicken Stew. Some of this work is fussy—getting just the right proportion and selection of ingredients—while other recipes require a good understanding of food science and an appetite for trying unusual methods and substitutions. For example, making a lighter Spaghetti Carbonara would seem an impossible task, given its huge amount of eggs and bacon fat. The solution included Canadian bacon, evaporated milk, and, oddly enough, mayonnaise. It sounds awful, but I tasted it and, believe it, it was well worth eating even a second helping.

The chapter names in *Light & Healthy* tell the story: Supper-Sized Salads, Soups and Stews, Poultry, Meat, Fish and Shellfish, Pasta and Pizza, Vegetarian Entrées, Fire Up the Grill, Great Grains and Beans, Perfect Vegetables, Breakfast and Baked Goods, and, of course, Desserts. What one notices immediately is that this table of contents sounds so normal—we wanted to give you the same types of big-flavored dishes that you have grown to expect from us but also do it with an eye toward healthy eating and a light hand in the kitchen. But hidden in these chapters are some real gems, such as using a strong blue cheese for a lower-fat dressing—it adds a lot of flavor with a very small portion—and how to caramelize seeded tomatoes as a base for many soups and stews. We also teach you tricks for developing flavor using secret ingredients and commonsense techniques, and which brand of the many supermarket options are the best, such as capers, orange juice, fish sauce, olive oil, and dozens more. Equipment reviews help you sort out items such as the best mandoline, fish spatula, pizza wheel, and juicer.

I can promise you that our family will be cooking out of this book on a regular basis. Sure, I am often happy munching on an apple or sitting down to a simple main-course salad, but the recipes in this book are a whole lot more intriguing, more complex in flavor, and, generally speaking, tastier than a last-minute "healthy" meal. This is real food, the only kind of food you and I like. We aren't playing with our food here; we really intend to eat it and, above all, enjoy every bite. So, start cooking from this book tonight and enjoy yourself and our recipes. (And, by the way, they are good for you, too.)

CHRISTOPHER KIMBALL
Founder and Editor,
Cook's Illustrated and *Cook's Country*
Host, *America's Test Kitchen* and
Cook's Country from America's Test Kitchen

POACHED SHRIMP SALAD WITH AVOCADO AND GRAPEFRUIT

SUPPER-SIZED SALADS

M = TEST KITCHEN MAKEOVER

CHICKEN CAESAR SALAD

MANY PEOPLE ASSUME THAT HAVING A SALAD FOR dinner is a safe bet for watching fat and calories. Think again. Consider one of the most celebrated dinner salads of all: chicken Caesar. The ideal version is made with crisp romaine lettuce and juicy chicken topped with grated Parmesan cheese and garlic croutons. And there's the dressing: a mix of garlic, anchovy, lemon juice, and Worcestershire sauce bound by a rich emulsion of egg yolks and olive oil. Healthy? When you consider the dressing, the cheese, the croutons, and sometimes even the chicken, it can add up to about 660 calories and 40 grams of fat per serving. We knew we could do better, but having tasted existing recipes for low-fat Caesar salads, we also knew it wouldn't be easy.

The dressing is one of the most crucial components of this salad, and many low-fat versions fall short because by omitting the egg yolk and most of the oil, they remove the creamy character of the dressing. What's left is an out-of-balance dressing without enough body to cling to the romaine. So we started by looking for a way to omit the egg and reduce the amount of oil without compromising taste or richness. Some low-fat recipes use ingredients like sour cream, yogurt, tofu, and buttermilk to emulsify the dressing. We found that sour cream and yogurt were too tart and dairy-rich. Soft tofu added a nice creamy texture but was too bland. Tasters, however, were impressed with buttermilk's tang and its silkiness, almost identical to that of egg yolks. Some complained that the dressing was still missing richness, so we added 3 tablespoons of light mayonnaise. This technique did the trick, and it also allowed us to decrease the amount of olive oil to 2 tablespoons from the ⅓ cup called for in the classic recipe.

Our dressing had perfectly balanced richness, so next we looked at finessing its flavor. Tasters liked 2 tablespoons of lemon juice, a modest teaspoon of Worcestershire sauce, and 2 teaspoons of minced garlic. Three anchovy fillets contributed a classic flavor, and Dijon mustard—an untraditional ingredient—added depth and helped further emulsify the ingredients. And instead of tossing the romaine with the grated Parmesan before dressing the salad (the traditional method), we found that stirring the Parmesan into the dressing itself spread the flavor of the cheese further and added good intensity to the dressing. With only ½ cup of cheese (many recipes called for twice that), our dressing now had big Parmesan flavor without unnecessary fat and calories.

As for the lettuce, romaine is standard, its fresh crunch a good match for the flavorful dressing. Some Caesar salads sport whole leaves of romaine, but tasters found these unwieldy on the plate, so we tore the leaves into bite-sized pieces.

We wanted the chicken in our salad to be fresh and moist, so leftover roast or grilled chicken was not an option. At the same time, we didn't want to make preparing the chicken a production. We wanted the flavor and color of browning, but browning both sides of the chicken breasts required more oil than we wanted to use, and it gave our chicken a tougher texture than we wanted. We found our answer in a half-sautéing, half-poaching method that required very little fat. First we browned the chicken on one side in 1 teaspoon of oil, then we flipped the chicken over, added water to the skillet, reduced the heat, and covered the skillet until the chicken was cooked through. This method yielded moist, flavorful chicken breasts.

Caesar salad wouldn't be complete without the crunch of croutons, and we found a way to make our croutons lighter than store-bought varieties (and those made with most traditional methods) by using vegetable oil spray and garlic powder rather than the traditional garlic oil. At last, we had a zesty main-course salad we could really dig into, and at 410 calories and 18 grams of fat, we knew it was a healthy choice.

MAKEOVER SPOTLIGHT: CHICKEN CEASAR SALAD

	CALORIES	FAT	SAT FAT	CHOLESTEROL
BEFORE	660	40g	7g	215mg
AFTER	410	18g	4g	110mg

Chicken Caesar Salad

SERVES 4

Parmesan cheese is a key ingredient in this classic salad, so be sure to use authentic Parmigiano-Reggiano and grate it yourself. Olive oil spray can be substituted for the vegetable oil spray in step 3.

DRESSING

- ⅓ **cup low-fat buttermilk**
- 3 **tablespoons light mayonnaise**
- 2 **tablespoons fresh lemon juice**
- 2 **tablespoons water**
- 2 **teaspoons Dijon mustard**
- 1 **teaspoon Worcestershire sauce**
- 2 **garlic cloves, minced**
- 3 **anchovy fillets, rinsed and patted dry**
- ½ **teaspoon pepper**
- ¼ **teaspoon salt**
- 2 **tablespoons extra-virgin olive oil**
- 1 **ounce Parmesan cheese (see note), grated (about ½ cup)**

SALAD

- 2 **slices high-quality white sandwich bread, cut into ½-inch cubes**
- **Vegetable oil spray (see note)**
- **Salt**
- ⅛ **teaspoon garlic powder**
- 4 **(6-ounce) boneless, skinless chicken breasts, trimmed**
- ⅛ **teaspoon pepper**
- 1 **teaspoon canola oil**
- 3 **romaine lettuce hearts (1 pound), torn into bite-sized pieces (about 12 cups)**

1. FOR THE DRESSING: Process the buttermilk, mayonnaise, lemon juice, water, mustard, Worcestershire, garlic, anchovies, pepper, and salt together in a blender until smooth, about 30 seconds, scraping down the sides as needed. With the motor running, add the olive oil in a steady stream. Transfer the mixture to a small bowl, stir in all but 1 tablespoon of the cheese, and set aside.

2. FOR THE SALAD: Adjust an oven rack to the middle position and heat the oven to 350 degrees.

3. Spread the bread cubes on a baking sheet and generously coat the cubes with the vegetable oil spray. Sprinkle with ⅛ teaspoon salt and garlic powder and toss to coat. Spread the bread cubes in an even layer and bake until golden brown, 20 to 25 minutes, tossing them halfway through. Set the croutons aside to cool to room temperature.

4. Meanwhile, pat the chicken breasts dry with paper towels and season with ⅛ teaspoon salt and the pepper. Heat the canola oil in a 12-inch nonstick skillet over medium-high heat until just smoking. Carefully lay the chicken in the skillet and cook until well browned on the first side, 6 to 8 minutes. Flip the chicken, add ½ cup water, and reduce the heat to medium-low. Cover and continue to cook until the thickest part of the breasts registers 160 to 165 degrees on an instant-read thermometer, 5 to 7 minutes longer.

NOTES FROM THE TEST KITCHEN

BRING OUT THE HELLMANN'S

Because mayonnaise is fatty by definition (it's mostly oil and egg yolks), low-fat mayonnaise is a popular product among the diet-conscious. In the past, Hellmann's Light Mayonnaise has been the winner of taste tests here in the test kitchen among leading brands of low-fat mayonnaise. (And among leading brands of full-fat mayos, Hellmann's Real Mayonnaise has also come in first.) Nowadays Hellmann's also makes a version with canola oil. We wondered how these two lighter versions stacked up against each other and the original, so we lined up all three for a test to find out, tasting them first plain and then in macaroni salad. The outcome? While the full-fat version remains our favorite, at 90 calories, 10 grams of fat, and 1.5 grams of saturated fat per tablespoon, it's not ideal for a lightened diet. Of the two lighter versions, tasters preferred **Hellmann's Light Mayonnaise** (35 calories, 3.5 grams of fat, 0 grams of saturated fat per tablespoon), finding it slightly sweeter than the original and praising its thick texture. Hellmann's Canola Cholesterol Free Mayonnaise (45 calories, 4.5 grams of fat, 0 grams of saturated fat per tablespoon) had a "tangier" flavor that some tasters disliked, though there were those who liked its bright flavor.

GOT ANCHOVIES?

Unless you plan on making Caesar salad, anchovy pizza, and pasta puttanesca all on the same day, you'd be hard-pressed to use up an entire tin of anchovies without having to store them. We tested multiple ways of storing anchovies over a two-week period and found that coiling them up individually, then freezing them on a plate before transferring them to a zipper-lock bag was the way to go. These frozen-and-thawed anchovies tasted nearly as good as the fresh fillets and were easier to handle than those we kept in the refrigerator beneath a blanket of olive oil.

FREEZE IN THE FLAVOR
Leftover anchovies coiled up and frozen in a zipper-lock bag taste almost as good as fresh.

5. Transfer the chicken to a carving board and let rest for 5 minutes. Cut the chicken crosswise into ½-inch-thick slices.

6. TO ASSEMBLE THE SALAD: Whisk the dressing to recombine. In a large bowl, toss the lettuce with all but 2 tablespoons of the dressing and divide among four plates. Add the chicken and the remaining 2 tablespoons dressing to the bowl and toss to coat. Arrange the chicken evenly on top of each salad. Sprinkle the croutons and the remaining 1 tablespoon cheese evenly over the salads and serve.

PER SERVING: **Cal** 410; **Fat** 18g; **Sat fat** 4g; **Chol** 110mg; **Carb** 14g; **Protein** 46g; **Fiber** 2g; **Sodium** 860mg

BUFFALO CHICKEN SALAD

SOME SALADS MIGHT BE CONSIDERED "LIGHT" ON flavor, but buffalo chicken salad makes a bold, spicy statement that proves a salad can

TEST KITCHEN
MAKEOVER

definitely pack a flavorful punch. Unfortunately, between the battered-and-fried chicken, the buttery, spicy sauce, and the creamy blue cheese dressing, this salad also tends to pack nearly 700 calories and 36 grams of fat in a serving. Could we reinvent this all-time classic and lighten it up while holding on to the addictive crispy-coated chicken, spicy sauce, and tangy, creamy dressing? We headed to the kitchen to find out.

The chicken was first on our list. We needed to figure out a way to give up the deep-fat frying without losing the crispy coating. We turned to a trick we had been developing for giving bone-in chicken a skin-like exterior that browned and crisped up—but without the fatty skin (see our recipe for Pan-Roasted Chicken Breasts with Lemon-Herb Sauce, page 61). For that recipe, we relied on a cornmeal-cornstarch coating, a combination that created both texture and browning, so all we had to do was adapt it to boneless breasts. We rolled our boneless, skinless chicken breasts in the same mixture and simply cooked them over lower heat for less time, since we didn't have the bone or skin protecting the meat. This coating worked perfectly. It was time to think about the spicy pepper sauce.

Classic buffalo chicken sauce is essentially hot sauce and melted butter. Many recipes called for an equal ratio of butter to hot sauce, but we found that much butter

simply wasn't necessary. A mere tablespoon of butter added to ½ cup of hot sauce gave us just the right amount of heat with a touch of richness, and there was plenty to coat the breasts. Tasters liked this simple combination, but they wanted some sweetness to offset the heat. We tried sugar, corn syrup, brown sugar, and molasses. A syrup was easier to incorporate than granulated sugar, and we all agreed that the caramelized flavor of molasses was best.

Next we moved on to the creamy dressing. Typically, full-fat blue cheese dressings have a mayonnaise base with one of, or a combination of, the following: sour cream, milk, buttermilk, heavy cream, yogurt, with water potentially for thinning it out. In low-fat recipes the higher-fat options are naturally off the list, and some get pretty imaginative for substitutes. We saw "imitation mayo" (a mixture of cottage cheese and apple juice concentrate), soft tofu, mashed white beans, tapioca, and even flaxseed oil, and we couldn't help but give them all a quick try. But these dressings were all lacking in both flavor and texture. More conventional options were the way to go.

Tasters immediately rejected nonfat mayonnaise and nonfat sour cream, citing a pasty sweetness in the former and unappealing tartness in the latter. Dressings made with their light counterparts, however, were a vast improvement. Better still was a version in which we replaced the reduced-fat sour cream with low-fat plain yogurt.

With the base settled, we were ready to add some zesty flavors. Typically, blue cheese dressings call for about ¾ cup of blue cheese, but quantity doesn't necessarily translate to intensity of cheese flavor. Stella and Danish blues are much milder than Stiltons and Roqueforts, so we reasoned that if we used a stronger blue cheese, we might be able to get away with using less. The result? Tasters were amazed that it took as little as ¼ cup of a stronger cheese to give our dressing the right zing. Adding some minced garlic brought a pleasant spiciness, and a splash of lemon juice added brightness. Now the consistency just needed some tweaking, as our dressing was too thick to coat the greens properly. A few tablespoons of water thinned it out perfectly without watering down the flavor.

While many recipes recommend dousing a salad for four with as much as 2 cups of dressing, we found that 1 cup was all it took. After cutting 20 grams of fat and more than 250 calories from the original, we knew that winning fans of this flavorful salad wouldn't be hard.

	CALORIES	FAT	SAT FAT	CHOLESTEROL
BEFORE	690	36g	15g	160mg
AFTER	430	16g	6g	12mg

Buffalo Chicken Salad

SERVES 4

We prefer Stilton or Roquefort here; other blues will work, but the dressing will have a milder cheese flavor. A milder cayenne pepper–based hot sauce (like Frank's RedHot) is essential; avoid hotter sauces like Tabasco.

DRESSING

- ⅔ cup plain low-fat yogurt
- ¼ cup light mayonnaise
- 3 tablespoons water
- 1 tablespoon fresh lemon juice
- 2 garlic cloves, minced
- ¼ teaspoon salt
- ⅛ teaspoon pepper
- 1 ounce blue cheese (see note), crumbled (about ¼ cup)

CHICKEN

- ½ cup hot sauce
- 1 tablespoon unsalted butter, melted
- 1 tablespoon light or mild molasses
- ½ cup cornmeal
- 1 tablespoon cornstarch
- 4 (6-ounce) boneless, skinless chicken breasts, trimmed
- ⅛ teaspoon salt
- ⅛ teaspoon pepper
- 1 tablespoon canola oil

SALAD

- 3 romaine lettuce hearts (1 pound), torn into bite-sized pieces (about 12 cups)
- 3 celery ribs, sliced thin
- 2 carrots, peeled and shredded

1. FOR THE DRESSING: Whisk the yogurt, mayonnaise, water, lemon juice, garlic, salt, and pepper together in a small bowl. Stir in the blue cheese and set aside.

2. FOR THE CHICKEN: Whisk the hot sauce, butter, and molasses together in a small bowl and set aside. Whisk the cornmeal and cornstarch together in a shallow dish.

Pat the chicken breasts dry with paper towels and season with the salt and pepper. Thoroughly coat the chicken with the cornmeal mixture, pressing to adhere.

3. Heat the oil in a 12-inch nonstick skillet over medium-high heat until just smoking. Carefully lay the chicken breasts in the skillet and cook until well browned on the first side, 6 to 8 minutes. Flip the chicken, reduce the heat to medium, and continue to cook until the thickest part of the breasts registers 160 to 165 degrees on an instant-read thermometer, 6 to 8 minutes longer.

4. Transfer the chicken breasts to a carving board and let rest for 5 minutes. Cut the breasts crosswise into ½-inch-thick slices.

5. TO ASSEMBLE THE SALAD: Whisk the dressing to recombine. In a large bowl, toss the lettuce, celery, and carrots with the dressing and divide among four plates. In a separate bowl, toss the chicken with the hot sauce mixture. Arrange the chicken slices evenly on top of each salad and serve.

PER SERVING: **Cal** 430; **Fat** 16g; **Sat fat** 6g; **Chol** 120mg; **Carb** 23g; **Protein** 46g; **Fiber** 4g; **Sodium** 650mg

NOTES FROM THE TEST KITCHEN

THE BEST HOT SAUCE

Considering that most hot sauces are made from a basic combination of red peppers, vinegar, and salt, does brand even matter? We rounded up eight supermarket samples to find out. We tried them simply sprinkled atop a portion of steamed white rice and in a Buffalo sauce for chicken. Across the board, tasters deemed one sauce a knockout: **Frank's RedHot** won points for its "bright" and "tangy" notes and potent heat. Other brands, such as Tabasco, had a searing heat that masked any other flavor in the sauce, and most tasters found the thin, watery body to be unappealing. We'll still use Tabasco for adding heat to recipes, but when it's flavor we're after, we'll reach for Frank's.

A BOLDER BLUE

Named for its veins of bluish green mold, blue cheese may be made from goat, sheep, or cow's milk, or a combination of these milks. At one extreme are the bold imports like Roquefort, a tangy, pungent sheep's milk cheese with a soft, almost spreadable texture, and Stilton, a crumbly English cow's milk cheese that is nutty and sharp. At the other end is the sliceably firm, and less complex-tasting Danish Blue. Using a bolder option in our dressing meant we could get maximum cheese flavor without using a lot—saving calories and fat but still keeping the flavor.

CHINESE CHICKEN SALAD

TYPICALLY COMPOSED OF A MIXTURE OF SHREDDED cabbage, bright vegetables, and shredded chicken tossed in a toasted sesame oil vinaigrette, Chinese chicken salad is quick to prepare and offers an enticing variety of tastes, textures, and visual appeal. The major problem is that most recipes produce a dressing that is overloaded with oil, coating the ingredients with a dull sheen that mutes any hint at freshness. And many versions are topped with handfuls of caloric cashews, peanuts, or sesame seeds. This dish would need some serious work to become a healthy salad. We headed to the test kitchen, set on creating a simple version that was light and flavorful, with a mixture of crisp, colorful vegetables and moist chicken tossed in a bright, well-balanced vinaigrette.

Since the dressing was responsible for most of the problems, that's where we decided to start. We began with a basic vinaigrette using ½ cup of oil, an amount called for in several of the recipes we found. Not surprisingly, this much oil made the dressing heavy and dull. With ¼ cup of oil the dressing was reasonably light, but tasters were convinced we could go lower still. We settled on only 2 tablespoons of oil, which added the perfect richness but ensured that the brighter flavors in the dressing would shine through. So our next task was to determine those flavors.

We found that rice vinegar was the most commonly used acid, though some recipes called for other vinegars. We tested a variety, and in the end rice vinegar proved best; its mild acidity and slight sweetness were ideal for keeping this salad fresh and light. Minced ginger seemed like a natural addition, as did soy sauce. But our dressing still lacked depth, so we rummaged through our pantry and settled on hoisin sauce. Hoisin added both sweetness and a hint of spiciness, which were a good contrast to the other flavors.

With the hardest part (the dressing) taken care of, we moved on to the chicken. Wanting it to be flavorful and moist, we decided to use the half-sautéing, half-poaching method we had just developed for our Chicken Caesar Salad (page 2). Once the breasts were cool, we sliced them and tossed the pieces with the noodles. But tasters commented that while the chicken was perfectly cooked, it seemed disconnected from the rest of the salad. And as an added problem, a fair amount of our flavorful dressing was pooling on the plate under the salad. We thought that for this particular salad, where

the chicken is incorporated, not rested on top, shredding might be the solution, so we tried again. This salad met with unanimous approval, as the meat incorporated nicely with the noodles and soaked up the dressing.

Now all we had left to do was decide which vegetables to include. Thinly sliced cabbage was a natural, and we found it worked well in combination with carrot and red bell pepper. Tasters also appreciated a few handfuls of bean sprouts for their fresh, crisp bite and earthy flavor. Thinly sliced scallions and minced cilantro added a fresh green quality to the salad. As a last touch, a sprinkle of crispy chow mein noodles lent a welcome crunch—and added far fewer calories and less fat than cashews or peanuts.

Chinese Chicken Salad
SERVES 4

Chow mein noodles, often sold in 5-ounce canisters, can be found in most supermarkets with other Asian ingredients; La Choy is the most widely available brand.

DRESSING
- ⅓ cup rice vinegar
- ¼ cup hoisin sauce
- 2 tablespoons canola oil
- 1½ tablespoons low-sodium soy sauce
- 1 tablespoon grated or minced fresh ginger
- ½ teaspoon toasted sesame oil

SALAD
- 1 pound boneless, skinless chicken breasts, trimmed
- ⅛ teaspoon salt
- ⅛ teaspoon pepper
- 1 teaspoon canola oil
- ½ head green or napa cabbage (about 1 pound), cored and sliced thin (about 4 cups; see page 7)
- 1 carrot, peeled and shredded
- ½ large red bell pepper, stemmed, seeded, and cut into ¼-inch-thick strips
- 1 cup bean sprouts
- 2 scallions, sliced thin on the bias
- 1 tablespoon minced fresh cilantro
- 1 cup chow mein noodles (see note)

1. FOR THE DRESSING: Whisk the vinegar, hoisin sauce, canola oil, soy sauce, ginger, and sesame oil together in a small bowl and set aside.

2. FOR THE SALAD: Pat the chicken breasts dry with paper towels and season with the salt and pepper. Heat the canola oil in a 12-inch nonstick skillet over medium-high heat until just smoking. Carefully lay the chicken in the skillet and cook until well browned on the first side, 6 to 8 minutes. Flip the chicken, add ½ cup water, and reduce the heat to medium-low. Cover and continue to cook until the thickest part of the breasts registers 160 to 165 degrees on an instant-read thermometer, 5 to 7 minutes longer.

3. Transfer the chicken to a carving board and let rest for 5 minutes. When the chicken is cool enough to handle, shred the meat into bite-sized pieces.

4. TO ASSEMBLE THE SALAD: Whisk the dressing to recombine. In a large bowl, toss the chicken, cabbage, carrot, red bell pepper, sprouts, scallions, and cilantro with the dressing. Divide the salad among four plates, sprinkle evenly with the chow mein noodles, and serve.

PER SERVING: Cal 350; Fat 13g; Sat fat 1.5g; Chol 65mg; Carb 27g; Protein 31g; Fiber 4g; Sodium 1030mg

NOTES FROM THE TEST KITCHEN

SHREDDING CABBAGE

1. Cut the cabbage into quarters, then trim and discard the hard core.

2. Separate the cabbage into small stacks of leaves that flatten when pressed.

3. Use a chef's knife to cut each stack of cabbage leaves into thin shreds.

OUR FAVORITE HOISIN SAUCE

Hoisin sauce, a thick, reddish brown mixture of soybeans, sugar, vinegar, garlic, and chiles, is used in many classic Chinese dishes, so it's a natural ingredient for our Chinese Chicken Salad. Taste tests of six hoisin sauces indicated that no two brands are identical, varying dramatically from gloppy and sweet to grainy and spicy. According to our tasters, the perfect hoisin sauce balances sweet, salty, pungent, and spicy elements. **Kikkoman Hoisin Sauce** came closest to this ideal; tasters praised its initial "burn" that mellowed into a blend of sweet and aromatic flavors.

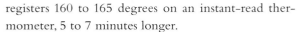

COLD SOBA NOODLE SALAD WITH CHICKEN

JAPANESE SOBA NOODLES, WHICH ARE MADE FROM buckwheat flour, possess a rich, nutty flavor and delicate texture that quickly wins fans, and as an added benefit, they also boast B vitamins, several minerals, and a healthy dose of protein and iron, among other things. While these noodles can be served hot, they are more widely seen in Japan as a cold appetizer accompanied by a soy-based dipping sauce seasoned with ginger and wasabi. These cold soba noodle dishes offer a delicate balance of key Japanese flavors and make for a refreshingly light meal. Inspired by the idea, we set out to create a chilled soba noodle salad. We would transform the dipping sauce into a dressing and add some chicken to pull it all together into a well-rounded meal with Western appeal.

Like all pasta, soba noodles require an ample amount of water for cooking; too little and you'll get a slimy mess of badly disintegrated noodles. We found it was best to cook the noodles in at least 4 quarts of salted water. Once they were cooked, we tried simply draining the noodles and spreading them on a baking sheet, the test kitchen method for prepping the pasta for most pasta salads, but the thin soba noodles turned gummy because they overcooked from residual heat. We found in this case it was better, as soon as they were just tender, to quickly rinse them under cold running water.

After the noodles were sufficiently cooled, we tossed them with a couple of teaspoons of sesame oil (a good choice to complement the noodles' nutty flavor) to prevent them from sticking, and we moved on to the dressing. We wanted to simulate the flavors of a classic dipping

COLD SOBA NOODLE SALAD WITH TOFU

sauce, so we began our dressing with traditional elements: soy sauce, mirin, sugar, and ginger. Tasters liked this simple dressing, but some craved a spicy component and suggested adding some wasabi (Japanese horseradish). A little went a long way, and we settled on ¼ teaspoon.

With our dressing settled, we turned to the chicken. Looking to our similarly assembled Chinese Chicken Salad (page 6), we knew that shredded chicken, cooked with our half-sautéed, half-poached method, was the best way to incorporate the chicken and soak up the dressing so it wouldn't pool on the plate. This method worked like a charm, so we moved on to exploring what vegetables would make the best additions. We tried daikon (a large Asian radish with a sweet flavor), pickled daikon, and red radishes, and we eventually settled on the radishes. Tasters thought their peppery flavor worked well with our dressing, and their bright red skin lent nice color to the dish (it didn't hurt that they're available year-round, unlike daikon, which can be hard to find). The crunch of carrots and cucumber and a garnish of sliced scallion rounded out our noodle salad perfectly.

Cold Soba Noodle Salad with Chicken

SERVES 4

To give this salad more heat, add additional wasabi paste to taste.

DRESSING

- ¼ cup low-sodium soy sauce
- 3 tablespoons mirin
- ½ teaspoon sugar
- ½ teaspoon grated or minced fresh ginger
- ¼ teaspoon wasabi powder or paste (see note)

SALAD

- 12 ounces dried soba noodles
   Salt
- 2 teaspoons toasted sesame oil
- 1 pound boneless, skinless chicken breasts, trimmed
   Pepper
- 1 teaspoon canola oil
- 6 large red radishes, trimmed, halved, and sliced thin
- 2 carrots, peeled and shredded
- 1 cucumber, halved lengthwise, seeded, and sliced thin
- 3 medium scallions, sliced thin on the bias

1. FOR THE DRESSING: Whisk the soy sauce, mirin, sugar, ginger, and wasabi together in a small bowl and set aside.

2. FOR THE SALAD: Bring 4 quarts water to a boil in a large pot. Add the noodles and 1 tablespoon salt and cook, stirring often, until tender. Drain the noodles and rinse them under cold running water until cool. Transfer the noodles to a large bowl, toss with the sesame oil, and set aside.

3. Meanwhile, pat the chicken breasts dry with paper towels and season with ⅛ teaspoon salt and ⅛ teaspoon pepper. Heat the canola oil in a 12-inch nonstick skillet over medium-high heat until just smoking. Carefully lay the chicken in the skillet and cook until well browned on the first side, 6 to 8 minutes. Flip the chicken, add ½ cup water, and reduce the heat to medium-low. Cover and continue to cook until the thickest part of the breasts registers 160 to 165 degrees on an instant-read thermometer, 5 to 7 minutes longer.

4. Transfer the chicken to a plate and let rest for 5 minutes. When the chicken is cool enough to handle, shred the meat into bite-sized pieces.

5. TO ASSEMBLE THE SALAD: Whisk the dressing to recombine. Add the dressing, chicken, radishes, carrots, cucumber, and half of the scallions to the bowl with the noodles and toss to combine. Season with salt and pepper to taste. Divide the salad among four plates, sprinkle evenly with the remaining scallions, and serve.

PER SERVING: Cal 520; Fat 7g; Sat fat 1g; Chol 65mg; Carb 76g; Protein 37g; Fiber 7g; Sodium 870mg

VARIATION

Cold Soba Noodle Salad with Tofu

We prefer the softer, creamier texture of medium or soft tofu here; firm or extra-firm tofu will also work, but it will taste drier. Be sure to handle the tofu gently, and thoroughly pat it dry before seasoning and coating. To give this salad more heat, add additional wasabi paste to taste.

DRESSING

- ¼ cup low-sodium soy sauce
- 3 tablespoons mirin
- ½ teaspoon sugar
- ½ teaspoon grated or minced fresh ginger
- ¼ teaspoon wasabi powder or paste (see note)

SALAD

12 ounces dried soba noodles

Salt

2 teaspoons toasted sesame oil

1 (14-ounce) package medium-firm or soft tofu, cut into
¾-inch pieces (see note)

⅓ cup cornstarch

2 tablespoons cornmeal

Pepper

3 tablespoons canola oil

6 large red radishes, trimmed, halved, and sliced thin

2 carrots, peeled and shredded

1 cucumber, halved, seeded, and sliced thin

3 medium scallions, sliced thin on the bias

1. FOR THE DRESSING: Whisk the soy sauce, mirin, sugar, ginger, and wasabi together in a small bowl and set aside.

2. FOR THE SALAD: Bring 4 quarts water to a boil in a large pot. Add the noodles and 1 tablespoon salt and cook, stirring often, until tender. Drain the noodles and rinse them under cold running water until cool. Transfer the noodles to a large bowl, toss with the sesame oil, and set aside.

3. Meanwhile, spread out the tofu on several layers of paper towels and let sit for 20 minutes to drain slightly. Place a wire rack over a baking sheet and set aside.

4. Whisk the cornstarch and cornmeal together in a shallow dish. Season the tofu with ⅛ teaspoon salt and ⅛ teaspoon pepper. Coat the tofu thoroughly with the cornstarch mixture, shaking off any excess, and transfer to the prepared wire rack.

5. Heat the canola oil in a 12-inch nonstick skillet over medium-high heat until shimmering. Carefully lay the tofu in the skillet and cook until crisp and light golden on all sides, 8 to 10 minutes, turning as needed. Transfer the tofu to a paper towel–lined plate.

6. TO ASSEMBLE THE SALAD: Whisk the dressing to recombine. Add the dressing, tofu, radishes, carrots, cucumber, and half of the scallions to the bowl with the noodles and toss to combine. Season with salt and pepper to taste. Divide the salad among four plates, sprinkle evenly with the remaining scallions, and serve.

PER SERVING: Cal 510; Fat 11g; Sat fat .5g; Chol 0mg; Carb 83g; Protein 19g; Fiber 7g; Sodium 790mg

---

NOTES FROM THE TEST KITCHEN

SOBA NOODLES

These delicate Japanese noodles possess a uniquely rich, nutty flavor that comes from the fact that they are made with buckwheat flour, an ingredient that also makes them nutrient-rich. But because buckwheat flour contains no gluten, a binder, usually wheat, is added to give the noodles structure and hold them together during cooking. The Japanese agriculture department requires that all noodles labeled as soba contain a minimum of 30 percent buckwheat flour, and the higher the percentage of buckwheat flour, the higher the price.

PESTO PASTA SALAD

A COOL PESTO PASTA SALAD WITH CHICKEN AND vegetables makes an appealing meal that certainly seems healthy (particularly when considered next to the heavier mayonnaise-based versions), but take one look at the fat and calories in a typical recipe and you'll do a double-take. In addition to the basil and garlic, you'll find nuts, cheese, and a generous amount of olive oil—it all adds up really quickly. But we couldn't resist thinking that with all its appeal, there had to be a way to lighten up this classic, so we set out to see what we could do.

Starting with the foundation, the pasta, we tried all shapes and sizes and learned that the best were those with a textured surface with nooks that could trap pesto. Farfalle, or bow tie pasta, beat out the competition. After a few trial runs, we noticed that its texture changed between the time it was done cooking and when it was cooled and on the plate. Pasta cooked to al dente took on a tough, chewy texture once it had cooled to room temperature. Completely tender pasta, on the other hand, cooled to a pleasant, bouncy texture. We knew from previous experience that rinsing the pasta to cool it would make the surface too slick for the pesto to take hold, so we went to our standard test kitchen method of letting the pasta cool in a single layer on a baking sheet, tossing it with olive oil to prevent sticking. This worked perfectly.

We moved on to the chicken and vegetables. Much as for the chicken in our Chinese chicken and soba noodle salads (see pages 6 and 7), tasters preferred shredded chicken to sliced or cubed chicken for the way it incorporated into the salads. Heartier vegetables, such as broccoli and beans, lent an unappealing toughness, and delicate vegetables like zucchini were disliked whether uncooked (they tasted too raw) or slightly cooked (too spongy). In the end, we liked the crisp texture (and bright colors) of bell peppers, shredded carrots, and cherry tomatoes. We stirred the peppers, carrots, and chicken into the pasta before adding the dressing, but we found it was best to wait until the end to gently fold in the tomatoes to prevent them from getting smashed from all the stirring.

Finally, we turned to the pesto. Most recipes rely on at least ½ cup of oil to emulsify and blend the sauce, but we wanted a pesto that wasn't fat-laden, so we began thinking about creative ways to reduce the amount of oil without taking away from pesto's trademark consistency. We decided we should give our Italian-style sauce a little hometown flair, borrowing a standard ingredient used in many American pasta salads: mayonnaise. We tried multiple batches with varying amounts of light mayo and thought the idea was getting there, but regardless of the amount, on its own the mayo was too rich and thick. We found that ⅓ cup of mayonnaise mixed with 2 tablespoons of lemon juice gave us a pesto with just the right consistency that wasn't too rich—and we cut about 20 grams of fat and almost 200 calories in the process.

Our pesto was on track, but now the flavors needed to come into balance. Garlic is a hallmark ingredient, but even a single clove created an overpowering raw flavor. Toasting the garlic worked wonders to tame the harshness, and adding a minced shallot further complemented the flavor. Pesto traditionally contains pine nuts and/or walnuts, but we decided to try leaving them out since they add so much fat. Tasters didn't have any problem with the flavor of our nutless pesto, but since the nuts did contribute bulk, we increased the amount of basil to compensate. Bruising the basil with a meat pounder helped release its oils and intensify its flavor.

Once the salad was tossed together, we found that it quickly became too dry. Simply adding more pesto didn't solve the problem; it just made the salad heavy, and the pesto overwhelmed the other ingredients. Looking for ways to add moisture to the salad without ruining the balance, we landed on the idea of adding some of the pasta cooking water. Just ½ cup loosened our pesto and kept our salad bright, fresh, and flavorful.

Pesto Pasta Salad with Chicken and Vegetables

SERVES 4

Instead of farfalle, 8 ounces of other short, bite-sized pasta such as penne, fusilli, or orecchiette can be used in this salad.

DRESSING

- 4 garlic cloves, unpeeled
- 3 cups lightly packed basil leaves
- 1 ounce Parmesan cheese, grated (about ½ cup)
- ⅓ cup light mayonnaise
- 1 shallot, minced (about 3 tablespoons)
- 2 tablespoons fresh lemon juice
- Salt and pepper

SALAD

- 8 ounces farfalle pasta (about 3 cups) (see note)
- Salt
- 1 tablespoon olive oil
- 1 pound boneless, skinless chicken breasts, trimmed
- Pepper
- 2 carrots, peeled and shredded
- 1 bell pepper, stemmed, seeded, and cut into ¼-inch-thick strips
- 12 ounces cherry tomatoes (about 2 cups), quartered

1. FOR THE DRESSING: Toast the garlic in a small skillet over medium heat, shaking the pan occasionally, until the color of the cloves deepens slightly, about 7 minutes. Transfer the garlic to a plate to cool, then peel the cloves and chop coarse.

2. Place the basil in a heavy-duty gallon-sized zipperlock bag. Pound the bag with the flat side of a meat pounder or rolling pin until all the leaves are lightly bruised.

3. Process the garlic, basil, cheese, mayonnaise, shallot, lemon juice, and ½ teaspoon salt in a food processor until smooth, about 30 seconds, scraping down the sides of the workbowl as needed. Transfer the mixture to a small bowl, season with salt and pepper to taste, and set aside.

4. FOR THE SALAD: Bring 4 quarts water to a boil in a large pot. Add the pasta and 1 tablespoon salt and cook, stirring often, until tender. Reserve ½ cup of the cooking water, then drain the pasta. Return the pasta to the pot and toss with 2 teaspoons of the oil. Spread the pasta on a rimmed baking sheet and cool to room temperature, about 30 minutes.

5. Meanwhile, pat the chicken breasts dry with paper towels and season with ⅛ teaspoon salt and ⅛ teaspoon pepper. Heat the remaining 1 teaspoon oil in a 12-inch nonstick skillet over medium-high heat until just smoking. Carefully lay the chicken in the skillet and cook until well browned on the first side, 6 to 8 minutes. Flip the chicken, add ½ cup water, and reduce the heat to medium-low. Cover and continue to cook until the thickest part of the breasts registers 160 to 165 degrees on an instant-read thermometer, 5 to 7 minutes longer.

6. Transfer the chicken to a plate and let rest for 5 minutes. When the chicken is cool enough to handle, shred the meat into bite-sized pieces.

7. TO ASSEMBLE THE SALAD: Whisk the dressing to recombine. In a large bowl, toss the pasta, chicken, carrots, and bell pepper with the dressing, adjusting the consistency with the reserved pasta cooking water as needed. Fold in the tomatoes and season with salt and pepper to taste. Divide the salad among four plates and serve.

PER SERVING: Cal 490; **Fat** 13g; **Sat fat** 3g; **Chol** 80mg; **Carb** 56g; **Protein** 40g; **Fiber** 5g; **Sodium** 690mg

---

NOTES FROM THE TEST KITCHEN

INEXPENSIVE JUICERS

Our lightened pesto sauce relies on lemon juice to bring the flavors into balance, and it helps to have a good juicer on hand. Ideally, a juicer should extract maximum juice from a lemon with minimum mess—and minimum expense. So we bought a bushel of lemons and compared several styles of inexpensive lemon-juicing tools. Our favorite of the five models we tested was the **Black and Decker CitrusMate Plus Model CJ525,** $19.95. With this model, it took no effort to squeeze all the juice from the lemons. As you press gently, the reamer rotates to clean out the fruit half, and an adjustable pulp screen keeps out seeds and lets you adjust the pulp level of the juice. It's also simple to assemble and clean.

STEAK AND POTATO SALAD

THE CLASSIC COMBINATION OF MEAT AND POTATOES is always a winner, but a big, juicy steak and a pile of potatoes overshadowing a little salad or a few sprigs of broccoli isn't exactly the pinnacle of a well-balanced meal. We felt as though a fresh, crisp-leafed salad topped with nicely seared steak and well-seasoned potatoes, all dressed in a flavorful vinaigrette, would be a great way to enjoy the duo and still be health-minded. We easily found existing steak and potato salad recipes, but most involved leftover steak draped over mundane greens and covered with a nondescript dressing. We were going to need to start fresh—literally.

Starting with the steak, we tested a number of leaner cuts. Some, like blade and shoulder steaks, tasted too livery, and others, like those from the round, were either gummy or tough. In the end, we liked the top sirloin steak best for its lean profile and nice beef flavor, and because it promised to cook quickly on the stovetop.

To get the perfect crust while pan searing our steak, we made sure of two things: that the skillet was just smoking before we added the steak, and that the skillet was large enough to give the steak plenty of room. If the skillet was not hot enough, or if the steak was crowded, the pan would cool down too dramatically, resulting in stewed, rather than seared, meat. And because moving the steak released its liquid—a potential cause for a steaming environment—we made sure not to move the steak once we placed it in the skillet. Getting a deep brown crust on the first side took about 3 minutes, then we flipped the steak, reduced the heat, and for a medium-rare steak continued cooking until it reached 125 degrees. By the time our steak was done resting, it had reached an internal temperature of 130 degrees, a perfect medium-rare.

With our steak nicely seared, we moved on to the potatoes. Looking at the fond left in the bottom of our now-empty skillet, we realized sautéing the potatoes would be a good way to infuse them with flavor and minimize the pans needed. We opted for red potatoes because their tender skin doesn't require peeling, saving us some prep time. In our initial tests we had trouble getting the potatoes simultaneously golden-crisp on the outside and tender on the inside—they were either burned on the outside and raw in the middle, or pale and completely blown out. The solution was to use the microwave to parcook them. While the steak seared, we popped the potatoes into the microwave, and by the time the steak was ready to rest, the potatoes were ready to finish up in the skillet with the fond. They needed only 5 to 10 minutes more, and by placing the potatoes in a single layer in the skillet, we were able to achieve deeply caramelized exteriors with creamy, moist interiors.

A simple but flavorful vinaigrette was all we needed to pull it together. Red wine vinegar, garlic, and shallot were all naturals to pair with the steak. Whole grain mustard added tang, and a touch of honey balanced the vinegar's acidity. Last, a little thyme added a nice herbal note. Romaine, with its fresh crunch, was preferred over the more delicate lettuce greens, and some sliced red onion added nice color and bite. This steak and potato entrée was still a blue-ribbon combination, but now there was no reason to feel guilty about eating every last bite.

Steak and Potato Salad

SERVES 4

Flap meat steak can be substituted for the boneless top sirloin in this recipe. We prefer this steak cooked to medium-rare, but if you prefer your steak more or less done, see our guidelines in "Testing Meat for Doneness" on page 86.

DRESSING

- 3 tablespoons red wine vinegar
- 3 tablespoons water
- 1 shallot, minced (about 3 tablespoons)
- 2 tablespoons extra-virgin olive oil
- 1 tablespoon honey
- 1 tablespoon whole grain mustard
- 1 garlic clove, minced
- ½ teaspoon minced fresh thyme
- ¼ teaspoon salt
- ⅛ teaspoon pepper

SALAD

- 1 (1-pound) boneless top sirloin steak (shell sirloin), trimmed of all visible fat, about 1¼ inches thick (see note)
  Salt and pepper
- 1 tablespoon canola oil
- 1 pound red potatoes (about 3 medium), cut into ¾-inch-thick wedges
- 3 romaine lettuce hearts (1 pound), torn into bite-sized pieces (about 12 cups)
- ⅓ cup thinly sliced red onion

1. FOR THE DRESSING: Whisk the vinegar, water, shallot, oil, honey, mustard, garlic, thyme, salt, and pepper together in a small bowl and set aside.

2. FOR THE SALAD: Pat the steak dry with paper towels and season with ⅛ teaspoon salt and ⅛ teaspoon pepper. Heat 2 teaspoons of the oil in a 12-inch non-stick skillet over medium-high heat until just smoking. Carefully lay the steak in the skillet and cook until well browned on the first side, about 3 minutes. Flip the steak, reduce the heat to medium, and continue to cook until the center of the steak registers 125 degrees on an instant-read thermometer (for medium-rare), 5 to 7 minutes longer.

3. Transfer the steak to a carving board, tent loosely with foil, and let rest for 10 minutes. Cut the steak across the grain into ¼-inch-thick slices.

4. While the steak is cooking, toss the potatoes with the remaining 1 teaspoon oil in a large microwave-safe bowl. Cover with plastic wrap and microwave on high until the potatoes are tender, 5 to 10 minutes, shaking the bowl halfway through.

5. Return the skillet to medium-high heat until just smoking. Add the potatoes in a single layer and cook until well browned on both sides, about 5 minutes, flipping them halfway through. Season with salt and pepper to taste.

6. TO ASSEMBLE THE SALAD: Whisk the dressing to recombine. In a large bowl, toss the lettuce and onion with ½ cup of the dressing and divide among four plates. Arrange the steak and potatoes evenly on top of each salad, drizzle with the remaining dressing, and serve.

PER SERVING: Cal 390; Fat 19g; Sat fat 4.5g; Chol 55mg; Carb 30g; Protein 24g; Fiber 4g; Sodium 380mg

WILTED SPINACH SALADS

DARK GREEN LEAFY GREENS LIKE SPINACH ARE A great source of nutrients, so it didn't take us long to come up with the idea of developing a recipe that would use this healthful green in a warm, wilted spinach salad. Warm spinach salad at its finest offers tender spinach leaves lightly wilted by a warm, aromatic dressing. But after several tests, we found this ideal is not achieved without a little know-how. Recipes ran the gamut from tough leaves covered with uninspired dressing to overdressed, oily piles of mushy greens. We would need to focus on the type of

WILTED SPINACH SALAD WITH PAN-SEARED SCALLOPS AND ORANGES

spinach and how to dress it. We wanted a hearty, warm salad that was simple enough to prepare midweek but could also serve as a nice weekend meal. We would make it a main course by bulking it up with quick-cooking proteins: one with briny scallops, another with a flavorful chicken sausage.

We tackled the spinach first. There are two categories: curly-leaf and flat-leaf. Curly-leaf spinach, a familiar variety sold at the grocery packaged in cellophane bags, didn't do well. Tasters felt the leaves were too dry and chewy, and the leaves didn't wilt when we poured over a warm dressing. We decided to reserve it for recipes in which the spinach is cooked.

When we tried flat-leaf spinach, our results were more encouraging. There are two types of flat-leaf commonly available: larger-leaf spinach, sold in bundles, and baby spinach, sold in the grocery in bags near the salads-in-a-bag. The larger-leaf spinach worked fine—its tender leaves were moist and wilted well. But the bunches we bought were full of dirt and required several washings. Discouraged by the prep, we tried a bag of the baby spinach. It worked perfectly. It came washed, trimmed, and ready to go, and it wilted perfectly.

It was time for the dressing. We knew the flavor of the acidic component in a warm dressing should be based on the featured salad ingredients. The scallops' delicate flavor would require a light, citrusy vinaigrette. We found that tasters preferred a mixture of orange juice and sherry vinegar. Because of sausage's more assertive flavors, we settled on a stronger dressing for that salad, combining apple cider, cider vinegar, and a touch of whole grain mustard.

As for the oil component of our dressings, we found we didn't need much. Too much olive oil bogged down the spinach, though too little made for an overly sharp vinaigrette. Vinaigrettes made with 1 tablespoon of olive oil tasted most balanced. When preparing the dressing, we found adding the acidic component in the early stages of cooking muted its flavors. Swirling in the acid after the pan had been removed from the heat restored its punch. These warm vinaigrettes wilted the spinach perfectly.

Now we just needed a few finishing flavors and textures. To the scallop salad we added a sweet burst of orange segments, crisp, sliced red onion, and crunchy toasted almonds. In our sausage variation, sliced apple and walnuts lent a rustic theme tasters appreciated. We now had two fresh-tasting spinach salads that were light, easy, and certainly hearty enough to serve as a main course.

Wilted Spinach Salad with Pan-Seared Scallops and Oranges
SERVES 4

For this recipe, we prefer large sea scallops. Depending on the size of your scallops, the cooking times may vary slightly.

1½ **pounds large sea scallops (about 16 scallops; see note), muscle removed (see page 16)**
    Salt and pepper
2 **tablespoons canola oil**
1 **tablespoon extra-virgin olive oil**
½ **cup thinly sliced red onion**
2 **large oranges, peel and pith removed, segmented (see page 16), and 1 tablespoon juice reserved**
1 **teaspoon minced fresh thyme**
2 **tablespoons sherry vinegar**
8 **ounces baby spinach (about 8 cups)**
¼ **cup sliced almonds, toasted (see page 16)**

1. Lay out the scallops on a paper towel–lined plate or baking sheet and season with ⅛ teaspoon salt and ⅛ teaspoon pepper. Lay a single layer of paper towels over the scallops and set aside.

2. Heat 1 tablespoon of the canola oil in a 12-inch non-stick skillet over high heat until just smoking. Meanwhile, press the paper towels flush to the scallops to dry them. Carefully lay half of the scallops in the skillet and cook until golden brown on the first side, 1 to 2 minutes. Using tongs, transfer the scallops to a large plate, with the seared side facing up, and set aside.

3. Wipe out the skillet with a wad of paper towels. Add the remaining 1 tablespoon canola oil to the skillet and return to high heat until just smoking. Add the remaining scallops and cook until golden brown on the first side, 1 to 2 minutes. Reduce the heat to medium, flip the scallops over, and return the first batch to the pan, browned side facing up. Cook until the sides have firmed up and all but the middle third of each scallop is opaque, 30 to 60 seconds longer. Transfer the scallops to a clean plate and set aside. Wipe out the skillet with a wad of paper towels.

4. Add the olive oil, onion, orange juice, thyme, and ¼ teaspoon salt to the skillet and return to medium-high heat. Cook until the onion is slightly softened, about 1 minute. Remove the pan from the heat, add the oranges and vinegar, and swirl to incorporate.

5. TO ASSEMBLE THE SALAD: In a large bowl, combine the spinach and almonds. Pour the warm dressing over the spinach mixture and gently toss to wilt. Divide the salad among four plates and arrange the scallops evenly on top of each salad. Serve.

PER SERVING: Cal 340; Fat 15g; Sat fat 1.5g; Chol 55mg; Carb 22g; Protein 32g; Fiber 5g; Sodium 580mg

VARIATION

Wilted Spinach Salad with Sausage and Apples

We found numerous chicken sausage flavors at our supermarket; choose those with flavors that will complement this salad, such as apple, herb, or garlic. Make sure to slice the apple just before serving to prevent it from turning brown.

 1 teaspoon canola oil
 1 pound chicken sausages (see note)
 ¼ cup plus 1 tablespoon apple cider or apple juice
 1 tablespoon extra-virgin olive oil
 ½ cup thinly sliced red onion
 1 teaspoon minced fresh thyme
    Salt and pepper
 2 tablespoons cider vinegar
 1 tablespoon whole grain mustard
 8 ounces baby spinach (about 8 cups)
 ¼ cup walnuts, toasted (see at right) and chopped coarse
 1 large apple, cored, halved, and sliced thin (see note)

1. Heat the canola oil in a 12-inch nonstick skillet over medium-high heat until just smoking. Carefully lay the sausages in the skillet and cook until well browned on all sides, about 8 minutes, turning as needed. Add ¼ cup of the apple cider and reduce the heat to medium-low. Cover and continue to cook until the sausages are no longer pink in the center, about 8 minutes.

2. Transfer the sausages to a carving board and let rest for 5 minutes. Cut the sausages into ¼-inch-thick slices.

3. Wipe out the skillet with a wad of paper towels. Add the remaining 1 tablespoon apple cider, olive oil, onion, thyme, ¼ teaspoon salt, and ¼ teaspoon pepper to the skillet and return to medium-high heat. Cook until the onion is slightly softened, about 1 minute. Remove the pan from the heat, add the vinegar and mustard to the skillet, and swirl to incorporate.

4. TO ASSEMBLE THE SALAD: In a large bowl, combine the spinach and walnuts. Pour the warm dressing over

the spinach mixture and gently toss to wilt. Add the apple and toss to combine. Divide the salad among four plates and arrange the pieces of sausage evenly on top of each salad. Serve.

PER SERVING: Cal 330; Fat 18g; Sat fat 3g; Chol 85mg; Carb 17g; Protein 24g; Fiber 5g; Sodium 990mg

POACHED SEAFOOD SALADS

POACHED SEAFOOD SALADS ARE A SPA MENU STAPLE, since seafood is a lean protein and poaching is one of the healthiest cooking techniques out there. Typically, salmon or shrimp is gently poached in an aromatic liquid, cooled, and tossed with a light vinaigrette and vegetables. But too many modern renditions have gone overboard with this classic's signature lightness, leaving us hungry for more. And all too often, the salad consists of dry, overcooked salmon or tough, tiny shrimp plopped onto lifeless lettuce leaves. We wanted to develop a salad featuring properly cooked seafood, fresh vegetables, and a flavorful dressing.

We started by exploring the seafood poaching methods. We began by bringing a mixture of water, lemon juice, bay leaf, and whole black peppercorns to a bare simmer, then added the seafood and cooked it for several minutes. This classic technique worked well for our salmon fillets, but when applied to the shrimp, which are smaller and more delicate than salmon, the result was chewy, overcooked shrimp. Our solution was to bring the poaching liquid to a boil, turn off the heat, add the shrimp, and cover the pot. The shrimp picked up flavor from the liquid and cooked through, but without any danger of overcooking.

We moved on to the dressings. We briefly considered straying from tradition and tested creamy dressings, but even with low-fat products, they were just too heavy for such a light salad. Tasters much preferred olive oil–based vinaigrettes. For the salmon salad we settled on a dressing with bolder flavors. Lemon was the logical starting point, to which we added whole grain mustard and dill, both flavors that are a good match for salmon. While the combination of olive oil and salmon gave our salad a higher amount of fat than we would have preferred, we were content with the fact that both contained heart-healthy fats (polyunsaturated Omega-3 fatty acids in the salmon, monosaturated fats in the olive oil, which also contains antioxidants; for more about olive oil, see page 21). For the more delicate shrimp, we opted for sweeter lime juice over lemon, complemented by a little honey and some grated ginger. With our simple yet flavorful dressings settled, now it was a matter of picking a few components to complement these flavors.

We focused on the salmon salad first. Green beans, cooked just to crisp-tender, and sliced potatoes worked perfectly with the bold flavor of the salmon and the mustardy dressing. From previous test kitchen experience, we knew that warm potatoes are great at soaking up dressing flavors, much better than when they are cooled, so we poured ¼ cup of the dressing over the potatoes right after they came out of the cooking liquid. After we'd cooked each component, it was just a matter of quick assembly. Before topping the lettuce with the beans, potatoes, and finally the salmon, we made sure to toss our beans in the dressing, ensuring that, like the potatoes, they were evenly coated and flavorful.

Next we worked on the shrimp salad, choosing to combine our perfectly poached crustaceans and bright dressing with avocado, snow peas, and grapefruit segments. After some testing, we happened on the idea of pureeing a quarter of the avocado in the dressing to help evenly distribute its buttery flavor. It added a nice complement to the shrimp's briny sweetness that tasters appreciated, and because the avocado lent our dressing body, we could eliminate the olive oil. The remaining avocado was diced and gently folded into the salad. We found that chopped mint added a freshness that nicely rounded out the salad.

These salads were an instant success in the test kitchen; tasters commented on how light and flavorful they were—and how surprisingly easy they were to prepare.

Poached Salmon Salad with Potatoes and Green Beans
SERVES 4

In this recipe, you will use the same water to cook the green beans and to poach the salmon. Remember not to drain the green beans in a colander; instead, use a slotted spoon to remove them from the water.

DRESSING

- 6 tablespoons whole grain mustard
- 6 tablespoons fresh lemon juice (about 2 lemons)
- 1 small shallot, minced (about 2 tablespoons)
- 3 tablespoons extra-virgin olive oil
- 2 tablespoons minced fresh dill
  Salt and pepper

SALAD AND SALMON

- 8 ounces green beans, trimmed and cut into 2-inch lengths
    Salt
- 1 lemon, halved
- 1 bay leaf
- ½ teaspoon black peppercorns
- 4 (4-ounce) skin-on salmon fillets, about 1½ inches thick
- ⅛ teaspoon pepper
- 1 pound red potatoes (about 3 medium), halved and sliced ¼ inch thick
- 2 heads Bibb lettuce (1 pound), torn into bite-sized pieces (about 16 cups)

1. FOR THE DRESSING: Whisk the mustard, lemon juice, shallot, oil, and dill together in a small bowl. Season with salt and pepper to taste and set aside.

2. FOR THE SALAD AND SALMON: Bring 2 quarts water to a boil in a large pot; have ready a medium bowl filled with ice water. Add the green beans and 1 tablespoon salt to the boiling water and cook until crisp-tender, about 5 minutes. Using a slotted spoon, transfer the green beans to the ice water to stop the cooking and let sit until chilled, about 3 minutes (do not drain the boiling water from the pot). Drain the green beans from the ice water and transfer to a medium bowl. Toss the green beans with ¼ cup of the dressing and set aside.

3. Squeeze the juice of both lemon halves into the water. Add the squeezed lemon halves, bay leaf, and peppercorns to the water, return to a boil over high heat, and cook for 2 minutes.

4. Pat the salmon dry with paper towels and season with ⅛ teaspoon salt and the pepper. Reduce the heat to a light simmer and slip the salmon fillets into the water. Cover and cook until the fish is still slightly pink in the middle, 4 to 6 minutes. Using a slotted spoon, gently transfer the salmon fillets to a large plate and let cool to room temperature. Remove the skin and refrigerate the fish until ready to serve.

5. Bring 6 cups water, the potatoes, and 1 tablespoon salt to a simmer in a large saucepan. Reduce the heat to medium-low and cook until the potatoes are tender, about 5 minutes. Drain the potatoes and transfer them to a medium bowl. Whisk the dressing to recombine. Toss the potatoes with ¼ cup of the dressing and set aside to cool to room temperature.

6. TO ASSEMBLE THE SALAD: Divide the lettuce among four plates and top evenly with the potatoes and green beans. Arrange a salmon fillet on top of each salad, drizzle with the remaining dressing, and serve.

PER SERVING (WILD SALMON): **Cal** 420; **Fat** 20g; **Sat fat** 2.5g; **Chol** 60mg; **Carb** 27g; **Protein** 27g; **Fiber** 5g; **Sodium** 730mg

PER SERVING (FARMED SALMON): **Cal** 470; **Fat** 26g; **Sat fat** 4g; **Chol** 65mg; **Carb** 27g; **Protein** 27g; **Fiber** 5g; **Sodium** 750mg

Poached Shrimp Salad with Avocado and Grapefruit
SERVES 4

If you can't get enough juice from your grapefruit to equal ¼ cup, add water to make up the difference. If your grapefruit is especially tart, you can add ½ teaspoon more honey to the dressing.

SHRIMP

- 1 lemon, halved
- 1 bay leaf
- ½ teaspoon black peppercorns
- 1 pound extra-large shrimp (21 to 25 per pound), peeled and deveined (see page 126)

SALAD AND DRESSING

- 2 medium ruby red grapefruits, peeled and pith removed, segmented (see page 16), and ¼ cup juice reserved (see note)
- 1 large avocado, pitted, peeled, and cut into ½-inch pieces (see page 19)
- 2 tablespoons fresh lime juice
- 1½ teaspoons grated or minced fresh ginger
- ½ teaspoon honey
- ¼ teaspoon salt
- ¼ teaspoon pepper
- 2 ounces snow peas, strings removed, cut lengthwise into ⅛-inch strips
- 1 tablespoon chopped fresh mint
- 2 heads Bibb lettuce (about 1 pound), torn into bite-sized pieces (about 16 cups)

1. FOR THE SHRIMP: Place 3 cups water in a medium saucepan and squeeze the juice of both lemon halves into the water. Add the squeezed lemon halves, bay leaf, and peppercorns to the water, bring to a boil over high heat, and cook for 2 minutes. Remove the pan from the heat, add the shrimp, cover, and let sit for 8 minutes; have ready a bowl filled with ice water.

2. Drain the shrimp, discarding the lemon halves, bay leaf, and peppercorns. Immediately transfer the shrimp to the ice water to stop the cooking and let sit until chilled, about 3 minutes. Drain the shrimp from the ice water, transfer them to a large bowl, and refrigerate until needed.

3. FOR THE SALAD AND DRESSING: Process the grapefruit juice, one-quarter of the avocado, lime juice, ginger, honey, salt, and pepper together in a blender until smooth, scraping down the sides as needed.

4. TO ASSEMBLE THE SALAD: Stir the dressing, remaining avocado, grapefruit segments, snow peas, and mint into the bowl with the shrimp. Divide the lettuce among four plates and arrange the shrimp salad evenly on top. Drizzle each salad with any remaining dressing left in the bowl and serve.

PER SERVING: Cal 290; Fat 10g; Sat fat 1.5g; Chol 170mg; Carb 27g; Protein 27g; Fiber 11g; Sodium 320mg

NOTES FROM THE TEST KITCHEN

PREPARING AVOCADOS

1. After slicing the avocado in half around the pit, lodge the edge of the knife blade into the pit and twist to remove. Use a large wooden spoon to pry the pit safely off the knife.

2. Use a dish towel to hold the avocado steady. Make ½-inch crosshatch incisions in the flesh of each avocado half with a knife, cutting down to but not through the skin.

3. Separate the diced flesh from the skin with a soup spoon inserted between the skin and the flesh, gently scooping out the avocado cubes.

WHEAT BERRY AND ARUGULA SALAD

MOST PEOPLE KNOW THAT WHOLE GRAINS ARE AN important part of a healthy diet, but daily servings don't have to stop with boring whole wheat toast or plain brown rice. Making a whole grain part of a salad with a bright dressing struck us as a great way to create a healthy, appealing meal. We knew we had several issues to tackle, so we started with the most important, choosing the right grain.

We began with amaranth and millet, but we found both to be too small, with a clumpy-sticky texture that didn't appeal in this setting. We wanted something with more individualized grains. Quinoa—which is a small, bead-shaped seed commonly treated as a grain—had better potential, but while tasters were excited about its earthy flavor, they didn't like its "caviar-like texture" for pairing with leafy greens. Then a fellow test cook suggested wheat berries—whole, unprocessed wheat kernels. Their nutty flavor, chewy texture, and larger shape won tasters over.

Now we needed to settle the best way to cook our wheat berries. Some recipes swore by simmering the kernels with exact proportions of water to wheat berries, though more relied on cooking the kernels like pasta, simply simmering the wheat berries in a large amount of water (both techniques required a long cooking time). We decided to go with the easier, more common method. After an hour of simmering, the grains had good texture, but we were disappointed to find the flavor had been somewhat diluted.

Taking another cue from pasta-cooking techniques, we added salt to the boiling water. Working with our standard ratio of 1 tablespoon of salt to 4 quarts of water, we cooked up another batch. This time we had an unexpected result; after an hour of cooking, the wheat berries were still incredibly hard. It turns out the salinity of the water was preventing the wheat from absorbing it. We decided to test separate batches, each with a different amount of salt. Right off the bat, tasters complained that the wheat berries cooked with 1 and 2 teaspoons of salt were still too hard. Those cooked with ¼ teaspoon and ½ teaspoon both produced grains with a pleasing texture and good flavor. In the end, we all agreed that just ½ teaspoon of salt allowed the wheat berries to achieve the proper tenderness and lent the best flavor boost. After draining and cooling the grains under running water, we were ready to move on.

WHEAT BERRY AND ARUGULA SALAD

With simplicity in mind, we considered the additional components for our salad. A bed of arugula worked best in this setting, lending a slightly peppery flavor that complemented the mild grain. A simple orange, lime, and cilantro vinaigrette spiked with cumin, paprika, and cayenne provided the perfect amount of spice and brightness. Tasters appreciated the sweet flavor and touch of color from roasted red peppers. Several test cooks also wanted some textural contrast, and chickpeas did this job well. At this point tasters loved our salad, but one suggested adding feta. Just 2 ounces crumbled into the salad continued the Mediterranean theme and created a cool, creamy counterpoint that made the perfect finishing touch.

Wheat Berry and Arugula Salad

SERVES 4

Wheat berries can be found in the health food section of most grocery stores. Once fully cooked, the wheat berries will still retain a chewy texture.

DRESSING

- 1 cup fresh orange juice (about 2 oranges)
- ¼ cup chopped fresh cilantro
- 2 tablespoons fresh lime juice
- 2 tablespoons water
- 1 tablespoon extra-virgin olive oil
- 2 teaspoons honey
- 2 garlic cloves, minced
- ¼ teaspoon salt
- ½ teaspoon ground cumin
- ¼ teaspoon paprika
- ⅛ teaspoon cayenne pepper

SALAD

- 1 cup wheat berries (see note)
  Salt
- 1 (15-ounce) can chickpeas, drained and rinsed
- ½ cup jarred roasted red peppers, drained, patted dry, and chopped
- 2 ounces feta cheese, crumbled (about ½ cup)
  Black pepper
- 8 ounces baby arugula (about 8 cups)

1. FOR THE DRESSING: Bring the orange juice to a simmer in a small saucepan over medium-high heat.

Reduce the heat to medium and cook until the juice is syrupy and reduced to ⅓ cup, 12 to 15 minutes.

2. Transfer the orange juice syrup to a small bowl and refrigerate until cool, about 10 minutes. Whisk in the cilantro, lime juice, water, oil, honey, garlic, salt, cumin, paprika, and cayenne and set aside.

3. FOR THE SALAD: Bring 4 quarts water to a boil in a large pot. Add the wheat berries and ½ teaspoon salt, partially cover, and cook, stirring often, until tender but still chewy, about 1 hour. Drain the wheat berries and rinse them under cold running water until cool. Transfer the wheat berries to a large bowl and set aside.

4. TO ASSEMBLE THE SALAD: Stir the chickpeas, roasted red peppers, feta, and half of the dressing into the bowl with the wheat berries. Season with salt and black pepper to taste. In a separate bowl, toss the arugula with the remaining dressing and divide among four plates. Arrange 1 cup of the wheat berry mixture on top of each salad and serve.

PER SERVING: Cal 410; Fat 8g; Sat fat 2g; Chol 10mg; Carb 69g; Protein 17g; Fiber 13g; Sodium 580mg

NOTES FROM THE TEST KITCHEN

THE BEST EXTRA-VIRGIN OLIVE OIL

We love extra-virgin olive oil drizzled over pasta or in a vinaigrette (we prefer not to use it for cooking since high heat destroys its distinctive taste). It not only provides a uniquely fruity flavor but it also plays a positive role in a healthy diet. Rich in monosaturated fats and antioxidants, olive oil has gained a lot of attention as a "good" fat that lowers "bad" cholesterol while maintaining or raising the "good" cholesterol—studies indicate that it helps protect against the effects of heart and artery disease, among other benefits. Used in moderation, it's definitely a positive. But health benefits aside, which one tastes the best? The options at the supermarket are overwhelming, so we set out to find our favorite. The best-quality oil comes from olives picked at their peak and processed as soon as possible, without heat (which can coax more oil from the olives but at the expense of flavor), and we found that our favorite oils were produced from a blend of olives and, thus, were well rounded. In our tasting, **Columela Extra Virgin Olive Oil** from Spain, $22 for 25.4 ounces, beat out the competition for its fruity flavor and excellent balance.

GARDEN MINESTRONE

SOUPS AND STEWS

M = TEST KITCHEN MAKEOVER

MINESTRONE

MINESTRONE, LITERALLY "BIG SOUP" IN ITALIAN, IS A broth- and tomato-based soup packed with vegetables, beans, herbs, and usually a starch (either pasta or rice). In some regions of Italy, minestrone is garnished with a potent dollop of pesto. There is no definitive recipe because Italian cooks typically use whatever vegetables and leftovers they have on hand. Generally speaking, a good minestrone captures the fleeting flavors of summer vegetables in a bowl. But this soup can easily turn stodgy and bland if you don't treat the vegetables right. We wanted to create a lighter, livelier version that would showcase a windfall of summer vegetables.

We began by sautéing onions and carrots in olive oil to build flavor, a step that appeared in almost every recipe we found, and one that proved to be a must. We passed up canned tomatoes in favor of chopped fresh tomatoes for a lighter, more summery flavor. For our liquid component, tasters preferred the mild flavor of chicken broth to tinny, overly sweet vegetable broth or heavier beef broth. We then added some ingredients that were givens in our minds—garlic, green beans, pasta (which we chose over rice), and summer squash—and let this soup cook until everything was tender.

This soup was lighter, all right. And far from lively. For bolder tomato flavor, we decided to cook some of the tomatoes with the onion and carrot until they broke down and began to resemble something like a fresh, sweeter tomato paste. A little white wine added a bright note of acidity, and fresh thyme lent a welcome herbal quality. When we added the chicken broth and more raw tomatoes (for another layer of garden-fresh flavor), our soup tasted like it was on track. We just needed to do a little fine-tuning.

During our tastings, test cooks had complained about the slimy texture of the summer squash (we used both yellow squash and zucchini). To fix this, we removed the watery seeds and browned the squash (we decided to add some of the garlic at the same time to mellow and deepen its flavor). We set this mixture aside so that we could add it back at the end of cooking, thus preserving its texture and preventing it from becoming soggy and overcooked.

Many minestrone recipes call for hearty greens like cabbage, collard greens, or kale, but these didn't seem summery enough. For a lighter feel, we tried fresh spinach, but its mild flavor faded quickly among the other vegetables. Since some recipes offer a pesto garnish, we wondered if fresh basil leaves could serve double duty as an herb and a "vegetable." A full 4 cups of roughly chopped basil added a texture and bold herbal flavor that tasters loved. To further lighten the soup, we eliminated heavy starches such as pasta and rice altogether. Instead, we relied solely on the creamy texture and delicate flavor of white navy beans to add a subtle heartiness to the soup. Now this was a minestrone that tasted like summer.

NOTES FROM THE TEST KITCHEN

SEEDING SUMMER SQUASH
Both yellow squash and zucchini are filled with small translucent seeds that can have a bitter taste and slimy texture. To avoid slippery squash, choose small to medium specimens that weigh 8 to 10 ounces (they contain fewer seeds), halve the squash lengthwise, and use a spoon or melon baller to scoop out the seeds.

SEEDS BE GONE
Avoid slimy soup by seeding the summer squash.

PUTTING THE GARDEN IN MINESTRONE

1. To preserve the delicate texture of summer squash while maximizing its sweet flavor, brown the seeded squash (with plenty of garlic) at the onset of cooking, remove it from the pot, and then add it back just prior to serving.

2. To add body to the soup without making it too heavy, make a fresh "tomato paste" by cooking half the seeded tomatoes until they begin to brown.

3. To add a bright herbal flavor and leafy texture, stir in freshly chopped basil just before serving.

Garden Minestrone

SERVES 8

You can use any combination of zucchini and yellow squash for this recipe. If desired, serve the minestrone with grated Parmesan cheese and a drizzle of extra-virgin olive oil.

1½ pounds summer squash (about 3 medium; see note), halved, seeded (see page 24), and cut into ½-inch pieces

2 teaspoons olive oil

Salt

6 garlic cloves, minced

1 onion, minced (about 1 cup)

1 carrot, peeled and cut into ½-inch pieces

2 pounds tomatoes (about 6 medium), cored, seeded, and chopped medium

Pepper

2 teaspoons minced fresh thyme, or ½ teaspoon dried

½ cup dry white wine

2 (15-ounce) cans navy beans, drained and rinsed

8 cups low-sodium chicken broth

8 ounces green beans, trimmed and cut into 1-inch pieces

4 cups loosely packed basil leaves

1. Combine the squash, 1 teaspoon of the oil, and ¼ teaspoon salt in a large Dutch oven. Cover and cook, stirring occasionally, over medium-low heat until the squash releases its juice, 3 to 5 minutes. Uncover, increase the heat to medium-high, and continue to cook, stirring occasionally, until the squash is golden brown and just tender, 2 to 3 minutes longer. Stir in half of the garlic and cook until fragrant, about 30 seconds. Transfer the squash to a plate.

2. Combine the remaining 1 teaspoon oil, onion, carrot, and ¼ teaspoon salt in the pot. Cover and cook, stirring occasionally, over medium-low heat until the onion is softened, 8 to 10 minutes. Uncover, increase the heat to medium-high, and continue to cook, stirring occasionally, until the onion is lightly browned, 4 to 6 minutes longer.

3. Stir in half of the tomatoes and ½ teaspoon pepper and cook until the juice has evaporated and the tomatoes begin to brown, 5 to 7 minutes. Stir in the remaining garlic and thyme and cook until fragrant, about 30 seconds. Stir in the wine, scraping up any browned bits.

4. Bring the wine to a simmer over medium-high heat and cook until reduced by half, about 2 minutes. Add the navy beans, broth, green beans, and remaining tomatoes and return to a simmer. Reduce the heat to medium-low and cook until the green beans are tender, about 15 minutes.

5. Place the basil in a heavy-duty gallon-sized zipper-lock bag. Pound the bag with the flat side of a meat pounder or a rolling pin until all the leaves are lightly bruised. Remove the leaves from the bag and coarsely chop.

6. Stir the squash and basil into the soup and cook until the squash is heated through, about 1 minute. Season with salt and pepper to taste and serve.

PER 1¾-CUP SERVING: Cal 270; Fat 3g; Sat fat 0g; Chol 0mg; Carb 52g; Protein 16g; Fiber 12g; Sodium 1050mg

SPRING VEGETABLE SOUP

FOUND IN MYRIAD INTERPRETATIONS, SPRING vegetable soup is sometimes inherently vegetarian, while other versions rely on beef bones and meat for flavor. Some are chunky, almost stew-like; others are silky purees. We were after a spring vegetable soup that was simple and clean-tasting and would make use of the tender green vegetables of the season. Moreover, while we wanted our soup to be light and fresh, it also needed to be substantial enough to serve for supper with just a crusty roll or a slice of whole grain bread.

Early in our recipe-testing process, we learned something critical about the inherent nature of a soup based on spring vegetables. While most other soups rely on their main ingredients for flavor, character, and overall heft, we found that spring vegetables are simply too delicate to carry this load. To make a good spring soup, these tender vegetables would need the support of a broth that was rich and multidimensional, not overwhelmed by any single, distinctive flavor. Because of this, we decided to turn our focus to building a flavorful liquid base.

Homemade vegetable broth was an obvious solution, but we were hoping to avoid making a broth from scratch. Doctoring store-bought broth was a more appealing approach. A few tests with canned vegetable broth, a natural starting point for vegetable soup, left us disappointed. These soups were too sweet, with tinny notes that overwhelmed the delicate vegetables and turned tasters off. Store-bought chicken broth, a test kitchen mainstay, was more promising, with a mellow flavor and sturdy character. On its own it didn't have enough vegetable flavor, but with a little tinkering we thought it would work well.

To see what combination would best boost the broth's flavor, we worked our way through a variety of vegetables, from carrots and onion to dried mushrooms and cauliflower. In the end, we found that the hallowed trio of carrot, celery, and onion, with some help from fennel, leek, and garlic, turned the broth into something rich and satisfying. Parsley, a sprig of thyme, and a bay leaf also helped reinforce the overall flavor change from store-bought to fresh.

Looking to streamline the process, we tried using a food processor to prepare the vegetables before adding them to the broth. However, the blades of the food processor battered and tore them up, eliciting an off, acidic flavor from the onions, leek, and fennel. Chopping the vegetables by hand was a necessity, and we realized the importance of cutting them into small pieces so they could release their flavors quickly. Sweating the vegetables lightly (which breaks down the vegetable cells, jump-starting the release of their flavor) before adding the canned broth deepened the flavor of the broth and reduced simmering time considerably. Finally, we had a quick broth that was chock-full of flavor. It was time to focus on the main characters in our soup: the spring vegetables.

We wanted an uncluttered, clean soup filled only with vegetables from the season. Leeks, green peas, asparagus, and baby spinach all made the cut. Their tender flavors, differing shapes, and varying shades of green made for a balanced and elegant lineup. Tomatoes added unwelcome acidity, and fava beans involved too much work. We found that while chard and arugula would have lent good color and flavor, their spicy bite overwhelmed the other flavors in our soup. Small red potatoes contributed some body, along with color and texture. Scallions, celery, and carrots were all omitted, since they did little but crowd and distract.

Cooking the five finalists—leeks, peas, baby spinach, asparagus, and red potatoes—was easy enough. The broth, still warm after being doctored and strained, was quickly brought to a simmer to poach our vegetables. The leeks and potatoes went in first, then the asparagus, and finally the spinach and peas just before serving. The vegetables took well to this gentle cooking process, and the flavorful broth brought out and reinforced the flavor of each. Garnished only with chopped tarragon, our soup had an unmistakable spring flavor.

Spring Vegetable Soup

SERVES 6

With its bright, fresh ingredients, this soup is best served immediately.

BROTH

- 2 onions, minced (about 2 cups)
- 1 carrot, peeled and chopped fine
- 1 celery rib, chopped fine
- 1 leek, white and light green parts only, chopped fine and rinsed thoroughly
- 1 fennel bulb (12 ounces), stalks removed, halved, cored, and chopped fine (see page 44)
- 3 garlic cloves, unpeeled and crushed
- 1 teaspoon canola oil
- ½ teaspoon salt
- 7 cups low-sodium chicken broth
- 2 whole black peppercorns
- 1 sprig fresh thyme
- 5 sprigs fresh parsley
- 1 bay leaf

SOUP

- 1 pound leeks, white and light green parts only, halved lengthwise, cut into 1-inch lengths, and rinsed thoroughly
- 12 ounces red potatoes (2 medium), scrubbed and cut into ¾-inch pieces
- ½ bunch asparagus (about 8 ounces), tough ends trimmed and cut into 1-inch lengths
- 1 cup frozen peas (4 ounces)
- 3 ounces baby spinach (about 3 cups)
- 2 tablespoons chopped fresh tarragon
  Salt and pepper

1. FOR THE BROTH: Combine the onions, carrot, celery, leek, fennel, garlic, oil, and salt in a large Dutch oven. Cover and cook over medium-low heat, stirring occasionally, until the vegetables are softened, 8 to 10 minutes.

2. Stir in the broth, peppercorns, thyme, parsley, and bay leaf. Bring to a simmer over medium-high heat, reduce the heat to medium-low, and cook for 15 minutes. Pour the broth through a fine-mesh strainer into a large bowl. Discard the solids in the strainer.

3. FOR THE SOUP: Bring the broth to a simmer in a clean Dutch oven over medium heat. Add the leeks and potatoes and cook for 5 minutes. Add the asparagus and cook until the vegetables are just tender, about 5 minutes.

4. Off the heat, stir in the peas, spinach, and tarragon, cover, and let sit until heated through, about 4 minutes. Season with salt and pepper to taste and serve.

PER 1½-CUP SERVING: **Cal** 140; **Fat** 1.5g; **Sat fat** 0g; **Chol** 0mg; **Carb** 26g; **Protein** 6g; **Fiber** 5g; **Sodium** 900mg

TORTELLINI SOUP

A SIMPLE COMBINATION OF TORTELLINI AND GREENS gently simmered in chicken broth, tortellini soup is naturally quick and easy to assemble. In its purest form, this soup relies on just three ingredients—homemade pasta, rich, flavorful chicken broth, and garden-fresh greens. The problem is, most home cooks don't have homemade pasta and long-simmered chicken broth on hand. Also, while the main ingredients of this soup are light, the garnishes—olive oil and Parmesan cheese—can cause the fat and calorie counts to spike if not used sparingly. We wanted a tortellini soup that we could make with common supermarket ingredients but that was still plenty flavorful, and we wanted to keep it light.

First we looked at the chicken broth. Since we didn't have time to make a broth from scratch, we looked for a few ways to infuse store-bought broth with flavor. Lightly browning onions in olive oil would impart some richness to the soup, and a generous hand with the aromatics—five minced garlic cloves and three bay leaves (most soups we make rely on just one or two bay leaves)—would add some depth.

Next we looked at our other key players: the pasta and greens. Fresh tortellini (the type in plastic packages found in the deli section of the supermarket) was the closest to homemade pasta and was much preferred over frozen tortellini. We then tested a variety of greens,

chopping them up and simmering them in our fortified chicken broth until tender. Kale was dismissed because it took too long to cook. Swiss chard and collards cooked more quickly, but tasters thought they were too hearty for this soup. Tender arugula had some promise, but its spiciness was overpowering. Spinach, however, was praised for its mild, earthy flavor and bright green color.

Right off the bat we were attracted to the convenience of bagged, prewashed baby spinach, but we were disappointed when the delicate leaves disintegrated in the simmering broth. The sturdy texture of both curly-leaf spinach and bunch spinach held up better, but stemming them was tedious. Revisiting bagged baby spinach, we considered our approach for our Spring Vegetable Soup (page 26). The answer, we realized, was to take the soup off the heat before stirring in the spinach. After a few minutes it was perfect, wilted but not broken down.

Our soup so far was fine, but not stellar. Something was missing. It was a little too light, and while tortellini soup is often finished with copious amounts of olive oil and Parmesan, we didn't want to load our soup with fat. Instead, we wondered if some additional vegetables might give us the bright flavors and depth we were looking for. We tried adding chopped fennel and asparagus, but their flavor overpowered the spinach. Cubed eggplant was slimy, and tasters agreed bell pepper and carrots were out of place. Zucchini and peas, however, fit the bill, adding texture and fresh garden flavor without being overwhelming. As we learned with our Garden Minestrone (page 25), simply chopping and tossing zucchini into a brothy soup can result in a slimy, unappealing texture. Seeding the zucchini, then browning it in the pot before starting the soup, solved this problem. To preserve its texture, we set the zucchini aside after browning and added it to the soup with the spinach at the end of cooking.

Looking for ways to further brighten the soup, we stirred in some lemon zest and chopped basil just before serving. This was so successful that we decided to add another flavor boost by stirring in some more garlic with the lemon and basil. Tasters were impressed with this final punch of fresh, vibrant flavor. Finally, we garnished each bowl with a little Parmesan cheese—just a touch was all our soup needed.

Tortellini and Vegetable Soup

SERVES 8

The choice of tortellini makes a big difference in this soup—we prefer fresh (the type in plastic packages found in the deli section of the supermarket).

6	garlic cloves, minced
1	zucchini, seeded (see page 24) and cut into ½-inch pieces
2	teaspoons olive oil
	Salt
1	onion, minced (about 1 cup)
1	teaspoon minced fresh thyme, or ¼ teaspoon dried
6	cups low-sodium chicken broth
3	bay leaves
1	(9-ounce) package fresh cheese tortellini (see note)
6	ounces baby spinach (about 6 cups)
1	cup frozen peas (4 ounces)
2	tablespoons chopped fresh basil
⅛	teaspoon grated lemon zest
	Pepper
¼	cup grated Parmesan cheese

1. Measure out and reserve 1 teaspoon of the minced garlic. Combine the zucchini, 1 teaspoon of the oil, and ⅛ teaspoon salt in a large Dutch oven. Cover and cook over medium-low heat, stirring occasionally, until the zucchini releases its juice, 3 to 5 minutes. Uncover, increase the heat to medium-high, and continue to cook, stirring occasionally, until the zucchini is golden brown and just tender, 2 to 3 minutes longer. Transfer the zucchini to a plate.

2. Combine the onion, the remaining 1 teaspoon oil, and ⅛ teaspoon salt in the pot. Cover and cook over medium-low heat, stirring occasionally, until softened, 8 to 10 minutes. Uncover, increase the heat to medium-high, and continue to cook, stirring occasionally, until the onion is lightly browned, 4 to 6 minutes longer.

3. Stir in the remaining garlic and thyme and cook until fragrant, about 30 seconds. Stir in the broth and bay leaves, scraping up any browned bits. Bring to a simmer, add the tortellini, and cook, stirring often, until just tender, 3 to 6 minutes.

4. Off the heat, stir in the zucchini, spinach, and peas, cover, and let sit until heated through, about 4 minutes. Stir in the reserved 1 teaspoon garlic, basil, and lemon zest. Season the soup with salt and pepper to taste, ladle it into bowls, and sprinkle each portion with some of the cheese before serving.

PER 1½-CUP SERVING: Cal 150; **Fat** 4g; **Sat fat** 1.5g; **Chol** 15mg; **Carb** 23g; **Protein** 8g; **Fiber** 3g; **Sodium** 710mg

NOTES FROM THE TEST KITCHEN

KEEPING BAY LEAVES FRESH

Many of our soup recipes rely on dried bay leaves for adding depth to the broth, and it certainly doesn't take many of the potent herb to do the job. But if they aren't stored properly, bay leaves won't do much of anything for flavoring, so we decided to find out what kind of storage was best for helping this intensely flavored herb retain its potency. We tested recipes using bay leaves from a freshly opened jar; from a jar that had been opened three months before, the lid replaced, and the jar stored at room temperature; and from a zipper-lock freezer bag that had been stored in the freezer for three months. We were amazed at the degree of flavor loss in the leaves stored in the jar; the fresh bay leaves tasted nearly twice as flavorful. The leaves stored in the freezer were nearly as good as those from the freshly opened jar.

THE BEST GARLIC PRESSES

Hand-mincing garlic is a chore many cooks avoid by turning to a garlic press. Our favorite model is **Kuhn Rikon's Easy-Squeeze Garlic Press** (left), $20. Though its plastic material seems less sturdy than other metal models, this garlic press performed best—its longer handle and shorter distance between the pivot point and the plunger help make pressing less work. The deeply curving plastic handles are also easier to squeeze together than straight handles. Another favorite is the **Trudeau Garlic Press** (right)—with its solid construction, it is sturdy and easy to use and is our best buy at a reasonable $11.99.

ASIAN CHICKEN NOODLE SOUP

HOMEMADE CHICKEN NOODLE SOUP IS A WHOLESOME, nourishing comfort food that is also inherently light. But while we love soup made from a long-simmered, homemade broth, making broth is a project that most of us just don't have time for. We wanted a quicker, easier chicken noodle soup that still had deep flavor and was full of tender vegetables, juicy meat, and perfectly cooked noodles. Looking for a new twist on traditional chicken noodle soup, we decided that incorporating some bright, aromatic Asian flavors would be a welcome change of pace.

Most recipes for fast homemade chicken soups are the same: Chunks of chicken and vegetables are dumped into store-bought chicken broth and quickly boiled. Sure, this method is fast, but it yields not only a weak-flavored broth but also dry, flavorless cubes of chicken. In a simple chicken noodle soup, the broth is a core ingredient that carries the flavors, so energizing the bland broth was our first task. Given our Asian theme, simmering minced garlic and ginger in the broth was a great first step toward boosting the flavor, and soy sauce and sherry took it to yet another level. Now our broth was greatly improved, but tasters felt it still needed a bit more depth. We had a feeling our chicken could help in that regard.

Boneless, skinless breasts have the appeal of a short cooking time, but from past experience we knew that simply simmering cubes of meat in broth would lead to dry nuggets of chicken. We found we could easily avoid this problem—and add great flavor to the soup—by using bone-in, skin-on split chicken breasts. First we browned the chicken breasts, which left a nice fond on the bottom of the pot that would serve as a good flavor base for our broth. After removing the skin, we set the browned chicken aside and added the broth and some vegetables to the pot. Then the chicken breasts went into the liquid to poach whole. By cooking the chicken this way, we ensured that the meat remained moist and tender, and we gave our broth a deeper, more chicken-y flavor. Tasters preferred shredded chicken to cubes or strips, so once the meat was poached, we shredded it into bite-sized pieces and stirred the pieces back into the broth just before serving.

Next up was fine-tuning the vegetables and noodles. Sautéing some onion in the fond further enriched the flavor of our broth, and both bok choy and shiitake mushrooms made natural additions to this Asian-inspired soup. Carrots lent a sweet flavor and some bright color. Tasters liked the chewy texture of fresh Chinese noodles, though dried linguine worked as well. Cooking the noodles after the chicken breasts had been removed from the pot to be shredded guaranteed that the noodles were not overcooked. Finally, we stirred in some thinly sliced scallions for their fresh flavor and mild bite. Our healthy Asian chicken noodle soup was as comforting as its traditional counterpart—but quick enough to make any night of the week.

NOTES FROM THE TEST KITCHEN

THE BEST CHICKEN BROTH

Among the many options lining the grocery store shelves, is there a single store-bought broth that is a worthy stand-in for a homemade broth? We discovered that the key was finding a broth with two important characteristics: less than 700 milligrams of sodium per serving and a short ingredient list that includes vegetables like carrots, celery, and onions. Our favorite broth, **Swanson Certified Organic Free Range Chicken Broth,** won tasters over with its "very chicken-y flavor" and "hints of roastiness."

OUR FAVORITE LADLE

You might think one ladle is pretty much the same as the next. But after dunking eight stainless steel models (plastic models stain and can melt on the stovetop) into pots of chicken noodle soup and hearty beef stew, scattered puddles on the test kitchen countertop made it clear that not all ladles are ergonomically equal. Ladles with handles shorter than 9 inches simply sank in deeper pots, and more than 10 inches of grip proved cumbersome to maneuver. Ladles with small bowls are better suited to sauces than soups, and an offset handle is a must—without some slight bend in the handle, cleanly transferring the ladle's contents to a bowl is nearly impossible. A handle that bends too dramatically, however, makes it difficult to dip the ladle into a tall, narrow stockpot. The **Rösle Ladle with Pouring Rim & Hook Handle,** $29.95, had everything we were looking for—including a hook handle and a drip-prevention pouring rim, which kept even wiggly noodles intact all the way to the bowl.

Asian Chicken Noodle Soup

SERVES 6

You can substitute 4 ounces dried linguine for the fresh Chinese noodles. Fresh noodles will take about 6 minutes to become tender; linguine will take about 15 minutes.

1½   pounds bone-in, skin-on split chicken breasts, trimmed (see page 29)

    Salt and pepper

1½   teaspoons canola oil

4   ounces shiitake mushrooms, stemmed and sliced ¼ inch thick

1   onion, minced (about 1 cup)

1   small head bok choy, greens and stalks separated, greens sliced thin and stalks chopped medium

1   large carrot, chopped medium

1   tablespoon grated or minced fresh ginger

2   garlic cloves, minced

8   cups low-sodium chicken broth

2   tablespoons low-sodium soy sauce

2   tablespoons dry sherry

6   ounces fresh Chinese egg noodles (see note)

2   scallions, sliced thin

1. Pat the chicken breasts dry with paper towels and season with ⅛ teaspoon salt and ⅛ teaspoon pepper. Heat the oil in a large Dutch oven over medium-high heat until just smoking. Carefully lay the chicken, skin-side down, in the pot and cook until golden brown on both sides, 10 to 12 minutes, flipping the breasts halfway through. Transfer the chicken to a plate and remove and discard the skin.

2. Add the mushrooms, onion, and ¼ teaspoon salt to the oil left in the pot, reduce the heat to medium-low, cover, and cook, stirring occasionally, until the vegetables are softened, 8 to 10 minutes. Uncover, stir in the bok choy stalks, carrot, ginger, and garlic, and cook until fragrant, about 30 seconds. Stir in the broth, soy sauce, and sherry, scraping up any browned bits.

3. Return the chicken, along with any accumulated juice, to the pot. Bring to a simmer over medium-high heat. Cover, reduce the heat to medium-low, and cook until the thickest part of the breasts registers 160 to 165 degrees on an instant-read thermometer, about 20 minutes.

4. Transfer the chicken to a plate. When the chicken is cool enough to handle, shred the meat into bite-sized pieces, discarding the bones.

5. While the chicken cools, return the soup to a simmer, add the noodles, and cook until just tender. Add the shredded chicken and bok choy leaves to the soup and cook until the leaves are just wilted, about 2 minutes. Stir in the scallions, season with salt and pepper to taste, and serve.

PER 1½-CUP SERVING: Cal 230; Fat 3.5g; Sat fat 0g; Chol 45mg; Carb 25g; Protein 25g; Fiber 3g; Sodium 1230mg

TORTILLA SOUP

IF YOU'RE MINDFUL OF FAT AND CALORIES, YOU might dismiss Mexican food as an option, and if you're thinking of the kind found in fast-food joints and mall food courts, you'd be absolutely right. However, some authentic Mexican cuisine can be quite healthful. Case in point: tortilla soup.

This heady chicken-tomato broth with chunks of chicken and colorful garnishes always satisfies with its intense flavors and contrasting textures. But we had a few issues: Authentic recipes call for some uniquely Mexican ingredients, such as *cotija* (a type of cheese) and *epazote* (a common Mexican herb). And the fried tortilla strips and typical overload of fattier garnishes (*crema* or sour cream, cheese, and avocado) don't make tortilla soup a light meal. We wanted to create a full-flavored version of this classic that not only was lighter, but would also rely on ingredients easily found in American supermarkets.

To begin, we broke down the soup into its three classic components: a flavor base made with fresh tomatoes, garlic, onion, and chiles; the chicken broth; and an array of garnishes. We zeroed in on the flavor base first. The recipes we found with the most flavor potential called for a basic Mexican cooking technique in which the vegetables are charred in a cast-iron skillet, then pureed and fried to create a concentrated paste. We started by charring our tomatoes, and the results were superb, but it took 25 attentive minutes to do. We wondered if adding chipotle chiles (smoked jalapeños) to the mix would allow us to skip charring the tomatoes altogether. Canned in a vinegary tomato mixture called adobo sauce, chipotles pack heat and roasted smoky flavor, and they're convenient. After pureeing the chipotles with the tomatoes, onion, and jalapeños, we found that cooking the mixture over high heat forced out water and further concentrated the flavors.

TORTILLA SOUP

It was time to move on to the broth. It's hard to beat homemade, but, as with our other lightened recipes, we wanted to move this soup into the express lane. Doctoring store-bought broth was yet again our preferred approach for getting a flavorful base but keeping the recipe's time line reasonable. We started with bone-in chicken breasts since they would contribute more flavor than boneless, and we decided that browning the chicken, which we had done for the noodle soup, wasn't necessary since this soup offered so many bold flavors. We tried poaching the chicken (skin removed) in broth bolstered with onion and garlic, knowing from experience that the chicken would both release and take on flavor while it cooked. The meat was done in just 20 minutes, so we removed the chicken from the liquid, shredded the meat, and waited to stir the pieces

back into the soup before serving. This chicken retained its juiciness and tenderness, and our broth was nicely flavored.

Authentic tortilla soup recipes call for fresh epazote, which imparts a heady flavor and fragrance, but this herb is difficult to find in most parts of the States. We found the pairing of strong, warm oregano with pungent cilantro was a close substitute, providing both intensity and complexity. We now had deeply flavored broth that, when combined with the tomato mixture, made for a soup that was close to tasting like the real thing.

Deep-fried corn tortillas are traditional, but frying is time-consuming and adds loads of calories. After some testing, we came up with a technique for crisping the tortillas that was quick and easy and didn't involve copious amounts of oil: lightly coating tortilla strips with vegetable oil spray and toasting them in the oven. The result? Chips that were crisp, not greasy, and much easier to prepare than their fried cousins.

For the garnishes, lime and cilantro added nice brightness, and a little avocado in moderation lent a creamy counterpoint to the bold flavors. This tortilla soup was light yet satisfying and loaded with flavors—no one even missed the cotija or crema.

NOTES FROM THE TEST KITCHEN

CORN TORTILLAS

We tasted six brands of corn tortillas and found that thicker tortillas did not brown as well in the oven and became more chewy than crisp. Thin tortillas, either white or yellow, quickly became feather-light and crisp when oven-fried. The same applied to steaming, and the thicker varieties quickly became leathery as they cooled. Flavor differences among brands were slight, but locally made tortillas did pack a bit more corn flavor than national brands. Our advice? Purchase the thinnest tortillas you can find and choose a locally made brand, if possible

THICK
Too Chewy

THIN
Just Right

REVIVING TIRED HERBS

You likely don't use an entire bunch of cilantro for one recipe, and after a few days of storage, the bunch of what's left might look a little weary. There's an easy way to refresh it (and, in the process, wash it) for the next recipe. Lop off the stems, submerge the leaves in a bowl of ice water, then swish them around to loosen any dirt and grit. Let them stand for 5 to 10 minutes, until they perk up and regain their lost vitality. To drain, instead of pouring the whole lot into a colander or salad spinner basket, which will upset the grit settled in the bottom of the bowl, lift the greens out of the water using your hands, leaving the dirt behind. This also works for parsley or mint. Of course, if the leaves remain utterly limp and lifeless after you try this trick, they are probably beyond resurrection.

Tortilla Soup

SERVES 6

If you prefer a soup with milder spiciness, cut the chipotle amount in half. We like this soup as is, but you can add a dollop of low-fat sour cream, minced jalapeño, and shredded reduced-fat Monterey Jack cheese.

TORTILLA STRIPS
- 8 (6-inch) corn tortillas, cut into ½-inch-wide strips
  Vegetable oil spray
  Salt

SOUP
- 8 cups low-sodium chicken broth
- 1½ pounds bone-in, skin-on split chicken breasts, trimmed (see page 61), skin removed
- 1 very large white onion (about 1 pound), root end trimmed, peeled and quartered
- 4 garlic cloves, peeled
- 8–10 sprigs fresh cilantro, plus 2 tablespoons chopped
- 1 sprig fresh oregano
  Salt

12 ounces tomatoes (about 2 medium), cored
and quartered

1 tablespoon minced canned chipotle chiles in
adobo sauce (see note)

1 teaspoon canola oil

1 avocado, pitted, peeled, and cut into ½-inch pieces
(see page 19)

Lime wedges, for serving

1. FOR THE TORTILLA STRIPS: Adjust an oven rack to the middle position and heat the oven to 425 degrees. Spread the tortilla strips on a rimmed baking sheet and lightly coat both sides with vegetable oil spray. Bake until the strips are deep golden brown and crisp, about 10 minutes, rotating the pan and shaking the strips to redistribute halfway through. Season the strips with salt to taste and transfer to a paper towel–lined plate.

2. FOR THE SOUP: Combine the broth, chicken breasts, 2 of the onion quarters, 2 of the garlic cloves, cilantro sprigs, oregano, and ¼ teaspoon salt in a Dutch oven. Bring to a simmer over medium-high heat. Cover, reduce the heat to medium-low, and cook until the thickest part of the breasts registers 160 to 165 degrees on an instant-read thermometer, about 20 minutes.

3. Transfer the chicken breasts to a plate. When the chicken is cool enough to handle, shred the meat into bite-sized pieces, discarding the bones. Meanwhile, pour the broth through a fine-mesh strainer; discard the solids in the strainer.

4. Process the remaining 2 onion quarters, remaining 2 garlic cloves, tomatoes, and chipotle together in a food processor until smooth, 15 to 20 seconds. Heat the oil in a clean Dutch oven over high heat until just smoking. Add the onion-tomato mixture and ⅛ teaspoon salt and cook, stirring often, until the mixture has darkened in color, about 10 minutes.

5. Stir the strained broth into the pot and bring to a simmer over medium-high heat. Reduce the heat to medium-low and cook until the flavors have blended, about 15 minutes. Add the shredded chicken to the soup and continue to simmer until the chicken is heated through, about 2 minutes.

6. Divide the tortilla strips among 6 bowls, then ladle the soup into the bowls. Top each serving with a portion of the avocado and sprinkle with some of the chopped cilantro. Serve, passing the lime wedges separately.

PER 1½-CUP SERVING: Cal 280; Fat 9g; Sat fat 1g; Chol 45mg; Carb 28g; Protein 21g; Fiber 5 g; Sodium 1110mg

BROCCOLI-CHEDDAR SOUP

GOOD BROCCOLI-CHEDDAR SOUP IS A PERFECT balance of earthy broccoli and the bite of cheddar cheese. For most recipes, you start by pureeing cooked broccoli florets and onions, then add heavy cream, chicken broth, and, of course, plenty of cheese. A typical version has 460 calories and 38 grams of fat per serving. We found lots of low-fat recipes out there, most of which used reduced-fat dairy products (milk, yogurt, sour cream, even cream cheese). We made a handful of them and were disappointed when they came out watery, curdled, gloppy, or sour—and sorely lacking in both broccoli and cheddar flavors. So we set out to make our own satisfying low-fat version of this all-time favorite.

TEST KITCHEN
MAKEOVER

We began by sautéing broccoli stems and some minced onion before adding the cooking liquid (tasters liked chicken broth more than vegetable broth) and the broccoli florets. Incorporating the broccoli stems, which have as much flavor as florets, maximized the broccoli flavor and was a healthy way to increase the soup's bulk. For a subtle bite that would complement the cheese, we added a few cloves of garlic to the broccoli stems and onions while they were sautéing. After several tests, we found the onions were causing issues. We tried every single variety, but tasters thought their pungency was masking the broccoli flavor. Switching to milder leeks was the answer, and when pureed, they also lent a silky texture to the soup.

As for the dairy component, we learned quickly that unlike more delicate creamy vegetable soups that include just a touch of cream, broccoli-cheddar soup has bold flavors that require a large dose of dairy. Simply replacing the heavy cream with milk or half-and-half resulted in a too-thin, watery texture, and we knew from our initial tests that many thicker low-fat dairy products would curdle. Then we remembered a test kitchen recipe for creamy macaroni and cheese that uses evaporated milk. Evaporated milk is made by removing more than half the water found in milk to concentrate its flavor, and it contains stabilizers that keep it from separating when cooked. We decided to give the fat-free version a try, and sure enough, it produced a perfectly rich and satiny soup.

Of course, you can't have broccoli-cheddar soup without the cheddar. Some recipes use as much as a full pound of this comparatively fatty cheese, which adds both flavor and creaminess, but since the pureed leeks and evaporated milk were already creating just the right silky texture, we needed only enough cheese to flavor the soup. Similar to what we had discovered when making blue cheese dressing for our Buffalo Chicken Salad (page 5), using a bolder cheese—extra-sharp cheddar instead of mild or sharp—allowed us to get distinct cheese flavor from just 4 ounces.

NOTES FROM THE TEST KITCHEN

PREPARING BROCCOLI

1. Place the head of broccoli upside down on a cutting board. Trim the florets very close to their heads and cut into 1-inch pieces.

2. Trim and square off the broccoli stalks, removing the tough outer ⅛-inch layer.

3. Slice the trimmed stalks crosswise into ¼-inch-thick pieces.

MAKEOVER MAGIC

We found two ingredients to be essential to making over Broccoli-Cheddar Soup.

FAT-FREE EVAPORATED MILK
Using fat-free evaporated milk instead of cream gives this soup creamy texture without the extra fat.

LEEKS
Leeks provide flavor, color, and silky consistency in the soup.

After pureeing the broccoli-leek-broth mixture in the blender, we transferred it to a Dutch oven and whisked in the evaporated milk and cheddar. We quickly discovered we would have to whisk in the cheese off the heat to prevent it from separating and ruining the smooth texture. A little Dijon mustard added with the cheese provided extra tang and made the small amount of cheese taste more potent. This lighter broccoli-cheddar soup was just as satisfying as the original.

MAKEOVER SPOTLIGHT: BROCCOLI-CHEDDAR SOUP

	CALORIES	FAT	SAT FAT	CHOLESTEROL
BEFORE	460	38g	15g	60mg
AFTER	210	11g	6g	25mg

Broccoli-Cheddar Soup

SERVES 5

Make sure to buy evaporated milk, not sweetened condensed milk, which is not the same and will be too sugary for this recipe. Don't boil the soup after adding the cheese or it will separate.

- 1   bunch broccoli (about 1½ pounds), florets cut into 1-inch pieces, stems trimmed and sliced ¼ inch thick (see photos)
- 1   pound leeks, white and light green parts only, halved lengthwise, sliced thin, and rinsed thoroughly
- 2   teaspoons canola oil
    Salt
- 2   garlic cloves, minced
- 3   cups low-sodium chicken broth
- 1   cup water
- ¾   cup fat-free evaporated milk (see note)
- 1   tablespoon Dijon mustard
- 4   ounces extra-sharp cheddar cheese, shredded (about 1 cup)
    Pepper

1. Combine the broccoli stems, leeks, oil, and ⅛ teaspoon salt in a large Dutch oven. Cover and cook over medium-low heat, stirring occasionally, until the vegetables are just beginning to soften, 6 to 8 minutes. Uncover, stir in the garlic, and cook until fragrant, about 30 seconds.

2. Stir in the broth and water and bring to a simmer over medium-high heat. Cover, reduce the heat to medium-low, and cook until the broccoli stems are softened, about 8 minutes. Add the broccoli florets, cover, and continue to cook until tender, about 5 minutes longer.

3. Working in 2 batches, process the broccoli mixture in a blender until smooth, about 1 minute. Transfer the broccoli mixture to a clean Dutch oven, whisk in the evaporated milk and mustard, and warm over low heat until very hot.

4. Off the heat, whisk in the cheese, one handful at a time, until the cheese is melted and the soup is smooth. Season with salt and pepper to taste and serve.

PER 1½-CUP SERVING: Cal 210; Fat 11g; Sat fat 6g; Chol 25mg; Carb 17g; Protein 11g; Fiber 3g; Sodium 700mg

QUICK CARROT SOUP

FRESH CARROTS ARE A FLAVORFUL AND WHOLESOME kitchen staple and an ideal base for a healthy soup. For the busy cook, the typical slow-simmered carrot soup is not an option, but the flavor of quicker versions often falls short because they lack the depth and richness that a long cooking time imparts. In the name of convenience, these shortcut carrot soups often use dry, tasteless "baby" carrots and load up on cream, which further masks the carroty flavor. We wanted a quick and healthy pureed carrot soup, one with a silky texture and that actually tasted like sweet carrots.

We started with the star: the carrots. In many of the carrot soup recipes we found in our research, the carrots are roasted before the soup is made. While we love the flavor that comes from roasting, for this particular soup we wanted a clean, fresh carrot flavor as well as a quick method, so we put the roasting idea aside. We began by peeling and chopping whole carrots and tossing them into a pot with a little oil and salt to sauté over gentle heat. Adding a minced onion to the carrots gave the soup some savory notes and enhanced the carrots' flavor. As for additional aromatics, carrots and ginger are a classic combination, and 2 tablespoons of grated fresh ginger provided the soup with a spicy bite that didn't overpower the carrot flavor.

We cooked the carrots and onion until they were just softened before stirring in the ginger. We then tried using vegetable broth as the soup base, but it brought with it more sweetness than we wanted (not surprising, since it is made with, among other vegetables, carrots).

Chicken broth proved to be a much better, more balanced choice. After stirring in the ginger, we added the broth to the pot, simmered until the carrots were tender, then pureed the mixture in a blender until smooth.

We had coincidentally found when researching our Broccoli-Cheddar Soup (page 34) that heavy cream is used in many carrot soup recipes, but it was obviously off-limits for a light soup. Following in the footsteps of the broccoli soup recipe, we tried using evaporated milk, but it was too sweet for pairing with the already-sweet carrots. We then tried half-and-half as well as milk. Half-and-half was good but a little too rich for our goal of a light, summery soup. Adding skim milk or 2 percent milk was the equivalent of adding more broth—these versions were too watery and not at all satisfying. But whole milk proved just right, making our soup smooth and creamy without overwhelming the carrot flavor.

Our soup was nearly there, but it needed some brightness. We found that supplementing the milk with orange juice lent the soup a citrusy freshness that other quick soups often lack. This light soup was bursting with fresh carrot flavor, highlighted by clean orange and ginger accents. A sprinkle of chives, a touch of grated nutmeg, or some plain low-fat yogurt all served as a good finishing touch.

Quick Carrot-Ginger Soup

SERVES 4

Serve with a dollop of plain low-fat yogurt, minced chives, or freshly grated nutmeg if desired.

1½   pounds carrots, peeled and chopped medium
 1   onion, minced (about 1 cup)
 2   teaspoons canola oil
     Salt
 2   tablespoons grated or minced fresh ginger
 3   cups low-sodium chicken broth
 ¾   cup whole milk
 ¼   cup orange juice
     Pepper

1. Combine the carrots, onion, oil, and ¼ teaspoon salt in a large Dutch oven. Cover and cook over medium-low heat, stirring occasionally, until the vegetables are softened, 8 to 10 minutes. Stir in the ginger and cook until fragrant, about 30 seconds.

2. Stir in the broth and bring to a simmer over medium-high heat. Cover, reduce the heat to medium-low, and cook until the carrots are tender, about 15 minutes.

3. Working in two batches, process the carrot mixture in a blender until smooth, about 1 minute. Transfer the mixture to a clean Dutch oven, stir in the milk and orange juice, and warm over low heat until very hot.

4. Season the soup with salt and pepper to taste, ladle it into bowls, and serve.

PER 1½-CUP SERVING: **Cal** 150; **Fat** 5g; **Sat fat** 1.5g; **Chol** 5mg; **Carb** 24g; **Protein** 4g; **Fiber** 6g; **Sodium** 710mg

---

NOTES FROM THE TEST KITCHEN

PUREEING SOUPS SAFELY

To prevent getting sprayed or burned by an exploding blender top, fill the blender jar only two-thirds full, hold the lid in place with a folded kitchen towel, and pulse rapidly a couple of times before blending continuously.

ROASTED BUTTERNUT SQUASH SOUP

ON A COLD WINTER'S EVENING, NOTHING BEATS THE rich flavor of a roasted butternut squash soup. Ideally, this soup should be smooth, silky, and bursting with sweet, caramelized squash flavor. But many versions we've tried are cloyingly sweet from too much brown sugar and overly rich and high in fat from a heavy hand with cream. Our challenge, then, was to develop a lighter recipe that featured a deep roasted-squash flavor and velvety texture, with its flavors and richness in perfect balance.

The first issue was how to prepare the squash for roasting. Recipes we found varied. In some, a whole squash is simply halved; in others, the squash is peeled and halved; and in still others, the squash is peeled and the flesh cubed before being tossed with oil. We tried

roasting squash prepared each way at 425 degrees (the high temperature would promote caramelization and quick cooking) and vastly preferred the peeled, cubed squash, which cooked fastest and developed more flavorful browning. However, this method used a generous amount of oil—a full ¼ cup—so we tried reducing the amount in increments. We found that 1 tablespoon was sufficient to coat the squash, prevent it from sticking to the pan, and still promote good browning. Boosting the oven temperature to 450 degrees further guaranteed consistently good caramelization and thorough cooking.

While the squash chunks roasted, we started the soup base by sautéing onions on the stovetop, then added chicken broth. We were happy to save time by cooking both the squash and the broth simultaneously, but then we realized we might be able to cook them not only at the same time, but in the same roasting pan in the oven. This would not only save us steps but also deepen the flavors even more. We started by tossing chopped onion with the oil and squash. Once the vegetables had browned, we added a little broth to deglaze the roasting pan and popped it back into the oven so the broth could reduce and concentrate in flavor. We then pureed the mixture in a blender and prepared to add the dairy.

Evaporated milk had worked as a low-fat alternative to cream for our Broccoli-Cheddar Soup (page 34), so we gave it a shot here. But just as we had learned with our Quick Carrot-Ginger Soup (page 35), the sweetness of evaporated milk was too much for the already-sweet squash. Next we tried using skim, low-fat, and whole milk, but all of these soups tasted too lean for a wintertime soup. In the end, we found half-and-half provided the right amount of dairy flavor and fat, making the soup smooth and creamy without overshadowing the vegetable.

The silky texture and deep flavor of the soup won approval from our tasters, but they also noticed a sharp onion flavor that stole a little thunder from the main ingredient. Switching to shallot, which has a sweeter, milder flavor than onion, fixed this problem. We finished our soup with a pinch of nutmeg, a classic squash seasoning, and just a tablespoon of maple syrup, which drew out the squash's natural sweetness without turning it into dessert. A little apple cider vinegar brightened everything up.

ROASTED BUTTERNUT SQUASH SOUP

PREPARING BUTTERNUT SQUASH

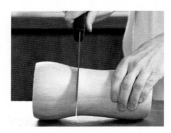

1. After removing the stem and root ends, cut the squash in half crosswise where the thinner neck meets the thicker base.

2. Use a vegetable peeler or paring knife to peel the skin from the squash, then cut the base in half to expose the seeds.

3. Use a large spoon to scrape the seeds and stringy pulp from the base of the squash. Chop each piece of squash as desired.

SQUASHED FOR TIME?

In addition to whole squash, most produce departments offer some time-saving alternatives: precut chunks of peeled butternut squash and peeled, halved butternut squash. Though both promised to streamline the prep, we were concerned that what we saved in time would be offset by poor texture and flavor. After making soups with both, and comparing them to soup made with fresh whole squash we had peeled and cubed ourselves, we weren't surprised that tasters preferred the "creamy" texture and "earthy sweetness" of the soup made with fresh squash. Still, tasters found the peeled, halved squash to be an acceptable substitute in the soup, lauding it as "balanced and nutty," though "not as squash-y" as the whole squash. The precut chunks, however, were "dry and stringy" with "barely any squash flavor."

Roasted Butternut Squash Soup

SERVES 5

Because the bulbous end of butternut squash contains the seeds and stringy fibers, purchase squash with a relatively long neck, as they have more usable flesh. If the soup is too thick after the half-and-half has been added, stir in additional water, ¼ cup at a time, to achieve the desired consistency. Garnish with freshly ground nutmeg if desired.

- 1 **butternut squash (about 3 pounds; see note), peeled, seeded, and cut into 1½-inch chunks (see photos)**
- 3 **shallots, peeled and quartered**
- 1 **tablespoon canola oil**
   Salt and pepper
- 4 **cups low-sodium chicken broth**
- ½ **cup water (see note)**
- ¼ **cup half-and-half**
- 1 **tablespoon maple syrup**
- 2 **teaspoons cider vinegar**
- ⅛ **teaspoon ground nutmeg**

1. Adjust an oven rack to the middle position, place a large roasting pan on the rack, and heat the oven to 450 degrees.

2. Toss the squash, shallots, oil, ½ teaspoon salt, and ¼ teaspoon pepper together in a large bowl, then spread the mixture in an even layer in the preheated roasting pan. Roast until the squash is softened and lightly browned, 50 to 60 minutes, stirring halfway through.

3. Add ½ cup of the broth to the pan and scrape up any browned bits. Return the pan to the oven and cook until the liquid has reduced and the vegetables are glazed, about 5 minutes.

4. Working in two batches, process the squash mixture, the remaining 3½ cups broth, and water in a blender until smooth, about 1 minute. Transfer the squash mixture to a Dutch oven and stir in the half-and-half, syrup, vinegar, and nutmeg. Warm over low heat until very hot.

5. Season the soup with salt and pepper to taste and serve.

PER 1½-CUP SERVING: Cal 190; Fat 4.5g; Sat fat 1g; Chol 5mg; Carb 38g; Protein 5g; Fiber 5g; Sodium 700mg

Curried Butternut Squash and Apple Soup

Serve with a dollop of plain low-fat yogurt, if desired.

Follow the recipe for Roasted Butternut Squash Soup, substituting 1½ pounds Golden Delicious apples (about 3), peeled, cored, and chopped, for half of the squash, and ½ teaspoon curry powder for the nutmeg. Omit the vinegar.

PER 1½-CUP SERVING: Cal 200; Fat 4.5g; Sat fat 1g; Chol 5mg; Carb 50g; Protein 4g; Fiber 5g; Sodium 700mg

Southwestern Butternut Squash Soup

Serve with a dollop of low-fat sour cream, if desired.

Follow the recipe for Roasted Butternut Squash Soup, substituting 1 tablespoon honey for the maple syrup, 2 teaspoons fresh lime juice for the vinegar, ½ teaspoon ground cumin for the nutmeg, and 2 tablespoons chopped fresh cilantro for the chives. Before serving, stir in 1 tablespoon minced canned chipotle chiles in adobo sauce.

PER 1½-CUP SERVING: Cal 190; Fat 5g; Sat fat 1g; Chol 5mg; Carb 38g; Protein 5g; Fiber 5g; Sodium 700mg

CAULIFLOWER SOUP

WE LOVE THE IDEA OF HIGHLIGHTING THE DELICATE flavor of cauliflower in a smooth, velvety soup. Many people boil the mild vegetable, but this results in overcooked cauliflower so bland that you can't even taste the cauliflower in the cauliflower soup. When properly prepared, cauliflower soup has a nutty, slightly sweet flavor that makes it an appealing meal or side dish any time of year. We wanted a healthy, flavorful recipe that would do this humble, underestimated vegetable justice.

First we set out to find the best way to cook the cauliflower. When we want to add flavor to vegetables we often turn to the oven and roast, a technique we had just used for our Roasted Butternut Squash Soup (page 38). It is a great way to coax big flavor from vegetables, as the dry heat caramelizes their natural sugars, creating a deep, smoky-sweet flavor. It seemed like a good choice for our cauliflower. We found three basic techniques for roasting cauliflower: roasting cauliflower that had been blanched, roasting cauliflower that had been steamed, and roasting raw cauliflower. In each preparation the cauliflower florets were also coated with oil, salt, and pepper at some point in the procedure. After tasting each side by side, we declared the cauliflower that had been roasted raw, with its attractive, browned exterior and well-developed flavor, the clear winner. The other two didn't brown as well and were less flavorful.

Now that the star of our soup had big flavor, we could turn to the other ingredients. As we had found with many of our soups, browned onion added flavor and depth. Taking a cue from how we had roasted the shallots with the squash in our Roasted Butternut Squash Soup, we tossed the onion with the oil and cauliflower and roasted them together in the oven to keep things simple. Because cauliflower is so mild-flavored, we felt it could take another flavor boost, so we then moved the vegetables to the stovetop and sweated them briefly in a Dutch oven with a little garlic, which would complement the roasty sweetness of the cauliflower and onions.

It was time to add the liquid. A base of chicken broth created the right balance, and tasters liked the hint of acidity that came from a splash of white wine. Simmering the wine before adding the chicken broth cooked off the alcohol and concentrated its flavor. At this point, because our cauliflower was already cooked, we only needed to add the florets to the pot to simmer just long enough for the flavors to meld. Then we pureed the mixture and were ready to move on to determining the dairy component.

Like most cream of vegetable soup recipes, the cauliflower soup recipes we came across relied on heavy cream for their dairy component. Looking for a substitute, we tested all types of milk, as well as half-and-half and evaporated milk. Milk didn't work here, because, as we had found with our squash soup recipe, it was simply too thin and flat for the fuller, deeper flavors of a roasted vegetable soup. Evaporated milk imparted its own sweetness that interfered with the more delicate taste of the cauliflower. In this situation, the half-and-half proved best (just as it had with the butternut squash soup), producing a soup with a smooth, velvety consistency and balanced roasted cauliflower flavor. We started with ¼ cup of half-and-half, but tasters thought this soup could take a larger dose of dairy, so we tested larger amounts and eventually settled on ½ cup. This soup was velvety and deeply flavorful, and we felt sure it would win over even the staunchest of cauliflower skeptics.

Roasted Cauliflower Soup

SERVES 4

If the soup is too thick after the half-and-half has been added, stir in water, ¼ cup at a time, to achieve the desired consistency.

- 1 head cauliflower (about 2 pounds), trimmed, cored, and cut into ½-inch florets (about 6 cups)
- 1 onion, halved and sliced ½ inch thick
- 4 teaspoons canola oil
- Salt and pepper
- 3 garlic cloves, minced
- ¼ cup dry white wine
- 1 bay leaf
- 3½ cups low-sodium chicken broth
- ½ cup half-and-half
- 1 tablespoon minced fresh chives

1. Adjust an oven rack to the middle position and heat the oven to 450 degrees.

2. Toss the cauliflower, onion, 1 tablespoon of the oil, ½ teaspoon salt, and ¼ teaspoon pepper together in a large bowl, then spread the mixture in an even layer on a rimmed baking sheet. Roast until the cauliflower is softened and lightly browned, 30 to 40 minutes, stirring halfway though.

3. Combine the roasted vegetables and remaining 1 teaspoon oil in a large Dutch oven. Cover and cook over medium-low heat, stirring occasionally, until the cauliflower is very soft, 3 to 5 minutes. Uncover, stir in the garlic, and cook until fragrant, about 30 seconds.

4. Stir in the wine and bay leaf and cook until the wine has reduced by half, about 1 minute. Stir in the broth and bring to a simmer over medium-high heat. Cover, reduce the heat to medium-low, and simmer for 5 minutes. Remove and discard the bay leaf.

5. Working in two batches, process the cauliflower mixture in a blender until smooth, about 1 minute. Transfer the cauliflower mixture to a clean Dutch oven, stir in the half-and-half, and warm over low heat until very hot.

6. Season with salt and pepper to taste, ladle into bowls, and sprinkle each portion with some of the chives before serving.

PER 1½-CUP SERVING: Cal 140; Fat 9g; Sat fat 2.5g; Chol 10mg; Carb 11g; Protein 4g; Fiber 3g; Sodium 830mg

VARIATION

Curried Roasted Cauliflower Soup

Follow the recipe for Roasted Cauliflower Soup, adding 1½ teaspoons curry powder to the pot with the roasted vegetables in step 3. Substitute 2 tablespoons minced fresh cilantro for the chives.

PER 1½-CUP SERVING: Cal 140; Fat 9g; Sat fat 2.5g; Chol 10mg; Carb 1g; Protein 4g; Fiber 3g; Sodium 830mg

MUSHROOM-BARLEY SOUP

THE EARTHINESS OF MUSHROOMS ADDS GREAT flavor to soups, and while a cream of mushroom soup always makes for a sophisticated meal, we already had plenty of creamy soups under our belts. Mushrooms can also make a hearty, rugged soup, especially when barley is added. That said, mushroom-barley soup often turns into barley-mushroom soup, meaning that the barley takes center stage and the mushrooms are left in the background. We wanted a soup that was all about the headiness of mushrooms, with barley lending a bit of texture and thickening power. In addition, we wanted our mushroom-barley soup to be able to stand on its own without leaning on a time-consuming homemade broth.

We started by cooking through a few mushroom-barley soup recipes we had come across. Some that caught our eye promised big flavor, starting with sautéing diced beef in some oil, cooking the mushrooms and other vegetables in the rendered beef fat, and then adding the liquid component to the pan. While this soup tasted rich and full-bodied, the beef flavor was overwhelming. We ruled out using any beef in our soup.

The other quick conclusion we made concerned the ratio of barley to liquid. In the recipes we found, this ratio varied from 2 teaspoons to 2 tablespoons of barley per cup of liquid. Barley can quickly take over a soup if not added in moderation. But, as it turned out, about 1 tablespoon per cup of liquid proved best. This balance allowed a couple of barley nuggets to find their way into each spoonful without overshadowing the other ingredients.

Although mushroom-barley soup isn't laden with tons of butter or heavy cream, a lot of recipes we found began with sautéing onion and white button mushrooms in a generous amount of oil—typically about ¼ cup. We were able to use just 1 tablespoon by relying on the technique we had developed for our Beef Stroganoff

TO WASH OR NOT TO WASH MUSHROOMS?

In the wild, mushrooms grow in damp forests where it rains all the time, so it actually makes no sense to claim that one should never wash mushrooms. You just want to avoid overdoing it. At some point, mushrooms can soak up water and become soggy. In the test kitchen, we place whole mushrooms in a colander, rinse them gently under cool running water, and then immediately pat them dry with towels. Because water beads up on the exterior of mushrooms, washing whole specimens is fine. Cut mushrooms are another story. The exposed flesh will soak up water like a sponge, so clean mushrooms before slicing them.

MUSHROOM MAGIC

In addition to using dried porcinis, we found a combination of two different fresh mushrooms was key for giving our soup its deep mushroom flavor.

PORTOBELLO

The heavyweight among cultivated mushrooms, portobellos gave our soup its intense mushroom flavor.

CREMINI

Also known as "brown buttons," creminis are simply tiny portobellos harvested before they mature. They gave our soup a rich, beefy flavor and visual appeal.

(page 94) in which we first covered the vegetables so they steamed in their own juices, then removed the lid and allowed them to brown. Once the mushrooms were browned, carrots, garlic, and thyme went into the pot. Chicken broth, barley, and a bay leaf were stirred in next, and the mixture was simmered until the barley was tender. This soup was good, but it was a bit washed out. We identified three different ingredients that might be able to boost the flavor and complexity: tomato paste, wine, and dried porcini mushrooms.

While some tasters found the flavor of the tomato paste appealing, most argued that its flavor and color (a burnished orange-red) made our recipe too much like canned soup. On the wine front, red wine muddied the flavors of the soup rather than bringing them together, and white wine made the soup harsh. Dried porcinis won over the crowd, providing a boost of mushroom essence and the depth we were looking for.

Up to this point, we had been using the supermarket staple, white button mushrooms. We felt as if the soup was pretty good, but we decided to tinker with different mushroom varieties. Not wanting to get too esoteric, we stuck to varieties that can usually be found in grocery stores: portobellos, creminis, and shiitakes. When we tried each of these different varieties, we realized what great potential this soup really had. While the shiitakes added an unwelcome pungency (and texturally became similar to fat rubber bands when cooked), the creminis and the portobellos (which are actually just grown-up creminis) gave our soup bravado. The creminis gave the soup an elegant look and somewhat "beefy" flavor, and the portobellos darkened the soup to an inky brown and gave it a more intense mushroom flavor.

Finally, we examined how to cut the mushrooms. We tried slicing, dicing, and cutting them into chunky quarters. We preferred cutting the smaller creminis into quarters. It was important to dice the portobellos small, however; otherwise they sautéed on the outside but steamed on the inside and were rubbery. All our soup needed was a few tablespoons of fresh parsley to add an herbal note and a touch of color.

Mushroom-Barley Soup

SERVES 6

If cremini or portobello mushrooms are not available, white button mushrooms can be substituted, though the soup won't be as flavorful.

- 1 **pound cremini mushrooms (see note), stemmed and quartered**
- 1 **pound portobello mushroom caps (4 medium; see note), cut into ¼-inch pieces**
- 1 **onion, minced (about 1 cup)**
- 1 **ounce dried porcini mushrooms, rinsed and minced**
- 1 **tablespoon canola oil**
  Salt
- 2 **carrots, peeled and chopped medium**
- 3 **garlic cloves, minced**
- 2 **teaspoons minced fresh thyme, or ½ teaspoon dried**
- 9 **cups low-sodium chicken broth**
- ½ **cup pearl barley**
- 1 **bay leaf**
- 2 **tablespoons minced fresh parsley**
  Pepper

1. Combine the creminis, portobellos, onion, dried porcinis, oil, and ½ teaspoon salt in a large Dutch oven. Cover and cook over medium-low heat, stirring occasionally, until the mushrooms are softened, 8 to 10 minutes. Uncover, increase the heat to medium-high, and continue to cook, stirring occasionally, until the mushrooms are well browned, 8 to 12 minutes longer.

2. Stir in the carrots, garlic, and thyme, and cook until fragrant, about 30 seconds. Stir in the broth, barley, and bay leaf, scraping up any browned bits. Bring to a simmer, reduce the heat to medium-low, and cook until the barley is tender, about 50 minutes.

3. Remove and discard the bay leaf. Stir in the parsley, season with salt and pepper to taste, and serve.

PER 1½-CUP SERVING: Cal 180; Fat 4g; Sat fat 0g; Chol 0mg; Carb 28g; Protein 8g; Fiber 6g; Sodium 1080mg

LENTIL SOUP

THICK AND HEARTY LENTIL SOUP HAS A LOT GOING for it: an appealing earthy flavor, and it's filling, healthy (lentils are high in protein, fiber, and a good source of iron), and inexpensive to make. But more often than not, what passes for lentil soup bears more similarity to thin slop or flavorless mud than soup. And even a picture-perfect bowlful of lentil soup can be an illusion—it still may have no flavor whatsoever. We set out to develop a recipe that would give this classic a lift.

Before we dealt with the flavor issues, we needed to pick the right lentil for the job. Many lentil soups resemble slop because some varieties of lentils fall apart when simmered. We wanted a soup with lentils that were still intact. We settled on testing the three varieties commonly found on supermarket shelves—brown, green, and red—as well as a couple of types found at specialty markets and natural foods stores, black and small French green lentils (lentilles du Puy). We made five pots of a basic lentil soup, each one using a different type. Red lentils were out—they disintegrated when simmered. The four remaining choices all produced soups with acceptable texture, but tasters most preferred, as expected, the earthy flavor and firm texture of the lentilles du Puy.

Now that we knew which lentil was best for our soup, we were ready to fine-tune our cooking method. A few recipes recommended soaking the lentils for a few hours, but this was unnecessary since lentils cook rather quickly.

Quite a few Indian cookbooks called for sweating the lentils in a covered pan before adding the liquid. So after cooking onions, carrots, and tomatoes until they began to soften, we added our aromatics and lentils, along with a little salt and pepper, to the pan. We found that sweating the lentils for about 10 minutes strengthened their outer skin and helped keep them intact while still ensuring a tender interior. These lentils were definitely firmer after simmering than lentils that had not been sweated.

It was time to move on to the other ingredients. A majority of recipes we found included pork, from ham bone and ham hock to prosciutto, pancetta, and bacon. Although bacon isn't first to come to mind when making a light recipe, we found it gave us the best bang for the buck for a number of reasons. Just two strips of chopped bacon was enough to infuse the entire soup with deep, smoky flavor. Another advantage of using the bacon was the rendered bacon fat, which we used to sauté the aromatics and add even deeper flavor.

Some recipes we found used water as the cooking liquid and relied entirely on the pork ingredient (in our case, the bacon) to flavor the cooking water. However, we found this approach gave us a soup base that was too bland. Chicken broth was a good start for adding depth, and a full ¾ cup of white wine added a necessary brightness. Tomatoes, garlic, onions, bay leaves, and fresh thyme all further rounded out the flavors.

Our soup tasted great, but it wasn't quite as hearty as we wanted. We found that simply pureeing some of the lentils thickened up the soup base perfectly but still left us plenty of whole, intact lentils for appealing texture.

Many recipes add vinegar or lemon juice just before the soup is served for an acidic contrast to the overall earthy flavor. We found that tasters preferred the flavor of balsamic vinegar most, as it added brightness as well as richness. It was the perfect finishing touch.

NOTES FROM THE TEST KITCHEN

SWEATING LENTILS
While French green lentils (also known as lentilles du Puy) are preferred in this soup because they hold their shape the best, even they can begin to fall apart. We learned that the trick to keeping lentils intact is sweating them, a technique we found in many Indian cookbooks. Sweating the lentils in the presence of salt and acid (in this case, the canned tomatoes) prevents the coating of the lentils from breaking down and allows the lentils to stay intact for a longer period of time.

Lentil Soup

SERVES 5

Lentilles du Puy (French green lentils) are our preferred choice for this recipe, but they can be hard to find. Plain green, brown, or black lentils will also work. Whichever type of lentil you decide to buy, we recommend that you buy them from a market with high turnover, since lentils lose flavor with age.

- 2 slices bacon, chopped fine
- 2 onions, minced (about 2 cups)
- 2 carrots, peeled and chopped fine
- 1 (14.5-ounce) can diced tomatoes, drained
  Salt
- 3 garlic cloves, minced
- 1 teaspoon minced fresh thyme, or ¼ teaspoon dried
- 1¼ cups (about 9 ounces) lentilles du Puy (French green lentils; see note), rinsed and picked through
  Pepper
- ¾ cup dry white wine
- 4 cups low-sodium chicken broth
- 1½ cups water
- 1 bay leaf
- 1 tablespoon balsamic vinegar

1. Cook the bacon in a large Dutch oven over medium-low heat, stirring often, until the fat is rendered and the bacon is crisp, 8 to 10 minutes. Add the onions, carrots, tomatoes, and ¼ teaspoon salt, cover, and cook, stirring occasionally, until the vegetables begin to soften, 2 to 4 minutes. Uncover, stir in the garlic and thyme, and cook until fragrant, about 30 seconds.

2. Stir in the lentils, ¼ teaspoon salt, and ¼ teaspoon pepper; cover and cook, stirring occasionally, until the vegetables are softened and the lentils have become darker, 8 to 10 minutes.

3. Uncover, increase the heat to medium-high, stir in the wine, and cook until reduced by half, about 1 minute. Stir in the broth, water, and bay leaf, and bring to a simmer. Partially cover, reduce the heat to medium-low, and cook until the lentils are tender but still hold their shape, 30 to 35 minutes. Remove and discard the bay leaf.

4. Process 3 cups of the soup in a blender until smooth, about 1 minute. Return the pureed soup to the pot and warm over low heat until very hot. Stir in the vinegar, season with salt and pepper to taste, and serve.

PER 1½-CUP SERVING: Cal 280; Fat 6g; Sat fat 1.5g; Chol 5mg; Carb 41g; Protein 13g; Fiber 9g; Sodium 1020mg

HEARTY CHICKEN STEW

SAY "BEEF STEW" AND MOST PEOPLE WILL PICTURE a belly-filling meal loaded with chunks of boneless browned beef along with vegetables in a rich, dark sauce. So what, then, is chicken stew? It seems a bit harder to define. Here in the test kitchen, we pictured making a dish similar to beef stew, but on the lighter side: tender, substantial chunks of chicken accompanied by a few bright, savory vegetables, enveloped in a glossy, flavorful sauce. We wanted a bowl of chicken stew that was healthy and hearty, a meal that was comforting but also lively with vibrant, fresh flavors.

For a starting point, we decided to mirror the method we use for making beef stew—brown the meat, make a sauce with aromatics, flour, wine, and broth, then simmer the meat and vegetables in the sauce until they are tender. Beginning with the chicken, we chose bone-in breasts since they are more flavorful and less likely to dry out than boneless, skinless breasts. As with the chicken-based soups we had made, we knew the bones would also add flavor to our stew. We also knew browning the meat would be an important step because the fond (the browned bits that cling to the bottom of the pot) would help us build flavor for the base of the stew. Keeping the skin in a light recipe wasn't an option, but browning the chicken without it caused the delicate breast meat to dry out. So we left the skin on to protect the meat during browning and removed it before adding the meat back to the stew.

Next up was bringing together some flavorful components, starting with a base of aromatics. Beef stew usually starts with onions; we chose leeks instead for their more delicate flavor that seemed better suited to the lighter profile we had in mind. The leeks would also give the sauce a silky texture as they broke down during cooking. The anise flavor of fennel paired well with the leeks, as did saffron, which we liked for its earthy flavor and bright color. Next to go into the pot were garlic, thyme, and bay leaves, all of which added depth without overwhelming. Flour is usually added with the aromatics to thicken beef stew. We started with 3 tablespoons, an amount we would normally add for beef stew, but this made our chicken stew thicker than we wanted. We found that 2 tablespoons of flour gave the sauce just the right body.

Next we stirred in broth, and while our beef stew relied on red wine for depth, we felt dry sherry, with its sweeter taste, would be a better match for chicken. We brought it to a simmer before returning the chicken to the pot along with some vegetables. We wanted a filling stew, so we chose a few select hearty vegetables. Tasters liked the earthy flavors of carrots and red potatoes.

At this point, we would transfer beef stew to the oven for a few hours to break down the beef's connective tissue and tenderize it, but because chicken breasts contain little connective tissue, there's no benefit to long cooking. Instead we continued to simmer our stew on the stovetop; it took only about 20 minutes for the chicken to cook through and the vegetables to become tender.

NOTES FROM THE TEST KITCHEN

PREPARING FENNEL

1. Cut off the stems and feathery fronds. (The fronds can be minced and used as a garnish, if desired.)

2. Trim a very thin slice from the base and remove any tough or blemished outer layers from the bulb.

3. Cut the bulb in half through the base. Use a small, sharp knife to remove the pyramid-shaped core.

4. Slice each fennel half into thin strips. If the recipe calls for chopping finely, then finely chop the strips crosswise.

Since we wanted a bowl of stew that didn't require a knife and fork to eat, we removed the meat from the bones and shredded it before adding it back to the pot. Finally, a sprinkling of parsley and a good dose of lemon juice brightened things up. Our hearty chicken stew was wholesome, satisfying, and ready in less than an hour.

Hearty Chicken Stew with Leeks, Fennel, and Saffron
SERVES 6

Buy saffron threads, not powder, and crumble them yourself for the best flavor.

3	pounds bone-in, skin-on split chicken breasts, trimmed (see page 61)
	Salt and pepper
1½	teaspoons canola oil
1	pound leeks, white and light green parts only, halved lengthwise, sliced thin, and rinsed thoroughly
1	large fennel bulb (about 1 pound), stalks removed, halved, cored, and cut into ¼-inch-thick strips (see photos)
4	garlic cloves, minced
2	teaspoons minced fresh thyme, or ½ teaspoon dried
¼	teaspoon saffron threads, crumbled (see note)
2	tablespoons unbleached all-purpose flour
3½	cups low-sodium chicken broth
½	cup dry sherry
1	pound carrots, peeled and sliced ¼ inch thick
1	pound red potatoes, scrubbed and cut into ½-inch pieces
2	bay leaves
¼	cup minced fresh parsley
2	tablespoons fresh lemon juice

1. Pat the chicken breasts dry with paper towels and season with ¼ teaspoon salt and ¼ teaspoon pepper. Heat the oil in a large Dutch oven over medium-high heat until just smoking. Carefully lay the chicken, skin-side down, in the pot and cook until golden brown on both sides, 10 to 12 minutes, flipping the breasts halfway through. Transfer the chicken to a plate and remove and discard the skin.

2. Add the leeks, fennel, and ¼ teaspoon salt to the oil left in the pot, reduce the heat to medium-low, cover, and cook, stirring occasionally, until the vegetables are softened, 8 to 10 minutes. Uncover, stir in the garlic, thyme, and saffron, and cook until fragrant, about 30 seconds. Stir in the flour and cook for 1 minute. Whisk in the broth and sherry, scraping up any browned bits.

3. Return the chicken, along with any accumulated juice, to the pot. Stir in the carrots, potatoes, and bay leaves. Bring to a simmer over medium-high heat. Cover, reduce the heat to medium-low, and cook until the thickest part of the breasts registers 160 to 165 degrees on an instant-read thermometer, about 20 minutes.

4. Transfer the chicken to a plate and remove and discard the bay leaves. When the chicken is cool enough to handle, shred the meat into large pieces, discarding the bones.

5. Return the shredded chicken to the pot and cook until heated through, about 2 minutes. Stir in the parsley and lemon juice, season with salt and pepper to taste, and serve.

PER 1⅔-CUP SERVING: Cal 390; Fat 4g; Sat fat 0.5g; Chol 105mg; Carb 37g; Protein 47g; Fiber 6g; Sodium 740mg

SPANISH SHELLFISH STEW

FIND A COUNTRY WITH A COASTLINE AND YOU WILL find fish stew in the culinary repertoire. One of our favorite versions hails from Spain. Though less well known than France's *bouillabaisse* and Italy's *cioppino,* Spain's tomato-based *zarzuela,* chock-full of shellfish like lobsters, clams, and mussels, is distinctively seasoned with saffron and paprika and thickened with a *picada,* a flavorful mixture of ground almonds, bread crumbs, and olive oil. Unlike most fish stews, zarzuela contains no fish stock—instead the shellfish release their rich liquors into the pot as they cook. The shells, too, serve to fortify the stew's liquid base, a combination of tomatoes and white wine. We liked the idea of a healthy fish stew that didn't rely on a finicky stock, so we set out to master this popular Spanish dish.

We gathered several recipes for zarzuela and started cooking. Like many other Spanish recipes, zarzuela starts with a *sofrito* of onions, garlic, and red bell peppers, cooked until softened. Then paprika, saffron, red pepper flakes, and bay leaves join the sofrito to create a distinctly Spanish flavor. Tomatoes and dry white wine are then added to the pot to form the liquid base. For simplicity we reached for canned tomatoes, and we considered both whole and diced. Although we had to chop the whole tomatoes, their flavor and texture in this stew were preferable to canned diced tomatoes. Some recipes include brandy in addition to white wine. After sampling the broth with and without, tasters favored the depth of flavor that brandy lent to the dish.

It was time to turn our attention to the shellfish. Typically, zarzuela includes lobster, shrimp, scallops, mussels, and clams. After some discussion, we decided to omit the fussy lobster, aware we'd have to do some fiddling to make up for the flavor it usually contributes.

Knowing that the shells contribute significant flavor to zarzuela, and given that we had decided to peel our shrimp before adding them to the stew (for easier eating), we thought we'd use the shrimp shells to enrich the broth's flavor. We sautéed the shells in a touch of olive oil and then steeped them in the wine. We chose to do this at the outset of cooking, so the shells would have plenty of time to infuse the wine with flavor while we prepared the other components. When it was time, we poured the wine through a strainer to remove the shells and added the wine to the pot. It provided a terrific flavor boost.

The final challenge was producing a stew with perfectly cooked shellfish. Since each type of shellfish was a different size and required a different cooking time, we knew we'd have to stagger the times when we added each variety. After some trial and error, we determined that the clams should be added to the stew first, followed by the mussels and scallops, and finally the shrimp.

A picada is stirred into this shellfish stew at the end to add both body and flavor. Most picadas contain ground almonds and fried bread crumbs. We found that fried bread, which requires a significant amount of oil, turned our stew greasy and added unwanted calories to what is otherwise a light dish. So instead, we toasted fresh bread crumbs with a little olive oil. To intensify the flavor of the almonds, we tossed them in with the bread crumbs to toast as well. Stirring the picada into the stew once the shellfish was cooked thickened the broth perfectly, and its rich, mellow flavor rounded out the meal. All that was left to do was sprinkle our stew with a handful of chopped fresh parsley and a squeeze of lemon for a bright, fresh finish.

SPANISH SHELLFISH STEW

Spanish Shellfish Stew

SERVES 4

Buy shrimp with their shells on and reserve the shells when cleaning the shrimp; they add important flavor to the cooking liquid in step 2. Buy saffron threads, not powder, and crumble them yourself for the best flavor.

PICADA

- 2 tablespoons slivered almonds
- 1 slice high-quality white sandwich bread, torn into quarters
- 1 teaspoon extra-virgin olive oil
  Pinch salt
  Pinch pepper

STEW

- 2 teaspoons olive oil
- 12 ounces extra-large shrimp (21 to 25 per pound), peeled and deveined, shells reserved (see note)
- 1½ cups dry white wine
- 1 onion, minced (about 1 cup)
- 1 red bell pepper, stemmed, seeded, and chopped fine
  Salt
- 3 garlic cloves, minced
- 1 teaspoon sweet paprika
- ¼ teaspoon saffron threads, crumbled (see note)
- ⅛ teaspoon red pepper flakes
- 2 bay leaves
- 2 tablespoons brandy
- 1 (28-ounce) can whole peeled tomatoes, juice reserved and tomatoes chopped medium
- 1½ pounds littleneck clams (about 16 clams), scrubbed
- 8 ounces mussels (about 16 mussels), scrubbed and debearded if necessary (see photo)
- 8 ounces large sea scallops (8 scallops), muscle removed (see page 16)
- 1 tablespoon chopped fresh parsley
- 1 teaspoon fresh lemon juice
  Pepper

1. FOR THE PICADA: Adjust an oven rack to the middle position and heat the oven to 375 degrees. Pulse the almonds in a food processor to fine crumbs, about 15 pulses. Add the bread, olive oil, salt, and pepper, and pulse the bread to coarse crumbs, about 10 pulses. Spread the mixture on a rimmed baking sheet and bake, stirring occasionally, until golden brown and dry, about 5 minutes. Set the crumbs aside to cool to room temperature.

2. FOR THE STEW: Heat 1 teaspoon of the oil in a medium saucepan over medium heat until shimmering. Add the reserved shrimp shells and cook until pink, 3 to 5 minutes. Off the heat, stir in the wine, cover, and let steep until ready to use.

3. Combine the remaining 1 teaspoon oil, onion, bell pepper, and ⅛ teaspoon salt in a large Dutch oven. Cover and cook over medium-low heat, stirring occasionally, until softened, 8 to 10 minutes. Uncover, increase the heat to medium-high, and continue to cook, stirring occasionally, until the vegetables are lightly browned, 4 to 6 minutes longer.

4. Stir in the garlic, paprika, saffron, pepper flakes, and bay leaves, and cook until fragrant, about 30 seconds. Stir in the brandy and cook until reduced by half, about 30 seconds. Stir in the tomatoes with their juice and cook until thickened slightly, 5 to 7 minutes.

5. Pour the wine mixture through a fine-mesh strainer into the Dutch oven, pressing on the shrimp shells to extract as much liquid as possible; discard the solids in the strainer. Bring to a simmer and cook until the flavors have melded, 3 to 5 minutes.

6. Add the clams, cover, and cook, stirring occasionally, until the first few clams begin to open, about 5 minutes. Add the mussels and scallops, cover, and cook until most of the clams have opened, about 3 minutes. Add the shrimp, cover, and continue to cook until the shrimp are pink and cooked through and the clams and mussels have opened, about 2 minutes longer.

7. Remove and discard the bay leaves and any clams or mussels that have not opened. Stir in the picada, parsley, and lemon juice, season with salt and pepper to taste, and serve.

PER SERVING: Cal 370; Fat 8g; Sat fat 1g; Chol 90mg; Carb 23g; Protein 29g; Fiber 2g; Sodium 910mg

NOTES FROM THE TEST KITCHEN

DEBEARDING MUSSELS

Some mussels contain a small, weedy beard that is easy to remove. Trap the beard between the side of a small paring knife and your thumb and pull it. Note that this should be done just before cooking the mussels.

RUSTIC WHITE BEAN STEW

CASSOULET, A FRENCH CLASSIC, MAKES FOR A HEARTY meal that's perfect any time there's a chill in the air. Typically composed of garlicky white beans, pork sausage, duck confit (a separate dish made by cooking duck in copious amounts of fat), and a variety of other meats, and occasionally topped with buttery bread crumbs, cassoulet can take three days to make, and the ingredients can be hard to find, not to mention the fact that this dish is notoriously high in fat. We wanted to use the basic flavors of cassoulet to create a lighter, simpler white bean stew that could be made in under an hour.

To start, we looked at the types of meat typically included: sausage, duck confit, and pork. We eliminated the duck confit entirely because in addition to being high in fat, it can be found only in very high-end grocers and takes an eternity to make at home. Fatty cuts of pork and sausage were out as well. We chose turkey kielbasa, a lower-fat version of traditional pork kielbasa that has a similar savory, smoky flavor and is available at most grocery stores. To get the most flavor out of the kielbasa, we chopped it into small pieces and browned it in a large Dutch oven, then set it aside while we built a flavorful base for the stew. A minced onion and some garlic were a good start. From the spice cabinet, we pulled out thyme, a bay leaf, and ground cloves, flavors that we thought would play off the beans and kielbasa nicely. One tablespoon of tomato paste brought out the sweet notes.

Cassoulet is traditionally prepared with Tarbais beans, a type of kidney-shaped white bean that is difficult to find stateside, but we thought that cannellini beans would work just fine. Since we were aiming for a quick stew, we reached for canned beans—there would be enough flavorful ingredients in this dish that we knew no one would miss the flavor of dried beans.

Turning to our sauce, we added chicken broth and vermouth to the pot; their flavors formed a bright base for our French-inspired dish. We then added the kielbasa and two cans of the beans, along with a can of diced tomatoes, to simmer in the broth and vermouth. So far our stew was looking good, but without all the meat, it needed something else, something that would contribute another flavor and texture. Although it is not a traditional ingredient in cassoulet, we stirred in some chopped kale, which added just the right earthiness and color and made the stew well rounded.

We liked the idea of the bread topping, but we wanted something less greasy than the traditional butter-soaked bread crumbs. We tore half a French baguette into 1-inch chunks and scattered them over the top of our stew. After coating the top of the bread with vegetable oil spray, we transferred the whole pot to the oven so that the topping could toast as the stew finished cooking. The bread emerged perfectly golden brown and crisp, and the stew, perfectly cooked. Our light and healthy white bean stew had a slow-cooked, countryside feel and flavor, but now it was happily streamlined for modern-day cooks.

Rustic White Bean Stew

SERVES 4

Canned navy or great Northern beans can be substituted for the cannellini beans.

- 2 teaspoons olive oil
- 4 ounces turkey kielbasa, halved lengthwise and sliced ¼ inch thick
- 1 onion, minced (about 1 cup)
  Salt
- 1 tablespoon tomato paste
- 1 tablespoon minced fresh thyme, or ¾ teaspoon dried
- 2 garlic cloves, minced
- 1 bay leaf
  Pinch ground cloves
- 1¾ cups low-sodium chicken broth
- 1 (14.5-ounce) can diced tomatoes, drained
- 1 cup dry vermouth or dry white wine
- 2 (15-ounce) cans cannellini beans (see note), drained and rinsed
- 8 ounces kale, stemmed (see page 49), leaves cut into 1-inch pieces
  Pepper
- 6 ounces rustic baguette (about ½ baguette), torn into 1-inch pieces (about 4 cups)
  Vegetable oil spray

1. Adjust an oven rack to the lower-middle position and heat the oven to 450 degrees.

2. Heat the oil in a large Dutch oven over medium-high heat until just smoking. Add the kielbasa and cook, stirring occasionally, until lightly browned, about 3 minutes. Transfer the kielbasa to a bowl.

3. Add the onion and ⅛ teaspoon salt to the oil left in the pot and return the pot to medium-low heat. Cover and cook, stirring occasionally, until the onion is softened, 8 to 10 minutes. Uncover, stir in the tomato paste, thyme, garlic, bay leaf, and cloves, and cook until fragrant, about 30 seconds. Stir in the broth, tomatoes, and vermouth, scraping up any browned bits.

4. Return the kielbasa, along with any accumulated juice, to the pot. Stir in the beans and bring to a simmer over medium-high heat. Stir in the kale, one handful at a time, and return to a simmer. Reduce the heat to medium-low, cover, and cook until the kale is just tender, about 15 minutes. Remove and discard the bay leaf and season with salt and pepper to taste.

5. Sprinkle the bread pieces evenly over the bean mixture to cover. Generously coat the bread with vegetable oil spray and season with a pinch salt and a pinch pepper. Bake until the bread pieces are toasted and golden brown, 15 to 20 minutes. Let sit for 10 minutes before serving.

PER SERVING: **Cal** 410; **Fat** 7g; **Sat fat** 1.5g; **Chol** 20mg; **Carb** 59g; **Protein** 18g; **Fiber** 8g; **Sodium** 1490mg

NOTES FROM THE TEST KITCHEN

HANDLING KALE

1. Hold the stem of each leaf over a bowl filled with water and slash the leafy portion from either side of the thick stem. Discard the stems, then wash and dry the leaves.

2. Stack some leaves in a short pile, roll the leaves into a tight cylinder, and slice crosswise into 1-inch pieces.

VEGETARIAN CHILI

ALTHOUGH THERE ARE COUNTLESS VERSIONS OF vegetarian chili, most come across as bland or one-dimensional, often relying on just one ingredient, such as beans or vegetables, making them more like a stew (or a bowl of baked beans) than chili. We wanted to create a vegetarian chili that was clearly chili, one that had some substance and complexity. We wanted a "meaty" chili that carnivores as well as vegetarians would want to eat.

Soy products are a staple protein source for vegetarians, so they seemed like the logical starting point for finding the meat stand-in for our chili. We gathered various options—tofu, tempeh, even textured vegetable protein (TVP)—and cooked up a simplified batch of chili using each. Tofu was an out-and-out failure, with silken and soft tofus disintegrating as expected. Even the extra-firm tofu crumbled into unappealing bits. TVP, a soy product that is sold dehydrated in flakes, became swollen when cooked, with a texture that won over no one. However, tasters were pleasantly surprised by the chili made with tempeh. Tempeh is a tender but firm soybean cake made from fermented whole soybeans, sometimes mixed with other grains such as rice or millet. While tempeh can taste slightly sour or yeasty on its own, it came across as mildly nutty when mixed with the bolder chili flavors. And the texture of this chili was actually "meaty."

Tempeh is usually marinated before cooking, but we decided against this step, knowing we'd be giving our chili plenty of flavor down the line with spices. However, we did feel that browning the tempeh, much as you might brown meat, would give its exterior good texture and boost its flavor a bit. We crumbled it and browned it in the pot, and even eaten on its own, tasters loved it.

While we didn't want to make beans the star, a balanced amount in our chili was a given. We narrowed a list of eight contenders down to three: red kidney, pinto, and black. We settled on red kidney beans, the most traditional choice for chili, but all three have an earthy flavor and firm texture that would have worked well.

It was time to consider the spices. Since our chili would be lacking the richness usually contributed by beef, we felt as though store-bought chili powder might fall a little flat. So first we tested making our own chili powder by toasting and pulverizing dried chiles. But this powder had too much kick and overwhelmed the mild tempeh. We decided commercial chili powder was the better option, even though it still had some bitterness that would need

VEGETARIAN CHILI

mellowing. Incorporating some vegetables struck us as a good way to balance out the bitterness and add color and texture. We added red bell pepper to a base of onion and garlic to see if it would help. It did. We then wondered if a cup of corn would tip the balance further. The flavor of the corn was great, and we appreciated its visual appeal. We liked it so much, in fact, that we decided to experiment more. Carrots added more sweetness and color, and they held up well. Zucchini, stirred in at the end (to preserve its texture), was surprisingly at home, adding a fresh accent to the long-cooked chili flavor.

Next we focused on the liquid. We had been relying on a simple combination of water bolstered by tomatoes. (We prefer diced tomatoes that we crush ourselves, rather than use canned crushed tomatoes, since brands of crushed vary so much.) Several recipes suggested using beer to build complexity in bean chili, so we thought we'd try it here. We found that it only added a sour note, so we left it out. Our chili was good, but the flavor was just a bit flat. Whole cumin seeds and the smoky heat of some minced chipotle chiles added just the right depth and a balanced complexity.

For our last few touches, a sprinkle of cilantro and a squeeze of lime just before serving brightened the flavors. With its mix of colorful vegetables, meaty tempeh, earthy beans, and great chili flavor, this chili won over everyone—carnivores included.

Vegetarian Chili

SERVES 6

Tempeh lends a meaty texture to this chili. You can substitute pinto beans or black beans for the kidney beans. If you like your chili spicier, add more minced chipotle chiles. Serve with low-fat sour cream, low-fat shredded cheese, chopped tomatoes, or minced onion if desired.

- 1 (28-ounce) can diced tomatoes
- 1 tablespoon canola oil
- 1 (8-ounce) package tempeh, crumbled into small pieces
- 1 tablespoon cumin seeds
- 2 carrots, peeled and chopped medium
- 1 onion, minced (about 1 cup)
- 1 red bell pepper, stemmed, seeded, and chopped fine
- 9 garlic cloves, minced
- 2 tablespoons chili powder
- 1 teaspoon minced canned chipotle chiles in adobo sauce (see note)
- Salt and pepper
- 3 cups water
- 1 (15-ounce) can kidney beans (see note), drained and rinsed
- 1 teaspoon dried oregano
- 1 cup frozen corn (4 ounces)
- 1 zucchini, halved, seeded (see page 24), and cut into ½-inch pieces
- ½ cup minced fresh cilantro
- 1 tablespoon fresh lime juice

1. Process the tomatoes, with their juice, in a food processor until smooth, about 10 seconds. Transfer to a bowl and set aside.

2. Heat 1 teaspoon of the oil in a large Dutch oven over medium-high heat until shimmering. Add the tempeh and cook, stirring occasionally, until browned, about 5 minutes. Transfer the tempeh to a bowl and set aside.

3. Reduce the heat to medium-low, add the cumin seeds, and cook, stirring often, until the seeds are toasted and very aromatic, about 1 minute. Add the remaining 2 teaspoons oil, carrots, onion, bell pepper, garlic, chili powder, chipotles, ½ teaspoon salt, and ¼ teaspoon pepper. Cover and cook, stirring occasionally, until the vegetables are softened, 8 to 10 minutes.

4. Uncover and stir in the processed tomatoes, water, beans, and oregano, scraping up any browned bits. Bring to a simmer and cook over medium-low heat until the chili is thickened slightly, about 45 minutes.

5. Stir in the reserved tempeh, corn, and zucchini, and cook until the zucchini is tender, 5 to 10 minutes. Off the heat, stir in the cilantro and lime juice and season with salt and pepper to taste. Serve with any desired accompaniments.

PER 1½-CUP SERVING: Cal 220; Fat 7g; Sat fat 1g; Chol 0 mg; Carb 30g; Protein 13g; Fiber 5g; Sodium 710mg

NOTES FROM THE TEST KITCHEN

GET TO KNOW TEMPEH
While tofu, drained and pressed soy-milk curds, has definitely hit the mainstream, its soy-based cousin, tempeh, might not be as familiar. Tempeh is made by fermenting cooked soybeans, which are formed into a firm, dense cake. Because it's better than tofu at holding its shape when cooked, it serves as a good meat substitute. It's also a healthy choice, since it is high in protein, cholesterol-free, and very low in fat. Tempeh is sold in most supermarkets.

SAUTÉED CHICKEN BREASTS WITH CHERRY TOMATOES, OLIVES, FETA, AND MINT

POULTRY

M = TEST KITCHEN MAKEOVER

SAUTÉED CHICKEN BREASTS

BONELESS, SKINLESS CHICKEN BREASTS ARE LIKELY A mainstay in the weekly rotation for anyone who wants to eat healthier. They are packed with protein and virtually fat-free—and they are also exceptionally easy to prepare. Though you could opt to broil or grill them, sautéing gives them that beautiful golden brown exterior that is both visually appealing and flavorful. Sautéing is also less fussy than grilling, and it allows for better control of the cooking than broiling. The major problem with sautéing is that it tends to dry out the meat—and eating dry chicken has about as much appeal as gnawing on cardboard. Ideally, a sautéed chicken breast should be juicy, with a golden, evenly browned crust. We felt sure we could nail down the best way to sauté boneless chicken breasts, and while we were at it we also wanted to transform them into an appealing, flavorful meal without relying on sauces full of butter and heavy cream, as so many recipes do.

We began by investigating what pan was best for sautéing. In the end, we found that a large, heavy-bottomed skillet was best. Pans smaller than 12 inches crowded our four chicken breasts and caused them to steam, resulting in pale, unappetizing-looking exteriors. We also preferred a traditional skillet to a nonstick one. This may seem counterintuitive since nonstick pans allow you to cook with less fat, but we found that regardless of skillet type, a certain amount of fat is necessary for a good sauté. We also liked using a traditional skillet because we wanted the fond, the browned bits that get left behind after browning in a traditional skillet, to build flavor for our topping or sauce.

So how much oil would we need? We wanted enough to brown the chicken evenly, while keeping the dish as light as possible. After cooking nearly 12 pounds of chicken, we found that 4 teaspoons was just enough. Sautéing the chicken with any less, even when we used vegetable oil spray, resulted in unattractive, spotty crusts (and slightly scorched pans).

In the test kitchen we know that a hot pan is necessary to get a good sear. We waited until our oil was just smoking before adding the chicken breasts to the skillet, but cooking the breasts at medium-high heat for the whole time resulted in a scorched pan and dry chicken. Turning the heat down when browning the second side of the breasts proved crucial to preventing the second side from turning to leather before the meat had cooked through.

Up to this point we had been using unfloured breasts, but we were curious whether flouring would make a difference. Indeed it did; the floured breasts were juicier, browned more evenly, and were less likely to stick to the skillet. A light coating was a definite plus.

Having nailed the cooking technique, we set out to determine how we would liven up our plain chicken breasts. Inspiration came in the form of a magazine photo of perfectly browned chicken breasts paired with

NOTES FROM THE TEST KITCHEN

THE BEST BONELESS, SKINLESS CHICKEN BREASTS

Given that they're affordable, easy to prepare, and an excellent low-fat source of protein, it's not surprising that boneless, skinless chicken breasts are standard in many home kitchens. To find out which brand is best, we gathered six popular brands of boneless, skinless chicken breasts, broiled them without seasoning, and had 20 tasters sample the chickens side by side. Among the contenders were one kosher bird, two "natural," and one "free-range." The remaining two were just "chicken."

The koshering process involves coating the chicken with salt to draw out any impurities; this process, similar to brining, results in moist, salty meat. Natural—in the case of chicken—simply means there are no antibiotics or hormones, and the birds are fed a vegetarian diet. "Free-range" means exactly what it says: The birds are not confined to small cages but are allowed to roam freely.

The tie for first place went to **Empire Kosher** (left) and the all-natural **Bell & Evans** (right). As the only kosher bird, Empire won points with tasters for its superior flavor, namely, salt.

BUYING KALAMATA OLIVES

Although kalamata olives are often packed in olive oil in their native Greece, on American soil we almost always find them swimming in a vinegary brine. We prefer the fresher kalamatas from the refrigerator section of the supermarket (also packed in brine), as the jarred, shelf-stable ones are bland and mushy in comparison. If you can't find kalamatas in the refrigerator section of your market, look for them at the salad bar.

a mixture of tomatoes, olives, and feta cheese. It looked colorful, inviting, and refreshingly light.

With a minimum of tests, the tomato relish came together in a flash. While the chicken rested, we tossed some garlic into the skillet, added cherry tomatoes and olives, and cooked the mixture just until the tomatoes began to wilt. The tomato juice mingled with the fond in the pan, picking up great flavor, and we ended up with a mixture that was part sauce, part side dish. Adding the feta cheese right to the hot pan caused our relish to lose some of its fresh-looking appeal (the cheese started to melt), so we poured the tomato-olive mixture over the chicken, then sprinkled the cheese over the top. The cool, tangy cheese was the perfect contrast to the warm, sweet tomatoes and briny olives. The finishing touch: a sprinkling of shredded mint leaves to add color and freshness. This chicken was light and refreshing, a satisfying meal perfect for a warm summer's night.

Sautéed Chicken Breasts with Cherry Tomatoes, Olives, Feta, and Mint
SERVES 4

If desired, basil can be substituted for the mint.

CHICKEN
- ½ cup unbleached all-purpose flour
- 4 (6-ounce) boneless, skinless chicken breasts, trimmed
- ⅛ teaspoon salt
- ⅛ teaspoon pepper
- 4 teaspoons canola oil

RELISH
- 2 garlic cloves, minced
- 12 ounces cherry tomatoes (about 2 cups), halved
- ⅓ cup kalamata olives, pitted and chopped
- 2 tablespoons water
- Salt and pepper
- 1 ounce feta cheese, crumbled (about ¼ cup)
- ¼ cup shredded fresh mint (see note)

1. FOR THE CHICKEN: Spread the flour in a shallow dish. Pat the chicken breasts dry with paper towels and season with the salt and pepper. Lightly dredge the chicken in the flour, shaking off the excess.

2. Heat the oil in a 12-inch skillet over medium-high heat until just smoking. Carefully lay the chicken breasts in the skillet and cook until well browned on the first side, 6 to 8 minutes. Flip the chicken, reduce the heat to medium, and continue to cook until the thickest part of the breasts registers 160 to 165 degrees on an instant-read thermometer, 6 to 8 minutes longer. Transfer the chicken to a platter, tent loosely with foil, and let rest while making the relish.

3. FOR THE RELISH: Add the garlic to the oil left in the skillet, return to medium heat, and cook until fragrant, about 30 seconds. Stir in the tomatoes, olives, and water, and cook, scraping up any browned bits, until the tomatoes are just softened, about 2 minutes. Stir in any accumulated chicken juice and season with salt and pepper to taste.

4. Pour the relish over the chicken breasts, sprinkle with the cheese and mint, and serve.

PER SERVING: Cal 310; Fat 12g; Sat fat 2.5g; Chol 100mg; Carb 8g; Protein 42g; Fiber 1g; Sodium 510mg

VARIATION

Sautéed Chicken Breasts with Cherry Tomatoes, Blue Cheese, and Scallions
Follow the recipe for Sautéed Chicken Breasts with Cherry Tomatoes, Olives, Feta, and Mint, omitting the olives and substituting 1 ounce blue cheese, crumbled (about ¼ cup), for the feta and 2 scallions, sliced thin, for the mint.

PER SERVING: Cal 300; Fat 9g; Sat fat 2.5g; Chol 105mg; Carb 10g; Protein 42g; Fiber 1g; Sodium 290mg

CHICKEN PICCATA

PICCATA WAS ORIGINALLY MADE WITH VEAL, BUT MOST recipes these days are made with chicken cutlets, which are floured, sautéed, then removed from the pan so a lemony, caper-studded pan sauce can be quickly assembled. When executed correctly, chicken piccata is a simple yet complex-tasting dish. Unfortunately, most recipes yield overcooked chicken and a sauce that is either bland or overbearingly tart. Plus, the dish is traditionally finished with lots of butter (the cutlets are also browned in it), tipping the scale on what would otherwise be a quick, healthy dinner. We wanted properly cooked chicken swathed in a bright but balanced sauce, one that was rich but didn't rely on so much fat to get there.

First, we considered how we would brown our cutlets. Though we wanted to cut back on the butter, we would still need some fat to achieve a golden brown crust.

CHICKEN PICCATA

Canola oil, which we had just successfully used to brown chicken breasts (see page 54), stood out as the best choice: It is lower in saturated fat than butter and is better for sautéing anyway because of its higher smoke point. We began by dredging cutlets in flour and browning them over medium-high heat, hoping to achieve a nicely browned, crisp crust quickly without drying out the meat. We found that while the cutlets got good color, even with short cooking times the high heat still dried out the thin-cut, lean meat. Moderate heat and a slightly shorter cooking time for the second side achieved the moist and juicy cutlets we were after. But now we had a new problem: The cutlets were on the second side for only about a minute, so the flour on that side wasn't cooking, and it turned unappealingly gluey. Omitting the flour altogether meant the first side didn't brown as well. A compromise was to flour only the first side of each cutlet, which gave us one nicely browned side ideal for presentation, while achieving the moist, juicy meat we wanted, and no unappetizing texture on the second side.

At this point in most recipes the chicken is removed and the pan is deglazed with lemon juice, but we found doing this muted the lemon's brightness. Deglazing instead with white wine and broth—and adding 4 teaspoons of lemon juice at the end of cooking—worked much better. To deepen the lemon flavor, we tried simmering lemon slices in the sauce as it reduced, but the pith (the white part between the peel and flesh) made the sauce too bitter. Grated zest added the right flavor, but tasters didn't like the chewy bits. Strips of zest proved to be the answer; they released their flavorful oils while the sauce cooked, and we could easily discard them before serving.

Salty, vinegary capers are an integral part of this dish, and we certainly were not going to skimp. Our tasters demanded a full 2 tablespoons. At this volume, there was no mistaking that this dish was piccata, but the sauce was beginning to taste a little too pickle-y. Quickly sautéing the capers (with a little garlic for added richness) before deglazing the pan perfectly tempered the harshness.

This piccata was almost perfect, but it tasted a little lean, even by our lightened-up standards. A teaspoon of flour added to the pan before deglazing and a tablespoon of butter added with the lemon juice went a long way toward enriching our sauce and creating a velvety consistency without adding a lot of fat. This piccata is plenty rich and flavorful—you won't even miss all the butter.

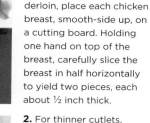

SERVES 4

Look for cutlets that are between ¼ inch and ½ inch thick, or make your own by slicing four 6-ounce boneless, skinless chicken breasts in half horizontally (see page 57).

- ¼ **cup plus 1 teaspoon unbleached all-purpose flour**
- 8 **(3-ounce) thin boneless, skinless chicken breast cutlets (see note)**
- ⅛ **teaspoon salt**
- ⅛ **teaspoon pepper**
- 2 **tablespoons canola oil**
- 2 **tablespoons drained capers, rinsed**
- 2 **garlic cloves, minced**
- 1 **cup low-sodium chicken broth**
- ½ **cup dry white wine**
- 4 **(2-inch) strips lemon zest plus 4 teaspoons fresh lemon juice**
- 1 **tablespoon unsalted butter, chilled**

1. Spread ¼ cup of the flour in a shallow dish. Pat the chicken cutlets dry with paper towels and season with the salt and pepper. Lightly dredge one side of each cutlet in the flour, shaking off the excess.

2. Heat 1 tablespoon of the oil in a 12-inch skillet over medium heat until shimmering. Carefully lay 4 of the chicken cutlets, floured-side down, in the skillet and cook until golden brown on the first side, about 3 minutes. Flip the cutlets and continue to cook until no longer pink, about 1 minute. Transfer the cutlets to a plate and tent loosely with foil. Return the skillet to medium heat and repeat with the remaining 1 tablespoon oil and the remaining 4 cutlets.

3. Add the capers and garlic to the oil left in the skillet, return to medium heat, and cook until fragrant, about 30 seconds. Stir in the remaining 1 teaspoon flour until incorporated. Whisk in the broth, wine, and lemon zest strips, scraping up any browned bits. Bring to a simmer and cook until thickened slightly and reduced to ½ cup, 10 to 15 minutes.

4. Return the chicken cutlets, along with any accumulated juice, to the skillet and simmer until heated through, about 30 seconds. Transfer the cutlets to a platter. Off the heat, remove the lemon zest and whisk in the lemon juice and butter. Spoon the sauce over the chicken and serve.

PER SERVING: Cal 310; Fat 12g; Sat fat 3g; Chol 105mg; Carb 4g; Protein 40g; Fiber 0g; Sodium 490mg

CHICKEN FLORENTINE

ALTHOUGH THE EARLIEST RECIPES FOR CHICKEN Florentine—chicken crowned with a bed of spinach and a cheesy cream sauce known as mornay—appeared in print as early as 1931, the concept really became popular 30 years later, when it was reinvented as a casserole, less appealingly made from frozen spinach, margarine, packaged bread crumbs, and condensed soups. Its decline continued in the decades following as it appeared on banquet hall buffets as rolled and fried chicken breasts stuffed with spinach and served with a gloppy sauce. Though it had begun as a relatively well-balanced meal, over the years chicken Florentine became bogged down by fat and calories. These days, a typical chicken Florentine recipe contains a whopping 670 calories and 53 grams of fat in each serving. We wanted to revisit this struggling dish and create a lighter version, a casserole that is easy to make but one that reflects its elegant—less heavy—past.

TEST KITCHEN
MAKEOVER

The sauce in chicken Florentine ties the dish together, but it also tends to be the calorie culprit. It made a logical starting place for our makeover. The base of the sauce in many Florentine recipes is heavy cream, which is simmered with cheese until it reduces to a velvety consistency. We needed a way to replace the reduced heavy cream and cheese and still achieve a smooth, rich sauce. We looked at three lower-fat dairy products—whole milk, evaporated milk, and half-and-half—and tested each in a basic sauce recipe. The milk-based sauce was disastrous, resulting in a gray, curdled mess, and the evaporated milk lent unwanted sweetness. Half-and-half proved best, but it still wasn't giving us a sauce with a luxurious consistency, and it lacked depth. A colleague suggested thickening chicken broth with a little flour and adding some cream at the end for richness. This produced a sauce with creamy body and rich flavor. Sautéing shallots and garlic at the outset, before adding the flour and broth, added even more. And with our sauce now touting bold flavor and creamy texture, there was no need to add cheese to it, so we reserved a small amount for garnish. With a minimum amount of cream and not a shred of cheese in our revamped sauce, our makeover was well on its way. We were ready to turn to the next crucial component—the chicken.

Many of the recipes we found for chicken Florentine called for sautéing the chicken until cooked, then setting it aside while preparing the sauce. We knew this standard method would work, but we wondered if we could marry the flavors of the sauce and the chicken earlier and streamline things. A fellow test cook suggested searing the chicken breasts and then poaching them in the simmering sauce to intensify the flavor of both. Opting to sear the chicken had multiple benefits: It gave the chicken breasts an attractive brown crust and created fond, which would flavor the sauce. This technique also provided another opportunity to lighten the dish, since a quick sear would require less oil than cooking the chicken through.

Back at the stove, we wilted a generous amount of baby spinach and set it aside to drain—key for avoiding a waterlogged mess. Then we added the chicken breasts to the hot skillet, seared them until they were brown on the outside, then set them aside as well. With the skillet empty, we proceeded to build the sauce as we had before, with the aromatics, broth, and flour—this time scraping up the browned bits from the bottom of the pan for added flavor. We added the chicken back to the sauce to finish up, but as it cooked, we realized the sauce would be reduced before the chicken was done. Adding more chicken broth was an easy way to build volume, but as the broth reduced, the sauce grew unpleasantly salty. Cutting the chicken broth with water gave us enough sauce, but it tasted flat. A squeeze of lemon juice and some zest added at the end, when we stirred in the cream, brightened up our sauce instantly.

To finish, we arranged the chicken in a casserole dish, topped it with the spinach and sauce, sprinkled on the Parmesan, and gave the dish a quick run under the broiler. With this casserole touting only 340 calories and 11 grams of fat per serving, we'd dropped a whopping 42 grams of fat and cut the calories from our starting recipe in half! This chicken Florentine looked elegant, fresh, and satisfying—you'd never guess how easy, or how light, it really was.

MAKEOVER SPOTLIGHT: CHICKEN FLORENTINE

	CALORIES	FAT	SAT FAT	CHOLESTEROL
BEFORE	670	53g	23g	200mg
AFTER	340	11g	3g	110mg

Chicken Florentine

SERVES 4

We prefer the tender leaves (and convenience) of bagged baby spinach in this recipe; if using curly-leaf, chop it before cooking. To avoid a watery dish, be sure to drain the spinach well in step 2.

- 4 teaspoons canola oil
- 2 (6-ounce) bags baby spinach (about 12 cups) (see note)
- 1½ pounds boneless, skinless chicken breasts, trimmed
  Salt and pepper
- 1 shallot, minced (about 3 tablespoons)
- 2 garlic cloves, minced
- 1 tablespoon unbleached all-purpose flour
- 2 cups low-sodium chicken broth
- 1¼ cups water
- 2 tablespoons heavy cream
- 1 teaspoon grated lemon zest plus 1 teaspoon fresh lemon juice
- 2 tablespoons grated Parmesan cheese

1. Position an oven rack 5 inches from the heating element and heat the broiler.

2. Heat 2 teaspoons of the oil in a 12-inch skillet over medium heat until shimmering. Add the spinach, one handful at a time, and cook, stirring frequently, until wilted, about 5 minutes. Transfer the spinach to a colander set over a bowl and press with a spatula to release any excess liquid. Wipe out the skillet with a wad of paper towels.

3. Pat the chicken breasts dry with paper towels and season with ⅛ teaspoon salt and ⅛ teaspoon pepper. Heat the remaining 2 teaspoons oil in the skillet over medium-high heat until just smoking. Carefully lay the breasts in the skillet and cook until lightly browned on both sides, 4 to 6 minutes, flipping them halfway through. Transfer the chicken to a plate and tent loosely with foil.

4. Add the shallot and garlic to the oil left in the skillet and cook over medium heat until fragrant, about 30 seconds. Stir in the flour until incorporated. Whisk in the broth and water, scraping up any browned bits.

5. Return the chicken breasts, along with any accumulated juice, to the skillet. Bring to a simmer, reduce the heat to medium-low, and cook until the thickest part of the breasts registers 160 to 165 degrees on an instant-read thermometer, 10 to 15 minutes, flipping the breasts halfway through. Transfer the chicken to a plate and tent loosely with foil.

6. Return the sauce to a simmer and continue to cook until thickened slightly and reduced to ¾ cup, about 15 minutes longer. Off the heat, whisk in the cream, lemon zest, and lemon juice. Season with salt and pepper to taste.

7. Cut the chicken breasts crosswise into ½-inch-thick slices and arrange in a broiler-safe 2-quart casserole dish. Scatter the spinach evenly over the chicken, then pour the sauce over the spinach. Sprinkle the cheese over the top and broil until golden brown, about 5 minutes. Serve.

PER SERVING: Cal 340; **Fat** 11g; **Sat fat** 3g; **Chol** 110mg; **Carb** 15g; **Protein** 44g; **Fiber** 4g; **Sodium** 670mg

NOTES FROM THE TEST KITCHEN

AVOIDING A WATERLOGGED MESS
As it cooks, spinach releases a lot of moisture, which can make dishes like our Chicken Florentine watery. To prevent that, we transferred the spinach to a colander immediately after we wilted it and pressed the leaves with a spatula to force the liquid out.

LOSE THE LIQUID
We drained nearly ¼ cup of liquid from the 12 ounces of spinach used in our Chicken Florentine.

PAN-ROASTED CHICKEN BREASTS

THERE ARE MANY WAYS TO COOK CHICKEN, BUT pan-roasting bone-in, skin-on chicken is one of the test kitchen's favorites. You get a deeply browned, flavorful exterior from starting on the stovetop, and cooking the chicken through in the oven guarantees extra-juicy, evenly cooked meat—not to mention that it's relatively fast. The problem is that the skin, as flavorful and attractive as it is, is also loaded with fat. Could we come up with a lighter version that had just as much flavor and also had good visual appeal?

The first decision we made was to use only chicken breasts, not the fattier dark meat pieces. Then we decided to remove the skin at the outset and pan-roast the breasts, following our go-to method. They emerged from the oven an attractive golden brown, but when we took a bite, it was like taking a bite of a tough old shoe. Skin normally protects the meat from the hot pan and seals in the moisture, and it was clear that the sizzling skillet was too much for the vulnerable, lean breast meat. We needed that protective barrier. What if we gave the breasts a faux skin, a coating to protect it from the hot pan?

Flour, cornstarch, and cornmeal all seemed like good candidates for a coating. We removed the skin from the chicken breasts, rolled a few in each coating, and left a few bare for comparison. After browning them in a hot skillet, we transferred them, skinned-side down, to a 450-degree oven to finish cooking. All of the coatings gave us more even browning and better texture than we got on the chicken without any coating. But the cornmeal was the clear winner. Its coarse texture created a substantial coating without making the chicken seem "battered." The cornstarch fared worst, as it was gummy and didn't create a distinct layer. However, the one bonus of the cornstarch was that the heat of the pan caramelized it to an attractive, mahogany brown. Hoping to incorporate this browning characteristic into our cornmeal coating, we experimented with adding different amounts of cornstarch to the cornmeal base. We found that 1 tablespoon of cornstarch and ½ cup of cornmeal gave the crust the perfect coating with the beautiful mahogany color we were after. The cornstarch also held on to some of the juice from the chicken, moistening the coating just enough that it started to bubble up in some places, looking just like real skin. Tasters in the test kitchen did a double-take when we told them the breasts were skinless!

Up to this point, coating aside, we had been following the test kitchen's recipe for pan-roasted breasts. But this technique had been developed using skin-on breasts, so to be sure this was also the best method for our skinless breasts, we tried roasting the breasts skinned-side up and at a range of oven temperatures. In each case, our working recipe of skinned-side down and a 450-degree oven proved superior. With our method determined, we developed some pan sauces with bright, bold flavors that would cook in minutes. By the time the chicken had finished resting, we were ready to spoon on our sauce and sit down to eat.

Pan-Roasted Chicken Breasts with Lemon-Herb Sauce

SERVES 4

If using kosher chicken, do not brine. If brining the chicken, do not season with salt in step 2. Make sure to use a 12-inch ovensafe nonstick skillet for this recipe.

CHICKEN

- ½ cup cornmeal
- 1 tablespoon cornstarch
- 4 (12-ounce) bone-in, skin-on split chicken breasts, trimmed (see photo), skin removed, and brined if desired (see note; see page 74)
- ⅛ teaspoon salt
- ⅛ teaspoon pepper
- 2 tablespoons canola oil

SAUCE

- 1 teaspoon canola oil
- 1 shallot, minced (about 3 tablespoons)
- 1 teaspoon unbleached all-purpose flour
- ¾ cup low-sodium chicken broth
- 1 tablespoon fresh lemon juice
- 1 tablespoon chopped fresh parsley
- 1 tablespoon minced fresh chives
- 1 tablespoon unsalted butter, chilled
  Salt and pepper

1. FOR THE CHICKEN: Adjust an oven rack to the lowest position and heat the oven to 450 degrees.

2. Whisk the cornmeal and cornstarch together in a shallow dish. Pat the chicken breasts dry with paper towels and season with the salt and pepper. Thoroughly coat the skinned sides of the chicken breasts with the cornmeal mixture, pressing to adhere.

3. Heat the oil in a 12-inch ovensafe skillet over medium-high heat until just smoking. Carefully lay the chicken breasts, skinned-side down, in the skillet and cook until golden brown on the first side, about 5 minutes. Flip the breasts and continue to cook until lightly browned on the second side, about 3 minutes longer.

4. Flip the chicken breasts skinned-side down and transfer the skillet to the oven. Cook until the thickest part of the breasts registers 160 to 165 degrees on an instant-read thermometer, 15 to 18 minutes.

5. Using potholders (the skillet handle will be hot), remove the skillet from the oven. Transfer the chicken

breasts to a platter, tent loosely with foil, and let rest while making the sauce.

6. FOR THE SAUCE: Heat the oil in a small saucepan and cook over medium heat until shimmering. Add the shallot and cook until softened, about 2 minutes. Stir in the flour and cook for 30 seconds. Whisk in the broth, bring to a simmer, and cook until thickened slightly and reduced to ½ cup, about 5 minutes.

7. Off the heat, stir in any accumulated chicken juice, lemon juice, parsley, chives, and butter. Season with salt and pepper to taste. Spoon the sauce over the chicken breasts and serve.

PER SERVING: Cal 400; Fat 14g; Sat fat 3.5g; Chol 135mg; Carb 12g; Protein 53g; Fiber 1g; Sodium 230mg

---

NOTES FROM THE TEST KITCHEN

TRIMMING SPLIT CHICKEN BREASTS

Using kitchen shears, trim off the rib section from each breast.

SECRETS TO HEALTHY PAN-ROASTED CHICKEN

Pan-roasting bone-in chicken breasts will give you ultra-juicy meat, but the fatty skin had to go for our lightened-up version. We made a coating from two key ingredients to create a protective skin-like barrier on our chicken breasts that was also attractive.

CORNMEAL

Its coarse texture creates a substantial coating without making the chicken seem "battered."

CORNSTARCH

The heat caramelizes the cornstarch, giving our chicken an attractive, mahogany color. It also helps moisten the coating so it bubbles up in spots, just like real skin.

VARIATIONS

Pan-Roasted Chicken Breasts with Spicy Thai Sauce

If using kosher chicken, do not brine. If brining the chicken, do not season with salt in step 2. Make sure to use a 12-inch ovensafe nonstick skillet for this recipe.

CHICKEN

- ½ cup cornmeal
- 1 tablespoon cornstarch
- 4 (12-ounce) bone-in, skin-on split chicken breasts, trimmed (see page 61), skin removed, and brined if desired (see note; see page 74)
- ⅛ teaspoon salt
- ⅛ teaspoon pepper
- 2 tablespoons canola oil

SAUCE

- ¼ cup packed light brown sugar
- 3 tablespoons fresh lime juice (about 2 limes)
- 1 tablespoon fish sauce
- 2 garlic cloves, minced
- 1 teaspoon Thai red curry paste
- ¾ cup low-sodium chicken broth
- 2 tablespoons chopped fresh cilantro

1. FOR THE CHICKEN: Adjust oven rack to lowest position and heat oven to 450 degrees.

2. Whisk the cornmeal and cornstarch together in a shallow dish. Pat the chicken breasts dry with paper towels and season with the salt and pepper. Thoroughly coat the skinned sides of the breasts with the cornmeal mixture, pressing to adhere.

3. Heat the oil in a 12-inch ovensafe skillet over medium-high heat until just smoking. Carefully lay the chicken breasts, skinned-side down, in the skillet and cook until golden brown on the first side, about 5 minutes. Flip the breasts and continue to cook until lightly browned on the second side, about 3 minutes longer.

4. Flip the chicken breasts skinned-side down and transfer the skillet to the oven. Cook until the thickest part of the breasts registers 160 to 165 degrees on an instant-read thermometer, 15 to 18 minutes.

5. Using potholders (the skillet handle will be hot), remove the skillet from the oven. Transfer the chicken breasts to a platter, tent loosely with foil, and let rest while making the sauce.

6. FOR THE SAUCE: Cook the brown sugar, 2 tablespoons of the lime juice, the fish sauce, garlic, and curry paste in a small saucepan over medium heat, stirring frequently, until thickened, about 3 minutes. Whisk in the broth, bring to a simmer, and cook until thickened slightly and reduced to ½ cup, about 5 minutes.

7. Off the heat, stir in any accumulated chicken juice, the remaining 1 tablespoon lime juice, and cilantro. Spoon the sauce over the chicken breasts and serve.

PER SERVING: Cal 410; Fat 10g; Sat fat 2g; Chol 130mg; Carb 24g; Protein 53g; Fiber 1g; Sodium 550mg

Pan-Roasted Chicken Breasts with Grapefruit-Tarragon Sauce

If using kosher chicken, do not brine. If brining the chicken, do not season with salt in step 2. Make sure to use a 12-inch ovensafe nonstick skillet for this recipe.

CHICKEN

- ½ cup cornmeal
- 1 tablespoon cornstarch
- 4 (12-ounce) bone-in, skin-on split chicken breasts, trimmed (see page 61), skin removed, and brined if desired (see note; see page 74)
- ⅛ teaspoon salt
- ⅛ teaspoon pepper
- 2 tablespoons canola oil

SAUCE

- 1 teaspoon canola oil
- 1 shallot, minced (about 3 tablespoons)
- ¾ cup low-sodium chicken broth
- 1 grapefruit, rind and pith removed, segments cut into ½-inch pieces, and juice (about ½ cup) reserved
- 1 tablespoon honey
- 1 tablespoon chopped fresh tarragon
- 1 tablespoon unsalted butter, chilled
  Salt and pepper

1. FOR THE CHICKEN: Adjust an oven rack to the lowest position and heat the oven to 450 degrees.

2. Whisk the cornmeal and cornstarch together in a shallow dish. Pat the chicken breasts dry with paper towels and season with the salt and pepper. Thoroughly coat the skinned sides of the breasts with the cornmeal mixture, pressing to adhere.

3. Heat the oil in a 12-inch ovensafe skillet over medium-high heat until just smoking. Carefully lay the chicken breasts, skinned-side down, in the skillet and cook until golden brown on the first side, about 5 minutes. Flip the breasts and continue to cook until lightly browned on the second side, about 3 minutes longer.

4. Flip the chicken breasts skinned-side down and transfer the skillet to the oven. Cook until the thickest part of the breasts registers 160 to 165 degrees on an instant-read thermometer, 15 to 18 minutes.

5. Using potholders (the skillet handle will be hot), remove the skillet from the oven. Transfer the chicken breasts to a platter, tent loosely with foil, and let rest while making the sauce.

6. FOR THE SAUCE: Heat the oil in a small saucepan over medium heat until shimmering. Add the shallot and cook until softened, about 2 minutes. Whisk in the broth, grapefruit juice, and any accumulated chicken juice, bring to a simmer, and cook until thickened and reduced to ¼ cup, about 14 minutes. Stir in the grapefruit segments and honey and return to a brief simmer.

7. Off the heat, stir in the tarragon and butter. Season with salt and pepper to taste. Spoon the sauce over the chicken breasts and serve.

PER SERVING: **Cal** 430; **Fat** 14g; **Sat fat** 3.5g; **Chol** 135mg; **Carb** 22g; **Protein** 53g; **Fiber** 2g; **Sodium** 320mg

CHICKEN IN A POT

OLD-FASHIONED CHICKEN IN A POT IS A SATISFYING, elegantly simple one-dish meal. Done right, the method produces a moist, velvety chicken and a deeply flavored broth that doubles as a sauce. True, the skin (which so many modern recipe writers, including some in our very own test kitchen, obsess about) is neither golden nor crisp. But its purpose here isn't to impress at the table but rather to protect the meat and flavor the vegetables and broth while cooking. So it's an ideal recipe for those eating light—you can simply discard the fatty skin before serving and still enjoy a flavorful, savory dinner.

Nineteenth-century recipes call for submerging the chicken in liquid and boiling it. After a few tests, we discovered that the problem with this technique is that all the meat cooks at the same temperature. This may have been well suited to a tough "free-range" bird (all birds were free-range before World War II) but not to the young, plump supermarket birds available now. By the time the chicken's legs were done, today's extra-lean breast meat was seriously dried out. We came across a Julia Child recipe for Casserole-Poached Chicken that noted that if the poaching liquid comes only partway up, the dark meat of the legs and thighs simmers and the white meat of the breast steams for a "beautifully tender and juicy chicken" and a "perfectly flavored … chicken broth." She cooked her chicken in the oven, which made sense to us—the oven braises gently and evenly. Following her lead, we cut the amount of water from 6 cups to 2 cups and baked our next chicken in the pot. Voilà! As promised, all parts were beautifully tender and juicy.

However, the "perfectly flavored" chicken broth was MIA. Frankly, the chicken didn't taste like much, either. So we replaced the water we'd been using with store-bought chicken broth, which helped, but tasters found it one-dimensional. A splash of white wine added both brightness and complexity. Searing the chicken before poaching it could add another layer of flavor, and even though it would also add fat (we'd have to put oil in the pan), we tried it anyway. Browning both sides, however, resulted in overcooked breast meat by the end of the cooking process. In the end, browning just the back elicited enough fond to intensify the broth and required only a tablespoon of oil. And flavorful broth equaled flavorful chicken.

Most recipes for chicken in a pot call for onions, carrots, and celery. Browning the vegetables seemed like another easy way to add more flavor to the broth. We kept it lean by pouring off all but a tablespoon of fat from our pot after browning the chicken and before browning the vegetables. The carrots held up nicely, but the onions and celery had a flabby, unfit-to-serve texture, so we kept them for flavor but discarded them after cooking. Cabbage, turnips, and potatoes are less common though not unheard-of additions, but our tasters found that the cabbage and turnips gave the broth off-flavors, so we left them out. Quartered potatoes nicely rounded out the one-pot meal. We discovered that arranging the chicken on top of the aromatics elevated the breast further, providing extra insurance against overcooking.

In many recipes the broth is finished with butter, but we found it unnecessary since the chicken was the star and it was tender, juicy, and plenty flavorful. All

NOTES FROM THE TEST KITCHEN

THE KEYS TO BUILDING FLAVOR

1. A rich, flavorful sauce starts with searing the chicken. To avoid over-cooking the breast meat, brown only the back.

2. Remove the chicken and brown the vegetables to bring out their natural sweetness and help flavor the sauce.

3. Arrange the chicken on top of the aromatics and place the potatoes around the chicken.

THE BEST INEXPENSIVE DUTCH OVEN

Dutch ovens are kitchen workhorses, useful for making not only Chicken in a Pot but stews, soups, and slow braises, and they're handy for deep-frying and baking crusty loaves of bread as well. We tested several inexpensive Dutch ovens by making stew, rice, and French fries, hoping to find a more affordable alternative to our favorites by Le Creuset and All-Clad (which run roughly $230 and $280, respectively). The **Tramontina 6.5-Quart Cast Iron Dutch Oven,** crafted from enameled cast iron, passed all our tests with flying colors. Comparable in size to our pricier favorites and performing almost as well, it's hard to beat with its price tag of $50.

we felt was needed was a touch of fresh parsley and chives for an herbal note, which we stirred in after we'd skimmed the sauce of fat. Finally, we had before us an old-fashioned meal, ready for the 21st century.

Chicken in a Pot

SERVES 4

You will need a Dutch oven with at least a 6-quart capacity and a tight-fitting lid to make this recipe. We prefer to use small red potatoes, measuring 1 to 2 inches in diameter, in this recipe. We strain the sauce into a saucepan in step 7 so that it can be reheated before serving if necessary. Serve the chicken with Dijon mustard, pickles, and horseradish as accompaniments, if desired.

1	(4½-pound) chicken, giblets discarded, trimmed
	Salt and pepper
1	tablespoon canola oil
1	pound carrots, peeled and cut into 1-inch pieces
1	onion, peeled and halved, root end left intact
1	celery rib, halved crosswise
6	garlic cloves, minced
1	cup dry white wine
1	cup low-sodium chicken broth
1½	pounds small red potatoes (about 9), scrubbed and quartered
1	tablespoon minced fresh chives
1	tablespoon minced fresh parsley

1. Adjust an oven rack to the lower-middle position and heat the oven to 350 degrees.

2. Pat the chicken dry with paper towels. Using your fingers, loosen the skin from the breasts and the legs of the chicken. Rub ½ teaspoon salt and ¼ teaspoon pepper all over the chicken and underneath the skin. Tuck the wings behind the back and tie the legs together with kitchen twine.

3. Heat the oil in a Dutch oven over medium-high heat until just smoking. Carefully lay the chicken, breast-side up, in the pot and cook until the back is lightly browned, 3 to 4 minutes. Transfer the chicken to a plate.

4. Pour off all but 1 tablespoon of fat from the pot. Add the carrots, onion, and celery and cook over medium-high heat, stirring occasionally, until browned, 6 to 8 minutes. Stir in the garlic and cook until fragrant, about 30 seconds. Whisk in the wine and broth and bring to a simmer, scraping up any browned bits. Place the chicken, breast-side up, on top of the vegetables and pour in any accumulated juice. Season the potatoes with ⅛ teaspoon salt and ⅛ teaspoon pepper and arrange around the chicken.

5. Place a large sheet of foil over the pot and press to seal, then cover tightly with the lid. Transfer the pot to the oven and cook until the thickest part of the breast registers 160 to 165 degrees and the thickest part of the thigh registers 175 degrees on an instant-read thermometer, 50 to 60 minutes.

6. Transfer the pot to a wire rack. Remove the lid and tent the pot loosely with the foil. Let the chicken rest for 20 minutes.

7. Transfer the chicken to a carving board. Using a slotted spoon, transfer the carrots and potatoes to a platter, discarding the onion and celery. Strain the sauce through a fine-mesh strainer into a small saucepan. Skim the fat off the surface of the sauce with a wide spoon. Whisk in the chives and parsley and season with salt and pepper to taste. Carve the chicken, discard the skin, and serve with the vegetables, passing the sauce separately.

PER SERVING: **Cal** 580; **Fat** 15g; **Sat fat** 3.5g; **Chol** 175mg; **Carb** 41g; **Protein** 59g; **Fiber** 6g; **Sodium** 670mg

CHICKEN BIRYANI

IN THE POPULAR INDIAN DISH *MURGH BIRYANI*, long-grain basmati rice takes center stage, enriched with saffron, fresh herbs, and pungent spices. Pieces of tender chicken and browned onions are layered with the rice and baked until the flavors have mingled. While the central ingredients—chicken, onions, rice, herbs—read like a light dish, biryani often contains a generous amount of butter, the onions are deep-fried, and the fat rendered by the chicken is soaked up by the rice, all leading to a heavy, unnecessarily caloric dish. On top of that, traditional biryani recipes are long in both ingredients and labor. We had in mind a modern take, something lighter, healthier, and true to the original dish that wouldn't take a whole day or a laundry list of special ingredients to make.

We prepared a few classic biryani recipes to better acquaint ourselves with the dish, which required a full day

in the test kitchen and produced a pile of dishes. But we made three time-saving discoveries. We learned that we could skip marinating the chicken (too much time, too little flavor enhancement). We also found that we could prepare the whole recipe on the stovetop, rather than dealing with moving the pot to the oven to finish. And finally, it was possible to cook the onions and the chicken one after the other in the same large skillet, saving a pan. The streamlined recipe, though not a 30-minute supper, now consisted of cooking the onions, browning the chicken, parboiling the rice, and then simmering the layered biryani until done.

The best-tasting biryani from our tests had one glaring flaw—it was made with two abundant layers of deep-fried onions, which not only turned the dish greasy but were an obvious roadblock to our lightening aspirations. After just a few batches, we found a method to brown our onions using significantly less fat. We tossed the onions with just 2 teaspoons of oil and some salt, turned the heat to medium, and put the lid on. The combination of the small amount of oil and the relatively low heat prevented the onions from burning, the salt drew their moisture out, and the cover trapped the moisture in the pan, allowing the onions to sweat in their own juices. We then took the lid off and turned the heat up to finish the browning process. Perfection.

As for the chicken, tasters preferred dark meat—it was juicier and more flavorful than white meat, which ended up dry. Bone-in thighs are a test kitchen favorite because they are so meaty, but they are also high in fat. Since most of this fat is in the skin, we decided to get rid of it. But first, we browned the thighs with the skin on. The skin protected the meat during browning and rendered enough fat that we didn't need to use any additional oil before layering everything in the pot. We simply stripped off the skin before layering the chicken pieces with the rice.

Biryani's subtle, delicate flavor and aroma are largely derived from the masala, a traditional Indian spice blend with myriad variations, stirred into the rice. In the end, tasters approved of a masala of cardamom, cinnamon, cumin seed, and fresh ginger sliced into coins. Sweet, earthy, sharp, and musky, the spices harmonized well. We tested both whole and ground, and whole spices won out, as the ground ones tasted raw. Lightly smashing the cardamom and ginger with a chef's knife intensified their flavor.

We were happy with the flavor that the whole spices imparted, but we weren't happy with having to fish them out of the rice before serving. So we bundled the spices in a piece of cheesecloth, then simmered the sachet in the water used to parboil the rice. We also found that adding a portion of this flavored liquid to the layered biryani—sort of like adding pasta cooking water to a pasta dish—further intensified the spice flavor.

Finally, a pinch of saffron added both color and flavor, and a fair amount of garlic and jalapeño lent needed heat, which we balanced with the addition of sweet currants. Most biryani recipes are finished with several tablespoons of butter, but we felt as if adding it would only weigh down the bold, fresh flavors in our dish, so we left it out. All it needed was a little cilantro, mint, and a dollop of yogurt sauce added at the end for the perfect finishing touches.

NOTES FROM THE TEST KITCHEN

THE BEST BASMATI RICE
Prized for its nutty flavor and sweet aroma, basmati rice is eaten worldwide in pilafs and biryanis and as an accompaniment to curries. The best Indian-grown rice is said to come from the Himalayan foothills, where the snow-flooded soil and humid climate offer ideal growing conditions. Choosing among the multitude of boxes, bags, and burlap sacks available today on supermarket shelves can be confusing.

To find a truly great grain, we steamed seven brands, five from India and two domestic options. Matched against Indian imports, the domestic brands suffered. They were less aromatic, and the grains didn't elongate as much. Their overall texture was mushy, too. While all of the imported brands were acceptable, tasters overwhelmingly chose the longest sample—**Tilda**—as their favorite.

STORING SPICES
Spices define Indian cooking, so their quality is of the utmost importance; they can ruin a dish or elevate it to the next level. All too often home cooks reach for old, stale bottles of spices, so it's important to be conscientious about how, and where, you store them. The biggest mistake home cooks make is keeping them close to the stove. Heat, moisture, air, and light quickly shorten the shelf life of spices, leaving them dull. Keep spices in a cool, dark, dry place in a well-sealed container.

Chicken Biryani
SERVES 4
Be sure to use a 3½- to 4-quart saucepan about 8 inches in diameter for this recipe. Do not use a large, wide Dutch oven, as it will adversely affect both the layering of the dish and the final cooking times. To make this dish spicier, add the chile seeds. Serve with Yogurt Sauce (recipe follows).

- 10 **cardamom pods, preferably green, crushed**
- 1 **cinnamon stick**
- 1 **(2-inch) piece fresh ginger, cut into ½-inch-thick coins and smashed**
- ½ **teaspoon cumin seeds**
- **Salt**
- 2 **onions, halved and sliced thin**
- 2 **teaspoons canola oil**
- 2 **jalapeño chiles, stemmed, seeded, and minced (see note)**
- 4 **garlic cloves, minced**
- **Pepper**
- 4 **(6-ounce) bone-in, skin-on chicken thighs, trimmed**
- 1¼ **cups basmati rice**
- ¼ **cup dried currants or raisins**
- ½ **teaspoon saffron threads, lightly crumbled**
- 2 **tablespoons chopped fresh cilantro**
- 2 **tablespoons chopped fresh mint**

1. Tie the cardamom pods, cinnamon stick, ginger, and cumin seeds in cheesecloth to make a sachet. In a large saucepan, bring the sachet, 3 quarts water, and 1 teaspoon salt to a boil over medium-high heat. Reduce the heat to medium and simmer, partially covered, for 20 minutes. Cover and set aside off the heat.

2. Meanwhile, combine the onions, oil, and ⅛ teaspoon salt in a 12-inch nonstick skillet. Cover and cook over medium-low heat, stirring occasionally, until softened, 8 to 10 minutes. Uncover, increase the heat to medium-high, and continue to cook, stirring occasionally, until the onions are well browned, 8 to 12 minutes longer. Stir in the chiles and garlic and cook until fragrant, about 30 seconds. Transfer the onion mixture to a bowl and season with salt and pepper to taste. Wipe out the skillet with a wad of paper towels.

3. Pat the chicken thighs dry with paper towels and season with ⅛ teaspoon salt and ⅛ teaspoon pepper. Return the skillet to medium-high heat. Carefully lay the chicken, skin-side down, in the skillet and cook until well browned on the first side, about 5 minutes. Flip the thighs and continue to cook until browned on the second side, 4 to 6 minutes longer. Transfer the chicken to a plate, remove and discard the skin, and tent loosely with foil.

4. Return the spice-infused water to a boil over high heat. Stir in the rice and cook for 5 minutes, stirring occasionally. Reserve ¾ cup of the cooking liquid, then drain the rice through a fine-mesh strainer. Remove and discard the sachet. Transfer the rice to a medium bowl and stir in the currants and saffron (the rice will turn splotchy yellow).

5. Spread half of the rice evenly over the bottom of the saucepan. Scatter half of the onion mixture over the rice, then arrange the chicken thighs, skinned-side up, on top of the onions, pouring any accumulated chicken juice over the top. Sprinkle with the cilantro and mint, then top with the remaining onions and the remaining rice. Pour the reserved cooking liquid evenly over the rice.

6. Cover the saucepan and cook over medium-low heat until the rice and chicken are tender, about 30 minutes. (If a large amount of steam is escaping from the pot, reduce the heat.)

7. Spoon the biryani into individual serving bowls, scooping from the bottom of the pot. Serve, passing the Yogurt Sauce separately.

PER SERVING: **Cal** 380; **Fat** 7g; **Sat fat** 1g; **Chol** 80mg; **Carb** 57g; **Protein** 24g; **Fiber** 4; **Sodium** 380mg

Yogurt Sauce

MAKES ABOUT 1 CUP

This cool and creamy sauce is a great complement to the spicy biryani.

1   **cup plain low-fat yogurt**
2   **tablespoons chopped fresh cilantro**
2   **tablespoons chopped fresh mint**
1   **garlic clove, minced**
    Salt and pepper

Combine all of the ingredients in a small bowl and season with salt and pepper to taste. Cover and refrigerate to let the flavors meld, at least 15 minutes or up to 1 day.

PER ¼-CUP SERVING: **Cal** 40; **Fat** 1g; **Sat fat** 0.5g; **Chol** 5mg; **Carb** 5g; **Protein** 3g; **Fiber** 0g; **Sodium** 45mg

ASIAN CHICKEN LETTUCE WRAPS

CONSIDERED COMMON STREET FOOD—FAST FOOD— in Thailand, the exotic-sounding *laab gai* consists of spicy, quickly cooked ground chicken that is eaten not with a fork but with the aid of a lettuce leaf. You spoon the ground filling onto a lettuce leaf, fold it shut, and eat it with your hands, much as you would a taco. Relying on a combination of fresh, bright aromatics for its flavor, laab gai is a naturally healthy dish. Though usually eaten as a starter, we thought it was the perfect inspiration for a light but not ho-hum weekday meal.

To start, we focused on the chicken. Most ground chicken is not finely ground, so it has an unappealing stringy texture when cooked. Wondering whether it would be better to mince boneless chicken breasts in the food processor or simply process store-bought ground chicken further, we gave each approach a try. The boneless chicken breasts that were processed in the food processor cooked into dry little morsels, and the ground chicken processed again in the food processor showed minimal improvement. We found that simply smashing store-bought ground chicken with the back of a spoon before cooking was the best option, and we made sure that we continued to break it into small pieces as it cooked.

Most laab gai recipes we found called for similar flavorings, including fish sauce, lime juice, scallions, and chiles. Lime zest gave our filling a good punch, which we tempered with brown sugar and fragrant basil. Though many laab recipes also include a unique ingredient, toasted rice powder, toasting and grinding rice just seemed too fussy for a weeknight meal, and tasters thought our filling was flavorful without it. However, it also serves as a thickener, so to keep our mixture from becoming too wet, we whisked a teaspoon of cornstarch with our liquid ingredients and let it briefly simmer until thickened.

To turn our recipe into a meal, we decided to spoon some cooked rice into our wraps to serve as a bed for the chicken filling. We tried long-grain rice, but the loose grains started falling out of the wrap as soon as we took a bite. Stickier short-grain sushi rice turned out to be the best choice. Spooned onto a lettuce leaf, it made a good bed for the chicken that absorbed the sauce and actually helped the wrap stay neatly together. Rinsing the rice was crucial, since rinsing rids rice of excess starch that coats the individual grains. We found that unrinsed rice

ASIAN CHICKEN LETTUCE WRAPS

had an unappealing, gluey consistency. We also found that if we used too much liquid when cooking our short-grain rice, it took on a creamy, risotto-like texture. We found that a 1½-to-1 ratio of water to rice was ideal. Although any type of lettuce leaves could be used here, we liked the small leaf size and pronounced curvature of Boston and Bibb lettuces. A few of these flavorful wraps left us feeling satisfied but not overstuffed, making them a perfect warm-weather meal.

Asian Chicken Lettuce Wraps

SERVES 4

To make this dish spicier, add the chile seeds. To make a lettuce cup, put a spoonful of rice in the middle of a lettuce leaf, top with the chicken, fold the leaf edges up to form a taco shape, and eat with your hands.

1½	cups water
1	cup short-grain rice, such as sushi rice, rinsed (see photo)
3	tablespoons fish sauce
3	tablespoons fresh lime juice plus 2 teaspoons grated lime zest (about 2 limes)
1½	tablespoons brown sugar
1	teaspoon cornstarch
1	pound ground chicken
2	teaspoons canola oil
1	Thai or jalapeño chile, stemmed, seeded, and minced (see note)
¼	cup chopped fresh basil
3	scallions, sliced thin
12	Bibb or Boston lettuce leaves (about 1 head)

1. Bring the water and rice to a boil in a medium saucepan over high heat. Cover, reduce the heat to low, and cook for 10 minutes. Remove the rice from the heat and let sit, covered, until tender, about 15 minutes.

2. While the rice sits off the heat, whisk the fish sauce, lime juice, brown sugar, and cornstarch together in a small bowl and set aside. In a medium bowl, mash the ground chicken using the back of a spoon until smooth and no strand-like pieces of meat remain.

3. Heat the oil in a 12-inch nonstick skillet over medium heat until shimmering. Add the chicken, chile, and lime zest and cook, breaking up the meat into small pieces with a wooden spoon, until the chicken is no longer pink, about 5 minutes.

4. Whisk the fish sauce mixture to recombine, then add it to the skillet and cook, stirring constantly, until the sauce has thickened, about 45 seconds. Off the heat, stir in the basil and scallions. Transfer the chicken to a shallow serving bowl and serve with the rice and lettuce leaves.

PER SERVING: Cal 430; Fat 15g; Sat fat 4.5g; Chol 135mg; Carb 50g; Protein 25g; Fiber 2g; Sodium 520mg

NOTES FROM THE TEST KITCHEN

THE BEST FISH SAUCE

Fish sauce, or *nam pla* or *nuoc cham*, is a salty, amber-colored liquid made from salted, fermented fish. Used in very small amounts, it adds a well-rounded, salty flavor to sauces, soups, and marinades. We tasted six brands of fish sauce—one from Vietnam, one from the Philippines, and the rest from Thailand. Tasters had preferences among the sauces, but those preferences varied from taster to taster. With such a limited ingredient list (most of the brands contained some combination of fish extract, water, salt, and sugar), the differences among sauces were minimal. If you are a fan of fish sauce and plan to use it often, you may want to make a special trip to an Asian market to buy a rich, dark sauce, like **Tiparos,** that is suitably pungent. We used Tiparos when making our Asian Chicken Lettuce Wraps, so keep in mind that if you use another brand, the sodium content of the dish will change.

RINSING RICE

To remove excess starch and prevent rice from becoming gluey, place the rice in a fine-mesh strainer, then rinse under cold water until the water runs clear.

CHICKEN SOFT TACOS

CHICKEN SOFT TACOS ARE EVERYWHERE, FROM THE $0.99 paper-wrapped ones at the food court to more satisfying versions at Mexican restaurants. The chicken filling can range from underseasoned, seared, and chopped white meat so bland it demands a smothering blanket of sour cream and cheese to whole chicken that's been broken down and poached to tender, fall-off-the-bone perfection. We wanted our tacos to be flavorful enough

NOTES FROM THE TEST KITCHEN

OUR FAVORITE ORANGE JUICE
Orange juice is a key ingredient for these tacos, and with a growing number of fresh-squeezed-style orange juices (called "super-premium juice") popping up in the produce department, we were curious whether these high-end juices tasted better and fresher than their not-from-concentrate cousins. So we tested five upscale juices with ordinary Tropicana Pure Premium, the winner of our previous middle-market tasting. Our winner, **Natalie's Orchid Island Juice Company Pasteurized Orange Juice**, (left) was the only juice to give

fresh-squeezed a run for its money. Tasters praised its "well-balanced and fresh-tasting" flavors. The surprise result was that the dairy case staple **Tropicana Pure Premium 100% Pure and Natural Orange Juice with Some Pulp** (right) came in second—above the rest of the fresh-squeezed-style pack.

WARMING TORTILLAS
Warming tortillas (either flour or corn) over the open flame of a gas burner or in a skillet gives them a toasted flavor; however, an oven or a microwave will also work. If your tortillas are dry, pat them with a little water first. If using a gas stove, toast the tortillas, one at a time, directly on the cooking grate over a medium flame until slightly charred around the edges, about 30 seconds per side. If using a skillet, toast the tortillas, one at a time, over medium-high heat until softened and speckled with brown, 20 to 30 seconds per side. Wrap the warmed tortillas in foil or a kitchen towel to keep them warm and soft until serving time. If using an oven, stack the tortillas in a foil packet and heat at 350 degrees until warm and soft, about 5 minutes. Keep them in the foil until serving time. To use a microwave, stack the tortillas on a plate, cover with microwave-safe plastic wrap, and heat on high until warm and soft, 1 to 2 minutes. Remove the plastic wrap and cover the tortillas with a kitchen towel or foil to keep them warm and soft.

on their own that fatty garnishes were not required, but we didn't want tacos that would take hours to make and require a mile-long list of exotic ingredients. We were in need of a healthy chicken soft taco recipe, one that offered the ease of the drive-through but the complex flavors and juicy texture of the real deal.

We looked at a variety of recipes and immediately crossed off those calling for 24-hour marinades and obscure ingredients. Some of the quick-cooking recipes we found called for briefly marinating boneless chicken breasts in lime juice, cilantro, garlic, and spices like chili powder and cumin, cooking them over high heat, chopping up the meat, then stuffing it in a tortilla. To begin our testing, we put together a simplified working marinade and moved ahead to settle on the cooking method. We soon learned that a quick marinade and a hot, fast sear wouldn't do—our chicken ended up with a leathery exterior and a dried-out interior.

In the test kitchen we often brine chicken in saltwater to keep it juicy, but this extra step takes about an hour and didn't fit into our short time frame. We also considered another test kitchen technique: reserving a few tablespoons of marinade to toss with the seared and chopped chicken, almost like dressing. We tested this idea, but if the goal was juicy chicken, we'd need more than a splash of liquid to disguise dry meat.

We also realized, inevitably, that sautéing the chicken would lead to a browned exterior and add texture that, while appreciated on simple sautéed breasts, wasn't something we wanted in our taco. We reconsidered the elaborate Mexican recipes where whole chickens are slowly simmered in flavored broths and wondered if we could borrow the technique. Poaching our chicken breasts would also have the added benefit of requiring no oil. We simmered chicken broth in a skillet, added the breasts, and cooked them, covered, for 10 minutes. The chicken emerged tender and moist. Unfortunately, it was also bland.

Could we use the marinade ingredients as the poaching liquid to get flavor into our chicken? The idea was good, but the flavors—garlic, lime juice, fresh jalapeños, and cilantro—were out of balance. Although bright, the chicken was aggressively tart. We discarded the lime and reached for orange juice. It did the trick, keeping the acidity while adding a note of sweetness. We replaced the jalapeños with 2 teaspoons of chipotle chiles for a smokier, more full-bodied flavor. Still, the meat lacked robustness.

CHICKEN SOFT TACOS

A fellow test cook who had grown up in Latin America suggested two seemingly unlikely ingredients: Worcestershire sauce and yellow mustard. These pantry items, she told us, are a mainstay in many Latin American kitchens and frequently find their way into basic chicken and beef marinades. A touch of Worcestershire mimicked the more complex flavor of dark meat, and a teaspoon of mustard pulled it together, adding a sharp tang that cut through the sweet juice and smoky chipotle.

Things were going well, but when the poaching was finished, a pool of flavorful liquid remained in the skillet. Reducing it into a sauce would add even more flavor to our tacos, so we made the recipe once more, this time sautéing the garlic and chipotle to build a base for the sauce. Fifteen minutes later, once the chicken was poached and the liquid reduced, we whisked in the mustard to help thicken and emulsify our sauce. Finally, we shredded the chicken (a side-by-side test showed that shreds absorbed more sauce than cubes) and tossed it with the sauce and more fresh cilantro. We reached for a steamy tortilla and tucked in chicken that was incredibly moist and laced with heat, spice, and tartness.

Chicken Soft Tacos

SERVES 6

We don't think toppings are essential for these tacos because they are so flavorful, but you can serve them with lettuce, tomato, avacado, or lime wedges if you like. Flour tortillas vary in fat content from brand to brand (we usually use one of our favorites, Mission Small Flour Tortillas), so make sure to read labels.

- 1 teaspoon canola oil
- 4 garlic cloves, minced
- 2 teaspoons minced canned chipotle chiles in adobo sauce
- ¾ cup chopped fresh cilantro
- ½ cup orange juice
- 1 tablespoon Worcestershire sauce
- 1½ pounds boneless, skinless chicken breasts, trimmed
- 1 teaspoon yellow mustard
  Salt and pepper
- 12 (6-inch) flour tortillas (see note), warmed (see page 70)

1. Heat the oil in a 12-inch skillet over medium heat until shimmering. Stir in the garlic and chipotles and cook until fragrant, about 30 seconds. Stir in ½ cup of the cilantro, orange juice, and Worcestershire.

2. Nestle the chicken into the skillet and bring the liquid to a simmer. Cover, reduce the heat to medium-low, and cook until the thickest part of the breasts registers 160 to 165 degrees on an instant-read thermometer, 12 to 18 minutes, flipping them halfway through.

3. Transfer the chicken breasts to a plate. Shred the chicken into bite-sized pieces using 2 forks. Meanwhile, continue to simmer the sauce over medium heat until thickened slightly and reduced to ¼ cup, about 5 minutes.

4. Off the heat, whisk the mustard into the sauce. Stir in the remaining ¼ cup cilantro and shredded chicken. Season with salt and pepper to taste. Serve with the tortillas and any desired accompaniments.

PER SERVING: Cal 350; **Fat** 7g; **Sat fat** 0g; **Chol** 65mg; **Carb** 36g; **Protein** 33g; **Fiber** 2g; **Sodium** 750mg

GROUND MEAT TACOS

SO MAYBE THEY'RE NOT AUTHENTIC MEXICAN FOOD, but ground meat tacos have earned a special place in the palates of at least a couple of generations of Americans. For a quick, crowd-pleasing weeknight meal, the comfort-food appeal of this variety of taco is undeniable, but the greasy ground beef versions we grew up on, loaded with cheese and sour cream, certainly don't come to mind when imagining a light meal. And while the supermarket taco kits do make taco making easy, their packets of stale, dusty seasoning produce flat-tasting fillings, reeking of dried oregano and onion powder. With a little effort we thought we could produce a lighter version of ground meat tacos, with a fiery, flavorful filling that even adults could enjoy.

We started with the meat. Most ground beef was too fatty to even be in the running. Tasters thought the tacos made with 95 percent lean ground beef were dry and sandy. Ground turkey, lower in fat but tender, seemed the best choice. We found three ground turkey options to choose from: ground dark meat with 15 to 20 percent fat (labeled 80 to 85 percent lean), ground white meat with 1 to 2 percent fat (98 to 99 percent lean), and a blend of the two (simply labeled ground turkey), which contains about 7 percent fat (93 percent lean). The dark turkey meat was moist and flavorful when cooked, but it was so high in fat and calories that we may as well have used ground beef. The white meat was exceedingly dry and devoid of flavor. The 93 percent lean ground turkey, however, was promising. It had a mild, meaty flavor and moderate juiciness without a surplus of fat.

With the meat selected, we move on to the key aspect—the seasoning. Most of the taco seasoning packets we looked at listed dehydrated onion and/or garlic, so we started our filling in a similar vein but with freshness in mind. We sautéed some minced onion and garlic to boost the moisture of the meat as well as flavor it. As for other spices, these packets indicate a hodgepodge of ingredients, including MSG, mysterious "spices," and even soy sauce. They all include chili powder, however, so we added that next, beginning with 1 tablespoon and quickly increasing it to 2 tablespoons for more kick. Dried oregano in a more modest amount—1 teaspoon— provided an herbal note. Instead of dumping the raw spices onto the meat, we first bloomed them with the onion and garlic in oil to bring out their complex flavors, and then we added the turkey. Since we weren't looking to brown the turkey (browning ground meat makes it tough), a nonstick skillet was ideal. It allowed us to use a mere 2 teaspoons of oil to soften the minced vegetables and to cook the turkey nearly through.

Because the turkey was lean, our filling needed some liquid, and a sauce would help carry the flavors of the spices. Many recipes call only for water, but water produced a thin, hollow-tasting mixture. We needed something to add meatiness. A combination of tomato sauce and chicken stock did just that, making the filling saucy and rich. Finishing with cider vinegar and brown sugar provided a sweet-and-sour tang with few calories.

Our taco filling was now, according to one taster, "perfect." We're certain no one will miss the taco kits or the beef.

Ground Turkey Tacos
SERVES 4

Feel free to top these tacos with low-fat cheese, lettuce, and tomatoes. Avocado, onion, low-fat sour cream, minced jalapeños, cilantro, and lime wedges are also worthy additions. We use plain tomato sauce (sold in 8-ounce cans) for this recipe.

1 onion, minced (about 1 cup)
1 teaspoon canola oil
Salt
2 tablespoons chili powder
3 garlic cloves, minced
1 teaspoon dried oregano
1 pound 93 percent lean ground turkey
½ cup tomato sauce (see note)
½ cup low-sodium chicken broth
2 teaspoons cider vinegar
1 teaspoon light brown sugar
Pepper
8 store-bought taco shells, warmed

1. Combine the onion, oil, and ⅛ teaspoon salt in a 12-inch nonstick skillet. Cover and cook over medium-low heat, stirring occasionally, until softened, 8 to 10 minutes. Stir in the chili powder, garlic, and oregano, and cook until fragrant, about 30 seconds.

2. Add the turkey to the skillet and cook, breaking up the meat with a wooden spoon, until almost cooked through but still slightly pink, about 2 minutes.

3. Stir in the tomato sauce, broth, vinegar, and brown sugar. Bring to a simmer and cook until thickened, about 4 minutes. Season with salt and pepper to taste.

4. Divide the filling evenly among the taco shells and serve with any desired accompaniments.

PER SERVING: Cal 300; Fat 13g; Sat fat 4g; Chol 65mg; Carb 23g; Protein 25g; Fiber 4g; Sodium 430mg

ROAST TURKEY BREAST

TURKEY MAKES A GREAT DINNER YEAR-ROUND, NOT just on Thanksgiving, but tackling the whole bird is a bit much for an everyday meal. Turkey breast, meanwhile, is an ideal, often overlooked alternative. The white meat is naturally lean, and many people prefer it to dark meat anyway, so there's not much waste. It's also much easier to handle than the whole bird, yet it still provides a substantial amount of food. But there is a downside: Turkey breast often ends up dry and chalky, especially when high heat is used. However, home cooks rely on high heat with the goal of achieving perfectly burnished, crispy skin, and we planned to remove the skin from our roast turkey breast since it's loaded with fat. This left us free to focus on achieving perfectly moist and juicy meat.

NOTES FROM THE TEST KITCHEN

BRINING

Both poultry and pork are quite lean, and in some preparations they can cook up dry. The salt in a brine changes the structure of the muscle proteins and allows them to hold on to more moisture when exposed to heat. In a sample test, tasters had no trouble picking out brined pork chops versus chops left untreated. Though we leave brining optional, if you have the time it will give you juicier meat in recipes like our Easy Roast Turkey Breast and Maple-Glazed Pork Tenderloin.

To brine, following the amounts in the chart, dissolve the salt (we use table salt) in the water in a container or bowl large enough to hold the brine and meat. Submerge the meat completely in the brine. Cover and refrigerate, following the times in the chart (do not overbrine or else the meat will taste too salty). Remove the meat from the brine, rinse, and pat dry with paper towels. The meat is now ready to be cooked.

There is one exception to brining: If you've purchased kosher poultry, frozen injected turkey, or enhanced pork (pork injected with a salt solution), don't brine them. These treatments will keep the chicken, turkey, and pork moist, and brining will make the meat way too salty.

Note that our nutritional data does not account for brining or using any of the types of meat or poultry mentioned above that should not be brined. If you brine or use any of those mentioned, be aware that the final sodium content for those recipes will be higher than what we have listed.

POULTRY OR MEAT	COLD WATER	SALT	TIME
Chicken 4 (12-ounce) bone-in, skin-on split chicken breasts and thighs	2 quarts	½ cup	½ to 1 hour
Turkey 1 (6-pound) whole bone-in, skin-on turkey breast	4 quarts	½ cup	3 to 6 hours
Pork 4 (6-ounce) boneless pork chops	2 quarts	¼ cup	½ to 1 hour
4 (8-ounce) bone-in pork chops	2 quarts	½ cup	½ to 1 hour
2 (1-pound) pork tenderloins	2 quarts	¼ cup	½ to 1 hour

Turkey breasts are available bone-in and boneless. Bones keep meat moist, especially during longer cooking times, so bone-in was the clear choice for roasting. We found that bone-in turkey breasts are sold in a few varieties—natural (untreated), self-basted (injected with a brine solution), and kosher (salted and rinsed). Although the test kitchen prefers the taste of natural turkey, which we most often brine ourselves, we found after a few basic tests that any of the options would work here, and that brining is optional. (Kosher and self-basting birds should not be brined since they have already been salted; for more on brining, see left.)

Chicken breasts can be roasted on a broiler-pan top, but larger cuts like a bone-in turkey breast do better in a V-rack, which promotes better air circulation. So back in the kitchen, we started by setting several turkey breasts skin-side up in V-racks placed inside roasting pans and tested a range of oven temperatures. We kept the skin on the meat, even though we'd discard it later, since it would protect the meat while it cooked and add flavor. Eventually, we found 325 degrees to be ideal: The breast cooked in a reasonable amount of time (two hours), and although it emerged with flabby, straw-colored skin, the meat was a different story. It was extremely tender and flavorful, by far the juiciest breast meat we'd ever had.

We were pleased with our recipe so far, but we had a few issues to work out. In the past when roasting turkey and chicken, often we pulled the skin away from the meat and massaged butter and herbs directly on the meat. The reasons for this are twofold. Loosening the skin helps it to lift and separate from the meat and creates crisper skin, and the butter and herbs flavor the meat during cooking. In this recipe, crisp skin wasn't a concern, but we were interested in the latter. We tried this technique side by side with a plain breast, and we were slightly surprised when tasters preferred the turkey without the butter and herbs. It turned out that when the skin was left intact, it provided better insulation, resulting in juicier turkey meat. We would simply remove the skin before serving.

Our turkey breast produced a lot less drippings than a whole turkey, but what drippings did result always burned in the pan and were difficult to clean. A quick solution was to add water to the roasting pan before cooking (a cup was the perfect amount; any more affected how the meat cooked).

Finally, there was the issue of what to serve with the turkey. A classic pan gravy made from drippings is usually loaded with fat, and our turkey breast didn't yield enough drippings anyway. Besides, rich gravies often serve to cover up cardboard-dry meat, and our breast meat was perfectly cooked and juicy on its own. So instead we paired the turkey with a fresh and easy sweet-tart cranberry sauce. This is Thanksgiving flavor any night of the week, but without the labor—or the calories.

Easy Roast Turkey Breast

SERVES 10

This recipe works equally well with any type of turkey breast, be it kosher, self-basting, or untreated. If using a kosher or self-basting turkey breast, do not brine. The ingredient list on the turkey breast's package will say whether it's been treated with salt. If brining the turkey breast, do not season with salt in step 2. Serve with Simple Cranberry Sauce or Simple Cranberry-Orange Sauce (recipes follow).

Vegetable oil spray
1 (6-pound) whole bone-in, skin-on turkey breast, trimmed, brined if desired (see note; see page 74)
½ teaspoon salt
¼ teaspoon pepper
1 cup water

1. Adjust an oven rack to the middle position and heat the oven to 325 degrees. Spray a V-rack with vegetable oil spray and set inside a large roasting pan.

2. Pat the turkey breast dry with paper towels and season with the salt and pepper. Place the turkey in the prepared rack, skin-side up. Pour the water into the roasting pan.

3. Roast the turkey until the thickest part of the breast registers 160 to 165 degrees on an instant-read thermometer, about 2 hours.

4. Transfer the turkey to a carving board, tent loosely with foil, and let rest for 20 minutes. Remove and discard the skin, carve the turkey, and serve, passing cranberry sauce separately.

PER SERVING: Cal 240; Fat 1.5g; Sat fat 0g; Chol 135mg; Carb 0g; Protein 53g; Fiber 0g; Sodium 220mg

Simple Cranberry Sauce

MAKES ABOUT 2½ CUPS

The cooking time in this recipe is intended for fresh berries. If you are using frozen cranberries, do not defrost them before use; just pick through them and add about 2 minutes to the simmering time.

1 cup sugar
¾ cup water
¼ teaspoon salt
1 (12-ounce) bag cranberries, picked through

Bring the sugar, water, and salt to a boil in a large saucepan over high heat, stirring occasionally to dissolve the sugar. Stir in the cranberries, reduce to a simmer, and cook until thickened slightly and about two-thirds of the berries have popped open, 7 to 10 minutes. Transfer to a serving bowl and cool to room temperature before serving. (The sauce can be covered and refrigerated for up to 1 week.)

PER ¼-CUP SERVING: Cal 90; Fat 0g; Sat fat 0g; Chol 0mg; Carb 24g; Protein 0g; Fiber 2g; Sodium 60mg

VARIATION

Simple Cranberry-Orange Sauce

Orange juice didn't add much flavor, but we found that orange zest and liqueur pack the orange kick we were looking for in this sauce.

Follow the recipe for Simple Cranberry Sauce, adding 1 tablespoon grated orange zest with the sugar. Before cooling, stir in 2 tablespoons orange liqueur (such as Triple Sec or Grand Marnier).

PER ¼-CUP SERVING: Cal 110; Fat 0g; Sat fat 0g; Chol 0mg; Carb 26g; Protein 0g; Fiber 2g; Sodium 60mg

PORK ROAST EN COCOTTE WITH APPLES AND SHALLOTS

MEAT

M = TEST KITCHEN MAKEOVER

SAUTÉED PORK CHOPS

NOWADAYS, BONELESS PORK CHOPS ARE A POPULAR choice for those looking to cook with leaner meat and who want an option beyond chicken breasts. But as we began our research, we realized that most pork chop recipes out there were more likely to result in sad, poorly cooked chops with bland, heavy sauces (usually relying on lots of butter and cream) than something you would proudly bring to the table. Our goal was to create a quick, perfectly cooked pan-seared pork chop with a light pan sauce that would be flavorful, rich, and anything but boring.

First we'd focus on the pork. Boneless pork loin chops are a great option for a quick meal, since they cook relatively quickly. After several tests with various sizes of pork chops, we discovered that extra-thick chops (those over 1 inch thick) required both the stovetop and the oven to cook properly; this felt like too much work. Thin chops (those about ¼ inch), on the other hand, were impossible to keep juicy. A ¾-inch chop proved perfect: thick enough to stay moist during sautéing, but thin enough that we could cook it entirely on the stovetop.

Next we experimented with cooking methods. The first technique we tried was to brown the chops, then cover them to finish cooking through. Doing this yielded a fairly moist piece of meat, but covering the pan created steam and ruined the chops' attractive and flavorful golden brown exterior. A more traditional approach was ultimately the most successful. We seared the chops on one side over medium-high heat, and once they developed a deep brown crust, we flipped the chops and reduced the heat to medium, allowing the chops to slowly reach 140 to 145 degrees. At this point we removed them from the pan to rest for 5 minutes, which allowed the juice to redistribute and the temperature to continue to rise (this is called carryover cooking) to the 150-degree mark. These chops were nicely browned and juicy.

During these tests, we found that the large surface area of a 12-inch skillet was necessary to build the exterior crust we desired—a pan that was any smaller crowded the chops and they simply steamed. Testing both traditional and nonstick skillets, we were surprised to see that the two performed similarly well. We opted to use a traditional skillet, however, so that we could take advantage of the fond left behind—an opportunity to build our pan sauce.

Looking for flavors that best complemented the pork, we found that a broth-based sauce with a sweet component had the most potential. Tasters preferred chicken broth over beef for its unobtrusive nature, and dried cherries for their sweet-tart concentrated flavor. Shallots, rosemary, and port also helped to deepen the flavors of the sauce. We didn't miss the more typical (and higher-fat) ingredients we'd seen elsewhere when we had such a bold, flavorful sauce topping our perfectly cooked chops.

Sautéed Pork Chops with Port Wine and Cherry Sauce

SERVES 4

If the pork is "enhanced" (see page 79 for more information), do not brine. If brining the pork, do not season with salt in step 1.

PORK

- 4 (6-ounce) boneless pork loin chops, ¾ inch thick, trimmed of all visible fat, brined if desired (see note; see page 74)
- ⅛ teaspoon salt
- ⅛ teaspoon pepper
- 1 tablespoon canola oil

SAUCE

- 1 shallot, minced (about 3 tablespoons)
- 1½ cups low-sodium chicken broth
- ½ cup ruby port
- ½ cup dried cherries
- 2 tablespoons whole milk
- 1 teaspoon cornstarch
- 2 teaspoons minced fresh rosemary
  Salt and pepper

1. FOR THE PORK: Pat the pork chops dry with paper towels and season with the salt and pepper. Heat the oil in a 12-inch skillet over medium-high heat until just smoking. Carefully lay the chops in the skillet and cook until browned on the first side, about 3 minutes. Flip the pork, reduce the heat to medium, and continue to cook until the centers of the chops register 140 to 145 degrees on an instant-read thermometer, 5 to 10 minutes longer.

2. Transfer the pork chops to a platter, tent loosely with foil, and let rest until the centers register 150 degrees on an instant-read thermometer, about 5 minutes.

3. FOR THE SAUCE: While the pork chops rest, add the shallot to the oil left in the skillet, return to medium heat, and cook until softened, about 2 minutes. Stir in the broth, port, and cherries, scraping up any browned bits. Bring to a simmer and cook until reduced to ¾ cup, about 5 minutes.

4. Whisk the milk and cornstarch together in a small bowl, then whisk the mixture into the simmering sauce, along with any accumulated juice from the pork. Continue to simmer the sauce until it has thickened, about 1 minute. Off the heat, stir in the rosemary and season with salt and pepper to taste. Spoon the sauce over the pork and serve.

PER SERVING: **Cal** 390; **Fat** 12g; **Sat fat** 3g; **Chol** 95mg; **Carb** 20g; **Protein** 39g; **Fiber** 2g; **Sodium** 400mg

VARIATION

Sautéed Pork Chops with Quick Ginger-Apple Chutney

If the pork is "enhanced" (see information at right), do not brine. If brining the pork, do not season with salt in step 1.

PORK

4 (6-ounce) boneless pork loin chops, ¾ inch thick, trimmed of all visible fat, brined if desired (see note; see page 74)

⅛ teaspoon salt

⅛ teaspoon pepper

1 tablespoon canola oil

CHUTNEY

1 pound Granny Smith apples (2 to 3), peeled, cored, and cut into ½-inch pieces

1 onion, minced (about 1 cup)
Salt

1 tablespoon grated or minced fresh ginger

¼ teaspoon ground allspice

⅛ teaspoon cayenne pepper

1 cup apple cider

¼ cup packed light brown sugar
Black pepper

1. FOR THE PORK: Pat the pork chops dry with paper towels and season with the salt and pepper. Heat the oil in a 12-inch skillet over medium-high heat until just smoking. Carefully lay the chops in the skillet and cook until browned on the first side, about 3 minutes. Flip the pork, reduce the heat to medium, and continue to cook until the centers of the chops register 140 to 145 degrees on an instant-read thermometer, 5 to 10 minutes longer.

2. Transfer the pork chops to a platter, tent loosely with foil, and let rest until the centers register 150 degrees on an instant-read thermometer, about 5 minutes.

3. FOR THE CHUTNEY: While the pork chops rest, add the apples, onion, and ¼ teaspoon salt to the oil left in the skillet. Cover and cook over medium-low heat, stirring occasionally, until the apples and onion have softened, 8 to 10 minutes. Uncover, stir in the ginger, allspice, and cayenne, and cook until fragrant, about 30 seconds. Stir in the cider and brown sugar, scraping up any browned bits. Bring to a simmer and cook until the sauce has thickened slightly, about 4 minutes.

4. Stir in any accumulated pork juice and return to a brief simmer. Season with salt and black pepper to taste. Spoon the sauce over the pork and serve.

PER SERVING: **Cal** 410; **Fat** 12g; **Sat fat** 3g; **Chol** 95mg; **Carb** 39mg; **Protein** 38g; **Fiber** 3g; **Sodium** 330mg

NOTES FROM THE TEST KITCHEN

ENHANCED OR UNENHANCED PORK
Because modern pork is remarkably lean and therefore somewhat bland and prone to dryness if overcooked, a product called "enhanced" pork has overtaken the market. Enhanced pork has been injected with a solution of water, salt, sodium phosphates, sodium lactate, potassium lactate, sodium diacetate, and varying flavor agents to bolster flavor and juiciness; these enhancing ingredients add 7 to 15 percent extra weight. (Pork containing additives must be labeled as such with a list of ingredients.) After several taste tests, we have concluded that, although enhanced pork is indeed juicier and more tender than unenhanced pork, the latter has more genuine pork flavor. Some tasters picked up artificial, salty flavors in enhanced pork. (Never brine enhanced pork, which only intensifies the saltiness, resulting in virtually inedible meat.) It can also leach juice that, once reduced, will result in overly salty sauces. We prefer natural pork, but the choice is up to you.

PORK ROAST EN COCOTTE

COOKING EN COCOTTE, OR CASSEROLE ROASTING, has long been relied on for delivering supremely tender and moist meat in a relatively healthful way. The method is simple: Brown a seasoned piece of meat in a Dutch oven, scatter in a small handful of chopped vegetables, cover, and bake slowly in a low-temperature oven. Unlike braising, in which liquid is added to the pot, cooking en cocotte relies only on the juice released from the meat to provide a moist cooking environment. The result is unbelievably tender and flavorful meat undiluted by additional liquid. We felt as if this might be a great way to prepare a lean pork roast. However, we'd have to be careful, as a lean roast would run the risk of steaming itself to inedible toughness in a covered pot. We headed to the test kitchen to see what we could do.

Pork loins can come in different shapes and sizes depending on how they've been butchered. Pieces that weigh the same can be long and thin or short and wide. For practical purposes, a shorter, wider piece was ideal simply because it fit in the pot. We also found that tying the meat made for easier browning and more even cooking.

We began by browning the meat on the stovetop in a large Dutch oven—a step we had found crucial in previous test kitchen en cocotte recipes for adding significant depth of flavor. We then tossed in a handful of aromatics, covered the pot, and placed it in the oven. Testing a range of oven temperatures, we found that while temperatures between 325 and 375 degrees produced decent results, even lower temperatures—around 250 degrees—produced incredibly tender meat.

Now that we had meat that was cooked just right, we needed to boost the flavor. We decided to try adding herbes de Provence, a fragrant mixture of dried basil, fennel seed, lavender, marjoram, rosemary, sage, summer savory, and thyme—a good match for pork. We seasoned the pork with salt and pepper and the herbs, then browned it and popped it into the oven. While the herbs simmered in the juice slowly being released as the pork cooked, their flavors bloomed and intensified. Tasters enjoyed the subtle flavors that the herbs lent the finished dish, but alone they weren't enough. We needed something more.

Since fruit is a traditional pairing with pork, and an easy, healthy option, we decided to try adding apples to the mix. We knew from experience that the apples would release a considerable amount of liquid, which would dull the flavor of the meat during cooking, so we would need to precook them on the stovetop before they went into the oven with our roast. After we browned the pork, we transferred it to a plate and cooked the apples in the now-empty pot to allow some of their juice to evaporate. We then added the roast back to the pot with the apples and let the dish finish in the oven. We were pleasantly surprised with the results—a rustic, chunky applesauce to accompany our juicy, flavorful pork. Adding some shallots to the apples not only helped offset the sweetness of the dish but also gave the mixture an appealing texture.

Pleased with our success, we created a more boldly flavored variation, substituting a spice rub for the herbes de Provence. Tasters liked a combination of coriander, paprika, brown sugar, cumin, and fennel, as well as a pinch of cayenne for heat. These spices had a tendency to burn, however, so we found it best to brown the roast lightly over more moderate heat. We replaced the apples and shallots with a couple of sliced onions, which we caramelized to provide a sweet contrast to the potent spice rub.

Pork Roast en Cocotte with Apples and Shallots
SERVES 6

We found that leaving an ⅛-inch-thick layer of fat on top of the roast is ideal; if your roast has a thicker fat cap, trim it to be about ⅛ inch thick. You can find herbes de Provence in most large grocery stores; however, 1 teaspoon each dried thyme, dried rosemary, and dried marjoram can be substituted.

- 1 **tablespoon herbes de Provence (see note)**
  Salt and pepper
- 1 **(2¼-pound) boneless center-cut pork loin roast, trimmed and tied at 1½-inch intervals (see page 81)**
- 2 **tablespoons canola oil**
- 8 **shallots, peeled and quartered**
- 1 **pound Golden Delicious or Granny Smith apples (2 to 3), peeled, cored, and cut into ½-inch-thick wedges**
- ¼ **teaspoon sugar**

1. Adjust an oven rack to the lowest position and heat the oven to 250 degrees.

2. Combine the herbes de Provence, ¼ teaspoon salt, and ¼ teaspoon pepper in a small bowl. Pat the pork dry with paper towels and rub the herb mixture evenly over the roast. Heat the oil in a large Dutch oven over medium-high heat until just smoking. Carefully lay the roast in the pot and cook until well browned on all sides, 7 to 10 minutes, turning as needed. Transfer the roast to a plate.

3. Add the shallots to the oil left in the pot, return to medium heat, and cook until golden, about 3 minutes. Add the apples and sugar and cook, stirring occasionally, until the apples are softened and golden brown, 5 to 7 minutes.

4. Off the heat, return the roast, along with any accumulated juice, to the pot. Place a large sheet of foil over the pot and press to seal, then cover tightly with the lid. Transfer the pot to the oven and cook until the center of the roast registers 140 to 145 degrees on an instant-read thermometer, 30 to 50 minutes.

NOTES FROM THE TEST KITCHEN

TYING PORK LOIN

Tying the roast tightly at 1½-inch intervals gives the roast an even shape, promoting even cooking.

THE BEST INSTANT-READ THERMOMETER

When cooking meat, we highly recommend using an instant-read thermometer to accurately gauge its temperature. Our favorite model is the **ThermoWorks Super-Fast Thermapen** (left), a true workhorse that quickly provides accurate readings across the board. But at $74, it isn't cheap. Recently, cheaper instant-read thermometers have come on the market, and we wondered if any of them could approach the performance of the Thermapen. We purchased eight models and put them through their paces in the test kitchen. None of the cheaper models could match the speed, temperature range, or accuracy of the Thermapen, but the no-frills **Maverick Redi-Chek Professional Chef's Digital Thermometer DT-01** (right), at $12.95, performed admirably enough to earn our endorsement.

5. Transfer the pot to a wire rack. Transfer the roast to a carving board, tent loosely with foil, and let rest until the center of the roast registers 150 degrees on an instant-read thermometer, about 20 minutes. Meanwhile, season the apple-shallot mixture with salt and pepper to taste and cover to keep warm.

6. Remove the twine from the roast, slice thin, and transfer to a platter. Spoon the apple-shallot mixture over the pork and serve.

PER SERVING: **Cal** 390; **Fat** 20g; **Sat fat** 5g; **Chol** 115mg; **Carb** 16g; **Protein** 37g; **Fiber** 2g; **Sodium** 200mg

---

VARIATION

Spice-Rubbed Pork Roast en Cocotte with Caramelized Onions

We found that leaving an ⅛-inch-thick layer of fat on top of the roast is ideal; if your roast has a thicker fat cap, trim it back to be about ⅛ inch thick. To prevent the spices from burning when browning the pork in step 2, be sure to use medium heat, adjusting the flame if necessary.

5 teaspoons ground coriander

2 teaspoons paprika

1 teaspoon brown sugar

¾ teaspoon ground fennel

¾ teaspoon ground cumin

Salt

Pinch cayenne pepper

1 (2¼-pound) boneless center-cut pork loin roast, trimmed and tied at 1½-inch intervals (see photo)

2 tablespoons canola oil

2 onions, halved and sliced thin

3 garlic cloves, minced

Black pepper

1. Adjust an oven rack to the lowest position and heat the oven to 250 degrees.

2. Combine the coriander, paprika, brown sugar, fennel, cumin, ½ teaspoon salt, and cayenne in a small bowl. Pat the pork dry with paper towels and rub the spice mixture evenly over the roast. Heat the oil in a large Dutch oven over medium heat until just smoking. Carefully lay the roast in the pot and cook until lightly browned on all sides, 5 to 7 minutes, turning as needed. Transfer the roast to a plate.

3. Add the onions and ¼ teaspoon salt to the oil left in the pot, cover, and cook, stirring occasionally, over medium-low heat until softened, 8 to 10 minutes. Uncover, increase the heat to medium-high, and continue to cook until the onions are well browned, 8 to 12 minutes. Stir in the garlic and cook until fragrant, about 30 seconds.

4. Off the heat, return the roast, along with any accumulated juice, to the pot. Place a large sheet of foil over the pot and press to seal, then cover tightly with the lid. Transfer the pot to the oven and cook until the center of the roast registers 140 to 145 degrees on an instant-read thermometer, 30 to 50 minutes.

5. Transfer the pot to a wire rack. Transfer the roast to a carving board, tent loosely with foil, and let rest until the center of the roast registers 150 degrees on an instant-read thermometer, about 20 minutes. Meanwhile, season the onions with salt and black pepper to taste and cover to keep warm.

6. Remove the twine from the roast, slice thin, and transfer to a platter. Spoon the onions over the pork and serve.

PER SERVING: **Cal** 360; **Fat** 21g; **Sat fat** 5g; **Chol** 115mg; **Carb** 7g; **Protein** 36g; **Fiber** 2g; **Sodium** 290mg

MAPLE-GLAZED PORK TENDERLOIN

FOR A WEEKNIGHT ROAST, A FINE-GRAINED, BUTTERY-smooth lean pork tenderloin is hard to beat—when done right. Unfortunately, today's pork tenderloin is quickly becoming the boneless, skinless chicken breast of the pork world: overcooked, dry, and flavorless. We set out to refine our cooking technique so that we would get perfectly cooked, juicy meat every time, and we also wanted to develop a simple, well-balanced glaze to pair with it.

We started with the cooking technique. After several trials, we found the best approach required both the stovetop and the oven. Searing the roasts first on the stovetop created a flavorful browned exterior, and this browning sealed in the juices so our meat stayed moist while it finished in the oven. We discovered that moving the tenderloins directly to the oven in the skillet led to an overcooked exterior, a result of the heat retained in the skillet from its time on the stovetop. Moving the roasts to a wire rack set over a baking sheet for their time in the oven solved the problem. We found 375 degrees for 12 to 20 minutes gave us moist meat every time.

We removed the roasts from the oven when they reached 140 to 145 degrees, since the meat would continue to cook as it rested.

Next we turned to developing a flavorful glaze. Enter New England's signature ingredient: maple syrup. Its rich, sweet flavor and subtle aroma complement pork beautifully. But, on its own, it made for an overwhelmingly sweet glaze. So we started with ¾ cup, which we mixed with ¼ cup of mildly bitter molasses. Some brandy added complexity, and cinnamon, cloves, and cayenne pepper played off the syrup and added a little spice. Now we just needed to work on how to apply it to the pork.

In the past we had found that the best way to glaze a pork loin roast was to brown the pork, add the glaze to the skillet, and place the meat in the oven, skillet and all, rotating the roast occasionally in the reducing syrup. But with our tenderloins raised on a rack, we didn't have this option. Reducing the glaze to the proper consistency on the stovetop, then coating the tenderloins and moving them to the oven on the rack, wasn't the answer either. The glaze ended up dripping through the rack, resulting in a perfectly glazed baking sheet and nearly bare tenderloins. We needed to find a way to make the glaze stick.

Could we somehow prepare the surface of the pork to hold the glaze, like priming a surface for painting? Coating the tenderloins with flour or cornstarch seemed promising, so we rolled one tenderloin in flour and the other in cornstarch before searing. The cornstarch-encrusted tenderloin did a better job grabbing glaze, but too much was still slipping away. Mixing a little sugar with the cornstarch did the trick. The sugar caramelized as the meat seared, creating a deep brown crust with the texture of sandpaper—perfect for holding a glaze.

We now had a surefire way of making our glaze stick to the meat, but after cooking up another round, tasters still wanted more glaze on the tenderloins. Thinking of our painting analogy, we considered that one key to good coverage is waiting between coats to allow each to dry. So we applied the first coat of glaze and let the meat roast in the oven until it was nearly done. Then we applied a second coat. When the tenderloins were done cooking, we added a third coat on top of the now-dry second coat. Finally, after letting the tenderloins rest, we glazed them once more, this time with a glaze that included whole grain mustard for a little extra zing. Slicing into the roasts revealed lustrous success—a thick maple glaze coating the juicy meat.

MAPLE-GLAZED PORK TENDERLOIN

Maple-Glazed Pork Tenderloin

SERVES 6

If the pork is "enhanced" (see page 79 for more information), do not brine. If brining the pork, omit the salt in the cornstarch mixture in step 2. Be sure to thoroughly shake off the cornstarch mixture in step 3, as any excess will leave gummy spots. If the tenderloins don't fit in the skillet initially, let their ends curve toward each other; the meat will shrink as it cooks. Make sure the tenderloins turn deep golden brown in step 3 or they will appear pale after glazing. Our preference is to use grade B maple syrup. (Don't be tempted to substitute imitation maple syrup, i.e., pancake syrup—it will be too sweet.)

- ¾ cup maple syrup (see note)
- ¼ cup light or mild molasses
- 2 tablespoons brandy
- ⅛ teaspoon ground cinnamon
  Pinch ground cloves
  Pinch cayenne pepper
- ¼ cup cornstarch
- 2 tablespoons sugar
- 2 teaspoons black pepper
- ½ teaspoon salt
- 2 (1-pound) pork tenderloins, silver skin removed (see photo), trimmed of all visible fat, brined if desired (see note; see page 74)
- 2 tablespoons canola oil
- 1 tablespoon whole grain mustard

1. Adjust an oven rack to the middle position and heat the oven to 375 degrees. Set a wire rack over a foil-lined rimmed baking sheet and set aside.

2. Combine ½ cup of the maple syrup, molasses, brandy, cinnamon, cloves, and cayenne in a small bowl and set aside. Whisk the cornstarch, sugar, black pepper, and salt together in a small bowl. Transfer the cornstarch mixture to a second rimmed baking sheet.

3. Pat the pork tenderloins dry with paper towels, then roll them in the cornstarch mixture until evenly coated on all sides, shaking off any excess. Heat the oil in a 12-inch nonstick skillet over medium heat until just smoking. Carefully lay both tenderloins in the skillet, spaced 1 inch apart, and cook until well browned on all sides, 8 to 12 minutes, turning as needed. Transfer the pork to the prepared wire rack.

4. Pour off any excess fat from the skillet and return to medium heat. Add the syrup mixture to the skillet, scraping up any browned bits, and cook until the mixture has reduced to ½ cup, 2 to 4 minutes. Measure out and reserve 2 tablespoons of the glaze.

5. Brush each pork tenderloin with 1 tablespoon of the remaining glaze. Transfer the baking sheet with the pork to the oven and roast until the thickest part of the tenderloins registers 130 to 135 degrees on an instant-read thermometer, 12 to 20 minutes. Brush each tenderloin with 1 tablespoon more glaze and continue to cook until the thickest part of the tenderloins registers 140 to 145 degrees on an instant-read thermometer, 2 to 4 minutes longer.

6. Brush the tenderloins with the remaining glaze and let rest, uncovered, until the thickest part registers 150 degrees on an instant-read thermometer, about 10 minutes.

7. While the tenderloins rest, stir the remaining ¼ cup maple syrup and mustard into the reserved 2 tablespoons of the glaze. Brush each tenderloin with 1 tablespoon of the mustard glaze. Transfer the tenderloins to a carving board and cut into ¼-inch-thick slices. Serve, passing the remaining mustard glaze separately.

PER SERVING: Cal 360; **Fat** 8g; **Sat fat** 1.5g; **Chol** 100mg; **Carb** 40g; **Protein** 32g; **Fiber** 0g; **Sodium** 200mg

---

NOTES FROM THE TEST KITCHEN

REMOVING THE SILVER SKIN FROM PORK TENDERLOIN

The silver skin is a thin, tough membrane covering parts of the tenderloin and should be removed before cooking. Slip a knife under the silver skin, angle it slightly upward, and use a gentle back-and-forth motion to remove it.

MOLASSES

Just as there are different grades of maple syrup, there is more than one kind of molasses: There are actually three. Each is produced from successive boilings of the cane sugar, and as more sugar is drawn from the juice, the resulting molasses gets stronger, darker, and more bitter. Light, or mild, molasses comes from the first boiling, dark from the second, and blackstrap from the third. Each type of molasses has a very distinctive flavor, and after we ran them through a test kitchen tasting to determine the "best," personal preference carried the day. Most preferred the milder varieties, which is what we like for our pork tenderloin recipe since it creates a not-too-bitter glaze that won't overwhelm the mild pork.

Maple-Glazed Pork Tenderloin with Smoked Paprika and Ginger

Follow the recipe for Maple-Glazed Pork Tenderloin, substituting dry sherry for the brandy and 1 teaspoon grated or minced fresh ginger and ¼ teaspoon smoked paprika for the cinnamon, cloves, and cayenne pepper. Omit the mustard in step 7.

PER SERVING: **Cal** 360; **Fat** 8g; **Sat fat** 1.5g; **Chol** 100mg; **Carb** 39g; **Protein** 32g; **Fiber** 0g; **Sodium** 140mg

Maple-Glazed Pork Tenderloin with Orange and Chipotle

Follow the recipe for Maple-Glazed Pork Tenderloin, substituting 2 tablespoons thawed frozen orange juice concentrate for 2 tablespoons of the molasses and 1 tablespoon minced chipotle chiles in adobo sauce for the cinnamon, cloves, and cayenne pepper. Omit the mustard in step 7.

PER SERVING: **Cal** 360; **Fat** 8g; **Sat fat** 1.5g; **Chol** 100mg; **Carb** 37g; **Protein** 32g; **Fiber** 0g; **Sodium** 135mg

PAN-SEARED INEXPENSIVE STEAK

FEW MEALS SEEM AS LUXURIOUS AS A PERFECTLY cooked, melt-in-your-mouth steak, and served in moderation, even a fine steak dinner can be healthy. But such bliss does not come cheaply, with premium cuts of beef—filet mignon, rib-eye, and strip steak, to name a few—often carrying a hefty price tag. While investing in these steaks is fine for a special occasion, we wanted to find an inexpensive steak that could still earn high praise. To keep our meal on the lighter side, we wanted to work with a lean cut of beef, and we also wanted to pair it with a rustic, hearty sauce that wouldn't be full of fat and calories.

Before narrowing down the cuts, we needed to understand a bit more about what makes certain cuts of beef inexpensive. In simple terms, the cost of a steak is driven primarily by its tenderness (the trait Americans prize most). As the animal grows and exercises, the tissues within each muscle grow, making the muscles bigger and tougher. The more tender meat comes from the least exercised part of the animal, the middle. This is why the cuts of beef from the rib (rib-eye) and the loin (filet mignon and strip steak) are so tender compared with any cut from the shoulder or front arms (top round) or the

back legs (blade steak and pot roast).

Armed with this knowledge, we went off to our local grocery store with an upper price limit of $6.99 per pound. We bought every cut within our price range, which turned out to be 12 different steaks. Back in the test kitchen, we determined that several of these steaks were simply too fatty even to be in the running for a light dinner, and others were too tough for a quick pan sear—these were better left for long, slow cooking. But a few showed tremendous potential. Tasters were particularly enthusiastic about the tenderness and flavor of the boneless top sirloin steak (also known as shell sirloin). This cut comes from the sirloin—right behind the middle of the steer—and not only was it a mere $5.99 per pound, but as an added bonus it was one of the leanest cuts we found. In fact, when we compared this steak with a porterhouse ($9.99 per pound), tasters were surprised at the similarities. Choosing a moderately sized 1-pound steak to serve four people worked perfectly since we were going to serve it with a hearty sauce.

Now the trick was to fine-tune our cooking method. Lean steaks are best when cooked quickly and with high heat—think filet mignon. For a perfectly seared steak, we found that a large skillet was key for maintaining even heat distribution. To achieve the perfect crust, it was also necessary to make sure that the oil in the skillet was just smoking before adding the steak. If the pan was not hot enough, the steak ended up stewing rather than searing. And because moving the steak released its liquid, once we placed the steak in the skillet, we made sure not to move it. Getting a deep brown crust on the first side took about three minutes, then we flipped the steak, reduced the heat, and for a medium-rare steak continued cooking until it reached 125 degrees, an additional five to seven minutes. We found it best to always undercook the steak a bit to allow for carryover cooking (an internal temperature of 130 degrees is medium-rare).

While our perfectly cooked steak rested, we worked on our pan sauce. For efficiency's sake, we kept things simple. The earthy flavor of sautéed mushrooms was a good match for the steak, and onion and garlic would add some depth. A quarter-cup of brandy to deglaze the pan added a rich caramelized flavor, and chicken broth provided a well-balanced base. Finishing with a little Dijon mustard—instead of butter—added richness without the fat, and thyme and lemon juice added fresh flavor to pull it all together. At last, we had a steak dinner that wouldn't break the bank or our scale.

Pan-Seared Inexpensive Steak with Hearty Mushroom Sauce

SERVES 4

We prefer this steak cooked to medium-rare, but if you prefer it more or less done, see our guidelines in "Testing Meat for Doneness" below. Be sure to add the brandy to the skillet off the heat to prevent it from igniting.

STEAK

- 1 (1-pound) boneless top sirloin steak (shell sirloin), trimmed of all visible fat
- ⅛ teaspoon salt
- ⅛ teaspoon pepper
- 2 teaspoons canola oil

SAUCE

- 10 ounces white mushrooms, sliced thin
- 1 onion, halved and sliced thin
- 2 teaspoons minced fresh thyme
- 1 teaspoon canola oil
  Salt
- 2 garlic cloves, minced
- ¼ cup brandy
- ¾ cup low-sodium chicken broth
- 1 teaspoon Dijon mustard
- 1 teaspoon fresh lemon juice
  Pepper

1. FOR THE STEAK: Pat the steak dry with paper towels and season with the salt and pepper. Heat the oil in a 12-inch skillet over medium-high heat until just smoking. Carefully lay the steak in the skillet and cook until well browned on the first side, about 3 minutes. Flip the steak, reduce the heat to medium, and continue to cook until the center of the steak registers 125 degrees on an instant-read thermometer (for medium-rare), 5 to 7 minutes longer. Transfer the steak to a carving board, tent loosely with foil, and let rest while making the sauce.

2. FOR THE SAUCE: Add the mushrooms, onion, thyme, oil, and ¼ teaspoon salt to the skillet. Cover and cook over medium-low heat, stirring occasionally, until the mushrooms and onion have softened, 8 to 10 minutes. Uncover, increase the heat to medium-high, and continue to cook, stirring occasionally, until the mushrooms and onion are well browned, 8 to 12 minutes longer. Stir in the garlic and cook until fragrant, about 30 seconds.

3. Off the heat, slowly stir in the brandy, scraping up any browned bits, and let sit until the bubbling subsides, about 30 seconds. Carefully return the skillet to medium heat and simmer until the brandy has almost completely evaporated, about 1 minute. Stir in the broth, bring to a simmer, and cook, stirring occasionally, until thickened slightly, about 5 minutes.

4. Off the heat, whisk in any accumulated steak juice, mustard, and lemon juice. Season with salt and pepper to taste. Cut the steak across the grain into ¼-inch-thick slices and serve, passing the sauce separately.

PER SERVING: Cal 260; Fat 12g; Sat fat 3.5g; Chol 55mg; Carb 7g; Protein 22g; Fiber 1g; Sodium 420mg

---

NOTES FROM THE TEST KITCHEN

TESTING MEAT FOR DONENESS
An instant-read thermometer is the most reliable method for checking the doneness of chicken, beef, and pork. To use an instant-read thermometer, simply insert it through the side of a chicken breast, steak, or pork chop. The chart below lists temperatures at which the meat should be removed from the heat, as the temperature of the meat will continue to climb between 5 and 10 degrees as it rests. (Cutlets cook too quickly for an actual doneness test and you will have to rely more on visual cues and cooking times.)

MEAT	COOK UNTIL IT REGISTERS	SERVING TEMPERATURE
Chicken and Turkey Breasts	160 to 165 degrees	160 to 165 degrees
Chicken Thighs	175 degrees	175 degrees
Pork	140 to 145 degrees	150 degrees
Beef		
Rare	115 to 120 degrees	125 degrees
Medium-rare	120 to 125 degrees	130 degrees
Medium	130 to 135 degrees	140 degrees
Medium-well	140 to 145 degrees	150 degrees
Well-done	150 to 155 degrees	160 degrees

BEEF AND VEGETABLE STIR-FRIES

WHILE MOST TAKEOUT STIR-FRIES ARE HEAVILY sauced and cooked in an excess of oil—not exactly light fare—homemade stir-fries can be the perfect option for a healthy meal. A properly prepared stir-fry avoids heaviness by using a minimal amount of oil and balancing a moderate amount of protein with lots of vegetables. We wanted to maximize its healthy potential and create a simply prepared stir-fry dressed in a light, flavorful sauce.

Technique and equipment are of utmost importance when making a stir-fry. The pan must get hot enough to caramelize sugars, deepen flavors, and evaporate unnecessary juices, all in a matter of minutes. It is also critical to avoid overloading the pan, as it will cause the meat and vegetables to be steamed rather than seared, leading to a soggy, unappealing stir-fry. We found a 12-inch nonstick skillet maximized the hot surface area and provided ample room for excess moisture to evaporate.

Because the protein would be featured in moderation, beef was certainly an acceptable choice. Beef stir-fries are best made with thinly sliced, tender meat, which will cook quickly and incorporate easily. We tried several cuts, including top round, tenderloin, flank steak, and blade steak. Top round and tenderloin toughened when stir-fried, and while both flank and blade steak remained moist and tender, the blade steak offered more flavor. We found it was easier to slice thin pieces of meat when the blade steak was slightly frozen; 15 minutes in the freezer was all it took.

As for the cooking method, we found that the continuous stirring suggested in many recipes detracted from browning and caused moisture to leach out of the beef. Lightly browning one side of the beef without stirring, then stirring once so that the second side could quickly brown, proved best, giving us lightly browned beef that stayed juicy.

After the beef was cooked, we removed it from the pan and moved on to the vegetables. Red bell pepper and broccoli were easy choices, as both are good matches for beef, but we found determining how to cook them required more consideration. The peppers cooked quickly, but the broccoli needed more time. So after cooking the peppers, we removed them from the pan and added the broccoli. Adding a bit of water to the pan and covering it with a lid steamed the broccoli in

minutes; once it was crisp-tender, the cover came off so excess water could evaporate.

In most recipes the aromatics are added at the outset, when the pan is empty, and are saturated with as much as ¼ cup of oil (which, in essence, fries them). By the time the stir-fry is done, the aromatics have burned, and all that unnecessary oil just makes the stir-fry greasy. We found we could avoid these problems by waiting to cook the aromatics until after we had cooked the vegetables. When the vegetables were done, we pushed them to the sides of the pan, added the aromatics and 2 teaspoons of oil to the center, and cooked until they were just fragrant, about 30 seconds. We then stirred them into the vegetables.

Now all we needed was our sauce. Chicken broth and sherry created the best base because the combination was not overpowering. Soy sauce, hoisin, and sesame oil were all excellent flavor enhancers, but we quickly learned a little of these ingredients goes a long way. The flavor of our sauce was good, but the consistency needed work—it was too thin and wouldn't adhere properly. The solution was as simple as adding a little cornstarch to help the sauce cling. We also found that marinating the meat in a simple soy sauce–sherry mixture mirrored the flavors of our sauce and tied it all together.

Our components and process were set: We mixed together the sauce, cooked the beef, and then cooked the vegetables and aromatics. We then added the beef back to the pan along with the sauce and cooked the whole dish just until the sauce thickened. Quick and simple, these stir-fries make a perfect light and healthy meal.

Stir-Fried Beef and Broccoli in Garlic Sauce
SERVES 4

Freezing the beef for 15 minutes before slicing makes it easier to cut thin slices. Letting the beef marinate as you prepare the vegetables will keep things efficient. If you like, add ½ teaspoon red pepper flakes to the garlic mixture in step 2 for more heat.

SAUCE
- ½ cup low-sodium chicken broth
- ¼ cup dry sherry
- 3 tablespoons hoisin sauce
- 1 tablespoon low-sodium soy sauce
- 2 teaspoons cornstarch
- 1 teaspoon toasted sesame oil

STIR-FRIED BEEF AND BROCCOLI IN GARLIC SAUCE

STIR-FRY

1 **(12-ounce) blade steak, trimmed of gristle and all visible fat (see page 90) and sliced ¼ inch thick (see note)**

2 **teaspoons low-sodium soy sauce**

2 **teaspoons dry sherry**

6 **garlic cloves, minced**

1 **tablespoon grated or minced fresh ginger**

3 **scallions, minced**

4 **teaspoons canola oil**

1 **red bell pepper, stemmed, seeded, and cut into ¾-inch pieces**

1 **bunch broccoli (about 1½ pounds), florets cut into 1-inch pieces, stems trimmed and sliced thin (see page 34)**

½ **cup water**

1. FOR THE SAUCE: Combine all of the ingredients in a small bowl and set aside.

2. FOR THE STIR-FRY: Toss the beef with the soy sauce and sherry in a medium bowl and let marinate for at least 10 minutes, or up to 1 hour. In a separate bowl, combine the garlic, ginger, scallions, and 2 teaspoons of the oil.

3. Heat 1 teaspoon more oil in a 12-inch nonstick skillet over high heat until just smoking. Carefully add the beef in a single layer, breaking up any clumps. Cook without stirring for 1 minute, then stir and continue to cook until the beef is lightly browned, 2 to 3 minutes longer. Transfer the beef to a clean bowl.

4. Add the remaining 1 teaspoon oil to the skillet and return to high heat until shimmering. Add the bell pepper and cook until crisp-tender, 1 to 2 minutes. Transfer the bell pepper to the bowl with the beef.

5. Add the broccoli and water to the pan, cover, and cook until the broccoli begins to turn bright green, 1 to 2 minutes. Uncover and cook, stirring frequently, until the liquid evaporates and the broccoli is crisp-tender, 2 to 4 minutes longer.

6. Clear the center of the skillet and add the garlic mixture. Cook, mashing the garlic mixture into the pan with the back of a spatula, until fragrant, about 1 minute. Stir the garlic mixture into the broccoli.

7. Return the bell pepper and beef to the skillet, along with any accumulated juices, and stir to combine. Whisk the sauce to recombine and add it to the skillet. Cook, stirring constantly, until thickened, about 1 minute. Serve.

PER SERVING: Cal 300; Fat 13g; Sat fat 3g; Chol 50mg; Carb 24g; Protein 23g; Fiber 5g; Sodium 820mg

VARIATION

Stir-Fried Beef and Eggplant in Oyster Sauce
Freezing the beef for 15 minutes before slicing makes it easier to cut thin slices. Letting the beef marinate as you prepare the vegetables will keep things efficient. If you like, add ½ teaspoon red pepper flakes to the garlic mixture in step 2 for more heat. We find it unnecessary to peel the eggplant here; however, you may peel it if desired.

SAUCE

6 **tablespoons dry sherry**

3 **tablespoons low-sodium chicken broth**

3 **tablespoons oyster sauce**

2 **tablespoons low-sodium soy sauce**

1 **teaspoon toasted sesame oil**

1 **teaspoon sugar**

1 **teaspoon cornstarch**

¼ **teaspoon pepper**

STIR-FRY

1 **(12-ounce) blade steak, trimmed of gristle and all visible fat (see page 90) and sliced ¼ inch thick (see note)**

2 **teaspoons low-sodium soy sauce**

2 **teaspoons dry sherry**

3 **garlic cloves, minced**

1 **tablespoon grated or minced fresh ginger**

3 **scallions, minced**

5 **teaspoons canola oil**

1 **eggplant (about 1 pound), trimmed and cut into ½-inch cubes (see note)**

8 **ounces shiitake mushrooms, stemmed and cut into ½-inch pieces**

1. FOR THE SAUCE: Combine all of the ingredients in a small bowl and set aside.

2. FOR THE STIR-FRY: Toss the beef with the soy sauce and sherry in a medium bowl and let marinate for at least 10 minutes, or up to 1 hour. In a separate bowl, combine the garlic, ginger, scallions, and 2 teaspoons of the oil.

3. Heat 1 teaspoon more oil in a 12-inch nonstick skillet over high heat until just smoking. Carefully add the beef in a single layer, breaking up any clumps. Cook without stirring for 1 minute, then stir and continue to cook until the meat is lightly browned, 2 to 3 minutes longer. Transfer the beef to a clean bowl.

4. Add 1 teaspoon more oil to the pan and return to high heat until shimmering. Add the eggplant and cook, stirring frequently, until browned and no longer spongy, about 5 minutes. Transfer the eggplant to the bowl with the beef.

5. Add the remaining 1 teaspoon oil to the skillet and return to high heat until shimmering. Add the mushrooms and cook until beginning to brown, about 3 minutes.

6. Clear the center of the skillet and add the garlic mixture. Cook, mashing the garlic mixture into the pan

with the back of a spatula, until fragrant, about 1 minute. Stir the garlic mixture into the mushrooms.

7. Return the eggplant and beef to the skillet, along with any accumulated juices, and stir to combine. Whisk the sauce to recombine and add it to the skillet. Cook, stirring constantly, until thickened, about 1 minute. Serve.

PER SERVING: **Cal** 410; **Fat** 13g; **Sat fat** 5g; **Chol** 75mg; **Carb** 42g; **Protein** 30g; **Fiber** 5g; **Sodium** 580mg

NOTES FROM THE TEST KITCHEN

TRIMMING BLADE STEAKS

1. Halve each steak lengthwise, leaving the gristle on one half.

2. Cut away the gristle from the half to which it is still attached.

THE BEST INEXPENSIVE NONSTICK SKILLET

We've always recommended buying inexpensive nonstick skillets because with regular use the nonstick coating inevitably scratches, chips off, or becomes ineffective. We rounded up eight models priced under $60 and pitted them against each other. We sautéed onions and carrots, cooked thin fillets of sole, made omelets, and fried eggs (with no added fat) in each pan; they all did an acceptable job cooking and releasing these foods. To gauge durability, we cooked frittatas while doing several things that manufacturers specifically forbid in each pan: broiling, cutting with a sharp knife, removing the slices with a metal pie server, and washing with an abrasive metal scrubber. The **Simply Calphalon Nonstick 12-inch Omelette Pan,** $55, which is ovensafe to 400 degrees, came out in front. It performed well thanks in part to its light weight and even, gently sloping sides. The nicely angled handle stayed cool, and the latest model's addition of a silicone grip lends added comfort.

BEEF AND VEGETABLE SHEPHERD'S PIE

A RICH MEAT AND VEGETABLE STEW CONCEALED under a creamy mashed potato crust, shepherd's pie is comfort food at its best, but we all know it isn't exactly the healthiest of meals, with a typical serving dishing

TEST KITCHEN
MAKEOVER

up 700 calories and almost 40 grams of fat. Would it be possible to come up with a lighter version that still had all the comfort of the classic?

Beef is one of the key ingredients in today's shepherd's pies, and it is also one of the main contributors of fat. So we picked the leanest ground beef we could find, 90 percent lean, knowing that what it lacked in flavor we could make up for with an extra-flavorful filling. However, we were a little more concerned about how it would cook. For a trial run, we sautéed a basic vegetable base of onion and carrots, cooked the meat until browned, then stirred in some broth as a basic working stew. We poured the mixture into a dish, topped it with mashed potatoes, and moved it to the oven (it didn't require long since the filling had already been cooking on the stovetop).

After one bite, we knew the meat needed work. It was dry, stringy, and rubbery—no doubt a result of the lack of fat. Looking at similar stew-like recipes that used lean ground beef, we discovered that many of them had good results when the meat wasn't browned. Instead, they called for cooking it until it just lost its color, then gently simmering it in the stew until it was perfectly done. Back in the kitchen, we tried the new technique, while at the same time also breaking up the beef to help avoid stringy pieces. The results were impressive: The meat was tender, moist, and not at all stringy.

Now our perfectly cooked beef needed a boost from a flavorful stew. Worcestershire sauce helped it taste beefier, and tomato paste added depth. Thyme is a traditional inclusion in shepherd's pie, and everyone approved of adding fresh, not dried. For the liquid ingredients, tasters preferred milder chicken broth to the "overwhelming" flavor of beef broth. Given that shepherd's pie is also a popular pub food, we felt a little beer was appropriate and would add great flavor without too many more calories. Guinness, our favorite pub beer, was too bitter. Most mild lagers and ales were fine, but it was an unlikely choice, O'Doul's nonalcoholic amber beer, that tasters deemed their favorite. Its sweet, malty flavor may not be terribly satisfying at a pub, but even a mere ¾ cup made a big difference here. Now our stew was a little thin, but cooking it down to the right consistency led to overcooked meat. A couple of tablespoons of flour added to the skillet before the liquid helped the sauce reach the proper consistency quickly. As a final touch, we stirred in 1 cup each of frozen peas and corn.

Now it was time to top our stew with a mashed potato crust. We knew our traditional mashed potato recipe, which contains nearly 30 grams of fat, would not work; the butter and heavy cream had to go. Testing a variety of broths and low-fat dairy, tasters liked mashed potatoes made with low-fat buttermilk best, commenting on the surprising creaminess and welcome tang. For added buttery texture, we used Yukon Gold potatoes instead of the traditional russets.

Ready for the final assembly, we poured the stew into a casserole dish, and, using a large rubber spatula, we spread the potatoes evenly across the top. We found it was important to completely cover the stew and seal the edges of the dish with the potato topping to prevent it from bubbling over. We baked it for 15 minutes to heat everything through, then ran the pie under the broiler for three to five minutes to create an appealing golden brown crust on top.

Our new version of shepherd's pie may have less fat and calories—26 grams less fat and almost 300 fewer calories, in fact—but it is still full on flavor and plenty comforting.

MAKEOVER SPOTLIGHT: SHEPHERD'S PIE

	CALORIES	FAT	SAT FAT	CHOLESTEROL
BEFORE	700	39g	20g	155mg
AFTER	410	13g	5g	75mg

Beef and Vegetable Shepherd's Pie

SERVES 6

Although just about any mild beer will work in this recipe, we prefer the sweet flavor of O'Doul's nonalcoholic amber. It is important to spread the potatoes to the very edge of the casserole dish to seal the top and prevent the filling from bubbling up and out of the dish.

FILLING

- 3 carrots, peeled and cut into ¼-inch pieces
- 1 onion, minced (about 1 cup)
- 1 teaspoon canola oil
  Salt
- 1½ pounds 90 percent lean ground beef
- 5 tablespoons unbleached all-purpose flour
- 1 tablespoon tomato paste
  Pepper
- 1½ cups low-sodium chicken broth
- ¾ cup beer (see note)
- 1 tablespoon Worcestershire sauce
- 2 teaspoons minced fresh thyme
- 1 cup frozen peas (4 ounces)
- 1 cup frozen corn (4 ounces)

TOPPING

- 1½ pounds Yukon Gold potatoes (3 to 4), peeled and cut into 2-inch pieces
  Salt
- 1 cup low-fat buttermilk
  Pepper

1. FOR THE FILLING: Adjust an oven rack to the upper-middle position and heat the oven to 375 degrees.

2. Combine the carrots, onion, oil, and ½ teaspoon salt in a 12-inch skillet. Cover and cook over medium-low heat until the carrots and onion have softened, 8 to 10 minutes. Uncover, increase the heat to medium, add the beef, and cook, breaking up the meat with a wooden spoon, until almost cooked through but still slightly pink, 5 to 6 minutes. Stir in the flour, tomato paste, and ½ teaspoon pepper, and cook for 1 minute.

3. Gradually whisk in the broth, beer, Worcestershire, and thyme. Bring to a simmer over medium-low heat and cook, stirring occasionally, until thickened but still saucy, 20 to 25 minutes. Off the heat, stir in the peas and corn, season with salt and pepper to taste, and transfer to a broiler-safe 2-quart casserole dish.

APPLYING THE POTATO TOPPING

Use a rubber spatula to scrape small piles of potatoes around the edge of the dish, then dollop more potatoes into the center and spread them until filling is covered and the topping is flush with the edge of the dish.

4. FOR THE TOPPING: While the filling simmers, bring 2 quarts water, the potatoes, and ½ teaspoon salt to a simmer in a large saucepan over high heat. Reduce the heat to medium-low and cook until the potatoes are tender, 15 to 20 minutes. Drain the potatoes and return to the saucepan. Mash the potatoes with the buttermilk until smooth, then season with salt and pepper to taste.

5. Following the photo, spread the potatoes over the filling and smooth the top. Bake until the filling is bubbling, about 15 minutes. Turn on the broiler and broil until the top is golden brown, 3 to 5 minutes. Transfer the casserole to a wire rack and let cool for 10 minutes before serving.

PER SERVING: Cal 410; **Fat** 13g; **Sat fat** 5g; **Chol** 75mg; **Carb** 42g; **Protein** 30g; **Fiber** 5g; **Sodium** 580mg

SLOW-ROASTED BEEF

WHEN PEOPLE THINK OF HEALTHY EATING, BEEF IS about the last thing that comes to mind. But just as we'd proven with our pan-seared steak recipe (see page 85), beef isn't unhealthy with the right cut and the proper serving size. Now we wanted an appealing meal for a larger group, and we wanted to keep the prep simple and the end result light. The answer? A beef roast.

First we searched for the most promising kind of roast. After a week in the kitchen, we had a clear winner: the eye round roast. Though less flavorful than fattier cuts and less tender than others, the eye round has one key attribute the others lack: a uniform shape from front to back. It would not only cook evenly but would look good on the plate.

We were pretty sure this tougher cut would benefit from a low-and-slow cooking approach, which would give the connective tissue time to break down, making the roast more tender. Some extreme recipes we found insisted the most tender, juicy roast is obtained by roasting at temperatures around 130 degrees for 20 to 30 hours. Tossing aside practicality, we set the one oven we have capable of maintaining such a low temperature to 130 degrees and popped in an eye round. Twenty-four hours later, we pulled out a roast with juicy, meltingly tender meat that tasters likened to beef tenderloin.

Looking into the science, we discovered that as the temperature of beef rises, enzymes within the meat begin to break down its connective tissues and act as natural tenderizers—but just until it reaches 122 degrees, at which point all action stops. Roasting the eye round in an oven set to 130 degrees allowed it to stay below 122 degrees far longer than when roasted in the typical low-temperature range (250 to 325 degrees), transforming this unassuming cut into something great. But knowing ovens don't heat below 200 degrees—and that most cooks don't want to run their ovens all day—we decided to take a more reasonable approach. We chose 225 degrees as our starting point.

After browning the roast for color and a flavorful crust, we cooked it in a 225-degree oven for about two hours. We were slightly disappointed. The roast was tender, but nothing like the one cooked at 130 degrees; the beef was still reaching the 122-degree mark too quickly. We wondered what we could do to keep the meat below 122 degrees longer. Someone suggested shutting off the oven just before the roast reached the threshold, so that the roast would continue to cook slowly as the oven cooled.

So we tried again, this time shutting off the oven when the meat reached 115 degrees. Sure enough, the meat stayed below 122 degrees 30 minutes longer than before, allowing its enzymes to continue the work of tenderizing, before creeping to 130 degrees for medium-rare. (We didn't have to account for carryover cooking once the roast was out of the oven since, in this case, the "carryover" happened when the roast was in the turned-off oven.) Tasters were definitely happy; this roast was remarkably tender and juicy, particularly for such a lean roast.

With the tenderness problem solved, it was time to tackle taste. So far we'd simply sprinkled salt and pepper on the roast before searing it. Perhaps the flavor would improve if the meat were salted overnight or even brined. Brining certainly pumped more water into the beef and made it very juicy, but it also made it taste bland and less beefy. Next we tried salting the meat for first 4, then 12, and finally 24 hours. As might be expected, the roast benefited most from the longest salting. As an added bonus, salt, like the enzymes in meat, breaks down proteins to further improve texture but without the negative effects of water absorption.

Finally, we had arrived at a tender and flavorful special-occasion beef roast. Served with a light horse-radish sauce, it was a meal that anyone would be proud to serve.

Slow-Roasted Beef with Horseradish Sauce

SERVES 8

Because this cut of meat is one muscle group with a fairly tight structure, tying the roast isn't necessary. If you prefer your meat more or less done, see our guide-lines in "Testing Meat for Doneness" on page 86. Open the oven door as little as possible in step 5 and remove the roast from the oven when taking its temperature.

BEEF

 2 teaspoons kosher salt or 1 teaspoon table salt
 1 (2-pound) boneless eye round roast (see note), trimmed of all visible fat
 1 tablespoon canola oil
 1½ teaspoons pepper

SAUCE

 ½ cup light mayonnaise
 ¼ cup low-fat sour cream
 2 tablespoons horseradish
 2 tablespoons fresh lemon juice
 ½ teaspoon garlic powder
 ½ teaspoon salt
 ¼ teaspoon pepper
 Water, as needed

1. FOR THE BEEF: Sprinkle the salt evenly over the roast. Place the roast on a plate, cover with plastic wrap, and refrigerate for at least 4 or up to 24 hours.

2. Pat the roast dry with paper towels, rub with 1 tea-spoon of the oil, and season with the pepper. Cover the roast loosely with plastic wrap and let sit at room temperature for 1 to 2 hours.

3. Adjust an oven rack to the middle position and heat the oven to 225 degrees. Set a wire rack over a foil-lined rimmed baking sheet and set aside.

4. Heat the remaining 2 teaspoons oil in a 12-inch skillet over medium-high heat until just smoking. Carefully lay the roast in the skillet and cook until well browned on all sides, 12 to 14 minutes, turning as needed. Transfer the roast, fat-side up, to the prepared wire rack and roast until the center registers 115 degrees on an instant-read thermometer, 1 to 1¼ hours.

5. Turn the oven off and let the roast continue to cook in the oven, opening the door as little as possible, until the center registers 130 degrees (for medium-rare), 30 to 35 minutes longer. If the roast has not reached the desired temperature in the time specified, heat the oven to 225 degrees for 5 minutes, shut it off, and continue to cook the roast to the desired temperature. Transfer the roast to a carving board, tent loosely with foil, and let rest for 30 minutes.

6. FOR THE SAUCE: While the roast cooks, combine all of the ingredients in a small bowl, adding water as needed to thin the sauce to the desired consistency. Cover and refrigerate until the flavors blend, about 30 minutes.

7. Slice the roast thin and serve, passing the sauce separately.

PER SERVING: Cal 220; Fat 11g; Sat fat 3g; Chol 55mg; Carb 3g; Protein 26g; Fiber 0g; Sodium 640mg

NOTES FROM THE TEST KITCHEN

THE BEST CARVING KNIFE

No other knife can cut with such precision in a single stroke as a carving knife, specially designed to cut neatly through meat's muscle fibers and connective tissues. We set out to find the best, and based on previous knife-testing experience, we were already aware of key attributes to look for: an extra-long, sturdy, tapered blade with a round tip for easy, trouble-free strokes; a granton edge, which means the knife has oval scallops carved into both sides of the blade, making a thinner edge possible without sacrificing the heft and rigidity carried by the top of the blade—perfect for producing thinner slices with little effort; and, finally, a comfortable handle. After we tested nine knives that fit these criteria, the **Victorinox Forschner Fibrox 12-inch Granton Edge Slicing Knife,** $44.95, came out in front, scoring top points in slicing, sharpness, and comfort.

BEEF STROGANOFF

THIS COMBINATION OF BEEF, MUSHROOMS, AND onions, simmered in a sour cream–enriched sauce and served over egg noodles is a Russian classic known for its richness. Could we develop a lighter version that was just as flavorful? We headed to the test kitchen to find out.

We started by choosing a cut of beef. Although some modern recipes turn to fatty steak tips because they are affordable, beef tenderloin is a more traditional choice, one that is much leaner. We gave the tenderloin a run, and while the meat was indeed tender and lean, we wondered if other lean cuts might bring more flavor to the pan. We tested stroganoffs with strips of sirloin and blade steak, and although the improved flavor was appreciated, in this setting these cuts were unpleasantly chewy, at odds with the notion of a plush main course. We went back to the tenderloin.

Recognizing that tenderloin can get pricey, we took a modest approach, stretching 12 ounces to serve four, which also kept things in check nutritionally. It is important not to overcook this lean cut, as it can quickly turn dry and metallic-tasting. We avoided this by cutting the meat into thin strips and cooking the strips until they just began to brown, then setting them aside while we cooked our vegetables and sauce. Just before serving, we would simply stir in the meat to heat it through.

The best stroganoffs have a strong mushroom and onion presence, and we found 10 ounces of mushrooms and one onion did the trick. Simmering the mushrooms and onions in the sauce required no additional oil, but they turned slimy and had little flavor. Sautéing the vegetables before adding the liquids would concentrate their flavor, but we wondered if we could cook them using less oil than the usual 1 tablespoon. We found if we covered the vegetables while they cooked, the pan needed only 1 teaspoon of oil. After they had cooked down, we removed the lid and increased the heat to cook off any liquid and allow the vegetables to brown.

Now our mushrooms and onions had deep flavor, and as a bonus they had left good fond in the skillet, perfect for building a flavorful sauce. Many recipes we found called for deglazing with brandy, but we also saw some with red wine. We tested both in a working broth-based sauce, and tasters quickly dismissed those with red wine. Its brash flavor didn't meld with the sour cream. On the other hand, everyone thought brandy added brightness and sweetness that balanced the dairy nicely. For the broth, we decided to test both chicken and beef broth.

On their own, the broths tasted one-dimensional, but when used together, our sauce was complex and flavorful. We settled on 1½ cups each of chicken broth and beef broth, with ⅓ cup brandy to deglaze the pan.

For additional flavorings, we abandoned ingredients like prepared mustard, paprika, and Worcestershire sauce, which only covered up the flavor of the beef and mushrooms. Small amounts of both tomato paste and brown sugar added depth and a balancing sweetness. Sour cream is key for lending richness and a creamy texture to stroganoff, and we found all we needed was ½ cup of low-fat sour cream. It provided just enough of that tangy richness we were after without weighing down our stroganoff.

At this point our sauce was a little thinner than we wanted, but just a couple of tablespoons of flour helped thicken it to the right luxurious consistency. A touch of lemon juice and parsley added at the end lent the perfect freshness. This stroganoff was certainly decadent, and no one would guess how light it really was.

Beef Stroganoff

SERVES 4

Be sure to add the brandy off the heat to prevent it from igniting. Stirring a little of the sauce into the sour cream, then adding the warmed sour cream mixture to the skillet prevents curdling. Serve with egg noodles.

- 1 tablespoon canola oil
- 2 (6-ounce) center-cut beef tenderloin steaks, about 1 inch thick, trimmed of all visible fat and cut into ⅛-inch strips (see page 95)
- 10 ounces white mushrooms, sliced thin
- 1 onion, minced (about 1 cup)
  Salt
- ⅓ cup brandy
- 2 tablespoons unbleached all-purpose flour
- 1 teaspoon tomato paste
- 1½ cups low-sodium chicken broth
- 1½ cups low-sodium beef broth
- 1½ teaspoons dark brown sugar
- ½ cup low-fat sour cream
- 1 tablespoon minced fresh parsley
- 2 teaspoons fresh lemon juice
  Pepper

1. Heat 2 teaspoons of the oil in a 12-inch nonstick skillet over medium-high heat until just smoking.

Carefully add the beef in a single layer, breaking up any clumps. Cook without stirring for 1 minute, then stir and continue to cook until the beef is lightly browned, 2 to 3 minutes. Transfer the beef to a bowl.

2. Combine the remaining 1 teaspoon oil, mushrooms, onion, and ½ teaspoon salt in the skillet. Cover and cook over medium-low heat, stirring occasionally, until the mushrooms and onion have softened, 8 to 10 minutes. Uncover, increase the heat to medium-high, and continue to cook, stirring occasionally, until the mushrooms and onion are well browned, 8 to 12 minutes longer.

3. Off the heat, slowly stir in the brandy, scraping up any browned bits, and let sit until the bubbling subsides, about 30 seconds. Carefully return the skillet to medium heat and simmer until the brandy has almost completely evaporated, about 1 minute. Stir in the flour and tomato paste and cook for 1 minute. Gradually whisk in the chicken broth, beef broth, and brown sugar, bring to a simmer, and cook, stirring occasionally, until thickened, 30 to 35 minutes. Return the beef to the skillet, along with any accumulated juice, and cook until warmed through, about 1 minute.

4. Off the heat, stir a few tablespoons of the sauce into the sour cream, then stir the sour cream mixture back into the skillet. Stir the parsley and lemon juice into the sauce and season with salt and pepper to taste. Serve.

PER SERVING: Cal 280; Fat 11g; Sat fat 4g; Chol 60mg; Carb 13g; Protein 22g; Fiber 1g; Sodium 600mg

NOTES FROM THE TEST KITCHEN

SLICING TENDERLOIN STEAK FOR STROGANOFF

1. Turn the tenderloin steak on its side and cut it in half to yield two ½-inch-thick medallions.

2. Cut the medallions across the grain into ⅛-inch-wide strips.

PHILLY CHEESESTEAKS

WITH ALL THE LOCAL PRIDE BEHIND THE ONE-OF-A-kind Philadelphia cheesesteak, it's a little intimidating to set out to re-create the famed sandwich at home. On top of that, what if we wanted a lighter version? After all, the typical cheesesteak is a greasy mix of beef and onions topped with gobs of provolone or, a local favorite, Cheez Whiz. Nevertheless, we felt up to the challenge.

TEST KITCHEN
MAKEOVER

The key to a good cheesesteak lies in the texture of the meat, so we took note of the cooking method used by most local cheesesteak stands. A good-sized rib-eye roast is sliced into credit card–thin slices on the deli slicer, then the meat is cooked on a well-greased griddle over a heap of browned onions. With two heavy-duty spatulas, the meat and onions are chopped together and as the meat finishes cooking, slices of cheese are draped over the top and melted. After a few final spatula swipes, the whole mixture is placed in a toasted sub, or hoagie, roll. This thinly sliced, spatula-chopped roast makes the sandwich.

We began by looking for the best cut of beef. Rib-eye, traditional as it is, was too fatty for our recipe. We considered blade, top sirloin, and top round, choosing steaks over roasts to better control the quantity. These steaks all worked well, tasting beefy and tender, but tasters preferred the leaner quality of the top round.

Next we needed to find a way to get those ⅛-inch-thick slices. Recognizing that our knife skills would most likely produce marginal results, we looked at the food processor on the kitchen counter, wondering if we could use it like a deli slicer.

For easier handling, after cutting the steaks into 1-inch-wide fingers, we placed the pieces in the freezer. Once they were frozen, we put them through the food processor using the slicing blade. This first attempt met with little success, as the solid blocks of frozen steak were too hard, and the blade had a difficult time cutting the meat neatly. Still, we felt we were on to something, so we tried freezing the steaks only partially, which turned out to be the solution. Using the feed tube plunger, we were able to make quick work of the task.

We were now ready to bring the remaining ingredients in line. Working with a nonstick skillet, which would require less oil than a traditional one, we started by quickly browning some chopped onion, then we added the bite-sized pieces of steak. Once the meat was cooked through, we were ready to add the cheese. We knew we needed

PHILLY CHEESESTEAKS

to keep the cheese at a minimum if we wanted to succeed at making our cheesesteak lighter, but our sandwich still needed to have enough to earn its name and have that gooey appeal. Tasters quickly voted in favor of provolone over Cheez Whiz. We cut back the typical number of cheese slices, down to 5 slices rather than 8, and used reduced-fat provolone, saving 8 grams of fat per serving. We layered the provolone cheese over the meat and onions, let it melt slightly, and then stirred the melted cheese into the meat and onions to ensure uniform dispersion. Even with less cheese, these sandwiches looked plenty appealing—and everyone appreciated that an overload of grease wasn't visible. We'd cut the calories in half and the fat down from 35 grams to 13 grams—even the native Philadelphians in our test kitchen were amazed at the great authentic flavor in our homemade Philly cheesesteak.

MAKEOVER SPOTLIGHT: PHILLY CHEESESTEAKS

	CALORIES	FAT	SAT FAT	CHOLESTEROL
BEFORE	640	35g	13g	115mg
AFTER	330	13g	1.5g	50mg

Philly Cheesesteaks

SERVES 4

Don't over-freeze the beef, as it will be difficult for the slicing disk of the food processor to shave the meat. Top with pickled hot peppers, sautéed bell peppers, sweet relish, or hot sauce, if desired.

- 1 **(1-pound) top round steak, trimmed of all visibile fat, cut into 1-inch-wide strips, and partially frozen (see photos)**
- 1 **onion, chopped (about 1 cup)**
- 2 **teaspoons canola oil**
  Salt and pepper
- 5 **slices reduced-fat deli-style provolone cheese**
- 4 **(6-inch) sub rolls, slit partially open and lightly toasted**

1. Following the photos, shave the partially frozen meat using a food processor fitted with the slicing disk. Set the shaved meat aside.

2. Combine the onion, 1 teaspoon of the oil, and ¼ teaspoon salt in a 12-inch nonstick skillet. Cover and cook over medium-low heat, stirring occasionally, until softened, 8 to 10 minutes. Uncover, increase the heat to

NOTES FROM THE TEST KITCHEN

PREPARING MEAT FOR PHILLY CHEESESTEAKS

1. Trim the fat from the steak and cut the meat into 1-inch-wide strips. Place the strips of meat on a large plate and freeze until the exterior hardens but the interior remains soft, 25 to 50 minutes.

2. Using a food processor fitted with the slicing disk, shave the partially frozen meat as thinly as possible.

THE BEST FOOD PROCESSOR

What should a food processor be able to do? It ought to chop, grate, and slice vegetables; grind dry ingredients; and cut fat into flour for pie pastry. Recently, we tested inexpensive food processors to find out which one performed best. Unfortunately, many brands failed basic tests: Vegetables were torn into mangled slices, soup leaked from the workbowl, and attempts to make pizza dough resulted in seriously strained motors and an acrid, smoky smell. We realized it would be necessary to open our wallet and check out the more expensive options. After we put the high-priced machines through a battery of tests, it was obvious that more money does indeed buy a better food processor—though you don't need to buy the most expensive one. Our top pick is the **KitchenAid 12-Cup Food Processor,** $199.95. It has a sturdy, sharp blade and a weighty motor that did not slow under a heavy load of dough. It performs almost every task as well as (or better than) its pricier competition.

medium-high, add the remaining 1 teaspoon oil, meat, ¼ teaspoon salt, and ⅛ teaspoon pepper, and cook until the meat is no longer pink, 2 to 3 minutes.

3. Reduce the heat to low, place the slices of cheese over the meat, and continue to cook until the cheese has melted, about 1 minute. Stir the melted cheese and meat together to combine. Spoon ½ cup of the meat mixture into each toasted bun and serve.

PER SERVING: Cal 330; Fat 13g; Sat fat 1.5g; Chol 50mg; Carb 24g; Protein 36g; Fiber 1g; Sodium 760mg

HALIBUT EN PAPILLOTE WITH ZUCCHINI AND TOMATOES

CHAPTER 5

FISH AND SHELLFISH

M   = TEST KITCHEN MAKEOVER

HALIBUT EN PAPILLOTE

THERE'S A REASON THE CLASSIC FRENCH TECHNIQUE of cooking fish *en papillote*—baking in a tightly sealed parchment paper packet—has held its own through countless culinary fads and fashions. It's an easy, mess-free way to obtain perfectly moist, flaky, and flavorful pieces of fish. Best of all, it requires little additional fat and by including vegetables, it can become a well-rounded "one-pouch" meal. We set out to make a streamlined recipe that would give us perfectly moist and tender pieces of fish, well-seasoned vegetables, and flavorful juices.

All the classic recipes we found for fish en papillote called for cutting parchment paper into attractive shapes such as teardrops, hearts, or even butterflies, then creasing the seams into painstakingly precise little folds. Sure, it would make an impressive presentation, but we wanted to get dinner on the table as quickly as possible, not create origami. So we immediately turned to aluminum foil, sandwiching the fish between two 12-inch squares, then crimping the edges to create an airtight seal that would lock in steam. This was admittedly not as glamorous as an intricately folded parchment packet, but it would definitely do the job.

We decided to start by determining the best vegetables for the situation. Since the fish and vegetables would have to cook at the same rate, we knew there would be some limitations. Dense vegetables like potatoes were immediately out of the running because they took far too long to cook through, as were absorbent vegetables like eggplant, which would simply cook to mush. Broccoli seemed a little bold for an otherwise light dish. Light, clean-tasting zucchini, sliced into thin rounds, was a winner. For sweetness, color, and some moisture that would encourage steaming, we also settled on chopped tomatoes.

Our next step was to figure out what type of fish worked best and how long it would take to cook. After trying a variety of fish fillets, we determined that tasters favored flaky, mild white fish, like halibut and cod, over more assertively flavored fish like salmon or tuna. In the moist atmosphere of the foil pouch, these oilier fish had a more concentrated flavor that would overpower the flavors of the milder vegetables; better to save them for poaching or grilling.

Determining when the fish was done proved more challenging: It was hard to nick and peek when the fish was sealed tightly in foil. The old rule of thumb for fish—10 minutes of cooking time per inch of thickness—failed in this case, as the fish was barely opaque within that period. After experimenting with oven temperatures, we found that 1-inch-thick fillets cooked best at 450 degrees for 15 minutes. While this seemed like an excessive length of time at such high heat, the fish was well insulated within the sealed packets and was flaky and moist.

But now we were ending up with diluted flavor by the end of cooking. The solution was to salt and drain the zucchini in a colander before assembling the packet—the moisture from the tomatoes was all we needed for the perfect steamy environment. Cooking the packets on the lower-middle rack of the oven helped concentrate the exuded liquid, further ensuring that neither the fish nor the vegetables became waterlogged and that the flavor was maximized.

For seasoning, we turned to garlic, red pepper flakes, and oregano for an assertive kick and to intensify the mild flavor of the fish. A dash of white wine along with some extra-virgin olive oil also helped boost flavor, and for a finishing touch, a sprinkling of chopped basil lent a pleasant fragrance. Our recipe was light, fresh, and incredibly easy to prepare.

Halibut en Papillote with Zucchini and Tomatoes

SERVES 4

Cod and haddock are good alternatives for the halibut. The packets can be assembled several hours ahead of time and refrigerated, but they should be baked just before serving. To prevent overcooking, open each packet promptly after baking.

- 2 zucchini (about 1 pound), sliced ¼ inch thick
  Salt
- 3 plum tomatoes, cored, seeded, and chopped medium
- 2 tablespoons extra-virgin olive oil
- 2 garlic cloves, minced
- 1 teaspoon minced fresh oregano
- ⅛ teaspoon red pepper flakes
  Pepper
- 4 (6-ounce) skinless halibut fillets, 1 to 1½ inches thick
- ¼ cup dry white wine
- ¼ cup chopped fresh basil
  Lemon wedges, for serving

1. Adjust an oven rack to the lower-middle position and heat the oven to 450 degrees.

2. Toss the zucchini with ¼ teaspoon salt in a colander set over a bowl and let sit for 30 minutes. Spread the zucchini on several layers of paper towels and gently press the tops of the slices dry with more paper towels. Meanwhile, combine the tomatoes, oil, garlic, oregano, ¼ teaspoon salt, pepper flakes, and ⅛ teaspoon pepper in a medium bowl.

NOTES FROM THE TEST KITCHEN

ASSEMBLING FOIL PACKETS

1. On a 12-inch square of heavy-duty foil, shingle one-quarter of the zucchini in the center, then sprinkle with 1 tablespoon of the wine. Place a halibut fillet on top of the zucchini and top with one-quarter of the tomato mixture.

2. Place a second square of foil on top of the tomato mixture. Crimp the edges together in a ½-inch fold, then fold over three more times to create an airtight packet.

THE TRUTH ABOUT PREPEELED GARLIC

We've never met a garlic product we like better than a fresh clove, but many supermarkets these days carry jars or deli containers of prepeeled garlic cloves, and we wondered how they compare to fresh garlic bought by the head. We tasted both kinds of garlic raw in aïoli, sautéed in spaghetti with garlic and olive oil, and lightly cooked in stuffed rolled flank steak. In all cases, results were mixed, neither freshly peeled nor prepeeled garlic claiming victory.

However, we did notice a difference in shelf life: A whole head of garlic stored in a cool, dry place will last for at least a few weeks, but prepeeled garlic in a jar (which must be kept refrigerated) lasts for only about two weeks before turning yellowish and developing an overly pungent aroma, even if kept unopened in its original packaging. (In fact, in several instances we found containers of garlic that had started to develop this odor and color on the supermarket shelf.) But if you go through a lot of garlic, prepeeled cloves can be an acceptable alternative. Just make sure they look firm and white with a matte finish when you purchase them.

3. Cut eight 12-inch square sheets of heavy-duty foil and lay four of them flat on the countertop. Pat the halibut fillets dry with paper towels and season with ⅛ teaspoon salt and ⅛ teaspoon pepper.

4. Following the photos, shingle one-quarter of the zucchini in the center of one of the pieces of foil. Sprinkle 1 tablespoon of the wine over the zucchini. Place a halibut fillet on top of the zucchini, then top with one-quarter of the tomato mixture. Place a second square of foil on top of the tomato mixture and crimp the edges together to make a packet. Repeat with the remaining vegetables and halibut to make 4 packets.

5. Set the packets on a rimmed baking sheet (overlapping slightly if necessary) and bake for 15 minutes.

6. Carefully open the packets, allowing the steam to escape away from you, and let cool briefly. Smooth out the edges of the foil and, using a spatula, gently transfer the halibut and vegetables, along with any accumulated juices, to individual plates. Sprinkle with the basil and serve with the lemon wedges.

PER SERVING: Cal 290; Fat 11g; Sat fat 1.5g; Chol 55mg; Carb 7g; Protein 37g; Fiber 2g; Sodium 320mg

GLAZED SALMON

WHEN YOU'RE TRYING TO EAT MORE HEALTHFULLY, it's good to have a repertoire of salmon recipes that are quick, flavorful, and easy. The meaty flesh of salmon takes well to a sweet, flavorful glaze, which can nicely complement the fish's natural richness (a glaze on a delicate white fish just doesn't work as well), and nothing really beats a moist salmon fillet with an appealingly crisp, golden crust to grab the glaze on the outside. So we set out to make a pan-seared salmon recipe with a perfect glaze—one that would complement the flavors of our fillets and form a glossy, attractive coating. First we would focus on cooking the fillets; then we would turn our attention to creating a flavorful glaze.

To prevent the fish from sticking and to allow for browning, salmon is typically sautéed in a traditional skillet with, at the very least, 3 tablespoons of oil (some recipes we found for four fillets called for as much as 5 tablespoons). Here in the test kitchen, we prefer to cook most fish fillets in a nonstick skillet, which would certainly allow us to cut out a significant amount of oil. However, we knew we'd still have to use some to promote even browning. We began testing quantities from 3 tablespoons of canola oil down to 1 tablespoon. While these amounts of oil may have been acceptable for frying battered fish, for our pan-seared salmon even 1 tablespoon of oil was too much and left a pool of oil in the pan after cooking. Eventually, we found that a mere teaspoon of oil in a large nonstick skillet was all we needed to promote a deep, even crust on both sides of the fillets. The fillets had the best texture when we removed them from the pan as their internal temperatures reached 125 degrees on an instant-read thermometer.

Next we shifted our attention to the glaze. Tasters wanted bold flavors, and our thoughts turned to balsamic vinegar. The concentrated, rich flavors and pungent sweetness make this vinegar an ideal candidate for creating glazes. Our plan was to reduce the vinegar along with orange juice, honey, and rosemary to a syrupy glaze that would coat the salmon while it finished cooking. The sweetness of the orange juice and honey would, we hoped, balance the acidity of the vinegar, and the rosemary would add an earthy flavor. After working with various amounts of each, we settled on ¼ cup of orange juice, 3 tablespoons of balsamic vinegar, 2 tablespoons of honey, and a sprig of rosemary. Tasters were pleased with the overall flavor of this glaze, but they wanted some more vibrancy. A little white vinegar helped add some punch without altering the flavor of the sauce, and a pinch of red pepper flakes gave a pleasant spiciness.

After searing the salmon on one side, we flipped it, added the ingredients for our glaze to the pan, and allowed the fish to finish cooking through while the sauce reduced to a glaze. But this proved to be more complicated than we anticipated. Trying to achieve just the right degree of doneness for the fish as well as the right consistency for the glaze was nearly impossible to do simultaneously, and the glaze had a tendency to develop an unpleasant fishy flavor when cooked directly with the salmon. The solution was a simple one—we would cook the glaze and the salmon separately. After searing the salmon, we set it aside to rest and then added the sauce to the skillet to reduce. The resulting syrupy glaze was an unbeatable combination of sweet and sour, fruity and earthy—the perfect match for our tender, golden-crusted salmon.

Balsamic Glazed Salmon
SERVES 4

If you can't find skinless salmon at the store, you can easily remove the skin yourself, following the photos on page 105.

SALMON
- 4 (6-ounce) skinless center-cut salmon fillets, about 1½ inches thick (see note)
- ⅛ teaspoon salt
- ⅛ teaspoon pepper
- 1 teaspoon canola oil

GLAZE
- ¼ cup orange juice
- 3 tablespoons balsamic vinegar
- 2 tablespoons honey
- 1 tablespoon white vinegar
- ⅛ teaspoon red pepper flakes
- 1 small sprig rosemary
- Salt and pepper

1. FOR THE SALMON: Pat the salmon fillets dry with paper towels and season with the salt and pepper. Heat the oil in a 12-inch nonstick skillet over medium-high heat until just smoking. Carefully lay the salmon, skinned-side up, in the skillet and cook until well browned on the first side, about 5 minutes. Flip the salmon and continue to cook until the sides are opaque and the thickest part registers 125 degrees on an instant-read thermometer, 3 to 5 minutes longer.

2. Transfer the salmon to a platter, tent loosely with foil, and let rest while making the glaze.

3. FOR THE GLAZE: Whisk the orange juice, balsamic vinegar, honey, white vinegar, and pepper flakes together in a small bowl. Wipe out the skillet with a wad of paper towels and return to medium heat. Add the glaze and rosemary to the skillet, bring to a simmer, and cook until the glaze is thick, syrupy, and reduced to about ¼ cup, about 5 minutes.

4. Remove and discard the rosemary sprig and season the glaze with salt and pepper to taste. Spoon the glaze over the salmon and serve.

PER SERVING (WILD SALMON): **Cal** 290; **Fat** 12g; **Sat fat** 2g; **Chol** 95mg; **Carb** 10g; **Protein** 34g; **Fiber** 0g; **Sodium** 150mg

PER SERVING (FARMED SALMON): **Cal** 360; **Fat** 20g; **Sat fat** 4g; **Chol** 100mg; **Carb** 10g; **Protein** 34g; **Fiber** 0g; **Sodium** 180mg

We could have settled for the simple solution of a fish poacher—a pan with perforated racks that would elevate the fish and allow it to cook evenly—but it seemed unreasonable to go out and buy an expensive new piece of specialty equipment. We needed something to lift the fish off the bottom of the pan and realized the solution was literally in our hands. Up until this point, we had been squeezing lemon juice into the poaching broth, but if we sliced the fruit into thin disks instead and lined the pan with them, we could infuse the poaching broth with lemon flavor while also raising the fillets to prevent the bottoms from overcooking. Placing the herb stems on top of the lemon slices guaranteed that our fillets would be infused with fresh flavors. Our salmon was now turning out perfectly cooked and full of flavor.

It was time to focus on the sauce. Looking at the list of ingredients in our poaching liquid, we recognized that we had the makings of a great wine reduction, perfect for preparing a vinaigrette. With the salmon cooked and resting, we simply enhanced the remaining broth by reducing and straining it, then mixing in a bit more shallot and fresh herbs. We also added a tablespoon of olive oil and a couple of tablespoons of capers; the capers enhanced the brininess of the fish, and the olive oil added some much needed richness. Last, a tablespoon of honey added just the right sweetness to complement the earthy and acidic flavors. Our simple vinaigrette paired exceptionally well with our poached salmon—all without losing valuable flavor or wasting ingredients.

Poached Salmon with Herb-Caper Vinaigrette

SERVES 4

If you can't find skinless salmon at the store, follow the photos to easily remove the skin yourself.

- 1 lemon, ends trimmed, sliced into ¼-inch-thick rounds
- 2 tablespoons chopped fresh parsley, stems reserved
- 2 tablespoons chopped fresh tarragon, stems reserved
- 1 large shallot, minced (about 4 tablespoons)
- ½ cup dry white wine
- ½ cup water
- 4 (6-ounce) skinless center-cut salmon fillets, about 1½ inches thick (see note)
- 2 tablespoons drained capers, rinsed and chopped
- 1 tablespoon honey
- 1 tablespoon extra-virgin olive oil
  Salt and pepper

HOW TO SKIN A SALMON FILLET

1. Insert the blade of a sharp boning knife just above the skin about 1 inch from the end of the fillet. Cut through the nearest end, keeping the blade just above the skin.

2. Rotate the fish and grab the loose piece of skin. Run the knife between the flesh and the skin, making sure the knife is just above the skin, until the skin is completely removed.

SALMON PRIMER

In season, we've always preferred the more pronounced flavor of wild-caught salmon to that of farmed Atlantic salmon, which has traditionally been the main farm-raised variety for sale in this country. With more species of wild and farmed salmon available these days, we decided to see what distinguishes one from the next.

The first difference we noted between farmed salmon and wild salmon was a nutritional one. Wild salmon, in general, is noticeably lower in fat than farmed, and the fat you do get from it is richer in heart-healthy Omega-3s than that from farmed. Farmed salmon is also fed antibiotics and is artificially colored, two factors that seemed worth avoiding when possible.

The differences in flavor and texture, meanwhile, required a few taste tests. We sampled three kinds of wild Pacific salmon alongside two farmed kinds; they ranged in price from $13 to $20 per pound. Farmed Atlantic salmon ($14/lb., year-round) was bland and had a texture that divided tasters. Farmed king salmon ($13/lb., year-round) had a richer yet still mild flavor and a custardy texture, but it is not widely available. Wild coho salmon ($16/lb., July through September) had a balanced flavor, but its texture was unimpressive. Boasting a strong flavor and a meaty texture, wild king salmon ($20/lb., May through September) often winds up on the menus of top restaurants, which increases the retail price. Our favorite is wild sockeye salmon ($20/lb., May through September). Characterized by a deep reddish color, the sockeye had a smooth, firm texture and an assertive flavor with clean, briny notes. While we loved the generally stronger flavor (and the nutritional profile) of the wild-caught fish, our tasting confirmed: If you're going to spend the extra money on wild salmon, make sure it looks and smells fresh and realize that high quality is available only from late spring through the end of summer.

1. Arrange the lemon slices in a single layer over the bottom of a 12-inch skillet. Scatter the parsley stems, tarragon stems, and half of the shallot over the lemon slices, and add the wine and water.

2. Lay the salmon fillets in the skillet, skinned-side down, on top of the lemons. Set the pan over high heat and bring to a simmer. Reduce the heat to low, cover, and cook the salmon until the sides are opaque and the thickest part registers 125 degrees on an instant-read thermometer, 10 to 15 minutes. Remove the pan from the heat and, using a spatula, carefully transfer the salmon and lemon slices to a paper towel–lined plate. Tent the salmon loosely with foil and let rest while making the vinaigrette.

3. Return the pan to medium-high heat and continue to simmer the cooking liquid until it has reduced to about 2 tablespoons, 4 to 6 minutes. Meanwhile, combine the remaining shallot, chopped parsley, chopped tarragon, capers, honey, and oil in a medium bowl. Strain the reduced cooking liquid through a fine-mesh strainer into the bowl with the shallot-herb mixture, whisk to combine, and season with salt and pepper to taste.

4. Season the salmon with ⅛ teaspoon salt and ⅛ teaspoon pepper. Using a spatula, carefully transfer the salmon fillets to individual plates, discarding the lemon slices. Pour the vinaigrette over the salmon and serve.

PER SERVING (WILD SALMON): Cal 320; Fat 14g; Sat fat 2g; Chol 95mg; Carb 6g; Protein 34g; Fiber 0g; Sodium 280mg

PER SERVING (FARMED SALMON): Cal 400; Fat 22g; Sat fat 4g; Chol 100mg; Carb 6g; Protein 34g; Fiber 0g; Sodium 310mg

VARIATION

Poached Salmon with Herb-Dijon Vinaigrette
Follow the recipe for Poached Salmon with Herb and Caper Vinaigrette, substituting 2 tablespoons chopped fresh dill, stems reserved, for the tarragon and 1 tablespoon Dijon mustard for the capers.

PER SERVING (WILD SALMON): Cal 320; Fat 14g; Sat fat 2g; Chol 95mg; Carb 6g; Protein 34g; Fiber 0g; Sodium 240mg

PER SERVING (FARMED SALMON): Cal 390; Fat 22g; Sat fat 4g; Chol 100mg; Carb 6g; Protein 34g; Fiber 0g; Sodium 270mg

BAKED COD PROVENÇAL

DURING THE SUMMER MONTHS IN THE SOUTH OF France, the markets are bursting with an abundance of fresh seafood and a bountiful selection of pungent herbs and ripe vegetables. It is the ideal environment for flavorful, light fare—everything is at its peak and needs little more than to be simply prepped and cooked to produce a delicious meal. We imagined creating a similar experience in our kitchen with an easy baked fish and vegetable dish with little fuss and big character. We wanted tender, flaky fish fillets paired with vegetables that would cook down into a sauce, lending flavor and additional moisture to the fish.

Our first step was to decide what type of fish we wanted to use. After trying a variety of fish fillets, tasters settled on flaky, mild fish for this recipe for the same reasons we had chosen it for our Halibut en Papillote with Zucchini and Tomatoes (page 100): This kind of fish would pair best with the flavors of more delicate vegetables. Cod became our first choice among the options, although haddock and halibut were close seconds. For our vegetable sauce, we wanted to stay true to our inspiration and turned to Provençal flavors: tomatoes, wine, capers, shallots, garlic, thyme, and olive oil all fit the bill. These seasonings would imbue our fish with good character without overpowering it.

We didn't want a precooked sauce—too much trouble. Plus we thought that if the tomatoes and seasonings cooked with the fish in the oven, they would better retain their fresh flavors and at the same time infuse the fish with flavor. We began our testing by combining the sauce ingredients we had selected, and then we spread the mixture over the bottom of a baking dish. The fish was then nestled into our vegetable sauce and cooked. We started off using seeded and diced plum tomatoes but, while the flavors worked well, the tomatoes cooked down too much and didn't retain the visual appeal we were hoping for. So next we tried quartered cherry tomatoes. These tomatoes still cooked down into a sauce, but they remained chunkier than the plum tomatoes. Tasters approved.

Tasters had also commented that, while the fish was good, it was definitely missing something—there were no contrasting textures. A flavorful crunchy topping seemed like a logical step in the right direction. We kept it simple, choosing crushed Melba toast for its sturdy texture, combined with olive oil and some seasonings.

We first tried applying the crumbs by spreading them on a plate and pressing the fish fillets into the mixture, but mere force wasn't enough to keep the crumbs on. Looking for an adhesive, we turned to Dijon mustard. This worked OK, but the flavor of the mustard overpowered the fish, and this idea was quickly dismissed. Turning to olive oil, we brushed the fish with it, then added the crumbs, pressing on them to get them to adhere—success at last. After baking, our fish was coated with a golden brown crust. Paired with the chunky tomato sauce, these crunchy-on-the-outside, tender-on-the-inside fillets made for a light but satisfying entrée.

NOTES FROM THE TEST KITCHEN

AN EASIER WAY TO PICK THYME LEAVES

Picking minuscule leaves of fresh thyme can really pluck at your nerves, even if it's just for the single teaspoon in our Baked Cod Provençal. In the test kitchen, we rely on some tricks to make this job go faster. If the thyme has very thin, pliable stems, just chop the stems and leaves together, discarding the tough bottom portions as you go. If the stems are thicker and woodier, hold the sprig of thyme upright, by the top of the stem; then run your thumb and forefinger down the stem to release the leaves and smaller offshoots. The tender tips can be left intact and chopped along with the leaves once the woodier stems have been sheared clean and discarded.

WHITE WINES FOR COOKING

When a recipe calls for dry white wine, it's tempting to grab whatever open bottle is in the fridge. Chardonnay and Pinot Grigio may taste different straight from the glass, but how much do those distinctive flavor profiles really come through in a cooked dish? To find out, we tried four varietals and a supermarket "cooking wine" in five different recipes. Only **Sauvignon Blanc** consistently boiled down to a "clean" yet sufficiently acidic flavor that played nicely with the rest of the ingredients. We also ran tests with sherry and vermouth, wines fortified with alcohol to increase their shelf life. Sherry's flavor was too distinct, but vermouth was surprisingly good. In fact, its clean, bright flavor bested all but the Sauvignon Blanc. (Note that in some recipes either vermouth or a dry white wine will work fine, so we give the option of both, but in other recipes, like our Spanish Shellfish Stew, only the wine is listed, as the vermouth is stronger in flavor and would overpower the dish.)

Baked Cod Provençal

SERVES 4

Halibut and haddock are good alternatives for the cod. Note that when shopping for fillets, look for those that are at least 1 inch thick—any less and the fillets will cook through before the vegetables are tender.

- 1¼ ounces Melba toast (about 5 crackers), crushed to coarse crumbs (about ¼ cup)
- 2 tablespoons extra-virgin olive oil
- ½ teaspoon grated lemon zest
  Salt and pepper
- 1½ pounds cherry tomatoes (about 4 cups), quartered
- 2 shallots, minced (about 6 tablespoons)
- ¼ cup dry white wine
- 2 tablespoons drained capers, rinsed
- 2 garlic cloves, minced
- 1 teaspoon minced fresh thyme, or ¼ teaspoon dried
- 4 (6-ounce) skinless cod fillets, 1 to 1½ inches thick (see note)
- 2 tablespoons chopped fresh basil
  Lemon wedges, for serving

1. Adjust an oven rack to the middle position and heat the oven to 400 degrees.

2. Toss the Melba toast crumbs with 2 teaspoons of the oil, lemon zest, ¼ teaspoon salt, and ¼ teaspoon pepper, and set aside. Toss 2 teaspoons more oil, tomatoes, shallots, wine, capers, garlic, thyme, ¼ teaspoon salt, and ¼ teaspoon pepper together, and spread evenly over the bottom of a 13 by 9-inch baking dish.

3. Pat the cod fillets dry with paper towels and nestle, skinned-side down, into the tomato mixture. Brush the tops of the cod with the remaining 2 teaspoons oil, season with ⅛ teaspoon salt and ⅛ teaspoon pepper, then sprinkle with the Melba crumbs, pressing on the crumbs to help them adhere.

4. Bake until the crumbs are crisp and the cod flakes apart when gently prodded with a paring knife, 20 to 25 minutes. Let rest for 5 minutes, then sprinkle with the basil and serve with the lemon wedges.

PER SERVING: Cal 300; Fat 9g; Sat fat 1.5g; Chol 75mg; Carb 18g; Protein 34g; Fiber 3g; Sodium 670mg

OVEN-FRIED FISH

OVEN-FRIED FISH

TEST KITCHEN
MAKEOVER

LIKE MOST DEEP-FRIED FOODS, FRIED FISH RANKS high on the list of unhealthy meals, which is a shame since fish is naturally healthy. A typical piece of fast-food fried fish can contain as much as 500 calories and 31 grams of fat, more than enough reason to consider giving it a serious makeover. There are already plenty of recipes out there for the lighter alternative, oven-fried fish, but most of these are disappointing, with dry, overcooked fish and bread-crumb coatings that range from thin and sandy to soggy and crumbly. We wondered if it was possible to bake moist and flavorful fillets in a crunchy coating that would not simply be a healthy alternative to fried fish, but would stand as a worthy dish in its own right.

Our first task was to select the fish. Tasters immediately ruled out dense varieties such as swordfish, as their firm flesh didn't lend the right contrast when paired with the crust. Thin fillets such as sole and flounder were also out—they ended up overcooked long before the coating was done. However, flaky cod and haddock were perfectly tender after baking, and they required enough time in the oven that we had a fighting chance to develop a crisp crust.

As for the coating, fresh crumbs made from sandwich bread had the right texture, but we had problems achieving a crisp enough crust by the time the fish was done. Toasting the bread crumbs first seemed as if it might give us a jump start on a crispy crust, so we gave it a shot.

To start, we pulsed the bread in a food processor and then tossed the crumbs with salt, pepper, and a little oil. We baked our seasoned crumbs in the oven until they were a deep golden brown. Working with one of the fillets at a time, we dredged them in flour, dipped them in beaten eggs, then pressed on the crumbs by hand. Baked on a foil-lined baking sheet in a 425-degree oven, our fish was done after just 20 minutes. When we pulled it out to check the results, we saw that the breading on the top and sides of the fish was much crispier than before, but the bottom crusts were still soggy. We tried again, this time working with a batch of larger, more coarsely processed crumbs. This helped, but it wasn't enough. Then a test cook suggested placing the fish on a wire rack set over the baking sheet to allow air to circulate underneath. This was a step closer, but we still needed something more.

When we realized that the bread crumbs were absorbing moisture released by the fish as it cooked, we tried salting the fillets. We let the salted fillets sit on a rack, then blotted them dry after 20 minutes and prepared the recipe as before. Yet again our hopes were quickly dashed: Not only were the bottom crusts still soggy, but the fish was now too salty.

We couldn't find the solution in the fish or the crumbs; we hoped it would be in the egg wash. Taking a cue from traditional deep-fried fish, we tried turning the egg wash into a buffer zone between the fish and the bread crumbs by adding few tablespoons of flour to thicken it to a batter-like consistency. We covered the fillets in a generous layer of this wash before pressing on the bread crumbs. When this fish came out of the oven, we held our breath. Success! The crust was crisp and dry all the way around and firmly bonded to the fish.

Having achieved a crunchy crust, we began work on fine-tuning the flavor. We tried mixing the bread crumbs with a range of herbs and aromatics. In the end, tasters preferred the subtler flavors of shallots and parsley, which we tossed with our bread crumbs once they had been toasted and cooled. As for the egg wash, some light mayonnaise worked well in adding richness and a welcome note of acidity. A combination of paprika, cayenne, and an unlikely addition—horseradish—also gave a nice bite to the fish.

These moist, tender fillets surrounded by a crisp, flavorful crust are great on their own, but we love them even more when served with a lightened-up tartar sauce. And at just 300 calories and 9 grams of fat per serving, we don't have an ounce of guilt when it's time to dig in.

MAKEOVER SPOTLIGHT: OVEN-FRIED FISH

	CALORIES	FAT	SAT FAT	CHOLESTEROL
BEFORE	500	31g	7g	135mg
AFTER	300	9g	1.5g	130mg

KEYS TO SUPER-CRISP OVEN-FRIED FISH

Soft, moist fish needs an extra-thick coating of bread crumbs to add flavor and crunch. Here's how we make it happen:

1. Processing fresh crumbs coarsely, then prebaking the crumbs, maximizes crunch.

2. Thickening the batter with flour and mayonnaise prevents the toasted crumbs from turning soggy and glues them firmly to the fish.

3. Baking the fish on a wire rack set over a baking sheet allows air to circulate underneath.

OUR FAVORITE SANDWICH BREAD

Picking a high-quality loaf is key if you want to have a great crust on our Oven-Fried Fish. We gathered eight leading brands of white sandwich bread, in country styles with larger slices whenever possible, and held a blind tasting. Tasters sampled the bread plain, in grilled cheese sandwiches, and prepared as croutons seasoned only with olive oil and salt. They gave top marks to the hearty texture of **Arnold Country Classics Country White** (left) and **Pepperidge Farm Farmhouse Hearty White** (right), which has larger-than-usual slices and what tasters called "perfect structure" and "subtle sweetness."

Oven-Fried Fish

SERVES 4

Halibut and haddock are good alternatives for cod. To prevent overcooking, buy fish fillets that are at least 1 inch thick. Serve with Tartar Sauce (recipe follows), if desired.

  Vegetable oil spray
4 large slices high-quality white sandwich bread, torn into pieces
1 tablespoon canola oil
  Salt and pepper
1 shallot, minced (about 3 tablespoons)
2 tablespoons minced fresh parsley
¼ cup plus 5 tablespoons unbleached all-purpose flour
2 large eggs
3 tablespoons light mayonnaise
2 teaspoons prepared horseradish (optional)
½ teaspoon paprika
¼ teaspoon cayenne pepper (optional)
4 (6-ounce) skinless cod fillets, 1 to 1½ inches thick (see note)
  Lemon wedges, for serving

1. Adjust an oven rack to the middle position and heat the oven to 425 degrees. Set a wire rack over a foil-lined rimmed baking sheet, lightly coat the rack with vegetable oil spray, and set aside.

2. Pulse the bread in a food processor to coarse crumbs, about 10 pulses. Transfer the crumbs to a bowl and toss with the oil, ¼ teaspoon salt, and ¼ teaspoon pepper. Spread the crumbs on a rimmed baking sheet and bake, stirring occasionally, until golden brown and dry, 8 to 10 minutes. Let the bread crumbs cool to room temperature, then toss with the shallot and parsley.

3. Place ¼ cup of the flour in a shallow dish. In a second shallow dish, whisk together the eggs, mayonnaise, horseradish (if using), paprika, cayenne (if using), and ¼ teaspoon pepper until combined, then whisk in the remaining 5 tablespoons flour until smooth. Spread the cooled bread-crumb mixture in a third shallow dish.

4. Pat the cod fillets dry with paper towels and season with ⅛ teaspoon salt and ⅛ teaspoon pepper. Dredge the cod in the flour and shake off the excess. Coat the cod with the egg mixture, allowing the excess to drip off. Coat all sides of the cod with a thick layer of the bread-crumb mixture, pressing to help the crumbs adhere. Lay the cod on the prepared wire rack.

5. Bake the cod until the thickest part registers 140 degrees on an instant-read thermometer, 18 to 25 minutes. Using a thin spatula, transfer the cod to individual plates and serve with the lemon wedges.

PER SERVING: **Cal** 300; **Fat** 9g; **Sat fat** 1.5g; **Chol** 130mg; **Carb** 18g; **Protein** 35g; **Fiber** 1g; **Sodium** 510mg

Tartar Sauce
MAKES ABOUT ½ CUP

This is a lighter version of the classic sauce for fried seafood. If cornichons are not available, substitute dill pickles. This sauce will keep in an airtight container in the refrigerator for up to 1 day.

¼ cup light mayonnaise
2 tablespoons low-fat sour cream
4 large cornichons, minced (about 2 tablespoons), plus 2 teaspoons cornichon juice (see note)
2 tablespoons minced red onion
1 tablespoon drained capers, rinsed and minced
⅛ teaspoon pepper
 Water

Mix the mayonnaise, sour cream, cornichons, cornichon juice, onion, capers, and pepper together in a small bowl, adding water as needed to thin the sauce. Cover and refrigerate until the flavors blend, about 30 minutes.

PER 2-TABLESPOON SERVING: **Cal** 60; **Fat** 5g; **Sat fat** 1g; **Chol** 5mg; **Carb** 3g; **Protein** 0g; **Fiber** 0g; **Sodium** 250mg

PAN-SEARED SCALLOPS

WE HAVE ALWAYS THOUGHT OF SCALLOPS AS A DINNER all-star, particularly from a healthy-diet point of view. They taste rich and indulgent, yet they carry with them a negligible amount of fat and few calories. One of our favorite ways to enjoy them is simply pan-seared. When they're cooked in a hot skillet, their rich, sweet characteristics shine through, offering a deliciously caramelized crust and tender interior. And while they are often served in a cream or butter sauce, we were looking to use only a minimal amount of fat while cooking our scallops. We wanted to come up with some light, flavorful sauces to pair with them that would really turn our scallops into a gorgeous yet simple-to-prepare meal.

In the test kitchen we have pan-seared everything from chicken to pork to salmon, so we have learned from experience that moisture is the enemy of a good crust and browned exterior. Since scallops in particular can often be bogged down by excess moisture, we knew something had to be done to ensure that they were perfectly parched going into the smoking-hot pan. To do this, we laid the scallops in a single layer on a paper towel–lined plate, seasoned them with salt and pepper, and placed paper towels over the top. The paper towels absorbed any moisture that the scallops released, and as an extra precaution just before they went into the pan, we pressed the paper towel flush to the surface of the scallops to ensure that every bit of moisture was absorbed.

Searing up a batch of scallops, we found that even though they were bone-dry going into the pan over high heat, they were still having trouble browning. It seemed that an overcrowded pan was the culprit; the scallops were so close together that they released moisture and steamed rather than sautéed. We decided to try cooking the scallops in two batches. Once half of the scallops were browned on one side but still had a rare interior, we transferred them to a plate (browned-side up) while the second batch seared. At this point, we knew our scallops wouldn't need much time in the pan to finish cooking through; achieving a good sear on the second side would only overcook them. So we settled on having just one browned side for presentation and then lowered the heat and returned the first batch to the pan to gently cook them through together. In addition to cooking in batches, we also found it was critical to place the scallops in the skillet one at a time, ensuring that the flat side was in good contact with the pan, and to leave them alone once they began cooking.

Now with the outside of the scallops browning beautifully, we looked to preserve the creamy texture of the flesh. Once they were all together in the pan and cooking on their second side, their soft flesh firmed up and an opaqueness that started at the bottom of the scallops, where they sat in the pan, slowly crept up toward the centers. The scallops were medium-rare when the sides had firmed up and all but about the middle third of the scallops had turned opaque, which took less than a minute.

Up until this point, we had been searing our scallops in a traditional skillet, and it was requiring almost 2 tablespoons of oil per batch. A nonstick skillet had worked wonders in dropping the amount of oil needed for our Balsamic Glazed Salmon (page 102), and we hoped it would do the same here. Also, since we were looking to use a minimal amount of fat, and because the scallops cooked quickly, we needed to choose a fat that browned efficiently. We tested butter, olive oil, vegetable oil, and a combination of butter and oil and settled on canola oil, which produced ideal browning and has a high smoke point. Working with canola oil in a nonstick skillet, we were able to reduce the amount of fat needed by half. These scallops were perfectly browned on the outside and cooked through just right.

When the scallops were ready to go, we considered accompaniments. Tasters agreed that they wanted some sort of sauce to drizzle over the scallops, and rich and creamy sauces were quickly nudged aside for the overpowering effect they would have on our delicate scallops. While some tasters liked the pairing of scallops with fruit salsas, others disliked the chunky nature of salsa and preferred a smoother fruit sauce. By simmering fruit juices until they had reduced to a syrup, we were able to create bold, fruit-flavored sauces. We settled on tangerine and pomegranate juices for their bright flavor. The syrups, which we found achieved the perfect silky-smooth drizzling viscosity when thickened with a little cornstarch, just needed a little honey to temper their acidity, as well as some

shallots and thyme to round out their rich fruit flavors. When we paired our flavorful sauces with the golden brown scallops, we had a light but decadent dish that was guaranteed to impress.

Pan-Seared Scallops

SERVES 4

For this recipe, we prefer using large sea scallops. Depending on the size of your scallops, the cooking times may vary slightly. If desired, make one of the sauces that follow ahead of time to serve with the scallops, or serve simply with lemon wedges.

1½ pounds large sea scallops (about 16 scallops; see note), muscle removed (see page 16)
⅛ teaspoon salt
⅛ teaspoon pepper
2 tablespoons canola oil
   Lemon wedges, for serving

1. Lay the scallops out on a paper towel–lined plate and season with the salt and pepper. Lay a single layer of paper towels over the scallops and set aside.

2. Heat 1 tablespoon of the oil in a 12-inch nonstick skillet over high heat until just smoking. Meanwhile, press the paper towel flush to the scallops to dry them. Carefully lay half of the scallops in the skillet and cook until golden brown on the first side, 1 to 2 minutes. Using tongs, transfer the scallops to a large plate, seared side facing up, and set aside.

3. Wipe out the skillet using a wad of paper towels. Add the remaining 1 tablespoon oil to the skillet and return to high heat until just smoking. Add the remaining scallops and cook until golden brown on the first side, 1 to 2 minutes.

4. Reduce the heat to medium, flip the scallops, and return the first batch to the pan, golden brown side facing up. Cook until the sides have firmed up and all but the middle third of each scallop is opaque, 30 to 60 seconds longer. Transfer all the scallops to a platter and serve with the lemon wedges.

PER SERVING: Cal 210; Fat 8g; Sat fat 0.5g; Chol 55mg; Carb 5g; Protein 29g; Fiber 0g; Sodium 350mg

Tangerine Juice Reduction

MAKES ABOUT ½ CUP

Though it is worth searching out tangerines for their bright flavor, if they aren't available, oranges can be used instead. If desired, add more honey to taste. Since it takes some time for this sauce to reduce, prepare the recipe before cooking the scallops, then cover and set aside until time to serve.

- 2 **cups fresh tangerine juice from 4 to 5 tangerines (see note)**
- 3 **sprigs fresh thyme**
- 1 **shallot, minced (about 3 tablespoons)**
- ½ **teaspoon cornstarch**
- ½ **teaspoon grated tangerine zest (see note)**
- ½ **teaspoon honey (see note)**

1. Simmer all but 1 tablespoon of the tangerine juice with the thyme and shallot in a small saucepan until the mixture has reduced to about ½ cup, 40 to 45 minutes.

2. Strain the sauce into a clean saucepan, discarding the solids, and return to a simmer. Whisk the remaining 1 tablespoon tangerine juice with the cornstarch in a small bowl, then whisk into the simmering sauce and cook until thickened, about 1 minute. Stir in the zest and honey and serve.

PER 2-TABLESPOON SERVING: Cal 60; Fat 0g; Sat fat 0g; Chol 0mg; Carb 14g; Protein 1g; Fiber 0g; Sodium 0mg

Pomegranate Juice Reduction

MAKES ABOUT ½ CUP

Pomegranate juice, which is high in antioxidants, is available at most supermarkets and natural foods stores. Be sure to purchase straight pomegranate juice, which is sweet and slightly tart, not a flavored variety. If desired, add more honey to taste.

- 2 **cups pomegranate juice (see note)**
- 3 **sprigs fresh thyme**
- 1 **shallot, minced (about 3 tablespoons)**
- ½ **teaspoon cornstarch**
- ½ **teaspoon honey (see note)**

1. Simmer all but 1 tablespoon of the pomegranate juice with the thyme and shallot in a small saucepan until the mixture has reduced to about ½ cup, 40 to 45 minutes.

2. Strain the sauce into a clean saucepan, discarding the solids, and return to a simmer. Whisk the remaining 1 tablespoon pomegranate juice with the cornstarch in a small bowl, then whisk into the simmering sauce and cook until thickened, about 1 minute. Stir in the honey. Drizzle over the scallops and serve.

PER 2-TABLESPOON SERVING: Cal 80; Fat 0g; Sat fat 0g; Chol 0mg; Carb 20g; Protein 1g; Fiber 0g; Sodium 15mg

CRAB CAKES

WE LOVE A GOOD CRAB CAKE, AND WE KNOW A GOOD one should taste of sweet crabmeat, not greasy filler ingredients. And while a cool and creamy dipping sauce is certainly complementary to a golden brown

TEST KITCHEN
MAKEOVER

crab cake, it doesn't have to be off the charts in terms of calories and fat. We wanted to make crab cakes (along with a few dipping sauces) that would showcase the flavor and texture of the crabmeat, while keeping the calories and fat in check.

Great crab cakes depend first and foremost on, naturally, the crabmeat. We tested all the options, and the differences were stark. Canned crabmeat is horrible, bearing little resemblance to the fresh product. Frozen crabmeat is stringy and wet. Fresh pasteurized crabmeat wasn't too bad and would work if we wanted to keep within a budget, but we found there just isn't a substitute for fresh blue crabmeat, preferably "jumbo lump," the largest pieces and highest grade. It costs a bit more per pound than the other types of fresh crabmeat, but since a one-pound container is enough to make crab cakes for four, in our opinion, it's money well spent.

Our next task was to find the right binder. A few tests proved that none of the usual suspects worked quite right. Crushed saltines were a pain to smash into small-enough crumbs, and fresh bread crumbs blended into the crabmeat too well, giving our cakes a pasty texture. We settled on fine dry bread crumbs. They don't have an overwhelming flavor, they are easy to mix in, and they didn't mask the texture of the crabmeat. The trickiest part was knowing when to stop; crab cakes need just enough binder to hold together but not so much that the filler takes over. We wanted crab cakes, not dough balls. We started out with 1 cup of crumbs and gradually worked our way down to just 2 to 4 table-spoons (the amount varied, depending on the crabmeat's juiciness).

We knew that we would need some moisture to keep our cakes from drying out, so we tried a range of low-fat options, starting with some more creative possibilities. Low-fat yogurt and buttermilk offered too much moisture, and light sour cream and cream cheese had too much tang. Traditional crab cake recipes call for full-fat mayonnaise, so our final test was to try the most obvious option, light mayonnaise. It provided the right amount of moisture, but it came across as somewhat sweet. Some Dijon mustard provided just the right sharpness, and we found we needed only ¼ cup of mayonnaise, leaving the crab as the star. To further help the binding, instead of the whole egg that most recipes call for, we used a single egg white to make it all meld together.

Recipes call for spiking crab cakes with everything from hot sauce to Worcestershire sauce, but we finally decided to go with Old Bay Seasoning, along with black pepper, minced scallions, and fresh herbs, a combination that tasters overwhelmingly approved.

Careful mixing is essential to a good crab cake—you don't want to beat the "lump" out of the lump crab you just invested in. We found that a rubber spatula works best, used in a folding rather than stirring motion.

When it came time to cook, we had trouble keeping our somewhat lean cakes together. Not wanting to add more binder, we tried chilling the cakes before cooking. As little as half an hour in the refrigerator made a huge difference. We also tried different cooking methods. After baking, pan-frying, and broiling, we settled on sautéing in a nonstick skillet over medium-high heat. It was fast but still gave us complete control over how brown and crisp the cakes got. Dredging the cakes very lightly in flour helped create a golden, crisp crust. We first tried sautéing in butter, but it burned and turned the flour coating gummy. Cut with canola oil, it was still too heavy and made a mess of the pan. Canola oil alone turned out to be ideal. It heated without burning (it has a high smoke point), it created a crisp crust, and it didn't overpower the delicate flavor of the crab.

Last but certainly not least were the dipping sauces. We already had a great lightened-up Tartar Sauce (page 111), but we wanted a few more options. We began with a creamy base of light mayonnaise and low-fat sour cream, which we jazzed up with fresh lemon juice, thyme, and parsley, and for a sauce with kick, we created another recipe with chipotle chiles in adobo sauce, lime juice, and cilantro added to the base. Paired with our perfectly tender crab cakes loaded with crab, we had a light dinner perfect for a warm summer evening.

MAKEOVER SPOTLIGHT: CRAB CAKES

	CALORIES	FAT	SAT FAT	CHOLESTEROL
BEFORE	340	24g	3g	140mg
AFTER	260	12g	1g	85mg

Crab Cakes

SERVES 4

Start with the smaller amount of bread crumbs, adjust the seasonings, and then add the egg white. If the cakes won't hold together at this point, add more bread crumbs as needed, 1 tablespoon at a time. The amount of bread crumbs you add will depend on the crabmeat's juiciness. Serve with Tartar Sauce (page 111), or Creamy Lemon-Herb Sauce or Creamy Chipotle Chile Sauce (recipes follow), if desired. The formed cakes can be kept, refrigerated and tightly wrapped in plastic wrap, for up to 24 hours.

- 1 **pound jumbo lump crabmeat, picked over to remove cartilage or shells**
- ¼ **cup light mayonnaise**
- 2-4 **tablespoons plain dry bread crumbs (see note)**
- 2 **tablespoons Dijon mustard**
- 4 **scallions, green parts only, minced**
- 4 **teaspoons minced fresh cilantro, dill, basil, or parsley**
- 1 **teaspoon Old Bay Seasoning**
  Salt and pepper
- 1 **large egg white**
- ¼ **cup unbleached all-purpose flour**
- 2 **tablespoons canola oil**
  Lemon wedges, for serving

1. Gently fold the crabmeat, mayonnaise, 2 tablespoons of the bread crumbs, mustard, scallions, herbs, and Old Bay together in a medium bowl, being careful not to break up the lumps of crab.

2. Season with salt and pepper to taste. Carefully fold in the egg white with a rubber spatula until the mixture just holds together, adding the remaining bread crumbs as needed.

3. Divide the crab mixture into 4 portions and shape each into a round cake, about 3 inches across and 1½ inches high. Transfer the crab cakes to a parchment paper–lined baking sheet. Cover with plastic wrap and refrigerate for at least 30 minutes and up to 24 hours.

4. Spread the flour in a shallow dish. Dredge the crab cakes in the flour and shake off the excess. Heat the oil in a 12-inch nonstick skillet over medium–high heat until shimmering. Carefully lay the chilled crab cakes in the skillet and cook until well browned on both sides, 8 to 10 minutes, flipping them halfway through. Transfer the crab cakes to a paper towel–lined plate to drain briefly. Serve with the lemon wedges.

PER SERVING: **Cal** 260; **Fat** 12g; **Sat fat** 1g; **Chol** 85mg; **Carb** 12g; **Protein** 26g; **Fiber** 1g; **Sodium** 790mg

NOTES FROM THE TEST KITCHEN

OUR FAVORITE DIJON
Dijon mustard is a staple here in the test kitchen, and we wanted to find out which nationally available brands were the best. We rounded up eight Dijon mustards and tasted them plain and in a simple vinaigrette. The result: Our tasters preferred the spicier mustards, and the most important factor was balance of flavor. Mustards that were too acidic or too salty or muddied with other flavors were downgraded. Our favorite Dijon mustard was **Grey Poupon Dijon Mustard,** which tasters described as having a "nice balance of sweet, tangy, and sharp."

ALL ABOUT OLD BAY
Old Bay Seasoning is a spice mix that's essential for crab boils, crab cakes, and many other seafood dishes, including some shrimp dishes. Created in the 1930s, this spice mix is a regional favorite in Maryland and Virginia along the coast. The predominant flavors in Old Bay are celery, mustard, and paprika. We like to use Old Bay to season steamed or boiled crustaceans and bivalves, in coatings for fried chicken and seafood, and in gumbos and seafood stews.

Creamy Lemon-Herb Sauce
MAKES ABOUT ½ CUP

This sauce will keep in an airtight container in the refrigerator for up to 1 day.

- ¼ cup light mayonnaise
- 2 tablespoons low-fat sour cream
- 1 tablespoon fresh lemon juice
- 2 teaspoons minced fresh parsley
- 2 teaspoons minced fresh thyme
- 1 scallion, minced
- ¼ teaspoon salt
- ⅛ teaspoon pepper
-    Water

Mix the mayonnaise, sour cream, lemon juice, parsley, thyme, scallion, salt, and pepper together in a small bowl, adding water as needed to thin the sauce. Cover and refrigerate until the flavors blend, about 30 minutes.

PER 2-TABLESPOON SERVING: **Cal** 50; **Fat** 4; **Sat fat** 1g; **Chol** 5mg; **Carb** 5g; **Protein** 1g; **Fiber** 0g; **Sodium** 280mg

Creamy Chipotle Chile Sauce
MAKES ABOUT ½ CUP

This sauce will keep in an airtight container in the refrigerator for up to 1 day.

- ¼ cup reduced-fat mayonnaise
- 2 tablespoons low-fat sour cream
- 1 tablespoon fresh lime juice
- 2 teaspoons minced fresh cilantro
- 1 teaspoon minced canned chipotle chiles in adobo sauce
- 1 garlic clove, minced
- ¼ teaspoon salt
- ⅛ teaspoon pepper
-    Water

Mix the mayonnaise, sour cream, lime juice, cilantro, chipotles, garlic, salt, and pepper together in a small bowl, adding water as needed to thin the sauce. Cover and refrigerate until the flavors blend, about 30 minutes.

PER 2-TABLESPOON SERVING: **Cal** 50; **Fat** 4g; **Sat fat** 1g; **Chol** 5mg; **Carb** 2g; **Protein** 1 g; **Fiber** 0 g; **Sodium** 280mg

PASTA WITH BUTTERNUT SQUASH AND SAGE

PASTA AND PIZZA

M = TEST KITCHEN MAKEOVER

PASTA WITH BUTTERNUT SQUASH AND SAGE

AMONG ALL THE TYPES OF SQUASH, WE PARTICULARLY love butternut squash, with its silky texture and appealing golden orange hue. It doesn't hurt that it also packs a nutritional wallop when it comes to vitamins A and C, along with respectable amounts of other vitamins and minerals. We tend to see this mildly flavored vegetable stuffed inside ravioli with sage (a classic Italian combination). While we love the idea of matching butternut squash, sage, and pasta, we didn't want to spend time rolling and filling raviolis. But there's a good reason butternut squash is usually hidden inside ravioli and swathed with a browned butter sauce or paired with crispy bacon or pancetta. Long on silky texture, it can be short on flavor and fairly watery. To make it worthy of an "outside job" without relying on lots of butter and pork fat (a task we felt was definitely worth the challenge), we would need to find a way to amplify its mild flavor.

First we tried roasting the squash. The high, dry heat did a nice job of evaporating the excess water and intensifying the flavor, but it took 45 minutes—a lot longer than we wanted to spend on this weeknight meal. Next we tried sautéing peeled and diced squash with a little olive oil. The squash cooked through in about 10 minutes, but because of an insufficient amount of oil, all the browning stuck to the bottom of the pan, not to the squash. Rather than adding more oil, we tried using a nonstick skillet and more moderate heat. It took a few extra minutes to sauté our squash, but we were rewarded with squash with a flavorful caramelized exterior.

Tossing the cooked squash with some penne (we liked the fact that its shape made it similar in size to the squash) and chopped sage, we hoped to call it a day. Not so fast. The flavor of the squash was still too delicate—especially with so potent an herb as sage—and the ingredients weren't really melding. We clearly needed a sauce to bring it all together.

We began by making a quick broth by boiling the squash's seeds and fibers in a little water. This made the dish more flavorful, but it wasn't so transformative as to justify the extra effort. Next we tried braising the squash with some chicken broth. We knew that too much liquid—or too long a simmer—would yield soggy squash, but if we used just enough to deglaze the pan, then simmered the squash briefly, it might give us squash with the right texture and the sauce we were looking for. After sautéing the squash over medium heat until just caramelized, we added 3 cups of chicken broth, then cooked it for a few minutes longer. This method produced silky squash and a flavorful sauce that was just the right consistency to cling to the penne.

But many tasters still weren't wowed; the dish needed more depth. Bacon, a classic companion to butternut squash and sage, was one obvious solution, but we didn't want to let pork fat enter the picture for our light recipe. In the past, dried mushrooms, such as porcinis (which are readily available in most markets), have helped impart deep, earthy flavors to some of our recipes. We wondered if they would help here. After some experimenting, we found that just ½ ounce of minced porcinis imparted a deep, robust flavor without being overpowering. To further fine-tune the sauce, we found that mincing and sautéing the sage helped tame its flavor and incorporate it throughout the dish. Chopped scallions added brightness, and a dash of nutmeg enhanced the caramelized flavors of the squash.

Just before serving, we tossed the squash and sauce with the pasta, then rounded out the dish with a touch of grated Parmesan and a squeeze of lemon. A modest handful of toasted almonds provided a crunchy final touch. This was a sophisticated, satisfying meal that was surprisingly light, and it didn't hurt that it easily cooked in under an hour.

Pasta with Butternut Squash and Sage

SERVES 6

Don't be tempted to use dried sage in this recipe; the simpler flavor of fresh sage is integral to the dish.

- 1 tablespoon olive oil
- 1 medium butternut squash (about 2 pounds), peeled, halved lengthwise, seeded, and cut into ½-inch pieces
- 6 scallions, sliced thin
- 2 tablespoons minced fresh sage (see note)
- ½ ounce dried porcini mushrooms, rinsed and minced
- ⅛ teaspoon freshly grated nutmeg
  Salt and pepper
- 3 cups low-sodium chicken broth
- 1 pound penne
- 1 ounce Parmesan cheese, grated (about ½ cup)
- 4 teaspoons fresh lemon juice
- ¼ cup sliced almonds, toasted (see page 16)

1. Heat the oil in a 12-inch nonstick skillet over medium heat until shimmering. Add the squash and cook, stirring occasionally, until spotty brown, 15 to 20 minutes.

2. Stir in the scallions, sage, mushrooms, nutmeg, ⅛ teaspoon salt, and ⅛ teaspoon pepper, and cook until the scallions are softened, about 1 minute. Add the broth, bring to a simmer, and cook, stirring occasionally, until the squash is tender, about 10 minutes.

3. Meanwhile, bring 4 quarts water to a boil in a large pot. Add the pasta and 1 tablespoon salt, and cook, stirring often, until al dente. Reserve ½ cup of the cooking water, then drain the pasta and return it to the pot.

4. Add the squash mixture, Parmesan, and lemon juice to the pasta, and toss to combine, adjusting the sauce consistency with the reserved cooking water as desired. Season with salt and pepper to taste. Sprinkle with the almonds and serve.

PER 1¾-CUP SERVING: **Cal** 420; **Fat** 7g; **Sat fat** 1.5g; **Chol** 5mg; **Carb** 76g; **Protein** 16g; **Fiber** 6g; **Sodium** 580mg

PENNE WITH CHICKEN AND SUMMER VEGETABLES

PENNE WITH CHICKEN IS A NO-LOSE COMBINATION. Add fresh summer vegetables and you have a perfect light summer dinner. Unfortunately, this simple combination often falls short—tough chicken, bland pasta, and soggy vegetables hiding beneath a heavy, oily sauce. We could do better. We wanted to bring the fresh flavors of summer back into focus with vegetables that were crisp and colorful, and to pair them with perfectly cooked chicken and a light, clean-tasting sauce.

We immediately decided that boneless, skinless chicken breasts were the best choice since they are lean and need little prep. We began by testing cooking methods, including microwaving, broiling, sautéing, and poaching. Not surprisingly, microwaving produced bland chicken with a steamed taste. Sautéing strips of chicken produced the most flavor, but the seared edges were too tough and stringy for this recipe. Poaching the chicken seemed to have good potential; this meat was tender and juicy, but its flavor was washed out.

Wanting the flavor from sautéing and the tenderness from poaching, we focused on combining the two methods. We started by cutting our chicken into strips and cooking the strips with a little olive oil in a skillet,

just until they began to turn golden. We removed the chicken pieces from the pan before they were cooked through and moved them to a pot of simmering water. It took only a minute for the meat to finish cooking. This chicken was tender and had decent flavor.

Feeling pretty good about the chicken, we moved on to creating a simple sauce. We added some garlic and red pepper flakes to the skillet, then poured in chicken broth for a base, which would add some richness without overwhelming the mild, summery vegetables, and let the liquid briefly cook down. After tossing our chicken with the sauce and some penne, we took a bite. It was a good start, but the chicken seemed a little flat. For our next test, instead of poaching the chicken in water, we poached it right in the sauce. This not only boosted the flavor of both the sauce and the chicken, but it was also efficient. All we had to do was sauté the chicken, remove it from the skillet, build the sauce, then add the chicken back to the pan and cook it through.

It was time to move on to the vegetables. We gathered a few of our summertime favorites: zucchini, cherry tomatoes, and bell pepper. Adding some onion lent the right bite. After sautéing the chicken, we quickly sautéed all the vegetables together until just softened, then removed them from the skillet to make the sauce and finish cooking the chicken. We tossed all the components together, along with some basil for brightness. The results were tasty, but our vegetables were cooked unevenly and their flavors were too homogeneous.

Perhaps adding the vegetables to the skillet in batches would allow them to retain their individual flavors and enable us to better control how much each was cooked. First, we sautéed the zucchini until browned, then we added the tomatoes and cooked them until they were just softened. Then we removed those vegetables and added the firmer onion and bell pepper, which we cooked covered to speed things up and allow us to use minimal oil. Once they were softened, we simply added the sauce ingredients and then the chicken to the skillet. This method yielded an assembly of perfectly cooked vegetables, chicken, and sauce, each with distinct flavor and perfect texture.

At this point our pasta dish was certainly very good, but we wanted more green. Chopped parsley added a nice burst of bright green color, but not much in the way of flavor. We then tried tossing in some baby spinach at the very end, when we were combining the components. The mild heat from the just-cooked pasta and sauce perfectly wilted the spinach. The spinach's delicate texture and earthy taste were just what was needed. This was a chicken and summer vegetable pasta that really tasted like summer.

Penne with Chicken and Summer Vegetables
SERVES 6

Yellow summer squash can be substituted for the zucchini. Freezing the chicken for 15 minutes before slicing makes it easier to cut thin slices. Serve with a light sprinkling of grated Parmesan cheese, if desired. Note that substituting other pasta shapes for the penne may affect the final portion size.

- 4 teaspoons olive oil
- 1 pound boneless, skinless chicken breasts, trimmed and sliced thin (see note)
- 1 zucchini (about 8 ounces), halved lengthwise and sliced ¼ inch thick (see note)
- 12 ounces cherry tomatoes (about 2 cups), halved
- 1 onion, halved and sliced thin
- 1 red bell pepper, stemmed, seeded, and cut into ¼-inch pieces
- Salt
- 3 garlic cloves, minced
- ⅛ teaspoon red pepper flakes
- 1½ cups low-sodium chicken broth
- 1 pound penne (see note)
- 3 ounces baby spinach (about 3 cups)
- ¼ cup shredded fresh basil
- Pepper

1. Heat 2 teaspoons of the oil in a 12-inch nonstick skillet over medium-high heat until shimmering. Carefully add the chicken in a single layer, breaking up any clumps. Cook without stirring for 1 minute, then stir and continue to cook until the chicken is almost cooked through, about 2 minutes longer. Transfer the chicken to a medium bowl, cover with foil, and set aside.

2. Add 1 teaspoon more oil to the skillet and return to medium-high heat until just smoking. Add the zucchini and cook, stirring often, until well browned, about 3 minutes. Add the cherry tomatoes and cook until the tomatoes are just softened, about 2 minutes. Transfer the vegetables to a medium bowl and set aside.

3. Combine the remaining 1 teaspoon oil, onion, bell pepper, and ⅛ teaspoon salt in the skillet. Cover and cook over medium-low heat, stirring occasionally, until softened, 8 to 10 minutes. Stir in the garlic and red pepper flakes and cook until fragrant, about 30 seconds. Stir in the broth, bring to a simmer, and cook until thickened slightly, about 1 minute. Stir in the chicken and cook until no longer pink, about 1 minute. Cover to keep warm and set aside.

4. Meanwhile, bring 4 quarts water to a boil in a large pot. Add the pasta and 1 tablespoon salt, and cook until al dente. Reserve ½ cup of the cooking water, then drain the pasta and return it to the pot.

5. Add the sauce, reserved vegetables, spinach, and basil to the pasta and toss until the spinach is wilted slightly, 1 to 2 minutes, adjusting the sauce consistency with the reserved cooking water as desired. Season with salt and pepper to taste and serve.

PER 2-CUP SERVING: Cal 430; Fat 5g; Sat fat 1g; Chol 45mg; Carb 66g; Protein 30g; Fiber 5g; Sodium 420mg

---

NOTES FROM THE TEST KITCHEN

STORING BASIL

When making pesto, storing leftover basil isn't usually an issue—the bunches bought in supermarkets get pretty much used up. But what about those occasions (such as when making our Penne with Chicken and Summer Vegetables) when you end up having most of a large bunch left over after preparing a single recipe? We wondered how long we could keep leftover store-bought basil and what would be the best way to store it.

Since leaving basil out on the counter wasn't an option (it wilted within hours), we were stuck with refrigerator storage, which is about 15 degrees colder than the recommended temperature for basil. We tested storing basil in unsealed zipper-lock bags (to prevent the buildup of moisture, which can cause basil to turn black), both plain and wrapped in damp paper towels (our preferred method for most leafy greens). After three days in the refrigerator, both samples were still green and perky. But after one week, only the towel-wrapped basil was still fresh-looking and fresh-tasting. Don't be tempted to rinse basil until just before you need to use it; when we performed the same tests after rinsing, the shelf life was decreased by half.

SPAGHETTI CARBONARA

TEST KITCHEN
MAKEOVER

THE ROMAN CLASSIC *SPAGHETTI ALLA CARBONARA* is typically made by crisping a lot of bacon, sautéing garlic in the drippings, then adding white wine and pepper and reducing the sauce. Beaten raw eggs and plenty of grated cheese (Parmesan, Pecorino, or a combination thereof) are combined in another bowl, pasta is added, the wine mixture is poured on top, and everything is tossed to create a dish of noodles coated in a silky, luscious sauce. Many recipes also include heavy cream, so it's no surprise that carbonara tips the scales at more than 600 calories and 28 grams of fat per serving. It seemed as if a lighter version of carbonara would require eliminating nearly every key player. Could we develop a recipe with lower-fat replacements and end up with a dish that actually tasted like carbonara?

We started by testing existing low-fat carbonara recipes. They were all unsuccessful. Egg substitutes produced bland, curdled sauces, and a version made with reduced-fat cream cheese horrified tasters with its sticky texture and sour flavor. The worst offender was the carbonara made with turkey bacon, which tasted bitter and artificial.

Starting over with the test kitchen's favorite full-fat recipe, we cut the bacon from eight strips to two, which still rendered enough drippings for sautéing some garlic. This pasta had decent smoky flavor, but tasters complained that pieces of crisp bacon were hard to find. To get more meat into the dish, we tested adding various leaner pork products to the mix, including ham and low-fat sausage, before settling on a few ounces of smoky, meaty, and relatively lean Canadian bacon. Bumping up the amounts of garlic, pepper, and wine gave us bigger flavor without excess fat and calories.

We opted to use all Pecorino Romano cheese because we prefer its saltiness and tang, and we tested varying amounts at decreasing intervals, starting at 2½ ounces. At 1⅓ ounces, tasters thought we still had great cheesy flavor; anything less was just too little. Most carbonara recipes use at least three eggs to add richness, but we were able to get away with using just one, adding one more egg white for structure. Our carbonara was

getting better, but it was still too dry and not creamy enough.

Many classic recipes address this issue by including a splash of cream. We turned to an ingredient we've used in other recipe makeovers for richness and a silky texture without big calories or fat: fat-free evaporated milk. Our first bite of the revamped recipe showcased just the right silkiness. Unfortunately, it was a short-lived thrill, as the pasta had soaked up all the sauce after a few minutes, making our carbonara unpalatably dry.

In traditional recipes, the fat coats the pasta, preventing it from absorbing too much sauce. What ingredient would coat the pasta without spiking the fat and calories? A colleague half-jokingly suggested mayonnaise, which after all is made from eggs and oil. We were skeptical but gave it a try anyway. Surprisingly, tossing the pasta with just ½ tablespoon of mayonnaise created a protective coating that prevented it from absorbing so much sauce. This trick was so successful that we wondered if adding some mayo directly to the sauce would help even more. Another 1½ teaspoons in the sauce added such great richness that we fooled tasters into thinking they were eating the real deal. We had been using regular mayonnaise, but in an attempt to cut a few more calories in fat we also tested using light mayo. But the light version just didn't coat our pasta as well as the full-fat. Since our recipe was already pretty trim, we felt as if a small amount of regular mayonnaise wasn't a problem.

So far we'd been whisking the sauce together in a bowl before tossing it with the pasta, but it wasn't coating the noodles as thoroughly as we would have liked. To increase the sauce's volume so it better covered the noodles without adding more ingredients, we whirled it in a food processor with some pasta water. This gave us a fuller, emulsified sauce that now easily coated our pasta. No one could deny that this lightened-up carbonara was still plenty creamy and rich.

MAKEOVER SPOTLIGHT: SPAGHETTI CARBONARA

	CALORIES	FAT	SAT FAT	CHOLESTEROL
BEFORE	620	28g	11g	150mg
AFTER	410	11g	3.5g	55mg

Spaghetti Carbonara

SERVES 6

An equal amount of Parmesan cheese may be substituted for the Pecorino Romano, if desired.

- 1⅓ **ounces Pecorino Romano cheese (see note), grated (about ⅔ cup)**
- ¼ **cup fat-free evaporated milk**
- 2 **tablespoons mayonnaise**
- 1 **large egg**
- 1 **large egg white**
- 2 **ounces Canadian bacon, chopped coarse**
- 2 **slices bacon, chopped coarse**
- 3 **garlic cloves, minced**
- 1 **teaspoon pepper**
- ⅓ **cup dry white wine**
- 1 **pound spaghetti**
- **Salt**
- 1 **tablespoon chopped fresh parsley**

1. Process the cheese, evaporated milk, 1½ tablespoons of the mayonnaise, egg, and egg white in a food processor until smooth, about 15 seconds; leave the mixture in the food processor.

2. Cook the Canadian bacon and bacon together in a 12-inch nonstick skillet over medium heat until the fat has rendered and the bacon is browned, about 7 minutes. Using a slotted spoon, transfer the bacon to a paper towel–lined plate and set aside.

3. Add the garlic and pepper to the fat left in the pan, and cook over medium heat until fragrant, about 30 seconds. Stir in the wine, bring to a simmer, and cook until thickened slightly, about 1 minute. Cover to keep warm and set aside.

4. Meanwhile, bring 4 quarts water to a boil in a large pot. Add the pasta and 1 tablespoon salt, and cook, stirring often, until al dente. Reserve ½ cup of the cooking water, then drain the pasta and return it to the pot. Toss the pasta with the remaining 1½ teaspoons mayonnaise until coated.

5. With the food processor running, slowly add the wine mixture and ¼ cup of the reserved cooking water to the egg mixture, and process until smooth and frothy, about 1 minute. Immediately pour the egg mixture over the pasta and toss to combine, adjusting the sauce consistency with the remaining reserved cooking water as desired. Stir in the bacon and season with salt to taste. Sprinkle with the parsley and serve.

PER 1-CUP SERVING: **Cal** 410; **Fat** 11g; **Sat fat** 3.5g; **Chol** 55mg; **Carb** 58g; **Protein** 16g; **Fiber** 3g; **Sodium** 420mg

NOTES FROM THE TEST KITCHEN

BIG FLAVOR WITHOUT THE FAT
For creamy, silky carbonara without the fat, three ingredients are essential:

CANADIAN BACON	**EVAPORATED MILK**	**MAYONNAISE**
We replace most of the bacon with Canadian bacon, which is meatier and contains far less fat.	Fat-free evaporated milk provides a thick, creamy texture.	Just 2 tablespoons of mayonnaise adds flavor and creaminess, allowing us to use less fat and fewer eggs.

SPAGHETTI AND MEATBALLS

IN A TRADITIONAL RECIPE FOR THIS ALL-TIME FAVORITE, the meatballs are fried in at least 1 cup of oil to get a crisp crust, then they're simmered in a tomato sauce also heavy on the olive oil. With 42 grams of fat per serving, it's a dinner far from healthy—not to mention making a flavorful tomato sauce can take all day. We set out to create meatballs healthier than their old-fashioned counterparts but still with the same comforting flavor. We also wanted a quick tomato sauce that tasted as if it had been simmered for hours.

TEST KITCHEN MAKEOVER

We started with the meat. Ground turkey seemed like a healthier option than beef, so we gathered the options: all-white-meat ground turkey, all-dark, and combinations of the two. Meatballs made with all dark meat were nearly as high in fat as ground beef meatballs, so we crossed that off the list. Meatballs made with all white meat were tough and grainy. Tasters unanimously preferred meatballs made with a combination of white and dark meat (labeled 93 percent lean). They had a meaty flavor and cooked up to a soft, moist texture, and by switching from beef to turkey, we quickly cut 12 grams of fat per serving.

SPAGHETTI AND MEATBALLS

Next, we moved on to binders, which keep the meatballs tender and prevent them from falling apart during cooking. We started with eggs. Our favorite classic meatball recipe relies on just a yolk (a whole egg makes the mixture too sticky), but we thought for this light version it was worth trying an egg white instead. These meatballs didn't hold together, and they tasted too lean, so we went back to the yolk. We weren't surprised that these meatballs were a breeze to handle.

Some form of bread, bread mixture, or cracker crumbs also typically serve as a binder. Both bread and cracker crumbs soaked up moisture, making the meatballs hard and dry. But meatballs made with bread soaked in milk, which acted more like a paste, were moist and rich. Still, we wondered if we could do even better. We made a batch of meatballs with buttermilk and found that they were even creamier and more flavorful than those made with whole milk, and buttermilk, though rich-tasting, is naturally low in fat. Parmesan cheese and garlic added the right classic flavors.

In search of a lighter cooking method, we tried roasting our meatballs, but they turned out dry and crumbly. Broiling was messy and also produced dry, unevenly cooked meatballs. We would have to make pan-frying work without using the usual 1 cup of oil. Rather than frying the meatballs start to finish, we wondered if we could brown them just enough to give them some flavor and a crust and then finish cooking them in the sauce. After testing varying amounts of oil, we found we needed a mere tablespoon to get a crisp crust and perfect browning. A brief stay in the refrigerator helped the meatballs firm up and stay intact.

Meatballs need a thick sauce, the kind produced by crushed tomatoes. Fresh tomatoes were off-limits because their quality is too variable. The answer was canned diced tomatoes, processing a good portion of them in the food processor to get the right consistency.

We wondered if we could save cleanup time and build more flavor into the sauce by making it in the same pan we used to brown the meatballs. After browning the meatballs, we set them aside, added some onion to the skillet, then stirred in garlic and some red pepper flakes. We added the tomatoes and meatballs and simmered until the meatballs were done. Not only was this method convenient, but it also gave the sauce depth, as the browned bits on the bottom of the pan dissolved into the sauce. The amount of sauce pushed the skillet's capacity, but it was well worth

it since we were able to both boost and marry the flavors for the final dish.

These guilt-free, easy-to-prepare meatballs and sauce had a rich, deep flavor that tallied merely 13 grams of fat when served over a pile of tender spaghetti, and it was a meal that left tasters thinking we'd spent all day in the kitchen.

MAKEOVER SPOTLIGHT: SPAGHETTI AND MEATBALLS

	CALORIES	FAT	SAT FAT	CHOLESTEROL
BEFORE	770	42g	10g	90mg
AFTER	550	13g	4g	105mg

Spaghetti and Meatballs

SERVES 6

Ground turkey is sold in a variety of package sizes; you can use between 1¼ and 1½ pounds of ground turkey in this recipe. It is important to let the meatballs chill for at least 1 hour before cooking, which allows them to firm up and remain intact during cooking. Do not use ground turkey breast meat (sometimes also labeled as 99 percent fat-free); it will make meatballs that are dry and grainy. You can substitute ½ tablespoon plain low-fat yogurt thinned with 1½ tablespoons milk for the buttermilk if desired. You will need a 12-inch skillet with at least 2-inch sides to accommodate both the meatballs and the sauce; the skillet will be quite full.

MEATBALLS

- 2 slices high-quality white sandwich bread, crusts removed, torn into pieces
- 3 tablespoons buttermilk
- 1 large egg yolk
- 1 (20.8 ounce) package 93 percent lean ground turkey (see note)
- 1 ounce Parmesan cheese, grated (about ½ cup)
- ¼ cup chopped fresh parsley
- 2 garlic cloves, minced
- ½ teaspoon salt
- ¼ teaspoon pepper
- 1 tablespoon olive oil

SAUCE AND PASTA

- 3 (14.5-ounce) cans diced tomatoes
- 1 onion, minced (about 1 cup)

Salt

4 garlic cloves, minced

¼ teaspoon red pepper flakes

1 pound spaghetti

Pepper

3 tablespoons shredded fresh basil

1. FOR THE MEATBALLS: Combine the bread, buttermilk, and egg yolk in a large bowl, cover, and set aside until the bread softens, about 5 minutes. When soft, mash the mixture to a smooth paste. Add the turkey, Parmesan, parsley, garlic, salt, and pepper. Combine the mixture gently, using your hands, until uniform, then form into 18 meatballs (each about 1½ inches in diameter). Spread the meatballs out on a large plate, cover, and refrigerate until firm, about 1 hour.

2. Heat the oil in a 12-inch nonstick skillet over medium heat until just smoking. Add the meatballs and cook until well browned on all sides, about 10 minutes, turning as needed. Transfer the meatballs to a paper towel–lined plate and set aside. (Do not wash the skillet.)

3. FOR THE SAUCE AND PASTA: Pulse 2 cans of the tomatoes, with their juice, in a food processor until mostly smooth, about 11 pulses. Add the onion and ⅛ teaspoon salt to the fat left in the skillet. Cover and cook over medium-low heat, stirring occasionally, until softened, 8 to 10 minutes. Stir in the garlic and pepper flakes, and cook until fragrant, about 30 seconds. Stir in the processed tomatoes and the remaining 1 can diced tomatoes with their juice, bring to a simmer, and cook for 10 minutes. Return the meatballs to the skillet, cover, and cook until the meatballs are cooked through, about 10 minutes.

4. Meanwhile, bring 4 quarts water to a boil in a large pot. Add the pasta and 1 tablespoon salt, and cook, stirring often, until al dente. Reserve ½ cup of the cooking water, then drain the pasta and return it to the pot.

5. Spoon several large spoonfuls of the tomato sauce (without the meatballs) into the pasta and toss to combine, adjusting the sauce consistency with the reserved cooking water as desired. Season with salt and pepper to taste. Divide the pasta among 6 individual bowls. Top each bowl with the remaining tomato sauce and meatballs, sprinkle with the basil, and serve.

PER SERVING (1½ CUPS SPAGHETTI WITH SAUCE AND 3 MEATBALLS): Cal 530; Fat 12g; Sat fat 3.5g; Chol 95mg; Carb 72g; Protein 35g; Fiber 3g; Sodium 1110mg

PASTA WITH SHELLFISH

PASTA WITH SHELLFISH APPEARS ON RESTAURANT menus both humble and fancy, and more often than not, the seafood is overcooked, the sauce is either watery and flavorless or intolerably heavy, and the pasta seems like an afterthought. These dishes are often finished with copious amounts of butter, which further masks the delicate shellfish. We were after a dish in which the shellfish was the star but the pasta, in a balanced and flavorful sauce, could hold its own rather than serve as a dispensable extra. We set out for the test kitchen to see if we could bring fresh life to this favorite combination.

We started our testing with a universal favorite for pairing with pasta—shrimp—and we focused on choosing a preparation method with the lowest risk of overcooking the crustaceans. Poaching proved to be the best: It was efficient since we could poach the shrimp right in the sauce, the shrimp could be cooked all at once (sautéing had to be done in batches), and the degree of doneness could be easily controlled. Once our sauce was ready, all we would have to do would be to stir in the shrimp, cover the pan, and let the shrimp cook through slowly off the heat, before tossing it all with the pasta.

With the shrimp settled, we moved on to the sauce. Fish stock seemed like a natural choice, but we didn't want to deal with making our own, so we turned to the next best option, bottled clam juice. On its own, the clam juice was overpowering. A combination of clam juice and chicken broth had the balance we were looking for. This sauce needed bright, bold flavor, so we started building our sauce with aromatics: one onion and a whopping eight garlic cloves. We added red pepper flakes for some subtle heat, and fresh thyme and a bay leaf rounded things out. Then we added the lemon juice, broth, and clam juice to the pan and simmered for about 10 minutes.

At this point, the flavor of the sauce was perfect, but it was too thin to coat the pasta. The time to thicken it was before we added the shrimp so that our recipe would stay streamlined. We wondered if adding a bit of cornstarch to the sauce would do the trick. We started with 3 tablespoons of cornstarch, which we mixed with water to make a paste (or slurry) to stir into the sauce along with some lemon juice. Tasters liked the fact that the sauce now clung to the pasta, but it tasted too starchy and chalky. When we cut the cornstarch back to 2 tablespoons, we got much better results. The texture was now just right, but we had another issue: The dish clearly needed some fat to add an undertone of creaminess and richness.

Looking for an ingredient that would add richness and body to our sauce without weighing it down, we thought light cream cheese might be the answer. We knew that a little cream cheese goes a long way, so we started with 3 tablespoons. When melted into the broth and clam juice, it gave our sauce just the right richness without imparting too much of an undesired "cream sauce" quality. For a touch of brightness, we added minced parsley. Coated in our lemon-garlic sauce, this pasta had enough flavor that we were happy eating it even without the shrimp—of course, our shrimp were so perfectly cooked it was hard to refuse.

We decided that a recipe with clams would make another classic match for linguine. We settled on littleneck clams, which we steamed in our lemon-garlic sauce just until they popped open, a technique that gave us the best control and most even cooking. Once they were ready, we transferred them to a bowl, thickened the sauce, and poured it over the pasta before nestling the clams snugly into the pasta. This second seafood and pasta dish was a cinch to prepare and looked as impressive as it tasted.

NOTES FROM THE TEST KITCHEN

DEVEINING SHRIMP

1. Hold the shelled shrimp between your thumb and forefinger and cut down the length of its back, about ⅛ to ¼ inch deep, with a sharp paring knife.

2. If the shrimp has a vein, it will be exposed and can be pulled out easily. Once you have freed the vein with the tip of the paring knife, just touch the knife to a paper towel and the vein will slip off the knife and stick to the towel.

Linguine with Shrimp, Lemon, and Garlic

SERVES 6

Take care not to overcook the shrimp or they will be tough. To make this dish spicier, increase the amount of red pepper flakes.

- 1 **onion, minced (about 1 cup)**
- 1 **teaspoon olive oil**
-   **Salt**
- 8 **garlic cloves, minced**
- 2 **teaspoons minced fresh thyme**
- ⅛ **teaspoon red pepper flakes (see note)**
- 2 **cups low-sodium chicken broth**
- 2 **(8-ounce) bottles clam juice**
- 1 **bay leaf**
- 2 **tablespoons cornstarch**
- 2 **tablespoons water**
- ½ **cup fresh lemon juice (about 4 lemons)**
- 3 **tablespoons light cream cheese**
- 1½ **pounds extra-large shrimp (21 to 25 per pound), peeled and deveined**
- 1 **pound linguine**
- 2 **tablespoons chopped fresh parsley**
-   **Pepper**

1. Combine the onion, oil, and ⅛ teaspoon salt in a 12-inch nonstick skillet. Cover and cook over medium-low heat, stirring occasionally, until softened, 8 to 10 minutes. Stir in the garlic, thyme, and pepper flakes, and cook until fragrant, about 30 seconds. Add the broth, clam juice, and bay leaf to the skillet. Bring to a simmer and cook until the sauce is reduced to about 2 cups, 7 to 10 minutes.

2. Whisk the cornstarch and water together in a small bowl, then whisk into the sauce. Continue to simmer the sauce until thickened, about 2 minutes longer. Off the heat, whisk in the lemon juice and cream cheese until smooth. Add the shrimp, cover, and let sit off the heat until the shrimp are firm and no longer translucent in the center, 7 to 10 minutes. Remove and discard the bay leaf, then cover to keep warm and set aside.

3. Meanwhile, bring 4 quarts water to a boil in a large pot. Add the pasta and 1 tablespoon salt, and cook, stirring often, until al dente. Reserve ½ cup of the cooking water, then drain the pasta and return it to the pot. Add the shrimp-sauce mixture and parsley to the pasta and gently toss to combine. Cover and let sit off the heat until the sauce is hot, about 1 minute. Adjust the sauce consistency with the reserved cooking water as desired. Season with salt and pepper to taste and serve.

PER 1⅔-CUP SERVING: Cal 440; Fat 4g; Sat fat 1.5g; Chol 175mg; Carb 65g; Protein 35g; Fiber 3g; Sodium 680mg

Linguine with Fresh Clam Sauce

SERVES 6

Be sure to discard any clams that are open or have broken shells prior to cooking. To make this dish spicier, increase the amount of red pepper flakes.

  1 onion, minced (about 1 cup)
  1 teaspoon olive oil
     Salt
  8 garlic cloves, minced
  2 teaspoon minced fresh thyme
  ⅛ teaspoon red pepper flakes (see note)
  2 cups low-sodium chicken broth
  2 (8-ounce) bottles clam juice
  1 bay leaf
  3 pounds littleneck clams (about 36 clams), scrubbed
  2 tablespoons cornstarch
  2 tablespoons water
  ½ cup fresh lemon juice (about 4 lemons)
  3 tablespoons light cream cheese
  1 pound linguine
  ¼ cup chopped fresh parsley
     Pepper

1. Combine the onion, oil, and ⅛ teaspoon salt in a 12-inch nonstick skillet. Cover and cook over medium-low heat, stirring occasionally, until softened, 8 to 10 minutes. Stir in the garlic, thyme, and pepper flakes, and cook until fragrant, about 30 seconds. Add the broth, clam juice, and bay leaf, bring to a simmer, and cook until the sauce is reduced to about 2 cups, 7 to 10 minutes.

2. Add the clams, cover, and continue to cook until the clams have opened, 4 to 8 minutes longer. Using tongs, transfer the clams to a large bowl, discarding any that did not open, cover to keep warm, and set aside. Whisk the cornstarch and water together, then whisk into the sauce. Continue to simmer the sauce until thickened, about 2 minutes longer. Off the heat, whisk in the lemon juice and cream cheese until smooth. Remove and discard the bay leaf, then cover to keep warm and set aside.

3. Meanwhile, bring 4 quarts water to a boil in a large pot. Add the pasta and 1 tablespoon salt, and cook, stirring often, until al dente. Reserve ½ cup of the cooking water, then drain the pasta and return it to the pot. Add the sauce and parsley to the pasta and toss to combine. Cover and let sit off the heat until the sauce is hot, about 1 minute. Adjust the sauce consistency with the reserved cooking water as desired. Season with salt and pepper to taste. Divide the pasta among 6 individual bowls and nestle the cooked clams into each serving, along with any accumulated juice.

PER SERVING (1¼ CUPS LINGUINE WITH 6 CLAMS): Cal 380; Fat 3g; Sat fat 5g; Chol 30mg; Carb 67g; Protein 23g; Fiber 3g; Sodium 560mg

PORK LO MEIN

THIS CLASSIC CHINESE DISH OF STIR-FRIED NOODLES with barbecued pork and vegetables has so much potential, but what you get when you order takeout pork lo mein almost always disappoints: overcooked, greasy noodles, dry pork, and sodden vegetables. We felt certain we could restore its fresher, more boldly flavored dignity. We wanted chewy noodles tossed in a salty-sweet sauce and accented with bits of perfectly cooked pork and vegetables that lent both texture and flavor.

Traditional versions rely on barbecued pork called *char siu*. While an occasional trip to Boston's Chinatown was fine, we wanted a recipe we could follow without making any special outings. Nor were we about to fire up the barbecue, so we thought, Why not stir-fry the pork since we would already be stir-frying the vegetables? Well-marbled pork shoulder is traditional for char siu, but we wanted something leaner. Pork tenderloin, which we've used with great success in stir-fries, seemed like the natural choice.

Char siu is usually marinated, so we decided to do the same. We sliced the tenderloin thin, then soaked it in a combination of classic Chinese ingredients: oyster sauce, soy sauce, toasted sesame oil, and five-spice powder, an aromatic blend of cinnamon, star anise, and other spices. Our marinade needed a touch of sweetness, and because hoisin sauce would spike the sodium count too high, instead we used a couple of tablespoons of sugar. After marinating the meat for 20 minutes, we seared it quickly over high heat (in a nonstick skillet, our choice for stir-fries), and after one bite we knew we had a good thing. The meat was tender and juicy on the inside with a crisp, browned exterior. To better imitate the smoky flavor of char siu, we added a few drops of liquid smoke.

We were ready to tackle the noodles. Traditional lo mein noodles are fresh, made from wheat and egg, and resemble thick spaghetti. Fresh noodles are used since they absorb the flavors of the sauce better than dried. We began by casting a wide net and trying a variety of fresh Chinese egg noodles. Not surprisingly, only those labeled "lo mein," which we had to buy from an Asian grocery, boasted the right wheaty taste and firm texture. The more readily available fresh "Chinese-style" egg noodles from the supermarket, sold in vacuum-packed containers in the produce aisle, had a pasty texture and an inferior taste that wouldn't do. In search of an accessible alternative, we found that dried linguine was the next best thing to the lo mein noodles. Despite their flat shape, the long strands are similar in width to the Chinese noodles, and when cooked to al dente, they shared the same firm chewiness of our top choice.

Avoiding the greasiness that plagues takeout lo mein proved easy. Restaurants typically slather the noodles in oil to keep them from clumping, only because they cook the noodles well ahead of serving for expediency's sake. Home cooking offered the advantage that we could simply boil the noodles right before tossing them with the other ingredients. Problem solved.

All that was left were the vegetables and sauce. We opted for traditional vegetables—cabbage, scallions, and shiitake mushrooms—stir-frying them in some canola oil with garlic and ginger after cooking the meat. By cooking the vegetables in stages, we ensured that they remained crisp and fresh-tasting. As for the sauce, tasters agreed the same ingredients we had used for the meat marinade would serve perfectly well as the base, with some chicken broth added for volume and balance and a teaspoon of cornstarch for body.

After cooking the meat and vegetables, we put them all together in the skillet and stirred in the sauce to cook down. All we had to do was toss everything with the noodles and dig in. We knew immediately we wanted a bigger proportion of meat and vegetables. We had been following tradition, making the noodles the star and treating the meat and vegetables more like garnishes, but we found that boosting the pork from 4 ounces to a pound and increasing the amount of vegetables by several cups actually made our lo mein taste richer and, surprisingly, fresher. A little Asian chili-garlic sauce lent just the right kick. At last, we had chewy noodles coated in a flavorful sauce and plenty of tender, browned pork and bold, fresh-tasting vegetables.

Pork Lo Mein

SERVES 4

Though optional, we feel the liquid smoke provides a flavor reminiscent of the Chinese barbecued pork that is traditional in this dish. It is important that the noodles be cooked at the last minute to avoid clumping. Look for fresh Chinese egg noodles labeled "lo mein." You can substitute 8 ounces dried linguine for the fresh Chinese noodles—just increase the noodle cooking time to 10 minutes in step 7 (note that the nutritional information will be different with linguine). Freezing the pork for 15 minutes before slicing makes it easier to cut thin slices.

- 3 tablespoons low-sodium soy sauce
- 2 tablespoons oyster sauce
- 2 tablespoons sugar
- 1 tablespoon toasted sesame oil
- ¼ teaspoon five-spice powder
- 1 (1-pound) pork tenderloin, trimmed of all visible fat and sliced into thin strips (see page 130)
- ¼ teaspoon liquid smoke (optional; see note)
- ½ cup low-sodium chicken broth
- 1 teaspoon cornstarch
- 4½ teaspoons canola oil
- 2 garlic cloves, minced
- 2 teaspoons grated or minced fresh ginger
- ¼ cup Chinese rice cooking wine (Shaoxing) or dry sherry
- 8 ounces shiitake mushrooms, stemmed and cut into thirds if large, halved if small
- 2 bunches scallions, white parts sliced thin and green parts cut into 1-inch pieces (about 2 cups)
- 1 small head Napa cabbage, halved, cored, and sliced crosswise into ½-inch strips (about 4 cups)
- 12 ounces fresh Chinese egg noodles (see note)
- 1 tablespoon Asian chili-garlic sauce

PORK LO MEIN

1. Whisk the soy sauce, oyster sauce, sugar, sesame oil, and five-spice powder together in a small bowl. Transfer 3 tablespoons of the mixture to a large zipper-lock bag and add the pork and liquid smoke (if using). Press out as much air as possible and seal the bag, making sure that all the pieces are coated with the marinade. Refrigerate for at least 15 minutes or up to 1 hour.

2. Whisk the broth and cornstarch into the remaining soy sauce mixture and set aside. In a separate small bowl, mix ½ teaspoon of the canola oil, garlic, and ginger together and set aside.

3. Heat 1 teaspoon more canola oil in a 12-inch non-stick skillet over high heat until just smoking. Carefully add half of the pork in a single layer, breaking up any clumps. Cook without stirring for 1 minute, then stir and continue to cook until the pork is lightly browned, 2 to 3 minutes more. Add 2 tablespoons of the wine to the skillet and cook, stirring constantly, until the liquid is reduced and the pork is well coated, 30 to 60 seconds. Transfer the pork to a clean bowl and repeat with 1 teaspoon more canola oil, the remaining pork, and the remaining 2 tablespoons wine. Wipe out the skillet with a wad of paper towels.

4. Return the skillet to high heat, add 1 teaspoon more canola oil, and heat until just smoking. Add the mushrooms and cook, stirring occasionally, until light golden brown, 4 to 6 minutes. Add the scallion whites and greens and continue to cook, stirring occasionally, until wilted, 2 to 3 minutes longer. Transfer the vegetables to the bowl with the pork.

5. Add the remaining 1 teaspoon canola oil and the cabbage to the skillet and cook, stirring occasionally,

---

NOTES FROM THE TEST KITCHEN

SLICING PORK FOR STIR-FRY

1. Place the pork tenderloin on a clean, dry work surface. Using a sharp chef's knife, slice the pork crosswise into ¼-inch-thick medallions.

2. Slice each medallion into ¼-inch-wide strips.

FIVE-SPICE POWDER

Though recipes for five-spice powder can vary, its trademark warmth and pungency traditionally derive from cinnamon, cloves, fennel seed, star anise, and Sichuan peppercorns (white pepper or ginger are common substitutes). Grinding whole spices produces the freshest and most aromatic results, but we wondered if we could save time and money by using a commercial blend. All five brands we tested turned out to be acceptable, but the best, **Dean & Deluca Five Spice Blend,** offered a "mellow" yet "sweet" and "fragrant" backdrop to our pork and noodle stir-fry.

NOODLES FOR LO MEIN

As we were developing the recipe for our Pork Lo Mein, we discovered that not any old noodle will do.

BEST BET
The slightly dry and curly fresh egg noodles labeled "lo mein" from an Asian market boasts firm texture and the best flavor.

BEST ALTERNATIVE
Dried linguine, though not authentic, offers a firm chewiness similar to that of lo mein.

NO THANKS
Vacuum-packed fresh noodles from the grocery store labeled "Chinese-style" are gummy and pasty.

until spotty brown, 3 to 5 minutes. Clear the center of the skillet and add the garlic mixture. Cook, mashing the garlic mixture into the pan with the back of a spatula, until fragrant, about 1 minute. Stir the garlic mixture into the cabbage.

6. Return the mushrooms and pork, along with any accumulated juices, to the skillet and stir to combine. Whisk the sauce to recombine and add it to the skillet. Cook, stirring constantly, until thickened, about 1 minute.

7. Meanwhile, bring 4 quarts water to a boil in a large pot. Add the noodles and cook, stirring often, until tender, about 4 minutes. Drain the noodles and return them to the pot. Add the cooked stir-fry mixture and chili-garlic sauce to the noodles and toss to combine. Serve.

PER 1⅔-CUP SERVING: Cal 520; Fat 12g; Sat fat 1.5g; Chol 85mg; Carb 64g; Protein 37g; Fiber 5g; Sodium 1530mg

SPINACH LASAGNA

THE AMERICANIZED VERSION OF THIS ITALIAN CLASSIC is thankfully simpler than the original (no homemade noodles, for one), but most stateside versions we've encountered are heavy and bland, with army-green spinach and béchamel that tastes mostly like glue. Then there's the fact that between all the sauce and cheese, one serving can tally nearly 500 calories and 27 grams of fat. That's far from the "healthier" alternative to meat lasagna you would imagine. We wanted a recipe we could put together on a weeknight that offered vibrant spinach, a flavorful sauce, and a healthy balance of cheese.

TEST KITCHEN
MAKEOVER

To begin, we tackled the spinach. We already knew that for most simplified recipes, the spinach's drab color and bland flavor are actually caused by the type of noodles used. Traditional Italian recipes use homemade fresh pasta, and because fresh pasta cooks in an instant, these lasagnas require only a brief stay in the oven, just enough time for the layers to bind. Meanwhile, most Americanized recipes call for convenient no-boil noodles, which certainly save you labor, but they require at least 50 minutes of baking to become tender. This long stint in the oven robs the spinach of its vibrancy.

We knew we could rescue the spinach by shortening the oven time, so we decided to use conventional dried lasagna noodles, cooked al dente, which would ensure that our lasagna would need just 20 minutes to bake.

Using this method, we made a lasagna with fresh spinach and one with frozen, and in a side-by-side tasting our test cooks were pleased with the flavor and color of both. So we settled on the more convenient frozen spinach. To guard against a waterlogged lasagna, we wrapped the defrosted spinach in a kitchen towel and wrung out excess liquid before proceeding.

Next we moved on to the béchamel. Béchamel is a classic milk sauce thickened with a roux, a mixture of flour and butter. We quickly cut out some fat by using low-fat milk instead of whole, but there was still the issue of thickening, since the roux, with its 5 tablespoons of butter, was out of the question. We were worried cornstarch might make the sauce gummy, but we gave it a try anyway, whisking 2 tablespoons into cold milk to make a slurry before stirring it into the sauce. This worked great. It thickened the sauce perfectly, and it didn't taste at all starchy.

To boost the flavor of our sauce, we sautéed 1 cup of onions with plenty of garlic before pouring in the milk. Adding two bay leaves and freshly grated nutmeg, typical béchamel seasonings, lent depth, and sprinklings of salt and pepper were the only other refinements needed. To simplify the layering process, we stirred grated Parmesan cheese into the sauce along with the spinach and set the mixture aside.

Most recipes for spinach lasagna call for both ricotta and mozzarella cheese. Tasters commented that the ricotta layer cooked up dry, so for our next test, instead of ricotta we covertly added scoops of cottage cheese, which we pureed with an egg to smooth out its curds. Tasters approved, and no one could identify the mystery ingredient. Although heretical to any "real" northern Italian cook, the cottage cheese provided a pleasing tang and the right creaminess. (We tried low-fat and fat-free cottage cheese in addition to the regular, but we all agreed the regular was a necessity.) Next we tried replacing bland shredded mozzarella with fontina, a semi-firm cheese with buttery, nutty tones that melts beautifully. Its complexity was a welcome addition, and though fontina contains more fat and calories than mozzarella, we found we could reduce the amount of shredded cheese from 2 cups to 1½ cups and still end up with bolder flavor.

By this point, we'd grown tired of dealing with parboiling conventional noodles and were determined to make easier no-boil noodles work. The solution—and key to this recipe—was to soak the no-boil noodles in boiling water for just 5 minutes. After only 20 minutes

SPINACH LASAGNA

in a 425-degree oven, the noodles in our lasagna were perfectly cooked and the spinach had maintained its vitality. The only cooking left to do involved a quick trip to the broiler to brown the cheese.

With its bright spinach, balanced layers of cheese and sauce, and far less fat than the original, this was one lasagna that really tasted fresh.

MAKEOVER SPOTLIGHT: SPINACH LASAGNA

	CALORIES	FAT	SAT FAT	CHOLESTEROL
BEFORE	480	27g	15g	105mg
AFTER	350	14g	7g	70mg

Spinach Lasagna

SERVES 8

We prefer Barilla no-boil lasagna noodles for their delicate texture resembling that of fresh pasta. Be sure to use Italian fontina rather than bland and rubbery Danish or American fontina. To make the cheese easier to shred, freeze it for 30 minutes to firm it up. You will need a broiler-safe baking dish for this recipe.

SAUCE

- 1 onion, minced (about 1 cup)
- 1 teaspoon canola oil
  Salt
- 4 garlic cloves, minced
- 3 cups 1 percent low-fat milk
- 2 bay leaves
- ½ teaspoon freshly grated nutmeg
- 2 tablespoons cornstarch
- 2 (10-ounce) packages frozen chopped spinach, thawed, squeezed dry, and chopped fine
- 1 ounce grated Parmesan cheese (about ½ cup)
  Pepper

LAYERS

- 8 ounces whole-milk cottage cheese (about 1 cup)
- 1 large egg
- ¼ teaspoon salt
- 12 no-boil lasagna noodles (see note)
  Vegetable oil spray
- 2 ounces Parmesan cheese, grated (about 1 cup)
- 6 ounces Italian fontina cheese, shredded (about 1½ cups; see note)

1. FOR THE SAUCE: Combine the onion, oil, and ⅛ teaspoon salt in a large saucepan. Cover and cook over medium-low heat, stirring occasionally, until softened, 8 to 10 minutes. Stir in the garlic and cook until fragrant, about 30 seconds. Stir in 2¾ cups of the milk, bay leaves, and nutmeg. Bring to a simmer over medium-low heat.

2. Whisk the cornstarch and remaining ¼ cup milk together, then whisk into the pot. Continue to simmer, whisking constantly, until thickened, about 6 minutes. Off the heat, remove and discard the bay leaves. Stir in the spinach and Parmesan until incorporated and no clumps of spinach remain. (You should have about 3½ cups sauce.) Season with salt and pepper to taste. Cover to keep warm and set aside.

3. FOR THE LAYERS: Position one oven rack 6 inches from the broiler element, adjust a second oven rack to the middle position, and heat the oven to 425 degrees.

4. Process the cottage cheese, egg, and salt in a food processor (or blender) until very smooth, about 30 seconds. Transfer to a bowl and set aside.

5. Pour 1 inch of boiling water into a 13 by 9-inch broiler-safe baking dish, then add the noodles one at a time. Let the noodles soak until pliable, about 5 minutes, separating them with the tip of a sharp knife to prevent sticking. Remove the noodles from the water and place in a single layer on clean kitchen towels. Discard the water, dry the baking dish, and coat the interior with vegetable oil spray.

6. TO ASSEMBLE AND BAKE: Spread ½ cup of the sauce evenly over the bottom of the baking dish. Position 3 of the noodles on top of the sauce. Spread ¾ cup more

NOTES FROM THE TEST KITCHEN

THE BEST NO-BOIL NOODLES

Over the past few years, no-boil (also called oven-ready) lasagna noodles have become a permanent fixture on supermarket shelves. Much like "instant rice," no-boil noodles are precooked at the factory. The extruded noodles are run through a water bath and then dehydrated mechanically. During baking, the moisture from the sauce softens, or rehydrates, the noodles, especially when the pan is covered as the lasagna bakes. For both our lasagna and manicotti recipes, we prefer **Barilla** no-boil noodles for their delicate texture, which resembles that of fresh pasta.

sauce evenly over the noodles, sprinkle evenly with the Parmesan, and top with 3 more of the noodles. Spread ¾ cup more sauce evenly over the noodles, sprinkle evenly with ¾ cup of the fontina, and top with 3 more of the noodles. Spread ¾ cup more sauce evenly over the noodles, followed by the cottage cheese mixture. Finish with the remaining 3 noodles, remaining ¾ cup sauce, and remaining ¾ cup fontina.

7. Cover the baking dish with foil and bake the lasagna on the middle oven rack until bubbling, about 20 minutes. Remove the baking dish from the oven and remove the foil. Heat the broiler. Transfer the baking dish to the upper oven rack and broil the lasagna until the cheese is spotty brown, 4 to 6 minutes. Let the lasagna cool for 15 minutes before serving.

PER SERVING: Cal 350; **Fat** 14g; **Sat fat** 7g; **Chol** 70mg; **Carb** 36g; **Protein** 24g; **Fiber** 3g; **Sodium** 870mg

SKILLET BAKED ZITI

BAKED ZITI CASSEROLE IS A FAMILY FAVORITE AND a great pick for church suppers and potlucks—it's approachable and it won't break the budget, requiring only cheese, sauce, and pasta. But the preparation is labor-intensive and messy: You need to cook the pasta in one pot, prepare a sauce in another, and assemble the dish in a third to bake. And after all this work, the result is often unappealingly heavy, a mess overloaded with fatty cheese in an attempt to compensate for an otherwise bland recipe. We saw no reason baked ziti should be off-limits to cooks who are looking for a fast, healthy dinner. We'd had some recent success in the test kitchen preparing pasta recipes made entirely in a skillet, and we felt this technique could help us make streamlined baked ziti with a lighter, fresher profile.

TEST KITCHEN **MAKEOVER**

Our most important breakthrough in developing skillet pastas was realizing we could eliminate the step of boiling pasta in a separate pot. Small amounts of pasta (12 ounces or less) cook very well in a 12-inch nonstick skillet with a brothy, creamy, or, as in this case, diluted tomato sauce that you want to cook down and thicken. If the pasta is cooked at a vigorous simmer, it absorbs the cooking liquid and becomes tender in a reasonable amount of time while also absorbing flavor. It seemed like an ideal technique to apply here.

We first considered the tomato sauce. This would be a streamlined recipe, so the sauce would have to be easy to make. We wanted a sauce that was smooth and pure-tasting, with a fresh tomato flavor. In the first test we tried canned crushed tomatoes, but they coated the ziti too heavily for our skillet method. Canned diced tomatoes, pulsed in a food processor, worked much better. To build the flavor base, we sautéed garlic and red pepper flakes in a modest amount of olive oil. To this we added the processed tomatoes and simmered the sauce for 10 minutes, just enough to develop the flavors of the sauce without losing the freshness.

Next we prepared to stir in water and the ziti. The right pasta-to-liquid ratio would be crucial. If you don't have enough liquid, the pasta won't cook through; too much and the resulting sauce will be too thin. After several tests, we found that 3 cups of water was just right. Covering the skillet while the pasta cooked prevented the tomatoes from reducing too much.

Traditionally, mozzarella cheese is used in baked ziti to bind the pasta together. But because mozzarella is so mild, we felt it was lost when mixed into the sauce, so we reserved it for the top, where it would brown and contribute gooey appeal. But now without dairy in the sauce, tasters thought the dish tasted too lean and somewhat acidic because of the dominant tomato sauce. Heavy cream is often added to tomato sauces to provide richness and mellow acidity, but it wasn't an option for our light recipe. Half-and-half had been a successful replacement for heavy cream in several of our other light recipes, so we gave it a shot. We found adding ¼ cup of half-and-half, after the pasta had become tender, gave the sauce the desired creaminess and balanced the acidity without making it overly rich. We also stirred in a touch of Parmesan and fresh basil to brighten the flavor, then topped it all off with our shredded mozzarella and moved the skillet to the oven. It took only 10 to 15 minutes at 475 degrees for the cheese topping to brown perfectly. We could hardly wait to dig in, and after cutting 11 grams of fat per serving from the original recipe, this was one casserole we didn't feel guilty about eating.

MAKEOVER SPOTLIGHT: BAKED ZITI

	CALORIES	FAT	SAT FAT	CHOLESTEROL
BEFORE	610	25g	13g	65mg
AFTER	500	12g	6g	25mg

Skillet Baked Ziti

SERVES 4

Substituting other pasta shapes for the ziti may affect both the dry measurement and the final portion size. Make sure to use a 12-inch nonstick ovensafe skillet for this recipe. If the sauce has thickened before the pasta is tender in step 3, stir in additional water, ¼ cup at a time, to loosen.

- 1 (28-ounce) can diced tomatoes
- 6 garlic cloves, minced
- 1 teaspoon olive oil
- ¼ teaspoon red pepper flakes
  Salt
- 3 cups water
- 12 ounces ziti (about 3¾ cups; see note)
- ¼ cup half-and-half
- 1 ounce Parmesan cheese, grated (about ½ cup)
- ¼ cup chopped fresh basil
  Pepper
- 4 ounces part-skim mozzarella cheese, shredded (about 1 cup)

1. Adjust an oven rack to the middle position and heat the oven to 475 degrees. Pulse the tomatoes, with their juice, in a food processor until mostly smooth, about 11 pulses.

2. Combine the garlic, oil, and pepper flakes in a 12-inch ovensafe nonstick skillet, and cook over medium heat, mashing the mixture with a spoon, until fragrant but not brown, about 1 minute. Stir in the processed tomatoes and ½ teaspoon salt. Bring to a simmer, reduce the heat to medium-low, and cook, stirring occasionally, until beginning to thicken, about 10 minutes.

3. Stir in the water, then add the pasta. Cover, increase the heat to medium-high, and cook, stirring often and adjusting the heat to maintain a vigorous simmer, until the pasta is tender, 15 to 18 minutes.

4. Stir in the half-and-half, Parmesan, and basil, and season with salt and pepper to taste. Sprinkle the mozzarella evenly over the top. Transfer the skillet to the oven and bake until the cheese has melted and browned, 10 to 15 minutes. Serve.

PER 2-CUP SERVING: **Cal** 500; **Fat** 12g; **Sat fat** 6g; **Chol** 25mg; **Carb** 73g; **Protein** 24g; **Fiber** 4g; **Sodium** 940mg

VEGETABLE PIZZAS

VEGETABLE PIZZA SOUNDS APPEALING AND HEALTHY, but most versions we've had taste like an afterthought, made by heaping a hodgepodge of raw vegetables onto a cheese pizza and throwing it in the oven. The vegetables release moisture, making the crust soggy before it can cook through. It's impossible to eat even if you wanted to. And with just as much cheese as a regular pizza, it's certainly not any healthier. We wanted to develop a vegetable pizza that was actually light, with flavorful, well-cooked vegetables that complemented each other, and a tender-crisp crust.

We started with the crust. The test kitchen's basic pizza dough is simple to make and shape, so we started with this bread flour–based recipe, omitting the 2 tablespoons of oil it called for in order to cut some fat. But this crust was a little more chewy than what we were after. Switching from bread flour to all-purpose flour gave us the crisp crust we were looking for. We also found that baking on a pizza stone is best for attaining a crisp crust, as the stone retains heat and lessens the effects of the oven's temperature fluctuations. (If you don't have a baking stone, we found that a rimless or inverted baking sheet preheated like a baking stone will also work.)

Next we considered the sauce. Thinking that a bright, fresh tomato flavor might be preferable here, we pitted a simple cooked sauce against a no-cook sauce in a tasting. The no-cook pizza sauce was favored for this fresh-flavored pizza, and we settled on a simple mix of canned diced tomatoes and garlic pureed in the food processor.

It was time to look at the toppings. First we wanted to decide on the best way to cook our vegetables. (Putting raw vegetables on our crust was not even considered.) We often turn to techniques such as roasting that use high, dry oven heat to draw out big flavor from vegetables, and with our oven already preheating for the pizza, it made sense to cook the vegetables there as well.

We loved the idea of a pizza featuring crisp-tipped broccoli florets; sweet onion was also great for roasting, and it would pair nicely with the broccoli. We roasted the two together in one pan for efficiency. A preheated pan is key for proper browning, so we had to preheat our pan on top of the baking stone and roast the vegetables there as well, which seemed a little odd but worked just fine. Instead of tossing the vegetables with oil before putting them in the oven as we typically do, we lightly coated them with vegetable oil spray and reserved 2 teaspoons

ROASTED VEGETABLE PIZZA WITH BROCCOLI AND FETA

of oil for drizzling over the vegetables after they were cooked. This way, we were able to use less oil, and it acted more like a dressing, giving the vegetables a fresher flavor.

We needed to use a sparing hand with cheese, so right off the bat we eliminated mozzarella—we would have needed a lot to make up for its mild flavor. We considered stronger cheeses, where a little would go a long way: goat, feta, and Parmesan. Tangy feta seemed like a good match for the onion and broccoli, and briny kalamata olives made this pizza bold but balanced.

Once the broccoli and onion were roasted, we placed them on our rolled-out dough, sprinkled on the cheese and olives, and slid the pizza into the oven. We all agreed the vegetables needed a little more intensity, and the crust drooped under their weight. To boost the flavor, instead of drizzling the vegetables with oil alone, we combined the oil with some minced garlic and tossed the warm vegetables in this garlicky oil after roasting. This gave them the punch of flavor they needed.

To fix the droopy crust, we found parcooking the dough for 5 minutes before adding the sauce and toppings gave it the necessary structure. We also learned that transferring our crust (and then pizza) to and from the oven was a lot easier with the help of a rimless (or inverted) baking sheet. This pizza had a perfect, slightly chewy crust, and our combination of vegetables and cheese could stand up to the best of the gourmet slices.

Roasted Vegetable Pizza with Broccoli and Feta

SERVES 4

While we think our homemade pizza dough and sauce taste best, you can substitute premade dough and sauce—just note that the nutritional information will change. Note that you will be roasting the broccoli in a baking sheet placed on top of the preheating baking stone. If you do not have a baking stone, bake the pizza on a rimless (or inverted) baking sheet that has been preheated just like a baking stone.

- 1 tablespoon olive oil
- 1 garlic clove, minced
- 12 ounces broccoli (about ½ bunch), florets cut into 1-inch pieces, stems trimmed and cut lengthwise into ½-inch-thick planks
- 1 onion, halved and sliced ½ inch thick
  Vegetable oil spray
  Salt and pepper
- 1 recipe Basic Pizza Dough or Whole Wheat Pizza Dough (recipes follow; see note)
- 1 recipe No-Cook Pizza Sauce (recipe follows; see note)
- ¼ cup kalamata olives, pitted and chopped fine
- 2 ounces feta cheese, crumbled (about ½ cup)

1. Adjust an oven rack to the lower-middle position, place a baking stone on the rack, and place a foil-lined rimmed baking sheet on the baking stone. Heat the oven to 500 degrees. Let the baking stone heat for at least 30 minutes (but no longer than 1 hour). Line a rimless (or inverted) baking sheet with parchment paper and set aside.

2. Combine 2 teaspoons of the oil and garlic in a small bowl and set aside. Combine the broccoli and onion in a large bowl, thoroughly coat with vegetable oil spray, and toss with ¼ teaspoon salt. Spread in an even layer on the preheated foil-lined baking sheet and roast until the vegetables are spotty brown, 9 to 11 minutes.

3. Return the roasted vegetables to the large bowl, drizzle with the garlic-oil mixture, and toss to coat. Season with salt and pepper to taste and set aside.

4. Turn out the dough onto a lightly floured counter. Press and roll the dough into a 14-inch round. Transfer the dough to the parchment-lined baking sheet and reshape as needed.

5. Slide the parchment paper and dough onto the hot baking stone. Bake the crust until just set and puffy and the bottom is spotty brown, about 5 minutes, poking air bubbles with a fork as needed. Remove the crust from the oven by sliding the parchment paper back onto the baking sheet.

6. Lightly brush the outer ½ inch of the crust with the remaining 1 teaspoon oil. Spread the sauce over the crust, leaving a ½-inch border around the edge. Scatter the roasted vegetables, olives, and cheese on top of the sauce.

7. Slide the parchment paper and pizza back onto the hot baking stone. Bake the pizza until the vegetables are hot and the cheese is melted, 5 to 8 minutes.

8. Slide the parchment paper and pizza back onto the baking sheet. Discard the parchment paper, slide the pizza onto a cutting board, and serve.

PER SERVING (WITH BASIC PIZZA DOUGH): Cal 400; Fat 11g; Sat fat 3g; Chol 15mg; Carb 63g; Protein 13g; Fiber 5g; Sodium 1090mg

PER SERVING (WITH WHOLE WHEAT PIZZA DOUGH): Cal 420; Fat 11g; Sat fat 3g; Chol 15mg; Carb 66g; Protein 15g; Fiber 8g; Sodium 1090mg

Vegetable Pizza with Eggplant, Mushrooms, and Goat Cheese

For this recipe, cooking the vegetables under the broiler gives them the best browning and flavor. While we think our homemade pizza dough and sauce taste best, you can substitute premade dough and sauce—just note that the nutritional information will change. If you do not have a baking stone, bake the pizza on a rimless (or inverted) baking sheet that has been preheated just like a baking stone.

4	teaspoons olive oil
1	garlic clove, minced
1	teaspoon minced fresh thyme
10	ounces cremini mushrooms, sliced ¼ inch thick
	Vegetable oil spray
	Salt and pepper
1	globe eggplant (about 1 pound), sliced crosswise into ¼-inch-thick rounds
1	recipe Basic Pizza Dough or Whole Wheat Pizza Dough (recipes follow; see note)
1	recipe No-Cook Pizza Sauce (recipe follows; see note)
2	ounces goat cheese, crumbled (about ½ cup)
1	ounce baby arugula (about 1 cup)
1	tablespoon fresh lemon juice

1. Position an oven rack 2½ to 3½ inches from the heating element and heat the broiler. (If necessary, set an inverted rimmed baking sheet on the oven rack to get closer to the heating element.)

2. Combine 2 teaspoons of the oil, garlic, and thyme in a small bowl and set aside. Place the mushrooms in a large bowl, thoroughly coat with the vegetable oil spray, and toss with ¼ teaspoon salt. Spread in an even layer on a foil-lined rimmed baking sheet and broil until the mushrooms are golden brown, 9 to 11 minutes, stirring halfway through.

3. Return the roasted mushrooms to the large bowl, drizzle with half of the garlic-oil mixture, and toss to coat. Season with salt and pepper to taste and set aside.

4. Arrange the eggplant in a single layer on a foil-lined rimmed baking sheet, lightly coat both sides with vegetable oil spray, and sprinkle with ¼ teaspoon salt. Broil the eggplant until well browned, 8 to 10 minutes, rotating the pan halfway through. Transfer the baking sheet to a wire rack and brush the slices with the remaining garlic-oil mixture. Season with salt and pepper to taste and set aside.

5. Adjust an oven rack to the lower-middle position, place a baking stone on the rack, and heat the oven to 500 degrees. Let the baking stone heat for at least 30 minutes (but no longer than 1 hour). Line a rimless (or inverted) baking sheet with parchment paper and set aside.

NOTES FROM THE TEST KITCHEN

GETTING PIZZA IN AND OUT OF THE OVEN

Maneuvering pizza in and out of the oven can seem intimidating, but it's actually very easy. We rely on a rimless baking sheet (an inverted rimmed sheet will also work) to easily transport it back and forth between the counter and the oven, and a piece of parchment paper allows you to transfer it from the sheet to the baking stone and vice versa. You will follow these steps twice in our recipe, once for parbaking the crust and once for cooking the pizza (with toppings) through.

1. To move the pizza (or dough round when parbaking) into the oven, pull the parchment paper and pizza off the baking sheet onto the hot baking stone. Just be careful not to touch the hot stone.

2. When the pizza is done (or when the crust is parbaked), gently tug on the parchment paper to slide the hot pizza back onto the baking sheet—the paper will not be hot, but it will be a bit brittle and look "toasted."

A CUT ABOVE

A shoddy pizza cutter drags melted cheese out of place and fails to cut through crisp crust cleanly. A good pizza cutter gets the job done quickly, neatly, and safely (and also makes an excellent tool for trimming the edges of rolled-out pastry dough). The basic wheel cutter is the most common variety, and we tested six of them to find the best one. Our favorite was the **Italian Kitchen by Mario Batali Pizza Wheel,** $15.95. It rolled through every shape and size of crust like a pro. Because of the comfortable soft-grip handle and heavy weight, we needed to apply less pressure when cutting our pizzas. We also liked the large metal guard, which protects fingers from the blade.

6. Turn out the dough onto a lightly floured counter. Press and roll the dough into a 14-inch round. Transfer the dough to the parchment-lined baking sheet and reshape as needed.

7. Slide the parchment paper and dough onto the hot baking stone. Bake the crust until just set and puffy and the bottom is spotty brown, about 5 minutes, poking air bubbles with a fork as needed. Remove the crust from the oven by sliding the parchment paper back onto the baking sheet.

8. Lightly brush the outer ½ inch of the crust with 1 teaspoon more oil. Spread the sauce over the crust, leaving a ½-inch border around the edge. Arrange the eggplant in an even layer on top of the sauce, then scatter the mushrooms and cheese on top.

9. Slide the parchment paper and pizza onto the hot baking stone. Bake the pizza until the vegetables are hot and the cheese is melted, 5 to 8 minutes.

10. While the pizza cooks, toss the remaining 1 teaspoon oil, arugula, and lemon juice together in a medium bowl. When the pizza is done, slide the parchment paper and pizza back onto the baking sheet. Discard the parchment paper, slide the pizza onto a cutting board, sprinkle the arugula over the top, and serve.

PER SERVING (WITH BASIC PIZZA DOUGH): Cal 390; Fat 10g; Sat fat 2.5g; Chol 5mg; Carb 62g; Protein 13g; Fiber 6g; Sodium 780mg

PER SERVING (WITH WHOLE WHEAT PIZZA DOUGH): Cal 410; Fat 10g; Sat fat 2.5g; Chol 5mg; Carb 65g; Protein 15g; Fiber 9g; Sodium 780mg

No-Cook Pizza Sauce

MAKES ABOUT 1 CUP, ENOUGH FOR ONE 14-INCH PIZZA

- 1 (14.5-ounce) can diced tomatoes, drained, juice reserved
- 1 garlic clove, minced
  Salt and pepper

Pulse the drained tomatoes and garlic together in a food processor until mostly smooth, about 8 pulses. Transfer the mixture to a liquid measuring cup and add the reserved canned tomato juice until the sauce measures 1 cup. Season with salt and pepper to taste. (The sauce can be refrigerated in an airtight container for up to 4 days.)

PER ¼-CUP SERVING: Cal 20; Fat 0g; Sat fat 0g; Chol 0mg; Carb 4g; Protein 1g; Fiber 0g; Sodium 280mg

Basic Pizza Dough

MAKES 1 POUND DOUGH, ENOUGH FOR ONE 14-INCH PIZZA

The dough can be made ahead of time; in step 2, don't let the dough rise, but refrigerate it overnight or up to 16 hours, then let the dough sit at room temperature for 30 minutes before using.

- 2–2¼ cups (10–11¼ ounces) unbleached all-purpose flour
- 1 teaspoon instant or rapid-rise yeast
- ½ teaspoon salt
- ¾ cup warm water (110 degrees)
  Vegetable oil spray

1. Pulse 2 cups of the flour, yeast, and salt together in a food processor (fitted with a dough blade if possible) to combine. With the processor running, pour the water through the feed tube and process until a rough ball forms, 30 to 40 seconds. Let the dough rest for 2 minutes, then process for 30 seconds longer. If after 30 seconds the dough is sticky and clings to the blade, add the remaining ¼ cup flour, 1 tablespoon at a time, as needed.

2. Turn the dough out onto a lightly floured counter and form it into a smooth, round ball. Lightly coat a large bowl with vegetable oil spray and place the dough in the bowl. Lightly coat a sheet of plastic wrap with vegetable oil spray and cover the bowl tightly. Let rise in a warm place until doubled in size, 1 to 1½ hours, before using.

PER SERVING: Cal 230; Fat 0g; Sat fat 0g; Chol 0mg; Carb 48g; Protein 7g; Fiber 2g; Sodium 290mg

VARIATION

Whole Wheat Pizza Dough

Follow the recipe for Basic Pizza Dough, substituting 1 cup whole wheat flour for 1 cup of the all-purpose flour.

PER SERVING: Cal 250; Fat 1g; Sat fat 0g; Chol 0mg; Carb 51g; Protein 9g; Fiber 5g; Sodium 290mg

VEGETABLE TART

M = TEST KITCHEN MAKEOVER

EGGPLANT PARMESAN

TEST KITCHEN
MAKEOVER

EGGPLANT PARMESAN IS A CLASSIC ITALIAN-AMERICAN comfort food, but once we found out that a typical serving contains 760 calories and 59 grams of fat, the idea of eating it suddenly became a little less comforting. We needed a fresh take on this timeless dish, and so we started developing our lighter recipe with a hard-line goal in mind: We wanted to cut the calories and fat in half at the very least, ideally more, if it was possible without sacrificing taste.

The reasons for the excess calories and fat in eggplant Parmesan are pretty obvious. In a typical recipe, slices of eggplant are coated with a standard breading of flour, egg, and bread crumbs, then fried in oil. Given its porous nature, the eggplant (and the crumbs) absorbs much of the oil. The fried—and now oil-soaked—eggplant is then layered with shredded mozzarella (which has about 7 grams of fat per ¼ cup) and topped with tomato sauce, which naturally includes grated Parmesan and more oil. This scenario was screaming for a major makeover.

We started with how to cook the eggplant. Hoping to avoid the frying process, we dispensed with the breading altogether, baking naked, salted eggplant slices on a baking sheet coated with vegetable oil spray—a method we often found in low-calorie recipes for eggplant Parmesan. The resulting eggplant earned negative reviews from tasters for its soft texture. Though baking the eggplant showed promise, we all agreed a crisp breading was essential. So we baked the eggplant again, this time in a breading. To lighten things up, we tweaked the standard dip in flour, then egg, then bread crumbs by trading in whole eggs for egg whites. This produced better results, but tasters had issues with the coating's bland flavor and pale color.

We decided to run a quick test, pitting breadings made with store-bought bread crumbs, homemade bread crumbs, and panko against each other. The panko's ultra-crisp texture won the day. We then decided to take it a few steps further for our next test. We toasted the panko in a skillet over medium heat until golden, then breaded the eggplant slices, sprayed their tops with a little vegetable oil for added crispness, and baked them. This eggplant had the perfect golden color and crisp, fried texture we were after. The flavor of the breading, however, still needed help. Adding a tablespoon of olive oil to the panko as they toasted gave them a nice "fried" flavor without turning them greasy or adding too many calories, and tossing them with some grated Parmesan helped boost their flavor. The eggplant now actually tasted like slices in a traditional eggplant Parmesan.

Figuring the hard part was done, we layered our eggplant in a casserole dish with a quick tomato sauce (which had just 1 teaspoon of oil), and, forgoing whole-fat mozzarella cheese, we substituted the shredded reduced-fat version and popped the casserole into the oven. Our hopes were dashed when we retrieved the dish. The once-crisp exterior of our eggplant had turned into the texture of wet cardboard, and tasters felt the breading was overwhelming, especially on the underside of the eggplant, which had dramatically absorbed moisture from the sauce and fat from the cheese.

Back at the drawing board, one taster suggested breading the eggplant on just one side and layering it, naked-side down, in the casserole. Less breading would mean not only less moisture and fat absorbed, but also less interference with the delicate eggplant flavor. Another colleague suggested we might also want to consider adding less tomato sauce to the casserole dish, instead saving a large portion of it to serve on the side. Though these ideas were unconventional, we decided to give them a try, and to our delight, they worked perfectly. The eggplant was no longer blanketed in a dull coating of crumbs, and our judicious use of tomato sauce led us to success. With a skinny 330 calories and only 12 grams of fat per serving, and plenty of comfort-food appeal and flavor, our makeover more than met our expectations.

MAKEOVER SPOTLIGHT: EGGPLANT PARMESAN

	CALORIES	FAT	SAT FAT	CHOLESTEROL
BEFORE	760	59g	13g	140mg
AFTER	330	12g	4g	15mg

Eggplant Parmesan

SERVES 6

Panko, Japanese-style bread crumbs, can be found in the international aisle of the supermarket. Three cups of fresh bread crumbs can be substituted for the panko (they will shrink as they toast).

SAUCE

- 2 **(28-ounce) cans diced tomatoes**
- 4 **garlic cloves, minced**
- 1 **tablespoon tomato paste**
- 1 **teaspoon olive oil**
- ⅛ **teaspoon red pepper flakes (optional)**
- ½ **cup chopped fresh basil**
  Salt and pepper

EGGPLANT

- 2 **eggplants (about 1 pound each), ends trimmed, sliced into ⅓-inch-thick rounds**
  Salt
  Vegetable oil spray
- 1½ **cups panko (see note)**
- 1 **tablespoon olive oil**
- 1 **ounce Parmesan cheese, grated (about ½ cup)**
- ½ **cup unbleached all-purpose flour**
- 1½ **teaspoons garlic powder**
  Pepper
- 3 **large egg whites**
- 1 **tablespoon water**
- 8 **ounces reduced-fat mozzarella cheese, shredded (about 2 cups)**
- 2 **tablespoons chopped fresh basil**

1. FOR THE SAUCE: Pulse 1 can of the tomatoes, with their juice, in a food processor until mostly smooth, about 11 pulses. Transfer the tomatoes to a bowl. Repeat with the remaining 1 can tomatoes. Cook the garlic, tomato paste, oil, and pepper flakes (if using) in a medium saucepan over medium heat, stirring frequently, until the tomato paste begins to brown, about 2 minutes.

2. Stir in the processed tomatoes, bring to a simmer, and cook until thickened, 20 to 25 minutes. Off the heat, stir in the basil and season with salt and pepper to taste. Cover and set aside until needed.

3. FOR THE EGGPLANT: Meanwhile, toss half of the eggplant with ½ teaspoon salt, then place in a large colander set over a bowl. Repeat with the remaining eggplant and ½ teaspoon more salt, and transfer to the

colander with the first batch. Let the eggplant sit for 30 minutes to drain.

4. Spread the eggplant over several layers of paper towels. Firmly press the tops of the eggplant dry with more paper towels.

5. Adjust the oven racks to the upper-middle and lower-middle positions and heat the oven to 475 degrees. Line 2 rimmed baking sheets with foil and lightly coat with vegetable oil spray.

6. Combine the panko and oil in a 12-inch skillet, and toast over medium heat, stirring often, until golden, about 10 minutes. Spread the panko in a shallow dish and let cool slightly, then stir in the Parmesan. In a second shallow dish, whisk the flour, garlic powder, and ½ teaspoon pepper together. In a third shallow dish, whisk the egg whites and water together.

7. Season the eggplant with pepper. Lightly dredge one side of each eggplant slice in the seasoned flour, shaking off the excess. Dip the floured side of the

---

NOTES FROM THE TEST KITCHEN

OUR FAVORITE SUPERMARKET PARMESAN

Can domestic Parmesan really stand up to imported Parmigiano-Reggiano? Simply put, no, it cannot. Our tasters effortlessly picked out the imports in our lineup of eight supermarket cheeses. The two genuine Parmigiano-Reggianos, sold by Boar's Head and Il Villaggio, were the clear favorites, and tasters deemed **Boar's Head Parmigiano-Reggiano** "best in show."

THE BEST CANNED DICED TOMATOES

Ten months out of the year, the quality of canned tomatoes easily surpasses that of fresh tomatoes. Picked at the peak of ripeness and canned immediately, they are sweet, flavorful, and convenient. We tasted several brands of canned diced tomatoes and discovered that not every brand was up to snuff. Some suffered from excessive sweetness or saltiness, while others had issues with texture. We suggest looking for canned tomatoes that are packed in juice rather than puree, which is heavier and pulpier than juice and contributes an unpleasant cooked flavor to the tomatoes. Our favorite brand is **Muir Glen Organic Diced Tomatoes,** which have a favorable balance of sweetness and saltiness. They also boast a vibrant, fresh-from-the-garden flavor.

eggplant into the egg whites, then coat the same side with the panko, pressing to help the crumbs adhere. Lay the eggplant slices, breaded-side up, on the baking sheets in a single layer.

8. Lightly coat the top of the eggplant slices with vegetable oil spray. Bake until the tops are crisp and golden, about 30 minutes, switching and rotating the baking sheets halfway through.

9. Spread 1 cup of the tomato sauce in the bottom of a 13 by 9-inch baking dish. Position half of the eggplant slices, breaded-side up, on top of the sauce, overlapping the slices to fit. Distribute ½ cup more sauce over the eggplant and sprinkle with half of the mozzarella. Layer in the remaining eggplant, breaded-side up, and dot with 1 cup more sauce, leaving the majority of the eggplant exposed so it will remain crisp; sprinkle with the remaining mozzarella.

10. Bake until bubbling and the cheese is browned, about 10 minutes. Let cool for 5 minutes. Sprinkle with the basil and serve, passing the remaining sauce separately.

PER SERVING: **Cal** 330; **Fat** 12g; **Sat fat** 4g; **Chol** 15mg; **Carb** 37g; **Protein** 21g; **Fiber** 6g; **Sodium** 1340mg

BLACK BEAN BURGERS

A RELIABLE STAPLE FOR THE HEALTH-MINDED COOK, black beans appear in various vegetarian entrées as the main protein source, from tacos and chili to casseroles and hearty salads. Recently they have emerged as the chief ingredient in their own version of vegetarian burgers. Black beans are mashed and combined with herbs, seasonings, and a binder, then formed into patties and pan-seared. With the meaty, satisfying flavor and satisfying appeal of black beans, we could certainly see the draw.

We started by testing a few existing recipes, and the common problems were clear. Most black bean burgers are a labor of love, requiring mashing, chopping, and measuring before mixing everything together—much more involved than their beef brethren. And many of these recipes were just not worth this effort—countless patties came out of the pan dry, pasty, or falling apart, not to mention bland in flavor. But, realizing the potential, we decided to develop our own recipe, one that would give us moist patties with appealing

texture, robust flavor, and the ability to go from pan to plate without falling into pieces.

We looked first at the black beans. Most of the recipes for burgers we had sampled called for two cans of beans. Canned beans were not only a time-saver compared to soaking and simmering dried, but two cans conveniently provided roughly the right amount to make six burgers. Although the canned beans have a mushier, slightly less pleasing texture than dried beans, we were confident we could overcome the issue with a little help from our prep and some additional ingredients.

Our test recipes had revealed two main preparation styles for the beans: mashing some and leaving some whole, or mashing all of them. Not surprisingly, burgers made with all mashed beans had an unappealing pasty consistency. The burgers with a combination of half mashed and half whole beans fared much better, offering a good textural contrast. But these burgers had another problem; we could rarely make a patty that didn't fall apart before it was cooked through, even in spite of the egg most of these recipes used for binding.

We wondered if more eggs would help hold our burgers together. Opening up a few more cans of beans, we experimented with batches of burgers made with two and three eggs. The batch with three eggs was too moist, making a mixture more like a batter than a burger. The batch with two eggs, however, had the proper amount of moisture and held together perfectly. Success!

It was time to look at additional ingredients. A few recipes we had come across included chopped vegetables, herbs, and spices. This idea seemed promising since it could result in more flavor and texture. We tested common choices for vegetables first: onion, garlic, shallot, celery, mushrooms, and bell pepper. Tasters felt that the onion and garlic were overpowering, but milder shallot provided a nice pungency. Celery and mushrooms both added a meaty texture and rich flavor, but they required precooking to avoid tasting raw—too much work for this recipe. But finely chopped raw bell pepper added the flavor and texture we were looking for. As for herbs and spices, tasters liked Southwestern flavors best—cilantro, cumin, and cayenne. As a final addition, a little olive oil brought our burgers' richness to just the right level.

Now our burgers had excellent flavor and texture, but with more ingredients in the mix, an old problem cropped up again: The burgers were struggling to hold together. Egg didn't seem like the answer this time, and recognizing that the mashed beans played a part in binding, we tried increasing the ratio of mashed beans to whole, finally settling on a 3-to-1 ratio. At this ratio, our burgers held together well, and with the whole beans and bell pepper lending texture, they weren't too mushy. To further ensure stability, we also incorporated bread crumbs—a binding ingredient often used in meat loaf and meatball recipes—to help absorb any excess moisture from the vegetables.

Served on buns with all the fixings, these black bean burgers were quickly gaining fame as a creative new way to enjoy a healthy, satisfying meal without a lot of work.

Black Bean Burgers

SERVES 6

Avoid overmixing the bean mixture in step 3 or the texture of the burgers will be mealy. Serve with your favorite toppings on whole wheat rolls or with a salad.

- 2 slices high-quality white sandwich bread, torn into pieces
- 2 large eggs
- 3 tablespoons olive oil
- 1 teaspoon ground cumin
- ½ teaspoon salt
- ⅛ teaspoon cayenne pepper
- 2 (15-ounce) cans black beans, drained and rinsed
- 1 red bell pepper, stemmed, seeded, and chopped fine
- ¼ cup chopped fresh cilantro
- 1 shallot, minced (about 3 tablespoons)

1. Adjust an oven rack to the middle position and heat the oven to 350 degrees.

2. Pulse the bread in a food processor to coarse crumbs, about 10 pulses. Spread the crumbs on a rimmed baking sheet and bake, stirring occasionally, until golden brown and dry, 10 to 12 minutes. Set aside to cool to room temperature.

3. Whisk the eggs, 1 tablespoon of the oil, cumin, salt, and cayenne together in a small bowl. Place 2½ cups of the beans in a large bowl and mash them with a potato masher until mostly smooth. Stir in the bread crumbs, egg mixture, remaining ½ cup beans, bell pepper, cilantro, and shallot until just combined. Divide the bean

mixture into 6 equal portions, about ½ cup each, and lightly pack into 1-inch-thick patties.

4. Heat 1 tablespoon more oil in a 12-inch nonstick skillet over medium heat until shimmering. Carefully lay half of the patties in the skillet and cook until well browned on both sides, 8 to 10 minutes, flipping them halfway through.

5. Transfer the burgers to a plate and tent loosely with foil. Return the skillet to medium heat and repeat with the remaining 1 tablespoon oil and the remaining burgers. Serve.

PER SERVING: Cal 170; Fat 9g; Sat fat 1.5g; Chol 70mg; Carb 20g; Protein 7g; Fiber 5g; Sodium 460mg

VARIATION

Black Bean Burgers with Corn and Chipotle Chiles
Follow the recipe for Black Bean Burgers, substituting 1 tablespoon minced canned chipotle chiles in adobo sauce for the cayenne pepper. Reduce the amount of red bell pepper to ¼ cup and add ¾ cup frozen corn, thawed and drained, to the bean mixture in step 3.

PER SERVING: Cal 190; Fat 9g; Sat fat 1.5g; Chol 70mg; Carb 24g; Protein 8g; Fiber 6g; Sodium 470mg

STUFFED PORTOBELLO MUSHROOMS

DURING THE HOLIDAYS WE SEE COUNTLESS TRAYS of stuffed mushrooms, and while the concept has a lot of appeal—meaty, earthy mushrooms paired with a flavorful filling—we decided it was long overdue for a makeover. First, we wanted an entrée-sized version, trading in the generic white button mushrooms for meatier portobellos (not an entirely new concept); and second, we wanted to rescue the stuffed mushroom from its all-too-common drab fate. Most we've seen are bland, watery mushroom caps weighed down by a soggy bread-crumb filling overloaded with cheese—not exactly appetizing, and certainly not light. We wanted lighter stuffed mushrooms that would satisfy a dinner crowd: meaty, earthy caps with a complementary, nicely textured filling.

Many stuffed portobello recipes called for stuffing raw caps and placing them in the oven. These invariably end up with soggy fillings. Portobellos are 80 to

STUFFED PORTOBELLO MUSHROOMS

90 percent water, so to avoid sogginess, some water would have to come out before any stuffing went in. The idea of salting the mushrooms struck us as one possible route, but we felt roasting might be a better avenue: We could dry out the mushrooms and deepen their flavor at the same time. Placing a batch of portobello caps in a 400-degree oven, we stood back and waited. And waited. Forty minutes later, we finally had mushrooms that were dry, with deep flavor, albeit a little leathery.

We needed to cut down on the roasting time. A colleague suggested first scoring the mushrooms with shallow cuts to expedite the release of moisture, and this trick worked wonders. The mushrooms lost enough water after about 20 minutes in the oven, becoming intensely flavored and sufficiently dry but still tender. We then wondered if we could get more intense flavor by caramelizing the exterior, so next we tried preheating the baking sheet before placing the mushrooms on top. These caps emerged from the oven perfectly dry and caramelized, full of deep flavor and ready for the filling.

When it comes down to it, you can stuff a mushroom with almost anything—cheese, meats, nuts, mashed potatoes—so long as it fits in the cap. But after testing dozens of combinations, we realized the more carried away we got, the more these fillings packed on fat, not flavor. The first ingredient we chose was an obvious one. A couple of chopped mushrooms and the stems (which we would have thrown out otherwise) would bolster the overall mushroom flavor. We thoroughly cooked the chopped stems until all the liquid had evaporated and they began to brown. Adding minced onion and garlic to the pan rounded out the savory mushroom flavor, and deglazing with dry sherry added depth.

Tasters liked our filling so far but asked for some contrasting bright flavor. In the end, we settled on spinach, but simply folded into the mushroom mixture, it leached moisture as it wilted, watering down our filling. Wilting the spinach in the microwave before adding it to the mix easily solved the problem.

Now we needed a binder. The most common choices are bread crumbs and cream sauces, but we found that each had problems. The bread crumbs became soggy and didn't do enough for flavor, while cream sauces (and their lighter alternatives) turned the filling gluey. Looking for other options, we considered cheese. After deglazing the pan with the sherry, we added some goat cheese and crossed our fingers. Success: The cheese kept the stuffing intact without weighing it down

and added a nice sharp contrast. And because of goat cheese's tangy flavor, we needed only about ¾ cup.

All our recipe needed now was a little tweaking. Tasters liked the fragrant addition of thyme and the brightness of lemon juice. For a bit of crunch, we sprinkled on some toasted bread crumbs. After a few minutes under the broiler, the stuffed mushrooms emerged sizzling from the oven with an appealing earthy aroma and a filling that was fresh-tasting and flavorful.

Stuffed Portobello Mushrooms
SERVES 4

The mushroom caps shrink significantly as they cook, so be sure to choose dense mushrooms that are 4 to 5 inches in diameter.

- 1 slice high-quality white sandwich bread, torn into pieces
- 2 tablespoons olive oil
  Salt and pepper
- 10 portobello mushrooms (each 4 to 5 inches in diameter), stems removed and reserved, caps wiped clean (see note)
- 12 ounces baby spinach (about 12 cups)
- 2 tablespoons water
- 2 onions, minced (about 2 cups)
- 1 teaspoon minced fresh thyme
- 4 garlic cloves, minced
- ½ cup dry sherry
- 3 ounces goat cheese, crumbled (about ¾ cup)
- 2 teaspoons fresh lemon juice

1. Adjust the oven racks to the upper-middle and lower-middle positions, place a rimmed baking sheet on the upper oven rack, and heat the oven to 400 degrees.

2. Pulse the bread in a food processor to coarse crumbs, about 10 pulses. Transfer the crumbs to a bowl and stir in 1 teaspoon of the oil, ¼ teaspoon salt, and ¼ teaspoon pepper. Spread the crumbs on a second rimmed baking sheet, place on the lower oven rack, and bake, stirring occasionally, until golden brown and dry, 8 to 10 minutes. Set aside to cool to room temperature.

3. Following the photos on page 148, use a sharp knife to cut ¼-inch-deep slits in a ½-inch crosshatch pattern on the tops of 8 of the mushroom caps. Cut the remaining 2 mushroom caps and reserved stems into ½-inch pieces and set aside.

4. Brush both sides of the caps with 1 tablespoon more oil and season with ¼ teaspoon salt. Carefully place the caps, gill-side up, on the preheated baking sheet and roast until the mushrooms have released some of their juice and begin to brown around the edges, 8 to 12 minutes. Flip the caps and continue to roast until the liquid has completely evaporated and the caps are golden brown, 8 to 12 minutes longer. Remove the mushrooms from the oven and heat the broiler.

5. Meanwhile, place the spinach and water in a large microwave-safe bowl. Cover the bowl and microwave on high power until the spinach is wilted and has decreased in volume by half, 3 to 4 minutes. Using potholders, remove the bowl from the microwave and keep covered for 1 minute.

6. Carefully uncover the spinach and transfer to a colander set in the sink. Using the back of a rubber spatula, gently press the spinach against the colander to release the excess liquid. Transfer the spinach to a cutting board and roughly chop. Return the spinach to the colander and press a second time.

7. Combine the remaining 2 teaspoons oil, chopped mushrooms, onions, thyme, and ⅛ teaspoon salt in a 12-inch nonstick skillet. Cover and cook over medium-low heat, stirring occasionally, until the vegetables are softened, 8 to 10 minutes. Uncover, increase the heat to medium-high, and continue to cook, stirring occasionally, until the vegetables are lightly browned, 4 to 6 minutes longer.

8. Stir in the garlic and cook until fragrant, about 30 seconds. Stir in the sherry and cook until almost no liquid remains, 1 to 2 minutes. Stir in the spinach and cheese, and continue to cook until the cheese is melted and the vegetables are well coated, 1 to 2 minutes longer. Off the heat, stir in the lemon juice and season with salt and pepper to taste.

9. Flip the mushroom caps gill-side up and distribute the filling evenly among them. Top each cap with the bread-crumb mixture and broil the mushrooms until the crumbs are deep golden brown, about 1 minute. Serve.

PER SERVING (2 MUSHROOM CAPS): **Cal** 280; **Fat** 12g; **Sat fat** 4g; **Chol** 10mg; **Carb** 31g; **Protein** 12g; **Fiber** 9g; **Sodium** 630mg

---

NOTES FROM THE TEST KITCHEN

SCORING MUSHROOMS

1. With the tip of a paring knife, carefully score the smooth (non-gill) side of the mushroom in one direction, ¼ inch deep, spacing the cuts about ½ inch apart.

2. Score the mushroom in the opposite direction to make a crosshatch pattern.

MUSHROOMS AND MOISTURE

To extract moisture from the whole mushroom caps in our stuffed portobello recipe, we tried salting and draining them before cooking—a trick we often use with watery veggies such as eggplant and zucchini. But the method succeeded only in making the caps slimy. It turns out that the exterior of any mushroom is covered with a layer of hydrophobic (water-repellent) proteins that prevents water from going in—and keeps moisture from going out. Instead, we removed liquid by cutting slits in the caps, which allowed water to drip out and evaporate as we precooked the mushrooms in a 400-degree oven.

NOT JUST FOR FISH

Fish spatulas, elongated versions of a standard pancake flipper, are designed with shimmying underneath delicate fillets in mind, but we've found no better tool for extracting sticky vegetables from a baking sheet—or transferring a loaded-up portobello to a plate. The best fish spatulas we tested were strong yet pliable and not too long. Tapered edges made easy work of digging beneath caramelized potatoes, and a gentle upward curve at the tip cradled slippery foods with panache. Sturdy yet nimble, the **Wüstof Gourmet 7.5-Inch Slotted Turner/Fish Spatula**, $34.95, sports a nicely arced blade and a comfortable handle that beat out the competition.

SPRING VEGETABLE RISOTTO

WE LOVE RICH, SATISFYING WINTERTIME RISOTTOS paired with squash or mushrooms, but spring-inspired versions of this Italian classic can be equally indulgent. Because they highlight bright, fresh springtime vegetables, they inherently offer a more balanced appeal in terms of lightness. We decided risotto would make a great vegetarian entrée, but there was certainly work to be done to perfect a light recipe. Regardless of their seasonal accents, traditional risotto preparations aren't exactly light. Typically, lots of butter and cheese are added to boost the richness and silkiness of the sauce (which is made when the rice grains release their starch during cooking), so we'd need to see what we could do to cut back on these fattier additions without taking away from the original dish's appeal. We'd also be faced with the challenge of making sure the natural richness of risotto's sauce didn't overwhelm our mild, delicate vegetables.

Previous experience with risotto in the test kitchen had already taught us a lot. Insofar as the type of rice, tasters agreed an Italian medium-grain rice was a must, preferring the arborio variety for its firm bite. We also found that while most recipes require adding the broth in painstakingly small increments and stirring continuously for up to 30 minutes, there was a simpler route. We found we could add about half the broth all at once at the beginning, allowing it to simmer for about half the cooking time and stirring only occasionally. Once the rice absorbed this broth, we added more, ½ cup at a time. At this point, stirring every minute or so was important; if we didn't, the rice stuck to the bottom of the pan.

So, confident about the basics of making a risotto, our focus for this recipe would be on the vegetables and lightening it up. We knew that pairing risotto with spring vegetables would be a challenge, as the vegetables' delicate flavors could easily be overpowered by the dense, creamy rice. Most existing spring risotto recipes turn to asparagus and leeks, so we began there. We weren't worried about the leeks. Added to the rice at the outset of cooking, they melted down and infused the dish. Our real challenge was to figure out how to maintain the bright flavor of the asparagus and keep it from turning to mush. We tried adding it partway through cooking, but since cooking rice to al dente is not an exact science, the asparagus frequently overcooked. Sautéing it separately, then stirring it into the rice just before serving proved to be the answer. For a third vegetable, we turned to peas. Frozen peas are a reliably consistent choice (much more so than fresh), and they worked well here. Sautéed along with the asparagus, they maintained their fresh flavor and firm texture.

This risotto tasted good, but everyone wanted more intense vegetable flavor. Up until this point, we had been using a combination of vegetable broth and water (tasters felt vegetable broth alone was too sweet), but then we realized the tough asparagus stems and the leek greens, which we had been throwing away, might be sources of more flavor. Simmering them for 20 minutes in the vegetable broth and water was all it took to intensify the vegetable flavor.

We still needed to tackle the butter and cheese. We started by testing four risottos, each finished with a different amount of butter, from 3 tablespoons down to none. The version with 3 tablespoons tasted great, but we eventually agreed the risotto made with 1 tablespoon was our best bet; some butter was beneficial, but the extra 22 grams of fat and 200 calories that came with another 2 tablespoons was just not worth it.

Turning to the Parmesan, we tried reducing the ¾ cup of cheese typically called for in risotto recipes, but our tasters only gave in a little—nothing less than a full ounce (about ½ cup of grated cheese) would do. However, since Parmesan packs a lot of flavor without adding too many calories and fat grams, we weren't too concerned.

Our risotto still needed a hit of freshness, and we thought that a gremolata (a garnish of minced parsley, lemon zest, and garlic) was the answer. But the raw garlic proved too strong, so we took it out, and some fresh mint added another spring accent. (At this point, we also found that adding the stems from the parsley and the mint made our amped-up vegetable broth even more flavorful.) This risotto was bursting with flavor, and we agreed it was just the refreshingly light entrée we were after.

Spring Vegetable Risotto

SERVES 4

Onions can be substituted for the leeks. If substituting onions, use 1 roughly chopped onion (1 cup) in the broth and 2 minced onions (2 cups) in the risotto. At the end of cooking, you may have up to 1 cup of broth left over.

GREMOLATA

- **2 tablespoons minced fresh parsley, stems reserved**
- **2 tablespoons minced fresh mint, stems reserved**
- **½ teaspoon grated lemon zest**

RISOTTO

- **1 bunch asparagus (about 1 pound), tough ends trimmed and reserved (see page 212), spears cut on the bias into ½-inch-thick pieces**
- **1 pound leeks (see note), greens reserved, white and light green parts halved lengthwise, sliced thin, and rinsed thoroughly (about 4 cups)**
- **4 cups low-sodium vegetable broth**
- **3 cups water**
- **1 tablespoon canola oil**
- **Salt and pepper**
- **½ cup frozen peas (2 ounces)**
- **2 garlic cloves, minced**
- **1½ cups arborio rice**
- **1 cup dry white wine**
- **1 ounce Parmesan cheese, grated (about ½ cup)**
- **1 tablespoon unsalted butter**
- **2 teaspoons fresh lemon juice**

1. FOR THE GREMOLATA: Combine the minced parsley, minced mint, and lemon zest in a small bowl and set aside.

2. FOR THE RISOTTO: Chop the tough asparagus ends and leek greens into rough ½-inch pieces. Bring the reserved parsley and mint stems, chopped asparagus ends, leek greens, broth, and water to a boil in a large saucepan over high heat. Reduce the heat to medium-low, partially cover, and simmer for 20 minutes.

3. Strain the broth through a fine-mesh strainer into a medium bowl, pressing on the solids with a spatula to extract as much liquid as possible. Discard the solids. Return the strained broth to the saucepan, cover, and set over low heat to keep warm.

4. Heat 2 teaspoons of the oil in a large Dutch oven over medium heat until shimmering. Add the asparagus spears, ⅛ teaspoon salt, and ¼ teaspoon pepper, and cook, stirring occasionally, until crisp-tender, 4 to 6 minutes. Add the peas and continue to cook until heated through, about 1 minute. Transfer the vegetables to a plate and set aside.

5. Combine the remaining 1 teaspoon oil, sliced leeks, ¼ teaspoon salt, and ¼ teaspoon pepper in the Dutch oven. Cover and cook over medium-low heat, stirring occasionally, until softened, 8 to 10 minutes. Uncover and increase the heat to medium. Stir in the garlic and cook until fragrant, about 30 seconds. Stir in the rice and cook, stirring often, until the ends of the rice kernels are transparent, about 3 minutes. Stir in the wine and cook until it has been completely absorbed, 2 to 3 minutes.

6. Stir in 3 cups of the hot broth and continue to simmer, stirring every few minutes, until the liquid is absorbed and the bottom of the pan is almost dry, about 12 minutes.

7. Stir in ½ cup more broth every few minutes as needed to keep the pan bottom from drying out (you may not need all of the broth), and cook, stirring often, until the rice is al dente, 10 to 12 minutes.

8. Off the heat, vigorously stir in the cheese, butter, and lemon juice, then gently fold in the reserved asparagus and peas. Season with salt and pepper to taste. Serve immediately, sprinkling each portion with some of the gremolata.

PER 1¾-CUP SERVING: Cal 380; **Fat** 9g; **Sat fat** 3.5g; **Chol** 15mg; **Carb** 53g; **Protein** 12g; **Fiber** 6g; **Sodium** 950mg

---

NOTES FROM THE TEST KITCHEN

THE BEST ARBORIO RICE

The stubby, milky grains of arborio rice, once grown exclusively in Italy, are valued for their high starch content and the creaminess they bring to risotto. But does the best arborio rice have to come from Italy? To find out, we cooked up batches of Parmesan risotto with two domestically grown brands of arborio rice and four Italian imports; all brands are widely available in supermarkets. To our surprise, the winning rice, **RiceSelect Arborio Rice,** hailed not from the boot, but from the Lone Star State. Its "creamy, smooth" grains won over tasters with their "good bite."

SPRING VEGETABLE RISOTTO

CREAMY POLENTA WITH SAUTÉED VEGETABLES

VELVETY POLENTA IS OFTEN SERVED AS A SIDE DISH to roasted meats, stews, and braises, but it also makes an excellent vegetarian entrée when topped with sautéed vegetables. It's a dish that can quickly become anything but light, however, as it's often finished with a good helping of butter and cheese. We wanted to come up with our own hearty recipe for polenta and vegetables that didn't require a heavy hand with fatty ingredients for flavor or texture.

We quickly learned that whisking cornmeal into boiling salted water until velvety (the traditional Italian method) was more complicated than it looked. For starters, not just any kind of cornmeal would do. We learned that the best polenta is made with evenly ground, medium- to coarse-ground cornmeal, often packaged and sold (not surprisingly) as "polenta." Fine-ground cornmeal, such as the Quaker brand sold in supermarkets, is too powdery and made gluey polenta, as did instant polenta. Stone-ground cornmeal also produced lousy polenta because the grind was so uneven.

Having the right type of cornmeal was half the battle; cooking was the rest. We found that tradition has it right: The polenta had to be slowly added to the salted water. We found that if added all at once, it seized into a nearly immovable mass. It also had to be stirred frequently to avoid clumping. We tested varying cooking temperatures and found that a gentle, even heat was the key to preventing scorching and unlocking the cornmeal's smooth texture. A double boiler did the best job of providing an evenly heated environment, but the cooking time was prohibitively long—a daunting hour and a half. A heavy-bottomed saucepan proved to be a reliable alternative. Although this method required a bit more stirring to prevent scorching, it was capable of providing the necessary moderate, even heat. Best of all, the polenta was done in a fraction of the time—a mere 10 to 15 minutes.

Most recipes recommended stirring in generous amounts of butter and Parmesan at this point—typically 4 tablespoons of butter and 1½ cups of Parmesan for 1 cup of polenta—to help encourage the polenta's creamy and rich qualities. Looking to cut fat and calories, we tested more modest amounts of both butter and cheese. We were surprised to find that because our polenta method was already producing incredibly creamy results, tasters

were satisfied with a tablespoon of butter and ½ cup of Parmesan for a final boost in texture and flavor. Our polenta was now ready for the topping.

Mushrooms have a natural affinity with polenta—their chewy, meaty texture and robust flavor are an ideal contrast to the mild, creamy polenta—so they were an easy starting point for our vegetable topping. In the Italian countryside, foraged wild mushrooms would be standard for this dish, but luckily an easier, more frugal approach was to combine dried porcini mushrooms with easy-to-find cultivated mushrooms. Tasters liked the smaller size and meaty flavor of cremini mushrooms better than other readily available varieties, and we simply cooked them with the porcinis until they had shed their liquid and were lightly browned. Tasters were immediately impressed with the deep mushroom flavor we were able to achieve.

Onion was a logical next step, capable of cooking down along with the mushrooms without additional oil, and it added a pleasant sweetness. Dense vegetables like carrots were out of the running for this simple recipe

---

NOTES FROM THE TEST KITCHEN

MAKING POLENTA

Pour the cornmeal into the boiling water in a very slow stream while whisking constantly in a circular motion to prevent the cornmeal from clumping.

TAMING THE FLAME

A flame tamer (or heat diffuser) is a metal disk that can be fitted over an electric or gas burner to reduce the heat to a bare simmer, a necessity for well-made polenta. If you don't have a flame tamer (it costs less than $10 at most kitchen supply stores), you can easily make one.

Take a long sheet of heavy-duty foil and shape it into a 1-inch-thick ring that will fit on your burner. Make sure that the ring is of an even thickness so that the pot will rest flat on it.

because they required too long to cook, and more delicate selections like zucchini tasted watered-down. Light, bright-tasting spinach was a crowd-pleaser and took minimal time to wilt once incorporated into the mushrooms. Halved cherry tomatoes also made the cut. Tossed in at the end of cooking, they not only added some acidity but also released just enough moisture to create the perfect sauce to tie everything together. As a final touch, we added rosemary and garlic, natural inclusions for our rustic topping. This was a hearty meal big on flavor but not on fat or calories.

Creamy Polenta with Wild Mushrooms, Spinach, and Tomatoes

SERVES 4

Do not use fine-ground, stone-ground, or instant polenta in this recipe. If you do not have a heavy-bottomed saucepan, be sure to use a flame tamer (see page 152), or else the bottom of the pan will scorch.

TOPPING

- 2 pounds cremini mushrooms, halved if small, quartered if large
- 1 onion, halved and sliced thin
- 2 teaspoons olive oil
- ¼ ounce dried porcini mushrooms, rinsed and minced
- 1 teaspoon minced fresh rosemary
  Salt
- 2 garlic cloves, minced
- 12 ounces baby spinach (about 12 cups)
- 12 ounces cherry tomatoes (about 2 cups), halved
  Pepper

POLENTA

- 4 cups water
  Salt
- 1 cup coarsely ground cornmeal (see note)
- 1 ounce Parmesan cheese, grated (about ½ cup)
- 1 tablespoon unsalted butter, cut into ½-inch pieces
  Pepper

1. FOR THE TOPPING: Combine the cremini mushrooms, onion, oil, porcini mushrooms, rosemary, and ¼ teaspoon salt in a large Dutch oven. Cover and cook over medium-low heat, stirring occasionally, until the vegetables are softened, 10 to 12 minutes. Uncover, increase the heat to medium-high, and continue to cook, stirring occasionally, until the vegetables are lightly browned, 4 to 6 minutes longer.

2. Stir in the garlic and cook until fragrant, about 30 seconds. Add the spinach, one handful at a time, and cook until wilted, 3 to 5 minutes. Stir in the tomatoes and cook until just softened, about 2 minutes. Season with salt and pepper to taste. Cover and set aside off the heat to keep warm.

3. FOR THE POLENTA: Meanwhile, bring the water and ½ teaspoon salt to a boil in a large heavy-bottomed saucepan. Following the photo on page 152, slowly add the cornmeal while whisking constantly in a circular motion to prevent clumping.

4. Bring to a simmer, stirring constantly. Reduce the heat to low, cover, and cook, stirring often and vigorously (making sure to scrape the corners of the pot), until the polenta becomes soft and smooth, 10 to 15 minutes. Off the heat, vigorously stir in 6 tablespoons of the cheese and butter. Season with salt and pepper to taste.

5. Divide the polenta among 4 bowls. Divide the vegetable mixture evenly among the bowls, arranging it on top of the polenta. Sprinkle each portion with the remaining 2 tablespoons cheese and serve.

PER SERVING: Cal 340; Fat 8g; Sat fat 3.5g; Chol 15mg; Carb 53g; Protein 15g; Fiber 9g; Sodium 720mg

GLAZED TOFU

MADE BY PRESSING SOY MILK CURDS INTO A CAKE, tofu appears in myriad vegetarian recipes because it is a great meatless, low-calorie protein source. Tofu is a relatively blank canvas because of its mild flavor, so it is a natural candidate for additions in flavor and texture. You often see crispy-coated, pan-fried tofu paired with a highly flavorful glaze, and while the sauce is usually relatively lean, the crisp coating is not, typically the result of pan-frying in a good amount of oil. We wanted a lighter version with an appealing crisp crust made with as little oil as possible. As for a glaze, a lively, well-balanced sweet and spicy combination would do the trick.

We started our testing with the tofu. In the past we had found extra-firm tofu to be the best type to stir-fry, and we felt confident this would also be the case with pan-frying. But to be sure, we coated ¾-inch-thick slabs of extra-firm, firm, and soft tofu in cornstarch (a technique the test kitchen uses when stir-frying to encourage browning) and pan-fried each. Surprisingly, tasters agreed that the extra-firm tofu was their least favorite. They unanimously preferred the soft tofu for its creamy, custard-like texture. Because of its soft texture, we decided not to press it under a weighted plate to expel excess moisture, since we didn't want it to lose its shape. Instead, we simply cut the tofu into planks and placed it on multiple layers of paper towels to drain.

Next we set out to fine-tune our coating. A pure cornstarch coating had proved itself to be the best choice for stir-fries in previous test kitchen tests, and for this application it yielded a decently thin, crispy coating, but it barely browned. We saw room for improvement—we would need to be a bit more adventurous.

In our library of authentic Chinese cookbooks, we found some recipes where cornmeal was added to the cornstarch coating. We tried ½ cup of cornmeal mixed with ½ cup of cornstarch, but this was too gritty, so we cut back to ¼ cup of cornmeal with ¾ cup of cornstarch. This combination was just right, giving us perfect browning and improved texture. In fact, tasters enjoyed the coating so much that they wanted more, so we cut each tofu slab in half to make "fingers." Now we had a greater coating-to-tofu ratio that everyone agreed provided the right balance of crispy to creamy.

Up to this point, we'd been pan-frying in a traditional skillet, which is always a good bet for encouraging nice browning, but it required ½ cup of oil. So our next goal was to cut back on the oil (we would still need at least some to promote browning). We began testing quantities of canola oil and eventually found that 3 tablespoons in a large nonstick skillet was all we needed to promote a deep, even crust on all sides of the tofu. So after we had sautéed our tofu, we moved it to the oven to stay warm and crisp and turned our attention to the glaze.

A spicy-sweet chili glaze is a classic match for mild, creamy tofu, and it seemed like a good healthy, flavorful fit for our recipe. A little research showed that this glaze typically consists of five simple ingredients simmered together in a saucepan. We started with equal parts sugar, water, and rice vinegar, then added 2 teaspoons each of Asian chili-garlic sauce and cornstarch (for thickening). This was a good start, but tasters complained it was too sweet; cutting the sugar down to ⅓ cup brought things into balance. Adding some cilantro to the sauce gave it the perfect fresh finish, so all that was left to do was gently toss our crispy tofu in the pan with the glaze and dig in.

Sweet Chili Glazed Tofu
SERVES 6

We prefer the creamier texture of soft tofu here, but firm or extra-firm tofu will also work (it will taste drier). Be sure to handle the tofu gently or else it may break apart. Adjust the amount of Asian chili-garlic sauce to your liking. Serve with white rice.

TOFU

- 2 (14-ounce) blocks soft tofu, sliced crosswise into ¾-inch-thick slabs, each slab sliced into two 1-inch-wide fingers (see note)
- ¾ cup cornstarch
- ¼ cup cornmeal
- ¼ teaspoon salt
- ¼ teaspoon pepper
- 3 tablespoons canola oil

GLAZE

- ½ cup water
- ½ cup rice vinegar
- ⅓ cup sugar
- 4 garlic cloves, minced
- 2–3 teaspoons Asian chili-garlic sauce (see note)
- 2 teaspoons cornstarch
- ¼ cup chopped fresh cilantro

1. FOR THE TOFU: Adjust an oven rack to the middle position, place a paper towel–lined plate on the rack, and heat the oven to 200 degrees. Place a wire rack over a rimmed baking sheet and set aside.

2. Spread the tofu over several layers of paper towels and let sit for 20 minutes to drain slightly.

3. Whisk the cornstarch and cornmeal together in a shallow dish. Season the tofu with the salt and pepper. Working with a few pieces at a time, coat the tofu thoroughly with the cornstarch mixture, pressing to help it adhere, then transfer to the prepared wire rack.

4. Heat 2 tablespoons of the oil in a 12-inch non-stick skillet over medium-high heat until shimmering. Carefully lay half of the tofu in the skillet and cook until crisp and lightly golden on all sides, 8 to 10 minutes, turning as needed. Using a spatula, gently lift the tofu and transfer to the plate in the oven. Return the skillet to medium-high heat and repeat with the remaining 1 tablespoon oil and the remaining tofu.

5. FOR THE GLAZE: Wipe out the skillet with a wad of paper towels. Whisk the water, vinegar, sugar, garlic, chili-garlic sauce, and cornstarch together in a small bowl. Add the glaze mixture to the skillet, bring to a simmer over medium heat, and cook until thick and syrupy and reduced to about 1¼ cups, 2 to 3 minutes.

6. Off the heat, stir in the cilantro, return the tofu to the pan, and turn to coat with the glaze. Serve.

PER SERVING: **Cal** 240; **Fat** 12g; **Sat fat** 1g; **Chol** 0 mg; **Carb** 21g; **Protein** 10g; **Fiber** 1g; **Sodium** 170 mg

VARIATION

Honey-Mustard Glazed Tofu

Follow the recipe for Sweet Chili Glazed Tofu, substituting ½ cup orange juice for the rice vinegar, ⅓ cup honey for the sugar, 3 tablespoons Dijon mustard for the Asian chili-garlic sauce, and 3 scallions, sliced thin, for the cilantro.

PER SERVING: **Cal** 280; **Fat** 12g; **Sat fat** 1g; **Chol** 0mg; **Carb** 32g; **Protein** 11g; **Fiber** 1g; **Sodium** 280mg

VEGETABLE CURRY

VEGETABLE CURRIES ARE AN IDEAL CHOICE FOR THE healthful cook—they are boldly flavored while low in fat and are as hearty and satisfying as a traditional meat curry. But vegetable curries can be complicated affairs. Sure, when flavorful beef or lamb is the main ingredient, even a mediocre recipe usually yields a decent outcome. But vegetable curry is a different story: It's all too easy to turn out a second-rate (if not inedible) dish. Delicate vegetables are often watery carriers for the sauce, offering little personality of their own. We wanted something worthwhile—a simple, streamlined vegetable curry that could still deliver tender, flavorful vegetables coated in a robust curry sauce.

Some curries are made with exotic whole and ground spices (fenugreek, asafetida, dried rose petals, and so on), but we decided to limit ourselves to everyday ground spices typical in curries, such as cumin, cloves, cardamom, cinnamon, and coriander. Most of the homemade spice mixtures we made were fine, but none proved remarkable. We had been reluctant to use store-bought curry powder and garam masala—both common spices added to curries—assuming their flavor would be inferior to that of our homemade blends, but at this point it seemed worth a try. We were surprised when tasters liked the store-bought versions nearly as well as our

homemade mix. It turns out that store-bought curry powder and garam masala contain some of the exotic spices we had dismissed at the outset. To improve their flavor, we tried cooking the spices with a little oil, a process known as "blooming," until their fragrance emerged. This simple step took less than a minute and turned commercial curry powder and garam masala into flavor powerhouses.

With the spices settled, we turned to building the rest of our flavor base. Many classic recipes begin with sautéing generous amounts of onion, which adds depth and body to the sauce, so we started there, adding the onion to the spices and oil already in the pot. In almost all curry recipes, equal amounts of garlic and ginger are then added to the onions, and we found no reason to stray from this well-balanced method. Wanting to take our meatless sauce to the next level, we also stirred in a minced fresh chile for heat and a spoonful of tomato paste for sweetness. The latter ingredient was decidedly inauthentic, but we found it really helped. As the onions caramelized with the other ingredients, the tomato paste began to darken and coat the bottom of the pan, mimicking the rich fond that develops when browning meat and supercharging our curry base.

For the vegetables, we decided to include chickpeas and potatoes for heartiness, along with one firm and one soft vegetable for balanced texture. Eventually, we settled on a classic pairing of cauliflower and peas. Although the combination of textures and colors was good, the vegetables were a bit bland; we needed to find a way to coax more flavor from them. Oven-roasting the potatoes was a good start, but it took too much time, so next we tried browning the potatoes along with the onions. This unconventional move was a huge success, substantially boosting the flavor of the potatoes.

Could other vegetables be amplified in flavor as well? An Indian cooking method called bhuna involves sautéing spices and main ingredients together to enhance and meld flavors. We tried this technique with the cauliflower, and all our tasters agreed it developed a richer, more complex flavor.

As for the peas, they turned to mush when cooked with the other vegetables, so we waited until the end to stir them in to ensure they held their bright flavor and color. Finally, we determined that a combination of water and pureed canned tomatoes, along with a little yogurt, stirred in at the end, provided the necessary liquid base for our curry; they provided good flavor but

VEGETABLE CURRY WITH POTATOES, CAULIFLOWER, PEAS, AND CHICKPEAS

didn't overpower the flavor of the vegetables. Cilantro stirred in at the end lent a last touch of brightness. With that, we had created a full-flavored, satisfying vegetable curry that was simple to prepare.

Vegetable Curry with Potatoes, Cauliflower, Peas, and Chickpeas

SERVES 6

To make this dish spicier, add the chile seeds. You can substitute ½ teaspoon ground coriander, ¼ teaspoon pepper, ⅛ teaspoon ground cardamom, and ⅛ teaspoon ground cinnamon for the garam masala in step 2. Serve with white rice.

1 (14.5-ounce) can diced tomatoes
3 tablespoons canola oil
4 teaspoons sweet or mild curry powder
1 teaspoon garam masala (see note)
2 onions, minced (about 2 cups)
12 ounces red potatoes (2 to 3 medium), cut into ½-inch pieces
3 garlic cloves, minced
1 tablespoon grated or minced fresh ginger
1 tablespoon tomato paste
1 serrano chile, stemmed, seeded, and minced (see note)
½ head cauliflower (about 1 pound), trimmed, cored, and cut into 1-inch florets (about 4 cups)
1¼ cups water
1 (15-ounce) can chickpeas, drained and rinsed

SALT

1½ cups frozen peas (about 6 ounces)
½ cup plain low-fat yogurt
¼ cup chopped fresh cilantro

1. Pulse the tomatoes, with their juice, in a food processor until mostly smooth, about 8 pulses.

2. Heat 2 tablespoons of the oil in a large Dutch oven over medium-high heat until shimmering. Add the curry powder and garam masala, and cook until fragrant, about 10 seconds. Add the onions and potatoes, and cook, stirring occasionally, until the onions are browned and the potatoes are softened slightly, about 10 minutes.

3. Reduce the heat to medium. Clear the center of the pot, stir in the remaining 1 tablespoon oil, garlic, ginger, tomato paste, and chile, and cook until fragrant, about 30 seconds. Add the cauliflower and cook, stirring occasionally, until the spices coat the florets, about 2 minutes.

4. Stir in the processed tomatoes, water, chickpeas, and ½ teaspoon salt, scraping up any browned bits. Bring to a simmer, cover, and cook, stirring occasionally, until the vegetables are tender, about 15 minutes.

5. Stir in the peas and continue to cook until heated through, about 2 minutes longer. Off the heat, stir in the yogurt and cilantro and season with salt to taste. Serve.

PER 1⅓-CUP SERVING: Cal 240; Fat 8g; Sat fat 1g; Chol 0mg; Carb 36g; Protein 9g; Fiber 8g; Sodium 440mg

VARIATION

Vegetable Curry with Sweet Potatoes, Eggplant, Green Beans, and Chickpeas

Follow the recipe for Vegetable Curry with Potatoes, Cauliflower, Peas, and Chickpeas, substituting 12 ounces sweet potatoes, peeled and cut into ½-inch pieces, for the red potatoes and 1 medium eggplant (about 1 pound), cut into ½-inch pieces, for the cauliflower. Add 6 ounces green beans, trimmed and cut into 1-inch pieces, with the eggplant in step 3, and omit the peas.

PER 1⅓-CUP SERVING: Cal 230; Fat 8g; Sat fat 1g; Chol 0mg; Carb 35g; Protein 7g; Fiber 9g; Sodium 450mg

NOTES FROM THE TEST KITCHEN

CURRY IN A HURRY
Hoping we could skip the step of grinding our own spices for curry, we substituted store-bought curry powder and garam masala. Tasters found this shortcut to be long on flavor, provided we chose the right brands and toasted the spice blends in a small amount of oil in a skillet. We prefer **Penzeys Curry Powder** (left) and **McCormick Garam Masala** (right).

VEGETABLE TART

AMONG ALL THE SAVORY TARTS AND PIES, ONE OF OUR favorites is the vegetable tart, a simple dish with a true emphasis on fresh vegetables. The other basic components—cheese and crust—simply play supporting roles. A vegetable tart makes a perfect vegetarian meal, but we knew right off the bat that the dish could use a leaner look, as the cheese and crust turn this seemingly light meal into a rare indulgence. With this in mind, we set out to come up with a fresh vegetable tart without the guilt.

We focused first on the crust. We liked the classic appearance of a traditional tart shell, and we needed one sturdy enough to support the toppings. We agreed puff pastry was out since it's too flaky, and we wanted something with less butter and shortening than regular pie dough. After some additional research, we learned that olive oil crusts are traditional in many regions of Italy. This sounded like a concept worth exploring.

Cobbling together our own recipe, we decided to avoid the more temperamental rolled-out crust in favor of a simpler press-in crust. Our first attempt at an olive oil press-in crust fared well, though its texture was much too tender—more like a shortbread than a sturdy tart crust. Reducing the amount of oil made it sturdier, but we had to be careful. Too little oil led to a chewy crust. Six tablespoons (compared to the 8 tablespoons we had been using) proved to be the happy medium. We also tried incorporating some whole wheat flour into the mix for additional strength and found that a 3-to-1 ratio of all-purpose to whole wheat flour worked the best, lending strength without making the crust tough. The whole wheat flour also gave the crust a rustic flavor that tasters appreciated.

Parbaking the crust before adding any filling ensured that the crust baked evenly, and at the recommendation of a fellow test cook, we also sprinkled a thin layer of Parmesan over the bottom of the shell. Not only did this add flavor and texture with little impact on the overall fat content, but it created a layer of protection from the moist vegetable topping, ensuring that our crust would stay crisp and sliceable.

Next we turned to the filling. Since we wanted the vegetables to be the star, we didn't need much cheese filling (over and above the Parmesan), just a thin, creamy layer to hold on to the vegetables. We made two tarts with shredded mozzarella—one with part-skim and one with reduced-fat—and a third tart with a mixture of part-skim ricotta and reduced-fat mozzarella. The two mozzarella-only versions yielded unappealing, rubbery layers of cheese that congealed when cooled. The ricotta mixture, however, was a hit. The ricotta provided just the right creamy texture, and the mozzarella helped hold the filling together and prevent it from oozing too much when the tart was sliced.

Moving on to the vegetables, first we had to determine which ones to use. Since our parbaked crust required little additional cooking, we needed to pick vegetables that would cook quickly. After some experimentation, we decided to stick with a fairly typical Italian combination of sliced zucchini and plum tomatoes—both capable of turning perfectly tender in a relatively short time. As we suspected, once in the oven, the zucchini and plum tomatoes exuded moisture during cooking, and the resulting tart was a waterlogged mess. To fix the problem, we salted the vegetables after slicing them and allowed them to drain on paper towels for 30 minutes, then blotted them dry and layered them in the shell over the cheese. This tart came out of the oven with just a slightly glossy sheen of moisture.

For a final flavor boost, we drizzled a touch of olive oil mixed with minced garlic and thyme over the tart before baking. When we pulled the tart out of the oven, we let it cool for a few minutes and sprinkled it with some chopped fresh basil. No longer in danger of tipping the scales, our vegetable tart was light but still full of bright vegetable flavor.

NOTES FROM THE TEST KITCHEN

OUR FAVORITE TART PAN

Tart pans can be divided into three basic categories based on materials: tinned steel, nonstick, and everything else—ranging from heavy ceramic to floppy silicone. Tarts baked in the tinned steel pan performed better than the rest. They browned evenly and released effortlessly. So stick with tinned steel pans like our favorite, the **Kaiser Tinplate 9-Inch Quiche Pan,** $9.00.

Vegetable Tart

SERVES 6

The filling in this tart is relatively thin, so be sure to press the dough only ¾ inch up the sides of the tart pan. We like the flavor and creaminess of part-skim ricotta here; do not use fat-free ricotta. Serve with a salad to round out this light, summery meal.

CRUST

- ¾ cup plus 3 tablespoons (about 4⅔ ounces) unbleached all-purpose flour
- ¼ cup plus 1 tablespoon (about 1¾ ounces) whole wheat flour
- 1 tablespoon sugar
- ½ teaspoon salt
- 6 tablespoons extra-virgin olive oil
- ¼ cup ice water
- 1 ounce Parmesan cheese, grated (about ½ cup)

FILLING

- 1 small zucchini (about 6 ounces), ends trimmed, sliced ¼ inch thick
  Salt
- 2 plum tomatoes, cored and sliced ¼ inch thick
- 2 teaspoons extra-virgin olive oil
- 1 garlic clove, minced
- ½ cup part-skim ricotta cheese (see note)
- 1 ounce reduced-fat mozzarella cheese, shredded (about ¼ cup)
  Pepper
- 2 tablespoons chopped fresh basil

1. FOR THE CRUST: Process the all-purpose flour, whole wheat flour, sugar, and salt together in a food processor until combined. Drizzle the oil over the flour mixture and pulse until the mixture resembles coarse sand, about 12 pulses. Add 3 tablespoons of the ice water and continue to process until large clumps of dough form and no powdery bits remain, about 5 seconds. If the dough doesn't clump, add the remaining 1 tablespoon water and pulse to incorporate, about 4 pulses. (The dough should feel quite sticky.)

2. Tear the dough into walnut-sized pieces and pat them into a 9-inch tart pan with a removable bottom, pressing the dough ¾ inch up the sides of the pan. Lay plastic wrap over the dough and smooth out any bumps using the palm of your hand. Leaving the plastic wrap on top of the dough, place the tart pan on a large plate and freeze the tart shell until firm, about 30 minutes.

3. Adjust an oven rack to the middle position and heat the oven to 375 degrees. Set the tart pan on a large baking sheet and remove the plastic wrap. Press a double layer of foil into the frozen tart shell and over the edges of the pan and fill with pie weights. Bake until the tart shell is golden brown and set, 30 to 40 minutes, rotating the baking sheet halfway through. Transfer the baking sheet to a wire rack and carefully remove the weights and foil.

4. Sprinkle the Parmesan evenly over the bottom of the tart shell, return the baking sheet to the oven, and continue to bake until the cheese is golden, 5 to 10 minutes longer. Let the tart shell cool on the baking sheet while making the filling. Increase the oven temperature to 425 degrees.

5. FOR THE FILLING: While the tart shell is cooling, spread the zucchini and tomatoes over several layers of paper towels. Sprinkle with ½ teaspoon salt and let drain for 30 minutes; gently blot the tops of the zucchini and tomatoes dry with more paper towels.

6. Combine 1 teaspoon of the oil and garlic in a small bowl. In a separate bowl, mix the remaining 1 teaspoon oil, ricotta, and mozzarella together and season with salt and pepper to taste.

7. Spread the ricotta mixture evenly over the bottom of the tart shell. Shingle the zucchini and tomatoes attractively on top of the ricotta in concentric circles. Drizzle the vegetables with the oil mixture. Bake the tart on the baking sheet until the cheese is bubbling and the vegetables are slightly wilted, 20 to 25 minutes, rotating the baking sheet halfway through.

8. Let the tart cool on the baking sheet for 10 minutes, then sprinkle with the basil. To serve, remove the outer metal ring of the tart pan, slide a thin metal spatula between the tart and the tart pan bottom, and carefully slide the tart onto a platter or cutting board. Serve warm.

PER SERVING: Cal 300; Fat 19g; Sat fat 4g; Chol 15mg; Carb 23g; Protein 9g; Fiber 2g; Sodium 540mg

SMOKED PORK LOIN

GRILLED GLAZED CHICKEN BREASTS

FROM A HEALTHY DINER'S PERSPECTIVE, THERE'S A lot to admire about a perfectly grilled chicken breast. Chicken is an ideal protein—convenient and lean— and the grill furthers its appeal by imparting smoky flavor while requiring little additional fat. Add a glaze and a grilled chicken breast is elevated to a flavorful, all-appealing dinner. But don't let the everyday nature of this grilled favorite fool you: This ideal isn't easy to achieve. Meat that is overcooked and dry and a glaze that is distractingly sweet and burned are too often the reality. In spite of these hurdles, we knew we could come up with a reliable method for producing tender, juicy chicken with an attractively glazed exterior that was both flavorful and balanced.

Just about every cookbook offers a way to grill bone-less, skinless chicken breasts, but we have found (after a lot of trial and error) that high heat and a single-level fire (where the heat is even across the grill) allow for the most success. Medium- and low-heat fires do not provide a good sear, and the interior of the chicken over-cooks by the time any color appears on the exterior. High heat produces the most attractive chicken breasts, turning them a deep golden brown; cooked at this tem-perature, the chicken is done in only three minutes per side, so it doesn't dry out.

Working with this method, we grilled up a few chicken breasts, and sure enough, they developed a beautiful, bronze exterior within minutes. But when we began adding a glaze (we went with a simple fruit preserve for our working glaze), things quickly went downhill. The glaze immediately began to burn from the high temperature of the grill, and by the time we developed a suitable coating on the breasts, they were completely overcooked.

We then tried cooking over a two-level fire, which provides a hotter side and a cooler side of the grill. We started the chicken breasts over high heat to brown the exterior, then moved them to the cooler part to fin-ish cooking and to coat them with the glaze. This meat was cooked through perfectly, and our glaze coated the chicken but wasn't burned. Now all we had to do was fine-tune the glaze.

A lot of glazes are overwhelmingly sweet because they are made mostly of honey, maple syrup, or brown sugar.

These types of glazes may be fine for a rich, salty ham, but when it comes to mild chicken, a glaze that is more savory makes better sense. We wanted to develop a vari-ety of glazes that would complement our chicken, and because we would already be out at the grill, we also wanted recipes that wouldn't require much precooking on the stovetop.

Our first stop was the test kitchen pantry, where we scanned the shelves for ingredients thick enough to serve as a base. We decided the fruit preserves we had been working with would be a good starting point for one of our glazes (we settled on apricot), though we would need to keep their sweetness in check. We also decided to make a glaze with ketchup and another with hoisin sauce. Neither of these latter options is overly sweet, and both have a thick, sticky consistency that we hoped would cling nicely to the chicken during grilling.

We began by adding hefty amounts of tangy Dijon and whole grain mustards to the preserves, then pulsed the mixture in a food processor to puree it. This glaze was mildly sweet and complemented the grilled chicken nicely. For our ketchup-based glaze, we created a fla-vor profile like a barbecue sauce with additions of cider vinegar, brown sugar, and liquid smoke, and the hoisin lent itself to an Asian-inspired angle with sesame oil, rice vinegar, and scallions.

Because these glazes weren't gloppy and thick like sugar-based glazes, a thin coating was all that clung to the chicken. No matter: Adding bold ingredients such as shallot, garlic, ginger, herbs, and spices ensured that a little went a long way, and passing extra glaze at the table to use as a dipping sauce boosted the flavor of every bite.

NOTES FROM THE TEST KITCHEN

HOW HOT IS YOUR FIRE?
To determine the heat level of the cooking grate itself, heat up the grill and hold your hand 5 inches above the cooking grate, counting how long you can comfortably keep it there. Note that this works with both charcoal and gas grills.

Hot fire	2 seconds
Medium-hot fire	3 to 4 seconds
Medium fire	5 to 6 seconds
Medium-low fire	7 seconds
Low fire	10 seconds

Grilled Chicken Breasts with Apricot-Mustard Glaze

SERVES 4

Before glazing the chicken, be sure to reserve ¼ cup of the glaze for serving.

GLAZE

- ½ cup apricot preserves
- 1 small shallot, minced (about 1 tablespoon)
- 4 teaspoons whole grain mustard
- 4 teaspoons Dijon mustard
- 1 tablespoon water
- ⅛ teaspoon salt
- ⅛ teaspoon pepper

CHICKEN

- 4 (6-ounce) boneless, skinless chicken breasts, trimmed
- 1 tablespoon canola oil
- ⅛ teaspoon salt
- ⅛ teaspoon pepper

1. FOR THE GLAZE: Process the apricot preserves, shallot, whole grain mustard, Dijon mustard, water, salt, and pepper together in a blender (or food processor) until smooth. Measure out and reserve ¼ cup of the glaze for serving.

2A. FOR A CHARCOAL GRILL: Open the bottom grill vents completely. Light a large chimney starter filled with charcoal briquettes (100 briquettes; 6 quarts). When the coals are hot, spread two-thirds of them evenly over the grill, then pour the remaining coals over half of the grill. Set the cooking grate in place, cover, and heat the grill until hot, about 5 minutes.

2B. FOR A GAS GRILL: Turn all the burners to high, cover, and heat the grill until hot, about 15 minutes. (Adjust the burners as needed to maintain a hot fire; see page 162.)

3. Clean and oil the cooking grate. Pat the chicken breasts dry with paper towels, brush with the oil, and season with the salt and pepper. Place the chicken on the grill (on the hotter part of the grill if using charcoal) and cook (covered if using gas) until well browned on both sides, 5 to 7 minutes, flipping the breasts halfway through.

4. Slide the chicken to the cooler part of the grill if using charcoal, or turn all the burners to medium (adjust the burners as needed to maintain a medium fire; see page 162) if using gas. Continue to cook, flipping and brushing the chicken with the remaining glaze, until well glazed and the thickest part of the breasts registers 160 to 165 degrees on an instant-read thermometer, 5 to 7 minutes longer.

5. Transfer the chicken to a platter, tent loosely with foil, and let rest for 5 minutes. Serve with the reserved ¼ cup glaze.

PER SERVING: Cal 330; Fat 6g; Sat fat 1g; Chol 100mg; Carb 28g; Protein 40g; Fiber 0g; Sodium 490mg

VARIATIONS

Grilled Chicken Breasts with Barbecue Glaze

Process ½ cup ketchup, 2 tablespoons brown sugar, 1 tablespoon low-sodium soy sauce, 1 tablespoon cider vinegar, 1 tablespoon Dijon mustard, 1 garlic clove, minced, ½ teaspoon chili powder, and ¼ teaspoon liquid smoke in a blender (or food processor) until smooth. Measure out and reserve ¼ cup of the glaze for serving. Follow the recipe for Grilled Chicken Breasts with Apricot-Mustard Glaze, substituting the barbecue glaze for the apricot–mustard glaze.

PER SERVING: Cal 280; Fat 6g; Sat fat 1g; Chol 100mg; Carb 15g; Protein 40g; Fiber 0g; Sodium 740mg

Grilled Chicken Breasts with Hoisin-Sesame Glaze

Process ⅓ cup hoisin sauce, 2 tablespoons rice vinegar, 1 tablespoon dry sherry, 1 teaspoon toasted sesame oil, 1 tablespoon grated or minced fresh ginger, 3 scallions, chopped, and 1 garlic clove, minced, in a blender (or food processor) until smooth. Measure out and reserve ¼ cup of the glaze for serving. Follow the recipe for Grilled Chicken Breasts with Apricot-Mustard Glaze, substituting the hoisin-sesame glaze for the apricot–mustard glaze.

PER SERVING: Cal 280; Fat 7g; Sat fat 1g; Chol 100mg; Carb 13g; Protein 40g; Fiber 0g; Sodium 910mg

GRILLED STUFFED CHICKEN BREASTS

HAVING MASTERED PERFECT GRILLED GLAZED chicken breasts (see page 162), we felt our next recipe should be about putting the flavor inside the chicken instead of outside. Stuffing a chicken breast is a great way to dress up an otherwise plain main course, but it is one that is rarely well executed. Most recipes insist on cramming the breasts full of ingredients that are short on flavor and full of fat and calories, and they do little besides take up space that is tight to begin with. Then there is the issue of getting the stuffing to actually stay put. We wanted to solve both problems and create a lighter grilled stuffed chicken breast recipe.

After testing both bone-in and boneless chicken breasts, we found that bones were awkward to navigate around when it came to stuffing, so we chose quick-cooking boneless, skinless breasts. With a quick swipe of the knife, we cut a stuffing-ready pocket in each breast, and as long as we kept the size of the opening to an inch or so, we figured we could easily seal each stuffed breast with a toothpick.

Because chicken breasts are so lean and mild, we wanted a filling that would add moisture as well as a big hit of flavor. We didn't have much room in each pocket, so we needed something potent. After a few batches, we ruled out stuffings whose ingredients were combined in a food processor—they held together well but were inevitably pasty. Chunkier vegetable fillings were also out, since they were too awkward and required too much work to stuff into the breasts. Herb mixtures (made with chopped herbs and a little olive oil) packed a lot of flavor and were easy to work with, but on the grill they oozed out of the chicken. But this concept had the most potential, so next we tried binding the herb filling with some Parmesan before stuffing the breasts. This particular cheese failed at keeping the filling inside the chicken, but the idea seemed sound, so we tried different cheeses. Creamy and strong-flavored fontina, pepper Jack, and feta worked better, and a little went a long way.

The cheese was a noticeable improvement (in both flavor and binding power), but our filling still needed a little help to hold together just right. We had been reluctant to use bread crumbs, a popular base in stuffed chicken breast recipes but one that has a tendency to make bland, dense stuffings. But we planned to add only a small amount to our herb stuffing, just enough to keep

it from oozing out. Sure enough, just 3 tablespoons of bread crumbs gave us a stable filling without turning it dense, and the flavorful herbs still took center stage. (When coming up with variations on this recipe, we found that crushed corn tortillas also worked well.)

Simply grilling the stuffed chicken breasts over high heat (which is how we cook plain boneless, skinless chicken breasts on the grill) caused the outside to burn before the inside was even warm. Next we tried a two-level fire, which had been the key to our grilled glazed chicken, starting on the hot side and finishing on the cooler side that had only minimal heat. But even this was too much for our stuffed chicken, and it overcooked on the outside before cooking through. A half-grill fire with all the heat concentrated on one side proved to be the answer. We seared the breasts on the hotter part of the grill, then transferred them to the cooler part and covered them with the lid, creating an oven-like effect, to finish up. For even more protection against drying out, we decided to employ a light marinade of olive oil, lemon juice, and garlic, which would also boost the flavor. A 30-minute soak gave the chicken the protection it needed and the extra flavor we were hoping for. We realized that some of our marinade could also be swapped in for the oil in the stuffing, adding an extra touch of zest while simultaneously cutting out some more fat. These chicken breasts were perfectly cooked, and they were flavorful inside and out.

Grilled Herb-Stuffed Chicken Breasts
SERVES 4

You will need 4 sturdy, uncolored wooden toothpicks for this recipe.

- 1 slice high-quality white sandwich bread, torn into pieces
- 2 tablespoons extra-virgin olive oil
- 1 tablespoon water
- 3 garlic cloves, minced
- 2 teaspoons fresh lemon juice plus ¼ teaspoon grated lemon zest
- ½ teaspoon sugar
- ¼ teaspoon salt
- ¼ teaspoon pepper
- 1 cup chopped fresh basil
- 2 ounces fontina cheese, shredded (about ½ cup)
- 4 (6-ounce) boneless, skinless chicken breasts, trimmed

1. Adjust an oven rack to the middle position and heat the oven to 350 degrees.

2. Pulse the bread in a food processor to coarse crumbs, about 10 pulses. Spread the crumbs on a rimmed baking sheet and bake, stirring occasionally, until golden brown and dry, 10 to 12 minutes. Meanwhile, whisk the oil, water, garlic, lemon juice, lemon zest, sugar, salt, and pepper together in a small bowl. Transfer the bread crumbs to a medium bowl and set aside to cool to room temperature, then stir in 2 tablespoons of the oil mixture, basil, and cheese.

3. Following the photos, use a sharp knife to cut a 1-inch opening in the thickest part of each chicken

breast, then cut the pocket for the filling. Place one-quarter of the filling in each pocket. Seal the pockets with toothpicks.

4. Transfer the chicken to a baking dish, pour the remaining oil mixture over the top, and turn to coat. Cover with plastic wrap and refrigerate for at least 30 minutes, or up to 1 hour.

5A. FOR A CHARCOAL GRILL: Open the bottom grill vents completely. Light a large chimney starter filled with charcoal briquettes (100 briquettes; 6 quarts). When the coals are hot, spread them in an even layer over half of the grill. Set the cooking grate in place, cover, and open the lid vents completely. Heat the grill until hot, about 5 minutes.

5B. FOR A GAS GRILL: Turn all the burners to high, cover, and heat the grill until hot, about 15 minutes. Leave the primary burner on high and turn off the other burner(s). (Adjust the primary burner as needed to maintain a hot fire and a low fire on opposite sides of the grill; see page 162.)

6. Clean and oil the cooking grate. Place the chicken on the hotter part of the grill, directly over the coals and flames. Cook (covered if using gas) until well browned on both sides, 5 to 7 minutes, flipping the breasts halfway through.

7. Slide the chicken breasts to the cooler part of the grill, away from the coals and flames. Cover (positioning the lid vents over the chicken breasts if using charcoal) and continue to cook until the thickest part of the breasts registers 160 to 165 degrees on an instant-read thermometer, 10 to 15 minutes longer.

8. Transfer the chicken to a platter, tent loosely with foil, and let rest for 5 minutes. Remove the toothpicks and serve.

PER SERVING: **Cal** 330; **Fat** 14g; **Sat fat** 4.5g; **Chol** 115mg; **Carb** 5g; **Protein** 44g; **Fiber** 0g; **Sodium** 400mg

VARIATIONS

Tex-Mex Grilled Stuffed Chicken Breasts

Adjust an oven rack to the lower-middle position and heat the oven to 350 degrees. Place 2 corn tortillas on a rimmed baking sheet, lightly coat with vegetable oil spray, and bake until golden brown, 20 to 25 minutes, flipping the tortillas halfway through. Set the tortillas aside to cool to room temperature, then crush into coarse crumbs. Follow the recipe for Grilled Herb-Stuffed Chicken Breasts, substituting the crushed corn tortillas for the bread crumbs, lime juice for the lemon

NOTES FROM THE TEST KITCHEN

STUFFING BONELESS CHICKEN BREASTS

1. Use a sharp paring knife to cut a 1-inch opening in the thickest part of the chicken breast.

2. Gently work the knife back and forth until the pocket extends deep into the breast.

3. Use a small spoon to scoop the filling into each chicken breast. Gently press down on the breast to distribute the stuffing evenly.

4. Seal in the filling by threading a toothpick through the center of the pocket about ¼ inch from the edge.

juice, lime zest for the lemon zest, cilantro for the basil, and pepper Jack cheese, shredded, for the fontina.

PER SERVING: Cal 350; **Fat** 15g; **Sat fat** 4g; **Chol** 115mg; **Carb** 9g; **Protein** 43g; **Fiber** 1g; **Sodium** 360mg

Greek Grilled Stuffed Chicken Breasts
Follow the recipe for Grilled Herb-Stuffed Chicken Breasts, substituting ¾ cup chopped fresh parsley plus ¼ cup chopped fresh oregano for the basil, and feta cheese, crumbled, for the fontina.

PER SERVING: Cal 320; **Fat** 13g; **Sat fat** 4g; **Chol** 110mg; **Carb** 6g; **Protein** 42g; **Fiber** 1g; **Sodium** 450mg

BARBECUED PULLED CHICKEN

PULLED PORK IS ALWAYS A BIG HIT AT BACKYARD barbecues, but this Carolina-style favorite—slow-cooked pork butt shredded and served on hamburger buns with a tangy sauce—isn't much of a hit on the health front because pork butt is inherently fatty. Luckily, a lighter alternative exists: barbecued pulled chicken. Dressed and served in the same way, this lesser-known player has the appealing smoked flavor and tender texture of its fattier counterpart without the guilt.

We had no problem finding existing pulled chicken recipes that were quick and simple. Boneless, skinless chicken breasts were quickly grilled, shredded, then tossed with a store-bought sauce, so it wasn't surprising that the results were dry, bland chicken covered in one-dimensional sauce. We needed to create a recipe that would make sure folks took the pulled chicken sandwich seriously.

Typical recipes for barbecued pulled chicken call for whole leg quarters, a reasonable choice since the additional fat in the legs and thighs helps to keep the meat moist. While this cut is certainly lower in fat than pork shoulder, we thought we could cut back even further. We began by testing two different versions of a lighter pulled chicken—one batch made with a half-and-half combination of bone-in breasts and thighs, and another made from only bone-in breasts—grilling each over direct heat, then shredding the meat and tossing it with a basic sauce. Tasters were pleased with both, but in the end they preferred the combination of breasts and thighs, accepting the slightly higher amount of fat for the added tenderness and moisture.

Ready to fine-tune the cooking method, we first placed a packet of wood chips on the fire, waited for it to begin smoking, then cooked the chicken right over the heat. Once it was cooked through and cooled, we discarded the skin, shredded the meat, and tossed it with our favorite homemade sauce. Tasters were quick to point out that the meat didn't develop much smoky flavor in the 20 minutes of cooking time, so we turned to indirect heat and a low-and-slow method. This time, we cooked the chicken for 45 minutes. This meat was moist and tender, and it had picked up that smoky flavor we were after. Cooking the chicken skin-side up enabled the rendered fat from the skin to baste the meat, ensuring it wouldn't turn dry, and setting a roasting pan beneath the chicken caught any fat that dripped through the cooking grate.

Up to this point, we had been shredding the meat by hand, but we wondered what would happen if we took a shortcut and pulsed the meat in the food processor. This meat was a bit too fine, but we noticed it absorbed sauce well—better, in fact, than the hand-shredded meat. So the next time we hand-shredded the larger

NOTES FROM THE TEST KITCHEN

MAKING SMOKE WITH WOOD CHIPS
Wood chips add great smoky flavor to grilled foods; we prefer to use chips rather than chunks since they're easier to handle and don't take as long to soak before they're put on the fire. Different types of wood will lend slightly different flavors to the food you are cooking. We don't call for a particular type in this book, so feel free to experiment.

OUR PICK OF THE PICKLES
Every good barbecue spread should include pickles in the mix, and we sampled seven brands of bread-and-butter pickles, beloved for their sweet-and-sour tang and snappy crunch, to find our favorite. We learned that although some form of sweetener is essential for preserving and flavoring a bread-and-butter chip, many brands have opted to replace real sugar with cheaper high-fructose corn syrup. Five of the seven pickle brands we sampled list this shelf-stable syrup as their second ingredient, which led to complaints about "artificial sweetness" and "syrupy" flavors. Our favorite brand, **Cascadian Farm Bread and Butter Chips,** are made with real sugar, and our tasters could tell the difference.

pieces, and the smaller, crustier bits went into the food processor. Mixed together, they gave us the perfect texture—the chicken looked, in fact, just like pulled pork. To enable the chicken to absorb even more sauce, we heated it up in a saucepan with some of the sauce just before serving. Flavorful and tender, our pulled chicken had now earned its spot with the best of the barbecue classics.

Barbecued Pulled Chicken
SERVES 4

If using kosher chicken, do not brine; if brining the chicken, do not season with salt in step 4. Serve the pulled chicken on hamburger buns or sandwich bread with pickles alongside.

SAUCE

- 1 small onion, minced (about ½ cup)
- 1 teaspoon canola oil
- Salt
- 1 garlic clove, minced
- ½ teaspoon chili powder
- ⅛ teaspoon cayenne pepper
- ⅔ cup ketchup
- 3 tablespoons molasses
- 4 teaspoons cider vinegar
- 1 tablespoon Worcestershire sauce
- 1 tablespoon Dijon mustard
- Black pepper

CHICKEN

- 1 (13 by 9-inch) disposable aluminum roasting pan (if using charcoal)
- 2 cups wood chips, soaked, drained, and sealed in a foil packet (see page 166)
- 1½ pounds bone-in, skin-on split chicken breasts, trimmed (see page 61), brined if desired (see note; see page 74)
- 1½ pounds bone-in, skin-on chicken thighs, trimmed, brined if desired (see note; see page 74)
- ⅛ teaspoon salt
- ⅛ teaspoon black pepper

1. FOR THE SAUCE: Combine the onion, oil, and ⅛ teaspoon salt in a small saucepan. Cover and cook over medium-low heat, stirring occasionally, until softened, 8 to 10 minutes. Stir in the garlic, chili powder, and cayenne, and cook until fragrant, about 30 seconds.

Whisk in the ketchup, molasses, vinegar, Worcestershire, and mustard.

2. Bring the sauce to a simmer, reduce the heat to medium-low, and cook, stirring occasionally, until thickened and reduced to about 1 cup, about 10 minutes. Season with salt and black pepper to taste.

3A. FOR A CHARCOAL GRILL: Open the bottom grill vents halfway and place the roasting pan in the center of the grill. Light a large chimney starter filled with charcoal briquettes (100 briquettes; 6 quarts). When the coals are hot, pour them into two even piles on either side of the roasting pan. Place the wood chip packet on top of one of the coal piles. Set the cooking grate in place, cover, and open the lid vents halfway. Heat the grill until hot and the wood chips begin to smoke heavily, about 5 minutes.

3B. FOR A GAS GRILL: Place the wood chip packet directly on the primary burner. Turn all the burners to high, cover, and heat the grill until hot and the wood chips begin to smoke heavily, about 15 minutes. Turn all the burners to medium-low. (Adjust the burners as needed to maintain the grill temperature around 350 degrees.)

4. Pat the chicken breasts and thighs dry with paper towels and season with the salt and black pepper. Clean and oil the cooking grate. Place the chicken, skin-side up, on the grill (in the center of the grill if using charcoal). Cover (positioning the lid vents over the chicken if using charcoal) and cook until the thickest part of the breasts registers 160 to 165 degrees and the thickest part of the thighs registers 175 degrees on an instant-read thermometer, about 45 minutes, rotating the chicken pieces halfway through (do not flip the chicken).

5. Transfer the chicken to a carving board, tent loosely with foil, and let rest until cool enough to handle. Remove and discard the skin, then pull the meat off the bones, separating the larger pieces from the smaller, drier pieces.

6. Pulse the smaller pieces of chicken in a food processor until coarsely chopped, about 4 pulses. Using your hands, pull the larger pieces of chicken into long shreds. Combine the shredded and processed chicken in a large saucepan with ¾ cup of the sauce. Cover and cook over medium-low heat, stirring occasionally, until hot throughout, about 10 minutes. Serve, passing the remaining ¼ cup sauce separately.

PER SERVING: Cal 460; Fat 10g; Sat fat 2.5g; Chol 220mg; Carb 25g; Protein 66g; Fiber 1g; Sodium 900mg

GRILLED TURKEY BURGER

GRILLED TURKEY BURGERS

A PERFECTLY GRILLED BURGER IS A QUINTESSENTIAL American favorite, but it's not too surprising that a standard beef hamburger is packed with fat and calories (about 28 grams of fat and 360 calories for a 5-ounce burger). To satisfy a juicy burger craving, many of us have turned to the lower-fat turkey burger, only to be disappointed with a patty that is dry, tasteless, and colorless. We wanted a turkey burger with all the appealing beef burger qualities—crusty on the outside and full-flavored and juicy on the inside. We knew with a little test kitchen know-how we could turn this turkey around.

To start, we took a close look at our options for types of ground turkey: all white meat, all dark meat, and a combination of the two. We had run a similar test when selecting the best ground turkey to use in our low-fat Spaghetti and Meatballs (page 122), and the results here were, not surprisingly, nearly identical. The turkey burgers made from all dark meat cooked up juicy and flavorful, but this type didn't save us much on fat or calories. Burgers made with all-white turkey meat were dry and bland; they contained so little fat that they tended to burn, and they shrank into inedible pucks. The burgers made with the mixture of dark and white meat (labeled 93 percent lean) were the most promising. They had a decent meaty flavor and were relatively juicy. This was a good starting point.

To add some moistness to the burgers, we tried a whole host of ingredients, including a milk-bread mixture (a panade), mashed beans, and rehydrated mushrooms, all with little success. The panade made our burger a bit too moist and seemed to steer us in the direction of a meatball or meatloaf, not a burger. The mashed beans failed to add enough moisture to the patties, and the rehydrated mushrooms had such a strong flavor that they overshadowed the turkey. Then we stumbled onto part-skim ricotta—it was exactly what we were looking for. The ricotta gave the turkey burgers a moist, chewy texture, and its mild flavor allowed the turkey flavor to stand out.

Flavoring the turkey patties was our next challenge. We tried every ingredient in the test kitchen that we thought would add a complementary meaty flavor to the burgers, from teriyaki sauce to fermented black beans to olive paste. After eating a lot of bad (and some good) burgers, we found two ingredients that gave our turkey burgers the optimal beefy flavor: Worcestershire sauce and Dijon mustard. These sharp, tangy flavors were just what our turkey burgers needed.

Because turkey must be cooked to well-done for safety reasons, figuring out how to maintain a juicy burger was difficult. If the heat was too high, the burgers burned before they were done; too low, and they were pale and virtually steam-cooked (and very unappealing). Experimenting with several different grill setups, we found that a two-level fire was the best way to cook the turkey burgers without drying them out. Beginning on the hotter side of the grill, we seared the burgers until well browned, then slid them over to the cooler part of the grill to finish cooking through. This resulted in a burger that had a flavorful crust and remained moist inside. We'd never mind trading in the full-fat beef burgers for one of these, which may have been low in fat but were certainly big on flavor.

NOTES FROM THE TEST KITCHEN

CHECKING THE PROPANE LEVEL
Gas grills aren't as complicated as charcoal, but if you own one, there is a detail you should always make sure of: Do you have enough gas? If your grill doesn't have a gas gauge or propane level indicator, don't worry. We've come up with the following trick:

1. Bring a cup or so of water to a boil in a saucepan or kettle, then pour the water over the side of the tank.

2. Where the water succeeds in warming the tank, the tank is empty; where the tank remains cool to the touch, there is propane inside.

Grilled Turkey Burgers

SERVES 4

Ground turkey is sold in a variety of package sizes; you can use between 1¼ and 1½ pounds of ground turkey in this recipe. Because these burgers are made of ground poultry, be sure to cook them until the centers register 160 to 165 on an instant-read thermometer. Serve the burgers on hamburger buns with your favorite toppings.

- 1 **(20.8-ounce) package 93 percent lean ground turkey (see note)**
- ½ **cup part-skim ricotta cheese**
- 2 **teaspoons Worcestershire sauce**
- 2 **teaspoons Dijon mustard**
- ½ **teaspoon salt**
- ¼ **teaspoon pepper**

1. Break the turkey into small pieces in a large bowl, then add the ricotta, Worcestershire, mustard, salt, and pepper. Using your hands, lightly knead the mixture until combined. Divide the meat into 4 equal portions, then form each into a loose ball and gently flatten into a 1-inch-thick patty. Cover and refrigerate the patties until the grill is ready.

2A. FOR A CHARCOAL GRILL: Open the bottom grill vents completely. Light a large chimney starter three-quarters full with charcoal briquettes (75 briquettes; 4½ quarts). When the coals are hot, spread two-thirds of them evenly over the grill, then pour the remaining coals over half of the grill. Set the cooking grate in place, cover, and open the lid vents completely. Heat the grill until hot, about 5 minutes.

2B. FOR A GAS GRILL: Turn all the burners to high, cover, and heat the grill until hot, about 15 minutes. (Adjust the burners as needed to maintain a hot fire; see page 162.)

3. Clean and oil the cooking grate. Place the burgers on the grill (on the hotter part of the grill if using charcoal) and cook (covered if using gas), without pressing on them, until well browned on both sides, 5 to 7 minutes, flipping them halfway through.

4. Slide the burgers to the cooler part of the grill if using charcoal, or turn all the burners to medium-low (adjust the burners as needed to maintain a medium-low fire; see page 162) if using gas. Continue to cook until the center of the burgers registers 160 to 165 degrees on an instant-read thermometer, 5 to 7 minutes longer, flipping them halfway through.

5. Transfer the burgers to a platter, tent loosely with foil, and let rest for 5 minutes before serving.

PER SERVING: Cal 240; Fat 11g; Sat fat 4g; Chol 95mg; Carb 3g; Protein 32g; Fiber 0g; Sodium 530mg

SMOKED TURKEY BREAST

SMOKED TURKEY BREAST IS A CLASSIC PREPARATION that is so simple and appealing that it will never go out of style (it doesn't hurt that turkey is also incredibly lean). Unfortunately, most people consider smoking a turkey breast to be a task better left to the professionals and don't bother trying it at home. We weren't going to make the same mistake. We set out to make a straightforward, flavorful smoked turkey on our backyard grill—plump, juicy meat, lightly perfumed with smoke—with a method that wouldn't intimidate any home cook.

Since we wanted to keep things light, we limited ourselves to bone-in, skin-on turkey breast—the bones and the skin would help keep the meat moist, especially during the longer cooking time on the grill, and we would simply discard the skin before serving to keep the fat in check. As with our Easy Roast Turkey Breast (page 73), we found that while the test kitchen preferred the taste of a brined natural turkey, any of the other common varieties of turkey breast—self-basted or kosher—would also work well. (Kosher and self-basting birds should not be brined since they have already been salted; for more on brining, see page 74.)

Cooking a turkey breast on the grill may seem straightforward, but it's not a snap to do. Our early tests yielded plenty of dry turkey. We quickly learned that cooking with indirect heat was key; placed directly over a fire, the outside of the turkey breast was sure to burn before the center was cooked through. With a hot fire isolated to one side of the grill and our turkey breast positioned skin-side up on the cooler part, opposite the coals and flames, we could allow the turkey breast to gently cook through. Removing the breast from the grill when the internal temperature reached between 160 and 165 degrees was also essential to ensuring that the meat did not overcook. This turkey was juicy and moist, but, smoke aside (which we'd tackle later), the flavor was pretty bland.

We tried rubbing salt and brown sugar under and over the turkey skin just before grilling. This gave us a tasty crust, but the seasoning wasn't penetrating the meat, which was problematic given that to keep things light, we would be tossing the skin out. When we tried leaving the rub on overnight, however, the resulting turkey breast was deeply seasoned. For good measure, we applied a second round of rub over and under the skin right before we put the breast on the grill. This second application added even more flavor, and by replacing the salt with pepper, we gave our turkey a spicy kick. Piercing the skin before grilling allowed more of the fat to render and further flavor the meat.

Finally, it was time to focus on the smoke. Many recipes require as much as 6 cups of wood chips for smoke flavor, but such a large amount of chips left our turkey tasting like the inside of the grill lid. Two cups of chips added just enough smokiness without overwhelming the mild meat. Now we had smoky, well-seasoned, juicy meat that our tasters were fighting over.

NOTES FROM THE TEST KITCHEN

PREPPING TURKEY BREAST FOR GRILLING

1. Carefully loosen the skin, then massage the brown sugar–salt mixture over and under the skin. After refrigerating at least 8 hours, wipe away excess moisture, then season with brown sugar and pepper.

2. Use a skewer or the tip of a sharp knife to poke numerous holes in the skin so the fat can render easily.

Smoked Turkey Breast

SERVES 10

This recipe works equally well with any type of turkey breast, be it kosher, self-basting, or untreated. If using a kosher or self-basting turkey breast, do not brine. The ingredient list on the turkey breast's package will say whether it's been treated with salt. If brining the turkey breast, do not use salt in step 1. Much like whole turkeys, turkey breasts come in a wide range of sizes. If your turkey breast is larger or smaller than 6 pounds, you will need to adjust the grilling time accordingly.

3   tablespoons brown sugar
1   tablespoon salt
1   (6-pound) whole bone-in, skin-on turkey breast, trimmed, brined if desired (see note; see page 74)
2   teaspoons pepper
1   (13 by 9-inch) disposable aluminum roasting pan (if using charcoal)
2   cups wood chips, soaked, drained, and sealed in a foil packet (see page 166)

1. Combine 2 tablespoons of the sugar and salt in a small bowl. Pat the turkey breast dry with paper towels. Following the photos, loosen the skin by sliding your fingers between the skin and the meat, and rub the sugar mixture evenly over and under the loosened skin. Tightly wrap the turkey breast with plastic wrap and refrigerate for at least 8 hours, or up to 24 hours.

2. Combine the remaining 1 tablespoon sugar and pepper in a bowl. Unwrap the turkey breast, pat it dry with paper towels, and rub the sugar mixture evenly both under and over the skin. Poke the skin all over with a skewer or the tip of a sharp knife.

3A. FOR A CHARCOAL GRILL: Open the bottom grill vents halfway and place the roasting pan in the center of the grill. Light a large chimney starter filled with charcoal briquettes (100 briquettes; 6 quarts). When the coals are hot, pour them into two even piles on either side of the roasting pan. Place the wood chip packet on top of one of the coal piles. Set the cooking grate in place, cover, and open the lid vents halfway. Heat the grill until hot and the wood chips begin to smoke heavily, about 5 minutes.

3B. FOR A GAS GRILL: Place the wood chip packet directly on the primary burner. Turn all the burners to high, cover, and heat the grill until hot and the wood chips begin to smoke heavily, about 15 minutes. Turn all the burners to medium-low. (Adjust the burners as needed to maintain the grill temperature around 350 degrees.)

4. Clean and oil the cooking grate. Place the turkey breast, skin-side up, on the grill (in the center of the grill if using charcoal). Cover (positioning the lid vents over the turkey if using charcoal) and cook until the thickest part of the breast registers 160 to 165 degrees on an instant-read thermometer, about 2 hours.

5. Transfer the turkey breast to a carving board, tent loosely with foil, and let rest for 20 minutes. Remove and discard the skin, carve the turkey, and serve.

PER SERVING: **Cal** 320; **Fat** 2g; **Sat fat** 0.5g; **Chol** 170mg; **Carb** 4g; **Protein** 67g; **Fiber** 0g; **Sodium** 830mg

GRILLED MARINATED STEAK

AMERICA'S LOVE AFFAIR WITH STEAK MARINATED IN a bottle of Italian-style salad dressing is both indisputable and curious. The flavor is often complex—or at least interesting—but the texture suffers terribly, with an exterior that turns mushy, a result of acids from the vinegar in the dressing. We wanted a fresh, Mediterranean-style marinated steak that was full of flavor and had a texture we could sink our teeth into.

Choosing the right steak was first. Steaks can be divided into two categories: tight-grained (like sirloin and strip) and loose-grained (like flank, flap meat, and skirt). Side-by-side tests determined that loose-grained steaks are able to absorb more marinade, and thus more flavor, than tight-grained. We settled on flank steak because it hit all the marks—it's tender, flavorful, relatively lean, and readily available.

After testing various grill setups, we found it best to use a half-grill fire with all the heat set up on one side. This allowed us to get a really hot fire, ideal for cooking flank steak (since it is a relatively thin cut of meat, it was done after we seared both sides).

As for the marinade, we wanted to avoid vinegars and other acids because of the mushy-meat issue. Fats carry flavor well, so oil would be necessary, but we wanted to use as little as possible. Minimizing the oil and no liquid acid meant our marinade would be more like a paste, so with that in mind we began testing marinades made with Mediterranean flavors. Our working recipe contained ¼ cup of olive oil and 1 tablespoon each of garlic and rosemary. We were pretty sure that heat would intensify the flavors, so we tested making flanks steaks with two different marinades—one made with raw garlic and rosemary, the other a heat infusion made by briefly cooking the garlic and rosemary in the oil. Tasters thought that the heat improved the flavor, but only slightly, so it didn't seem worth the bother. We found simply increasing the amounts of garlic and rosemary—to 2 tablespoons each—was far more effective. We tried adding other ingredients to the marinade, but only shallots made the cut. Among the losers were parsley (too subtle), Worcestershire sauce and tomato paste (both toughened the meat), and anchovy paste (just plain fishy).

We had been finely mincing the paste ingredients by hand and then stirring them with the oil. We wondered if we could just throw everything in the blender, but the blender failed to mince things finely enough, and the rough bits didn't contribute as much flavor as a fine mince. Mincing the garlic, rosemary, and shallots with a knife and then combining them with the oil in the blender gave us an extremely fine, well-blended paste that flavored the steak in just one hour.

NOTES FROM THE TEST KITCHEN

KEYS TO MAXIMIZING THE MARINADE FLAVOR

1. Prick the steak with a fork all over (20 times on each side) to speed up the flavor absorption.

2. Rub both sides of the steak with the garlic-rosemary paste, then wrap it with plastic wrap and refrigerate for at least 1 hour.

Our steak was pretty good, but tasters wanted more flavor inside the meat. Pricking the surface of the steak before rubbing on the paste was the answer, since the perforations allowed the marinade to penetrate the steak. We thought we were done, but one colleague suggested we try a final test and marinate the meat overnight to see if we could give it even more flavor. This steak ended up being potently flavored, but so was the one-hour version, so it really didn't matter within that range how long the meat was marinated. Because the marinade could be applied to the steak well before cooking it, it gave us some flexibility as to when to prep for getting this healthy dinner on the table.

Grilled Marinated Flank Steak with Garlic and Rosemary
SERVES 6

We prefer this steak cooked to medium-rare, but if you prefer it more or less done, see "Testing Meat for Doneness" on page 86.

- ¼ cup olive oil
- 1 shallot, minced (about 3 tablespoons)
- 6 garlic cloves, minced
- 2 tablespoons minced fresh rosemary
- ¼ teaspoon salt
- ¼ teaspoon pepper
- 1 (1½-pound) flank steak, trimmed of all visible fat

1. Process the oil, shallot, garlic, rosemary, salt, and pepper together in a blender (or food processor) until smooth. Following the photos on page 172, prick the steak with a fork about 20 times on each side, then rub both sides of the steak evenly with the paste. Wrap the steak with plastic wrap and refrigerate for at least 1 hour, or up to 24 hours.

2A. FOR A CHARCOAL GRILL: Open the bottom grill vents completely. Light a large chimney starter filled with charcoal briquettes (100 briquettes; 6 quarts). When the coals are hot, spread them in an even layer over half of the grill. Set the cooking grate in place, cover, and heat the grill until hot, about 5 minutes.

2B. FOR A GAS GRILL: Turn all the burners to high, cover, and heat the grill until hot, about 15 minutes. (Adjust the burners as needed to maintain a hot fire; see page 162.)

3. Clean and oil the cooking grate. Place the steak on the grill (on the hotter part of the grill if using charcoal) and cook (covered if using gas) until well browned on both sides and the thickest part of the steak registers 120 to 125 degrees on an instant-read thermometer (for medium-rare), 8 to 12 minutes, flipping the steak halfway through.

4. Transfer the steak to a carving board, tent loosely with foil, and let rest for 10 minutes. Slice the steak thin, against the grain and on the bias, and serve.

PER SERVING: **Cal** 240; **Fat** 15g; **Sat fat** 3.5g; **Chol** 40mg; **Carb** 2g; **Protein** 25g; **Fiber** 0g; **Sodium** 160mg

VARIATION

Grilled Marinated Flank Steak with Garlic and Chiles
To make this dish spicier, add the chile seeds to the marinade.

Follow the recipe for Grilled Marinated Flank Steak with Garlic and Rosemary, substituting canola oil for the olive oil, 2 scallions, minced, for the shallot, and 1 tablespoon minced canned chipotle chiles in adobo sauce plus 1 medium jalapeño chile, stemmed, seeded, and minced, for the rosemary.

PER SERVING: **Cal** 250; **Fat** 15g; **Sat fat** 3g; **Chol** 40mg; **Carb** 2g; **Protein** 25g; **Fiber** 0g; **Sodium** 160mg

SMOKED PORK LOIN

WHILE TOUGHER CUTS OF PORK, LIKE THOSE FROM the shoulders and ribs, require a low-and-slow cooking technique to become tender, lean loin roasts are ideal for the higher heat and quicker cooking time of grill-roasting, making them a great option for feeding a healthy meal to a small group. Add some smoke, and the grill-roasted pork loin sounds like a real winner—juicy, flavorful meat, permeated with smoke and spice. We tested a few recipes that seemed worthwhile, but most of the results just went up in, well, smoke. We set out to see what we could do.

We already had a foolproof test kitchen technique for grill-roasting a pork loin, so we started there. Build a fire with hot and cool sides, sear the meat over high heat so that the exterior browns, then move the pork loin to the cool side of the grill so that it can finish cooking through gently with indirect heat without drying out. Adding smoke seemed like an easy proposition since various cuts of beef are also smoked over indirect heat— all we'd need to do would be to add a packet of soaked wood chips to the fire, sear as usual, and sit back to let the smoke and low fire work their magic.

There was only one problem: the leanness of the pork loin. Fatty cuts, like those from the shoulder and ribs, take to smoke well because they have enough richness to balance the assertive smoke flavor. Pork loin isn't rich or fatty, and when we tried smoking it this way, the smoke overwhelmed the subtle flavor of the meat. Using fewer wood chips gave us inconsistent results. We were going to have to find ways to add more flavor to the pork loin so that it could stand up to a healthy dose of smoke.

A basic barbecue spice rub (paprika, chili powder, cumin, oregano, cayenne, brown sugar, salt, and pepper) helped, but searing the rubbed meat at the onset meant putting it directly over the smoking wood chips on the hot side of the grill, resulting in pork that tasted sooty and ashy. Starting the meat on the cooler side and saving the searing until the end of cooking, when the wood chips had already surrendered their smoke, proved a better way to develop flavor, at least on the outside of the meat. But we found we still needed to boost the flavor on the inside.

We decided to try making a marinade with flavors that would complement the smoke. We started with one of our favorite marinade ingredients, soy sauce, which penetrates the meat (much like a saltwater brine), helping to season it and keep it moist. Garlic, Worcestershire sauce, Dijon mustard, and brown sugar lent boldness to the mild pork, but we wanted something that would specifically reinforce the smoke flavor. Though many recipes rely on liquid smoke, we decided to fill its spot with whiskey, which offered a smoky flavor as well as a bold kick. Between the marinade, the spice rub, and the smoke, this pork loin was about as flavorful as you could get.

Smoked Pork Loin
SERVES 6

Leaving a ⅛-inch-thick layer of fat on top of the roast is ideal; if your roast has a thicker fat cap, trim it to be ⅛ inch thick. You can substitute bourbon for the whiskey, if preferred.

MARINADE

- ¼ **cup Dijon mustard**
- ¼ **cup American whiskey, such as Jack Daniel's (see note)**
- ¼ **cup low-sodium soy sauce**
- ¼ **cup packed brown sugar**
- 2 **tablespoons Worcestershire sauce**
- 4 **garlic cloves, minced**
- 1 **(2¼-pound) boneless center-cut pork loin roast, fat on top scored lightly (see note), tied at 1½-inch intervals (see page 175)**

SPICE RUB

- 1 **tablespoon paprika**
- 1 **tablespoon brown sugar**
- 2 **teaspoons chili powder**
- 2 **teaspoons ground cumin**
- 1 **teaspoon dried oregano**
- 1 **teaspoon black pepper**
- 1 **teaspoon salt**
- ¼ **teaspoon cayenne pepper**
- 2 **cups wood chips, soaked, drained, and sealed in a foil packet (see page 166)**

1. FOR THE MARINADE: Whisk the mustard, whiskey, soy sauce, brown sugar, Worcestershire, and garlic together in a small bowl. Place the marinade and pork in a gallon-sized zipper-lock bag. Press the air out of the bag, seal, and refrigerate for at least 2 hours, or up to 8 hours, flipping the bag halfway through.

2. FOR THE SPICE RUB: Combine the paprika, brown sugar, chili powder, cumin, oregano, black pepper, salt, and cayenne in a small bowl. Remove the pork from the marinade and pat dry with paper towels. Rub the meat evenly with the spice mixture, wrap in plastic wrap, and let sit at room temperature for at least 1 hour, or refrigerate for up to 24 hours. (If refrigerated, let sit at room temperature for 1 hour before grilling.)

3A. FOR A CHARCOAL GRILL: Open the bottom grill vents halfway. Light a large chimney starter filled with charcoal briquettes (100 briquettes; 6 quarts). When the coals are hot, pour them into a steeply banked pile against one side of the grill. Place the wood chip packet on top of the coals. Set the cooking grate in place, cover, and open the lid vents halfway. Heat the grill until hot and the wood chips begin to smoke heavily, about 5 minutes.

3B. FOR A GAS GRILL: Place the wood chip packet directly on the primary burner. Turn all the burners to high, cover, and heat the grill until hot and the wood chips begin to smoke heavily, about 15 minutes. Leave the primary burner on high and turn off the other burner(s). (Adjust the primary burner as needed to maintain the grill temperature between 350 and 400 degrees.)

4. Clean and oil the cooking grate. Place the pork, fat side up, on the cooler part of the grill, away from the coals and flames. Cover (positioning the lid vents over the meat if using charcoal) and cook until the meat registers 130 to 135 degrees on an instant-read thermometer, about 1 hour, flipping and rotating the roast halfway through.

5. Slide the pork to the hotter part of the grill, directly over the coals and flames, and continue to cook, covered, until well browned on all sides and the center of the meat registers 140 to 145 degrees, 5 to 10 minutes longer.

NOTES FROM THE TEST KITCHEN

PREPARING PORK LOIN FOR THE GRILL

1. To encourage the fat to render so it can baste the meat as it cooks, use a sharp knife to cut a shallow crosshatch pattern into the fat. Avoid cutting through the fat and into the meat, as this may result in moisture loss.

2. Tying the roast tightly at 1½-inch intervals gives it an even shape, promoting even cooking on the grill.

6. Transfer the pork to a carving board, tent loosely with foil, and let rest until the very center of the meat reaches 150 degrees, about 20 minutes. Remove the twine, slice the pork ½ inch thick, and serve.

PER SERVING: **Cal** 340; **Fat** 16g; **Sat fat** 5g; **Chol** 115mg; **Carb** 8g; **Protein** 36g; **Fiber** 1 g; **Sodium** 820mg

GRILLED PORK CHOPS AND PEACHES

WHEN YOU'RE FIRING UP THE GRILL FOR A LIGHT meal and pork is what you want, lean chops are the way to go. But because of their lack of fat, pork chops have a tendency to dry out on the grill. We wanted a chop with a deeply browned crust and meat that would be tender and juicy. And to contrast with the savory pork, the flavors of sweet grilled fruit seemed like a perfect pairing.

We knew bone-in chops were our best bet for grilling. We like center-cut chops and rib chops, both of which are cut from the middle of the pig's loin. Both are tender and flavorful, but tasters voted in favor of the center-cut chops, which are leaner but still juicy.

In past test kitchen experience we have found single-level fires to be problematic when cooking bone-in chicken breasts and T-bone steaks, and sure enough, they didn't work with our bone-in pork chops either. The chops developed a beautiful bronze exterior within minutes, but when we checked their temperature, they were completely raw inside. Leaving the chops on the grill longer would only burn the perfect crust.

Next we tried a two-level fire, which had been successful in other recipes, like our grilled glazed chicken breasts (see page 162), when we needed a high-heat zone to start and get a good sear and a lower-heat zone where the interior could cook through slowly without fear of burning the outside. We seared the chops over high heat, moved them to the cooler part of the grill, then covered them with the lid to create an oven-like effect and finish up the cooking. After less than 10 minutes on the cool side, the interior of the chops registered between 140 and 145 degrees, so we took them off the grill to rest and finish cooking through from residual heat. This time we had just what we were after: a crisp crust and flavorful, juicy meat.

Now that we had perfectly cooked pork chops, we wanted to pair them with a grilled fruit—a nice complement to the pork—and decided on peaches. To give the peaches another dimension of flavor, we thought a honey glaze might do the trick. So while the chops rested, we tossed some peaches in honey, placed them skin-side up on the hotter part of the grill, and cooked them until tender. Tasters liked the caramelized flavor the honey lent, but everyone agreed these sweet, heavily glazed peaches seemed better suited for dessert than for accompanying our pork chops.

Looking to make a more savory dressing, we whipped up a few different flavor combinations for tasters to sample. They particularly liked a combination that wasn't far from our original idea—a sweet-tangy mixture of honey and whole grain mustard. Some balsamic vinegar added a pleasant piquancy, and a little extra-virgin olive oil provided just the right roundness. Tossing our peaches in this dressing prior to grilling gave them the sweet-savory flavor we were after, and tasters enjoyed the flavor so much that they wanted a little extra dressing to drizzle over the pork as well. With a final sprinkle of tarragon for freshness, our pork chops and peaches had a summery, fresh flavor that made them a great light meal off the grill.

NOTES FROM THE TEST KITCHEN

STORING PEACHES

While it may seem like a good idea to put your just-purchased peaches in the refrigerator to prolong their life, doing so can come at a price. Refrigerating not-yet-ripe peaches, we have found, can make them mealy, a fact that a study proved a few years ago and that we decided to test for ourselves. We divided a single case of peaches into two batches, allowing one to ripen immediately without refrigeration and storing the other for a week in the fridge before allowing it to finish ripening for a couple of days at room temperature. Both sets of peaches were placed in containers sealed with plastic wrap in order to prevent moisture from evaporating. True to the study, our tasters found that despite being soft and ripe to the touch, the peaches that had spent time in the fridge were significantly mealier than those kept at room temperature. The moral of the story? Don't refrigerate your peaches unless you're sure they're ripe. You may prolong their shelf life, but the loss of quality isn't worth it.

Grilled Pork Chops and Peaches

SERVES 4

If the pork is "enhanced" (see page 79 for more information), do not brine. If brining the pork, omit the salt in step 3.

- 2 tablespoons balsamic vinegar
- 2 tablespoons olive oil
- 1 tablespoon honey
- 1 tablespoon whole grain mustard
  Salt and pepper
- 4 ripe but firm peaches (7 to 8 ounces each), halved and pitted
- 4 (8-ounce) bone-in center-cut pork loin chops, about 1 inch thick, trimmed of all visible fat, brined if desired (see note; see page 74)
- 2 teaspoons chopped fresh tarragon

1. Whisk the vinegar, oil, honey, mustard, ⅛ teaspoon salt, and ⅛ teaspoon pepper together in a large bowl. Measure out and reserve 3 tablespoons of the balsamic dressing for serving. Add the peaches to the remaining balsamic dressing and toss to coat.

2A. FOR A CHARCOAL GRILL: Open the bottom grill vents completely. Light a large chimney starter filled with charcoal briquettes (100 briquettes; 6 quarts). When the coals are hot, spread two-thirds of them evenly over the grill, then pour the remaining coals over half of the grill. Set the cooking grate in place, cover, and open the lid vents completely. Heat the grill until hot, about 5 minutes.

2B. FOR A GAS GRILL: Turn all the burners to high, cover, and heat the grill until hot, about 15 minutes. (Adjust the burners as needed to maintain a hot fire; see page 162.)

3. Clean and oil the cooking grate. Pat the pork chops dry with paper towels and season with ⅛ teaspoon salt and ⅛ teaspoon pepper. Place the pork chops on the grill (on the hotter part of the grill if using charcoal) and cook (covered if using gas) until well browned on both sides, 6 to 10 minutes, flipping the chops halfway through.

4. Slide the pork chops to the cooler part of the grill if using charcoal, or turn all the burners to medium (adjust the burners as needed to maintain a medium fire; see page 162) if using gas. Cover and continue to cook

until the center of the chops registers 140 to 145 degrees on an instant-read thermometer, 5 to 6 minutes longer, flipping the pork halfway through.

5. Transfer the pork chops to a platter, tent loosely with foil, and let rest until the center of the chops registers 150 degrees, 5 to 10 minutes.

6. While the pork chops rest, place the peach halves, skin-side up, on the hotter part of the grill if using charcoal, or turn all the burners to high (adjust the burners as needed to maintain a hot fire; see page 162) if using gas. Cover and cook until caramelized and slightly softened, about 10 minutes, flipping the peaches halfway through.

7. Transfer the peaches to the platter with the pork chops. Whisk the reserved balsamic dressing to recombine and drizzle over the pork chops and peaches. Sprinkle with the tarragon and serve.

PER SERVING: **Cal** 330; **Fat** 14g; **Sat fat** 3g; **Chol** 70mg; **Carb** 22g; **Protein** 30g; **Fiber** 3g; **Sodium** 300mg

WOOD-GRILLED SALMON

THE PREMISE OF WOOD-GRILLED SALMON IS SIMPLE: Salmon fillets are set on a soaked plank of aromatic cedar wood, which is then placed on the grill. Soaking the plank keeps the fish moist during cooking and prevents the soft, resinous cedar from smoking too heavily or, in the worst case, combusting. There was a lot to like about this concept right off the bat: Fish is inherently healthy (particularly salmon), it's quick-cooking, and the perfume of the cedar adds a whole other layer of flavor that sounded pretty hard to resist. It was a shoo-in for adding to our light cooking repertoire.

After taking a trip to pick up some cedar planks from our local specialty foods store, we settled in and got to work. We soaked the planks for an hour, topped them with salmon fillets, and put them on the cooking grate over moderate heat. With a bit of fiddling (and yes, we did ignite a plank during one failed, though memorable, test), we were able to produce moist salmon tinged with a nice wood flavor. Now that we knew what we were after, we wondered if we could achieve the same results without having to make a special trip just for a set of planks.

Wood chips are generally by our side throughout the grilling season and seemed like a good option. We knew we couldn't simply swap them for the plank because the chips would just fall through the cooking grate, so we made individual foil trays to hold the chips and salmon. We tossed a handful of soaked chips in each tray, laid our fillets on top, and set the trays on the grill's hot cooking grate. About 10 to 15 minutes later, our salmon was cooked perfectly, but we ran into a slight problem. The soaked wood chips were doing a great job of lending woody flavor to the fish, but they also ended up stuck to the salmon, making for mangled fillets when it came to serving time. To remedy this, we left the skin on the salmon, which protected the flesh from the chips; once the fish was cooked, we could easily separate the skin and discard it. The resulting fillets were moist and fully intact, but though they had some wood flavor, we wanted more. Poking a few holes in the bottom of the foil allowed even more heat to reach the wood chips, causing them to release more of their woody flavor without making our fish taste overly smoky.

Though the flavor was now spot-on, the fillets were looking unappealingly pale. Following the lead of a few recipes we had come across, we tried coating the fillets with some brown sugar. The sugar caramelized into an appealing golden hue but made the fish candy-sweet. A better solution was to coat each fillet with a thin layer of olive oil and a light sprinkling of granulated sugar. These fillets were perfectly golden, and the mildly sweet exterior surrounding the smoky-rich salmon tasted just as good as it looked.

Wood-Grilled Salmon
SERVES 4

Any variety of wood chips will work here, but aromatic woods such as cedar and alder give the most authentic flavor.

- 1½ teaspoons sugar
- ½ teaspoon salt
- ¼ teaspoon pepper
- 4 (6-ounce) skin-on salmon fillets, about 1½ inches thick
- 1 tablespoon olive oil
- 2 cups wood chips, soaked and drained

1. Combine the sugar, salt, and pepper in a small bowl. Pat the salmon fillets dry with paper towels, then brush the flesh sides with the oil and rub them evenly with the sugar mixture. Following the photos, use heavy-duty foil to make four 7 by 5-inch trays. Perforate the bottom of each tray with the tip of a knife. Divide the wood chips among the trays and place a salmon fillet, skin-side down, on top of the wood chips in each tray.

2A. FOR A CHARCOAL GRILL: Open the bottom grill vents completely. Light a large chimney starter filled with charcoal briquettes (100 briquettes; 6 quarts). When the coals are hot, spread them in an even layer over the grill. Set the cooking grate in place, cover, and heat the grill until hot, about 5 minutes.

2B. FOR A GAS GRILL: Turn all the burners to high, cover, and heat the grill until hot, about 15 minutes. (Adjust the burners as needed to maintain a hot fire; see page 162.)

3. Clean and oil the cooking grate. Place the trays on the grate. Cook (covered if using gas) until the sides of the salmon are opaque and the thickest part of the fillets registers 125 degrees on an instant-read thermometer, 10 to 15 minutes.

4. Transfer the trays to a wire rack, tent loosely with foil, and let rest for 5 minutes. Slide a metal spatula between the skin and the flesh of the salmon, transfer to a platter, and serve.

PER SERVING (WILD SALMON): **Cal** 280; **Fat** 14g; **Sat fat** 2g; **Chol** 95mg; **Carb** 2g; **Protein** 34g; **Fiber** 0g; **Sodium** 370mg

PER SERVING (FARMED SALMON): **Cal** 350; **Fat** 22g; **Sat fat** 4g; **Chol** 100mg; **Carb** 2g; **Protein** 34g; **Fiber** 0g; **Sodium** 370mg

VARIATIONS

Chinese Wood-Grilled Salmon

Look for Chinese five-spice powder in either the spice aisle or the international aisle of the supermarket.

Follow the recipe for Wood-Grilled Salmon, adding 1½ teaspoons Chinese five-spice powder and ¼ teaspoon cayenne pepper to the sugar mixture, and substituting 2 tablespoons hoisin sauce for the oil.

PER SERVING (WILD SALMON): **Cal** 270; **Fat** 11g; **Sat fat** 1.5g; **Chol** 95mg; **Carb** 7g; **Protein** 34g; **Fiber** 0g; **Sodium** 640mg

PER SERVING (FARMED SALMON): **Cal** 340; **Fat** 19g; **Sat fat** 3.5g; **Chol** 100mg; **Carb** 7g; **Protein** 34g; **Fiber** 0g; **Sodium** 640mg

Barbecued Wood-Grilled Salmon

Follow the recipe for Wood-Grilled Salmon, adding ¾ teaspoon chili powder and ¼ teaspoon cayenne pepper to the sugar mixture, and substituting 1 tablespoon Dijon mustard mixed with 1 tablespoon maple syrup for the oil.

PER SERVING (WILD SALMON): **Cal** 270; **Fat** 11g; **Sat fat** 1.5g; **Chol** 95mg; **Carb** 6g; **Protein** 34g; **Fiber** 0g; **Sodium** 460mg

PER SERVING (FARMED SALMON): **Cal** 340; **Fat** 19g; **Sat fat** 3.5g; **Chol** 100mg; **Carb** 6g; **Protein** 34g; **Fiber** 0g; **Sodium** 460mg

Lemon-Thyme Wood-Grilled Salmon

Follow the recipe for Wood-Grilled Salmon, adding 2 teaspoons minced fresh thyme and 1½ teaspoons grated lemon zest to the sugar mixture, and substituting 2 tablespoons Dijon mustard for the oil.

PER SERVING (WILD SALMON): **Cal** 260; **Fat** 11g; **Sat fat** 1.5g; **Chol** 95mg; **Carb** 3g; **Protein** 34g; **Fiber** 0g; **Sodium** 550mg

PER SERVING (FARMED SALMON): **Cal** 330; **Fat** 18g; **Sat fat** 3.5g; **Chol** 100mg; **Carb** 3g; **Protein** 34g; **Fiber** 0g; **Sodium** 550mg

---

NOTES FROM THE TEST KITCHEN

MAKING WOOD-GRILLED SALMON

1. Cut out four rectangles of heavy-duty aluminum foil and crimp the edges until each tray measures 7 by 5 inches. Using a paring knife, poke small slits in the bottom of the trays.

2. Place the soaked wood chips in the foil trays and arrange the salmon skin-side down directly on top of the wood chips.

3. Once the salmon is cooked, slide a metal spatula between the flesh and the skin; the fish should release easily.

WOOD-GRILLED SALMON

GRILLED FISH TACOS

POPULAR IN SOUTHERN CALIFORNIA AND PARTS OF Mexico, fish tacos are being seen more and more often throughout the States. The fish in these tacos can be prepared several ways, but grilled is one of the more popular versions. Grilled pieces of fish, topped with crisp shredded lettuce and a tangy sauce, are wrapped up in warm, soft corn tortillas. One bite of this summery meal and you're hooked. We wanted a recipe for fish tacos that we could make at home, one that offered the same great flavors and light, refreshing ingredients we'd find at any California taco shack.

Most of the recipes we found for fish tacos called for a sturdy white fish, so we tried halibut, swordfish, cod, and mahi-mahi. We found them all acceptable, although mahi-mahi was the leanest of the group and easiest to manage on the grill. Tasters also liked its meaty flavor and firm texture. To serve four people, we first tried grilling two larger 12-ounce fillets with the idea that we would divide the fish up for the tacos once cooked, but we quickly decided it would be easier to work with four smaller 6-ounce fillets, each of which we could easily cut into three pieces (to give us one piece per taco).

To help firm up the fillets and make them easier to handle, and remain in one piece during cooking, we refrigerated the fish on a wire rack set over a baking sheet until our grill was ready. Because fish cooks relatively quickly, we knew a hot single-level fire, one with an even amount of heat over the entire grill, would be our best bet. This would allow our fish a chance to develop a nicely crisped exterior in a short amount of time without being overcooked in the interior. We did note that we had to be thorough when cleaning and oiling the cooking grate; otherwise, our fish stuck to the grill. Tasters agreed that this fish was good, but it needed a flavor boost. Salt and pepper weren't enough, so we put together a boldly flavored rub that seemed appropriate to a taco recipe: chili powder, coriander, and cumin. This combination gave us well-seasoned, flavorful fish.

Happy with our mahi-mahi, we turned our attention to the accompaniments. Up to this point, our working taco sauce was pretty simple—nothing more than some light mayonnaise mixed with lime juice. Looking to add another flavor dimension, we mixed in some garlic and fresh cilantro, as well as minced chipotle chiles for their smoky heat. Meanwhile, the shredded lettuce was bland and turned limp in a matter of seconds when added to the warm fish. Many fish taco purveyors rely on shredded cabbage since it is better able to hold on to its crunch, but on its own it didn't add much more flavor than plain lettuce. Tossing it with a few extra ingredients—sliced scallions, cilantro, cider vinegar, salt, and a touch of oil—brought it up to par while keeping things light. Our cool, simply flavored cabbage slaw was the perfect match for our smoky, spice-rubbed fish and bright sauce. Sitting back with our fish tacos, we all agreed we had created a little bit of paradise right in our own kitchen.

Grilled Fish Tacos

SERVES 4

If your fish fillets are thicker or thinner than 1 inch, the cooking times may vary slightly. Halibut or swordfish can be substituted for the mahi-mahi if desired. To make this dish more or less spicy, adjust the amount of chipotle chiles. Serve with lime wedges.

- ½ small head green cabbage (about 8 ounces), cored and shredded (about 4 cups) (see page 7)
- 5 tablespoons chopped fresh cilantro
- 3 scallions, sliced thin
- 2 tablespoons cider vinegar
- 1 tablespoon canola oil
   Salt
- ¾ cup light mayonnaise
- 1 tablespoon fresh lime juice
- 2 teaspoons minced canned chipotle chiles in adobo sauce (see note)
- 1 garlic clove, minced
   Pepper
- 2 teaspoons chili powder
- ½ teaspoon ground coriander
- ¼ teaspoon ground cumin
- 4 (6-ounce) skinless mahi-mahi fillets, about 1 inch thick (see note)
- 12 (6-inch) corn tortillas, warmed (see page 70)

1. Toss the cabbage, ¼ cup of the cilantro, scallions, vinegar, 1 teaspoon of the oil, and ¼ teaspoon salt together in a medium bowl, and set aside for serving. In a separate bowl combine the mayonnaise, remaining 1 tablespoon cilantro, lime juice, chipotles, and garlic. Season with salt and pepper to taste.

2. Combine the chili powder, coriander, cumin, ⅛ teaspoon salt, and ⅛ teaspoon pepper in a small bowl. Pat the mahi-mahi fillets dry with paper towels, brush with the remaining 2 teaspoons oil, then rub evenly with the spice mixture. Place the mahi-mahi on a wire rack set over a rimmed baking sheet and refrigerate until the grill is ready.

3A. FOR A CHARCOAL GRILL: Open the bottom grill vents completely. Light a large chimney starter filled with charcoal briquettes (100 briquettes; 6 quarts). When the coals are hot, spread them in an even layer over the grill. Set the cooking grate in place, cover, and heat the grill until hot, about 5 minutes.

3B. FOR A GAS GRILL: Turn all the burners to high, cover, and heat the grill until hot, about 15 minutes. (Adjust the burners as needed to maintain a hot fire; see page 162.)

4. Clean and oil the cooking grate. Place the mahi-mahi on the grill, perpendicular to the bars of the cooking grate. Cook (covered if using gas) until the fillets are opaque and flake apart when gently prodded with a paring knife, 10 to 14 minutes, gently flipping the fillets halfway through with two spatulas. Transfer the fish to a carving board, tent loosely with foil, and let rest for 5 minutes.

5. Cut each fillet into 3 equal pieces. Smear 1 tablespoon of the mayonnaise mixture on each warm tortilla, top with the cabbage salad and a piece of mahi-mahi, and serve.

PER SERVING: Cal 520; Fat 18g; Sat fat 2g; Chol 130mg; Carb 51g; Protein 36g; Fiber 5g; Sodium 890mg

GRILLED LEMON SHRIMP

WE LOVE THE BRINY, SWEET TASTE OF SHRIMP, AND it doesn't hurt that they are a great source of low-fat, low-calorie protein. While this little crustacean can be prepared in countless ways, one of our favorites is fairly straightforward: on the grill with lemon. It's a simple flavor combination, but a good recipe for grilled shrimp with lemon is actually hard to find. Most recipes lead to overcooked shrimp swimming in a bath of mouth-puckering sauce. We wanted to find a way to get perfectly cooked shrimp with a smoky, charred crust and citrus flavor that was more than just superficial.

Lean, quick-cooking shrimp can easily become tough and dry, especially when seared over the high heat of the grill. But with the help of past test kitchen experience, we knew how to avoid these issues. Packing the shrimp tightly on skewers would ensure that they cooked more slowly, and sprinkling one side of the shrimp with sugar would promote caramelizing and accentuate the shrimp's natural sweetness, nicely setting off their inherent sea-saltiness. We also knew we'd need the grill set up with a hot side for searing and a cooler side for cooking through. We grilled our shrimp, sugared-side down, over the hot side for a few minutes. When a nice crust had developed, we flipped the skewers and moved them to the cool part of the grill to finish up. We found that a good sear on one side provided plenty of flavor, and searing the second side only resulted in overcooking. This method worked like a charm, allowing the interior to stay moist and tender while the exterior developed a flavorful char.

So what we really needed to concentrate on was the lemony kick. Starting with an ample but not overpowering amount of lemon juice (the amount we squeezed out of two lemons), we added a little olive oil, lemon zest, garlic, parsley, and red pepper flakes and brushed the mixture on the shrimp as they came off the grill. They tasted fine, but the flavor of the sauce wasn't permeating the shrimp. Our next batch fared better: We used some of the flavorful mixture as a 15-minute marinade, reserving the rest to employ as a finishing sauce.

We were on the right track, but we wanted to get still more flavor inside the shrimp. Making the marinade more powerful overwhelmed the delicate shrimp

GRILLED LEMON SHRIMP

flavor, and marinating for more than 15 minutes wasn't an option since the acid in the marinade started cooking the shrimp after that point. Then it hit us: If we wanted more flavor, why not butterfly the shrimp to expose more meat to the marinade? Sure enough, the butterflying worked perfectly and produced the most flavorful shrimp yet. This recipe was quick, easy, and gave us perfectly juicy, flavorful shrimp every time.

Tasters raved over our lemon shrimp recipe so much that we were inspired to come up with a few variations, with the idea of keeping the vibrancy created in our original recipe. We used the pungent, spicy flavors of chiles and ginger to create an Asian-inspired marinade, and for some bold flavors of the bayou, we developed a New Orleans–style variation with a little beer, garlic, herbs, and Worcestershire. These marinades won tasters over as quickly as the original.

Grilled Lemon Shrimp

SERVES 4

Don't let the shrimp marinate for longer than 15 minutes or else the acid in the marinade will begin to "cook" the shrimp and turn them rubbery. We prefer to use extra-large shrimp for this recipe; if your shrimp are smaller or larger, they will have slightly different cooking times.

MARINADE

- ¼ cup fresh lemon juice plus 1 teaspoon grated lemon zest (about 2 lemons)
- ¼ cup chopped fresh parsley
- 2 tablespoons olive oil
- 6 garlic cloves, minced
- ½ teaspoon salt
- ⅛ teaspoon red pepper flakes

SHRIMP

- 1½ pounds extra-large shrimp (21 to 25 per pound; see note), peeled, deveined, and butterflied (see photo)
- ½ teaspoon sugar

1. FOR THE MARINADE: Combine the lemon juice, lemon zest, parsley, oil, garlic, salt, and pepper flakes in a medium bowl. Measure out and reserve 2 tablespoons of the marinade for serving.

2. FOR THE SHRIMP: Pat the shrimp dry with paper towels, add them to the bowl with the remaining marinade, and toss to coat. Cover and refrigerate for 15 minutes. Following the photo, remove the shrimp from the marinade and thread onto skewers. Sprinkle one side of the shrimp with the sugar.

3A. FOR A CHARCOAL GRILL: Open the bottom grill vents completely. Light a large chimney starter filled with charcoal briquettes (100 briquettes; 6 quarts). When the coals are hot, spread them in an even layer over half of the grill. Set the cooking grate in place, cover, and open the lid vents completely. Heat the grill until hot, about 5 minutes.

3B. FOR A GAS GRILL: Turn all the burners to high, cover, and heat the grill until hot, about 15 minutes. (Adjust the burners as needed to maintain a hot fire; see page 162.)

4. Clean and oil the cooking grate. Place the shrimp, sugared-side down, on the grill (over the coals if using charcoal). Cook (covered if using gas) until lightly charred, 3 to 4 minutes.

5. Flip the shrimp and slide to the cooler part of the grill if using charcoal, or turn off all the burners if using gas. Cover and continue to cook the shrimp until the second side is no longer translucent, 1 to 2 minutes longer.

6. Remove the shrimp from the skewers, toss with the reserved 2 tablespoons marinade, and serve.

PER SERVING: Cal 250; Fat 10g; Sat fat 1.5g; Chol 260mg; Carb 5g; Protein 35g; Fiber 0g; Sodium 550mg

---

NOTES FROM THE TEST KITCHEN

BUTTERFLYING AND SKEWERING SHRIMP

1. Using a paring knife, make a shallow cut down the outside curve of the shrimp to open up the flesh.

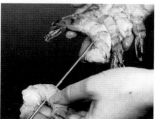

2. Alternate the direction of the shrimp as you pack them tightly on the skewer. This allows you to fit about a dozen shrimp snugly on each skewer.

Grilled Shrimp with Chiles and Ginger

To make this dish spicier, add the chile seeds to the marinade in step 1. A jalapeño chile can be substituted for the small red chiles. Serve with lime wedges.

Combine 2 small red chiles, stemmed, seeded, and minced, 1 scallion, minced, 3 tablespoons rice vinegar, 2 tablespoons low-sodium soy sauce, 1 tablespoon toasted sesame oil, 1 tablespoon grated or minced fresh ginger, 2 teaspoons sugar, and 1 garlic clove, minced, in a small bowl. Follow the recipe for Grilled Lemon Shrimp, substituting the chile and ginger marinade for the lemon marinade.

PER SERVING: Cal 240; Fat 7g; Sat fat 1g; Chol 260mg; Carb 8g; Protein 36g; Fiber 1g; Sodium 520mg

New Orleans Grilled Shrimp

Combine 5 tablespoons room-temperature beer, 3 garlic cloves, minced, 1 tablespoon canola oil, 1 teaspoon minced fresh thyme, 1 teaspoon minced fresh rosemary, 1 teaspoon Worcestershire sauce, ½ teaspoon dried oregano, ½ teaspoon red pepper flakes, ½ teaspoon salt, and ⅛ teaspoon cayenne pepper in a small bowl. Follow the recipe for Grilled Lemon Shrimp, substituting the beer marinade for the lemon marinade.

PER SERVING: Cal 230; Fat 7g; Sat fat 1g; Chol 260mg; Carb 4g; Protein 35g; Fiber 0g; Sodium 560mg

GRILLED SCALLOPS WITH ORANGE-CHILI VINAIGRETTE

GRILLING BUTTERY, RICH SCALLOPS IS A GREAT WAY to amplify their sweetness and briny flavor and introduce another dimension of flavor without adding much in terms of fat or calories. The problem is keeping the scallops on the grill long enough for the meat to pick up flavor without drying out. We wanted to make grilling scallops a fail-safe process, and to complement the flavor from the grill, we also wanted to pair our scallops with a robust but balanced sauce.

We settled on using sea scallops for this recipe over small bay and calico varieties (both are about ½ inch in diameter), since their larger size would allow them to spend more time on the grill and soak up the smoke. Smaller scallops would overcook before they picked up

any grill flavor and wouldn't brown in the minute or two it would take for them to cook through.

In addition to choosing the right type of scallop, we also found it was important to inquire about processing when purchasing them. Some scallops are dipped in a phosphate and water mixture that can also contain citric and sorbic acids. This processing extends shelf life but harms the texture and masks the scallops' naturally delicate, sweet flavor. Even worse, during processing, scallops absorb water. Besides the obvious objections (why pay for water weight or processing that detracts from their natural flavor?), processed scallops are much more difficult to grill (and cook in general), since they essentially steam on the cooking grate, making it impossible for them to brown. A caramelized exterior was paramount for tasters; processed scallops simply would not cut it, so we made sure to ask our fishmonger if the scallops were processed before purchasing.

Finally having settled on our scallops, we were able to move on to grilling them. To preserve the creamy texture of the flesh, we wanted to cook the scallops to medium-rare—hot all the way through with slightly translucent centers—to ensure they would not become dry and tough. We also wanted them to develop a caramelized crust. A hot, single-level fire—an even amount of heat over the entire grill—was the answer. The high heat gave our scallops a chance to develop a nicely caramelized exterior in the short cooking time without causing the interior to overcook. We also had to be thorough when cleaning and oiling the cooking grate; otherwise, our scallops stuck to the grill. Finally, tossing the scallops with a little oil and double skewering them before grilling helped to further prevent sticking and ensured that their flat sides were in contact with the cooking grate for maximum browning.

Similarly to our Pan-Seared Scallops (page 111), tasters preferred a smoother, fruit-based sauce to accompany our grilled scallops. With our scallops already boasting the smokiness of the grill, our minds naturally wandered to the vivid flavors of the Southwest. After sampling a variety of reduced citrus juices combined with a little olive oil, we settled on the warm flavor of orange juice but wanted a little more vibrancy. A bit of red wine vinegar helped solve that problem, along with the addition of some minced shallot. Finished with a little cilantro for brightness and chili powder for spice, our vinaigrette was now the perfect finishing touch to our scallops.

Grilled Scallops with Orange-Chili Vinaigrette

SERVES 4

For this recipe, we prefer using larger sea scallops. Depending on the size of your scallops, the cooking times may vary slightly.

VINAIGRETTE

- 1 cup orange juice
- 2 shallots, minced (about 6 tablespoons)
- ½ teaspoon chili powder
- 2 tablespoons olive oil
- 2 tablespoons chopped fresh cilantro
- 1 tablespoon red wine vinegar
- 1 tablespoon water
- 1 teaspoon honey
- ¼ teaspoon salt
- ⅛ teaspoon pepper

SCALLOPS

- 1½ pounds large sea scallops (about 16 scallops; see note), muscle removed (see page 16)
- 1 tablespoon olive oil
- ⅛ teaspoon salt
- ⅛ teaspoon pepper

1. FOR THE VINAIGRETTE: Bring the orange juice, shallots, and chili powder to a simmer in a small saucepan over medium-high heat. Reduce the heat to medium and cook until the orange juice mixture is syrupy and reduced to ⅓ cup, 12 to 15 minutes.

2. Transfer the orange juice syrup to a small bowl and refrigerate until cool, about 10 minutes. Whisk in the oil, cilantro, vinegar, water, honey, salt, and pepper, and set aside.

3. FOR THE SCALLOPS: Toss the scallops and oil together in a large bowl and season with the salt and pepper. Following the photo, thread the scallops onto doubled skewers.

4A. FOR A CHARCOAL GRILL: Open the bottom grill vents completely. Light a large chimney starter filled with charcoal briquettes (100 briquettes; 6 quarts). When the coals are hot, spread them in an even layer over the grill. Set the cooking grate in place, cover, and open the lid vents completely. Heat the grill until hot, about 5 minutes.

4B. FOR A GAS GRILL: Turn all the burners to high, cover, and heat the grill until hot, about 15 minutes. (Adjust the burners as needed to maintain a hot fire; see page 162.)

5. Clean and oil the cooking grate. Place the scallops on the grill (over the coals if using charcoal). Cook the scallops (covered if using a gas grill) until golden brown on both sides and the sides are firm and all but the middle third is opaque, 6 to 8 minutes, flipping them halfway through.

6. Remove the scallops from the skewers and transfer to a platter. Drizzle with the vinaigrette and serve.

PER SERVING: Cal 280; Fat 12g; Sat fat 1.5g; Chol 55mg; Carb 15g; Protein 29g; Fiber 0g; Sodium 500mg

---

NOTES FROM THE TEST KITCHEN

PREPARING SCALLOPS FOR THE GRILL

Thread the scallops onto doubled skewers so that the flat sides of each scallop will directly touch the cooking grate.

BUYING SCALLOPS

When buying sea scallops, look first at their color. Scallops are naturally ivory or pinkish tan; processing (dipping them in a phosphate and water mixture to extend shelf life) turns them bright white. Processed scallops are slippery and swollen and are usually sitting in a milky white liquid at the store. You should look for unprocessed scallops (also called dry scallops), which are sticky and flabby; they will taste fresher than processed scallops and will develop a nice crust when browned because they are not pumped full of water.

GRILLED GLAZED TOFU

WHETHER YOU ARE TRYING TO EAT HEALTHIER OR just looking for a convenient dinner option, tofu is great to have on hand because it stays fresh much longer than raw meat, and it's quick-cooking. We had come across some recipes for grilled tofu, and we were intrigued— we had already prepared a glazed tofu (page 153) on the stovetop but hadn't thought about grilling it. It seemed simple enough, but we wondered if there were challenges waiting to be discovered. There was only one way to find out.

First we needed to find the best way to prepare tofu for the grill. Starting with two 14-ounce blocks, we cut planks, strips, as well as 1-inch cubes that we skewered with the hope it might make the task of flipping the delicate tofu easier. We rubbed them all with oil and threw them onto the grill to see how they fared. The skewered cubes were a failure; they were no easier to flip, and the small cubes stuck to the grate immediately. We found it was best to cut the tofu crosswise into six 1-inch-thick slabs. This shape maximized surface contact with the grill, and there weren't as many pieces of tofu to manage and flip. As with our Grilled Fish Tacos (see page 180), we found that using two spatulas provided the best leverage for flipping the planks.

Next we tested types of tofu. We grilled soft, medium-firm, firm, and extra-firm tofu and had tasters try them side by side. The extra-firm tofu was the easiest to grill, but it had a dry, crumbly texture that most tasters found unappealing. The others were all well liked for their smooth, custardy texture. However, since the soft and medium-firm tofus had a higher tendency to stick to the grill, we settled on the firm variety.

We knew adding enough flavor to the tofu—which is very mild-tasting on its own—would be key to the success of this recipe. Marinating seemed promising, but after an hour the marinade had still not permeated far enough into the tofu to flavor it significantly, and the excess moisture it absorbed made it messy to grill. Glazing had been successful with our previous tofu recipe, so what about a thick glaze, applied toward the end of grilling?

Back in the kitchen, we made a basic glaze of soy sauce, sugar, mirin (a sweet Japanese rice wine), and water, which diluted the saltiness of the soy sauce without muting its rich flavor. To thicken our glaze we added a bit of cornstarch and simmered it for a few minutes until it developed a clingy, syrupy texture. The addition of ginger, garlic, and Asian chili-garlic sauce gave our glaze a final flavor boost.

To prepare our tofu for the grill, we simply brushed it with a little oil and seasoned it with pepper. Working with a high-heat, single-level fire, we placed the tofu on the well-oiled cooking grate (important to prevent sticking) and allowed our tofu planks to sear on both sides, carefully flipping them once. Our tofu browned well and looked pretty, but when we started adding the glaze, the exterior quickly began to burn from the high heat. We'd run into a similar problem during our testing for grilled glazed chicken (page 162), so we thought using a two-level fire with two different heat zones, which had been successful with our chicken, was worth a shot with the tofu. We grilled the tofu on the hotter side until it was lightly browned on both sides, then moved it to the cooler part of the grill to finish cooking and brushed it with a layer of glaze. This time the sugar in the glaze caramelized beautifully and gave us the flavorful crust we were after. Giving the tofu another thick slather of glaze off the grill gave it another boost. The final touch was the addition of cilantro (a generous ¼ cup) to brighten the dish and balance the sweetness of the glaze.

Grilled Glazed Tofu
SERVES 6

Mirin is a sweet Japanese rice wine available in the international aisle of most supermarkets; if unavailable, substitute dry sherry or white wine. Be sure to handle the tofu gently or else it may break apart. This dish pairs well with brown rice or soba noodles and a green salad.

- 2 **(14-ounce) blocks firm tofu, cut lengthwise into 1-inch-thick slabs**
- ⅓ **cup low-sodium soy sauce**
- ⅓ **cup water**
- ⅓ **cup sugar**
- ¼ **cup mirin (see note)**
- 1 **tablespoon grated or minced fresh ginger**
- 2 **garlic cloves, minced**

2 teaspoons cornstarch

1 teaspoon Asian chili-garlic sauce

2 tablespoons canola oil

¼ teaspoon pepper

¼ cup chopped fresh cilantro

1. Spread the tofu on several layers of paper towels and let sit for 20 minutes to drain slightly.

2. Meanwhile, combine the soy sauce, water, sugar, mirin, ginger, garlic, cornstarch, and chili-garlic sauce in a small saucepan. Bring to a simmer over medium-high heat and cook until thickened and reduced to ¾ cup, about 5 minutes. Set aside.

3A. FOR A CHARCOAL GRILL: Open the bottom grill vents completely. Light a large chimney starter filled with charcoal briquettes (100 briquettes; 6 quarts). When the coals are hot, spread two-thirds of them evenly over the grill, then pour the remaining coals over half of the grill. Set the cooking grate in place, cover, and heat the grill until hot, about 5 minutes.

3B. FOR A GAS GRILL: Turn all the burners to high, cover, and heat the grill until hot, about 15 minutes. (Adjust the burners as needed to maintain a hot fire; see page 162.)

4. Clean and oil the cooking grate. Pat the tofu dry with paper towels, brush with the oil, and season with the pepper. Gently place the tofu on the grill (on the hotter part of the grill if using charcoal) and cook (covered if using gas) until lightly browned on both sides, 6 to 10 minutes, gently flipping the tofu halfway through with two spatulas.

5. Slide the tofu to the cooler part of the grill if using charcoal, or turn all the burners to medium (adjust the burners as needed to maintain a medium fire; see page 162) if using gas. Brush the tofu with some of the glaze and cook until well browned on both sides, 2 to 4 minutes, flipping and brushing the tofu with more glaze halfway through cooking.

6. Transfer the tofu to a platter and brush with the remaining glaze. Sprinkle with the cilantro and serve.

PER SERVING: Cal 250; Fat 13g; Sat fat 2g; Chol 0mg; Carb 19g; Protein 15g; Fiber 2g; Sodium 510mg

GRILLED VEGETABLE AND BREAD SALAD

WHAT'S NOT TO LOVE ABOUT FRESH VEGGIES combined with the heat and smoke of the grill? We could think of two things. First, there is the challenge of grilling them to just the right point—gently charred on the outside and tender within—while avoiding blackened and mushy vegetables. Then there's the issue with flavor: Usually there's just not enough of it. They may be appealing from a health point of view, but plain grilled vegetables are sure to get boring fast. That's when the idea for an Italian-style vegetable and bread salad came to mind. Pair grilled vegetable chunks with cubes of rustic bread, fresh herbs, and a bright vinaigrette, and very little else is needed. With a little testing, we figured we'd have a surefire winner.

We began by determining the vegetables to use, focusing on Mediterranean flavors. Mindful of complementary cooking times, we matched zucchini with sweet red onion and red bell peppers. Cutting the zucchini lengthwise and the bell peppers into quarters gave us large pieces that were easy to handle on the grill. Once they cooked, they would be easy enough to cut up into bite-size chunks. For the grilling itself, most recipes we found for these vegetables suggested a total of 10 minutes for both sides over high heat. But when we tried this method, our vegetables were incinerated on the outside when the time was up. Trying again, we built a more moderate, medium-heat fire. Ten minutes later, our vegetables were perfectly browned and tender and full of smoky flavor. During this testing we also found that no matter how hard we tried to keep the onion rings intact, they always came apart and fell through the grate. Threading the onion slices onto metal skewers was an easy solution to ensure that not an onion was lost.

The bread cubes were up next. We knew the quality of the bread would be fundamental to the success of this dish, so we tried several varieties. Sliced white or supermarket bread was immediately out. Its overly smooth texture meant it turned to mush when tossed with the vinaigrette (at this point a simple combination of lemon juice and extra-virgin olive oil), and its surprisingly sweet flavor conflicted with the savory flavors

GRILLED VEGETABLE AND BREAD SALAD

of the salad. We thought breads containing dried fruits or nuts might add a nice touch to the salad, but their garnishes seemed random and out of place. A high-quality rustic loaf or baguette worked the best. The sturdy texture and strong wheaty flavor paired well with the bolder grilled flavor of the vegetables, and it held up reasonably well once dressed. To make it a little sturdier and add appealing crunch, we decided to toast the bread in the oven before tossing it with the vegetables and dressing. This was exactly the texture the salad needed.

We thought we were on our last run-through when we noticed we had a fair amount of room left on the grill while the vegetables were cooking. We realized there was no need to toast the bread in the oven because it could be done quickly and easily right on the grill. Lightly coated with vegetable oil spray and seasoned with some salt and pepper, the bread toasted up to a beautiful golden brown. And as we did with our vegetables, we grilled the bread in larger pieces for easier handling, then cubed it once cooked.

Now all we need to do was put the finishing touches on our vinaigrette. Keeping with our Mediterranean theme, we started with a basic lemon juice and extra-virgin olive oil combination and added some mustard and garlic for tanginess and chopped basil and lemon zest for freshness. All we had to do was toss everything together. Tasters were raving over our grilled vegetable salad with bread, but one suggested adding a little goat cheese for a creamy contrast. Just 2 ounces crumbled on top of the salad made the perfect finishing touch.

Grilled Vegetable and Bread Salad

SERVES 4

A rustic round loaf, or a baguette sliced on the extreme bias, works best for this recipe. Be sure to use high-quality bread.

- 3 tablespoons extra-virgin olive oil
- 2 tablespoons chopped fresh basil
- 4 teaspoons fresh lemon juice plus 1 teaspoon grated lemon zest
- 1 teaspoon Dijon mustard
- 1 garlic clove, minced
  Salt and pepper

- 1 red onion, sliced into ½-inch-thick rounds
- 2 red bell peppers, stemmed, seeded, and quartered
- 2 zucchini, halved lengthwise
  Vegetable oil spray
- 6 ounces French or Italian bread, cut into 1-inch-thick slices (see note)
- 2 ounces goat cheese, crumbled (about ½ cup)

1. Whisk the oil, basil, lemon juice, lemon zest, mustard, garlic, ⅛ teaspoon salt, and ⅛ teaspoon pepper together in a large bowl and set aside.

2. Thread the onion rounds, from side to side, onto two metal skewers. Lightly coat the onion, bell peppers, and zucchini with vegetable oil spray, and season with ⅛ teaspoon salt and ⅛ teaspoon pepper.

3A. FOR A CHARCOAL GRILL: Open the bottom grill vents completely. Light a large chimney starter half full with charcoal briquettes (50 briquettes; 3 quarts). When the coals are hot, spread them in an even layer over the grill. Set the cooking grate in place, cover, and open the lid vents completely. Heat the grill until hot, about 5 minutes.

3B. FOR A GAS GRILL: Turn all the burners to high, cover, and heat the grill until hot, about 15 minutes. Turn all the burners to medium. (Adjust the burners as needed to maintain a medium fire; see page 162.)

4. Clean and oil the cooking grate. Place the vegetables on one half of the grill and cook (covered if using gas) until spottily charred on both sides, 10 to 15 minutes, flipping them halfway through. Transfer the vegetables to a cutting board and remove the onion from the skewers.

5. While the vegetables cook, lightly coat the bread slices with vegetable oil spray and season with ⅛ teaspoon salt and ⅛ teaspoon pepper. Place the bread slices on the grill, opposite the vegetables, and cook (covered if using gas) until golden brown on both sides, about 4 minutes, flipping the slices halfway through. Transfer the bread to the cutting board with the vegetables.

6. Cut the vegetables into 1-inch pieces and the bread slices into 1-inch cubes. Add the vegetables and bread to the bowl with the vinaigrette and toss to coat. Divide the salad evenly among individual plates, sprinkle the cheese evenly over the salads, and serve.

PER SERVING: Cal 290; Fat 15g; Sat fat 3.5g; Chol 5mg; Carb 31g; Protein 8g; Fiber 3g; Sodium 510mg

HERBED RICE PILAF

CHAPTER 9

GREAT GRAINS AND BEANS

M = TEST KITCHEN MAKEOVER

HERBED RICE PILAF

AT ITS MOST BASIC, RICE PILAF IS A SEEMINGLY LIGHT, simple dish. It begins with toasting long-grain rice in butter or oil to develop a rich, nutty flavor. Liquid is then added, the pot is covered, and the rice is cooked over low heat until tender. In addition to deepening the flavor, toasting the rice creates a light and fluffy pilaf with evenly cooked, discrete grains, making it an appealing change from the more starchy and compact regular steamed rice. Rice pilaf is a nice side as is, but it naturally lends itself to additional flavorings—typically aromatics, spices, and herbs—that can be sautéed with the rice at the beginning or stirred into the cooked rice just before serving, making for a side that is simple to prepare but unique and flavorful. Unfortunately, there's more to it than meets the eye. Rice pilaf is often made with a generous amount of fat (some classic recipes call for 1 cup of butter to cook 1 cup of rice!), turning a side dish that should be light and fluffy into one that's dense and greasy. Could we scale back the fat and come up with a foolproof recipe that produced perfectly cooked rice pilaf, deeply flavored with fragrant herbs?

From previous testing of rice pilafs, we already had the basics of the perfect pilaf in place. We knew that long-grain rice—preferably basmati—was the best choice, as medium- and short-grain rice, inherently starchy varieties, made sticky pilafs. We've also found that most pilaf recipes call for too much liquid, resulting in soggy, bland rice. Rather than the standard 2-to-1 ratio of water to rice, the test kitchen has found that 2¼ cups of water and 1½ cups of rice produce a perfect pilaf with fluffy grains. We followed this technique, then tried replacing the water with chicken broth. Not surprisingly, this made our pilaf taste more savory. Following the lead of many classic recipes, we also sautéed some minced onion and several garlic cloves in the oil before adding the broth, which lent a welcome depth.

During these previous tests, we had also learned a few tricks that helped create a perfectly fluffy pilaf. The first is to thoroughly rinse the rice until the water runs clear enough to see the grains distinctly. We believe this step to be essential for producing rice with separate, light, and fluffy grains. Second, we discovered that allowing the rice to steam for 10 minutes after being removed

from the heat ensures that the moisture gets evenly distributed throughout. Placing a clean kitchen towel between the pan and the lid, right after removing the rice from the heat, prevents condensation from forming. The towel absorbs the excess moisture, preventing water from dripping back into the pan during steaming, which in turn produces drier, fluffier rice.

With our pilaf basics in place, we were ready to test toasting the rice using less fat. We made four separate pilafs, each with a different amount of fat—varying from 1 teaspoon to 2 tablespoons—and lined up the finished products for a side-by-side tasting. Right off the bat, tasters complained that the pilaf made with 1 teaspoon of fat was too dry and sticky. Pilaf made with 2 teaspoons proved a bit more promising, but it still seemed somewhat clumpy and dry. The winner wound up being 1 tablespoon of fat, which beat out 2 tablespoons, an amount that tasters complained was a tad too heavy. One tablespoon of fat perfectly coated the rice, making the grains separate and tender and giving the pilaf a good balance of flavor and moisture.

In most recipes for herb pilaf a handful of fresh herbs is tossed in just before serving, but we wanted deep, layered herb flavor. Adding an aromatic bay leaf with the garlic provided a nice base. We tested adding parsley, rosemary, sage, and thyme (alone and in combination) to the pot at various stages, and our tasters were unanimous in preferring the potent simplicity of a teaspoon of fresh thyme, quickly sautéed with the garlic and bay leaf, and a handful of chopped fresh parsley mixed in just before serving. With toasted sliced almonds added for crunch, this fluffy pilaf has the perfect balance of flavors and textures and none of the grease.

NOTES FROM THE TEST KITCHEN

STEAMING RICE

After the rice is cooked, cover the pan with a clean kitchen towel, replace the lid, and allow the pan to sit for 10 minutes.

Herbed Rice Pilaf

SERVES 6

Jasmine or Texmati rice (both of which have a fragrant, nutty aroma) can also be used in this recipe. A wide-bottomed saucepan with a tight-fitting lid works best for evenly cooked rice.

1 onion, minced (about 1 cup)
1 tablespoon canola oil
  Salt
1½ cups basmati or long-grain white rice (see note), rinsed (see page 69)
2 garlic cloves, minced
1 teaspoon minced fresh thyme
1 bay leaf
2¼ cups low-sodium chicken broth
¼ cup sliced almonds, toasted (see page 16)
¼ cup chopped fresh parsley
  Pepper

1. Combine the onion, oil, and ¼ teaspoon salt in a large saucepan. Cover and cook over medium-low heat, stirring occasionally, until softened, 8 to 10 minutes. Add the rice and cook, stirring constantly, until the ends of the rice kernels are transparent, 1 to 2 minutes. Stir in the garlic, thyme, and bay leaf, and cook until fragrant, about 30 seconds.

2. Stir in the broth and bring to a simmer over medium-high heat. Reduce the heat to low, cover, and cook until the liquid is absorbed and the rice is tender, 16 to 20 minutes.

3. Remove the pot from the heat and lay a clean, folded kitchen towel underneath the lid. Let sit for 10 minutes, then discard the bay leaf and fluff the rice with a fork. Stir in the almonds and parsley, season with salt and pepper to taste, and serve.

PER ¾-CUP SERVING: Cal 210; Fat 4.5g; Sat fat 0g; Chol 0mg; Carb 39g; Protein 5g; Fiber 1g; Sodium 310mg

CURRIED RICE SALAD

CURRIED RICE SALAD SHOULD BE A LIGHT AND EASY side dish with fluffy grains and balanced flavors. Unfortunately, most recipes yield sticky clumps of rice coated with a dressing that is surprisingly bland. We wanted a recipe for curried rice salad that yielded perfectly cooked rice and a flavorful dressing, the type of crowd-pleasing and healthy dish you could whip up at the last minute for a potluck or weeknight dinner.

While the concept of a rice salad seems quite simple, the texture of rice—both short- and long-grain—presents a problem from the get-go. Long-grain rice, though promising texturally when just cooked, normally just isn't good cold; it tends to turn into a solid, clumpy mess. Both short- and medium-grain rice hold up better as they cool, but they have an inherent stickiness that you don't want in a rice salad, making them nonstarters for this situation. If we were to achieve a tender, fluffy, and light rice salad, we needed a cooking method for long-grain rice that would preserve its fresh-from-the-pan characteristics once cooled.

We started by cooking long-grain rice (we preferred aromatic basmati rice over regular long-grain rice) using the conventional absorption method (simmered in a covered pot with just enough water). As expected, once cooled, the rice solidified into a sticky mass. We tried rinsing the rice before cooking to remove some excess starch, as we had done with our Herbed Rice Pilaf (page 192), and this made for a slight improvement, but it still didn't produce the fluffy texture we wanted once the rice cooled.

We needed to get rid of even more starch, so we tried cooking the rice as we would pasta: boiling it in a large volume of water until it was just cooked through and then draining it. The drawback was that it tended to turn out rice that tasted waterlogged, but we found after a few tests that the light and separate consistency of the rice held up well and it remained fluffy after cooling—just what we were looking for. To solve the waterlogging problem, we spread the drained rice on a baking sheet to cool off, creating a large surface area that allowed the excess moisture to evaporate. Spreading out the rice also promoted less clumping and quicker cooling.

Many basic recipes simply have you toss the cooled rice with a curry vinaigrette made with raw curry powder. The results are predictably dull and dusty. From our

CURRIED RICE SALAD

experience with Indian curries, we've found that blooming curry powder in some oil unlocks its flavor. Using the same pot as we'd used for the rice, we first sautéed onion and jalapeño to add depth and heat, then added the curry powder, along with some garlic and ginger, and cooked them until they were fragrant. A little curry powder went a long way: 1½ teaspoons was flavorful without being overpowering.

For the acid component of our salad, lime juice delivered the right fruity-tart note, and ¼ cup of juice tempered with a little sugar produced the most well-balanced salad. Raisins (which we plumped in the lime juice and sugar) added chewy sweetness. Chopped cilantro provided just the right fresh finish to this summery salad.

Curried Rice Salad

SERVES 6

For more heat, add the jalapeño ribs and seeds when mincing.

⅔ cup raisins or currants
¼ cup fresh lime juice (about 2 limes)
¾ teaspoon sugar
1½ cups basmati or long-grain rice
　Salt
1 onion, minced (about 1 cup)
1 jalapeño chile, stemmed, seeded, and minced (see note)
1 teaspoon canola oil
1 tablespoon grated or minced fresh ginger
1½ teaspoons curry powder
1 garlic clove, minced
3 tablespoons chopped fresh cilantro
　Pepper

NOTES FROM THE TEST KITCHEN

GRATING GINGER SAFELY

Peel a small section of a large piece of ginger. Then grate the peeled portion, using the rest of the ginger as a handle.

1. Combine the raisins, lime juice, and sugar in a small bowl and set aside. Bring 4 quarts water to a boil in a Dutch oven. Add the rice and 1 tablespoon salt, and cook, stirring often, until just tender, 12 to 14 minutes. Drain the rice, spread it on a rimmed baking sheet, and cool to room temperature.

2. Combine the onion, jalapeño, oil, and ¼ teaspoon salt in the pot. Cover and cook over medium-low heat, stirring occasionally, until the vegetables are softened, 8 to 10 minutes. Stir in the ginger, curry powder, and garlic, and cook until fragrant, about 30 seconds. Off the heat, stir in the raisin mixture, then transfer to a large bowl and cool to room temperature.

3. Add the rice and cilantro to the bowl with the raisin mixture and toss to combine. Season with salt and pepper to taste and serve.

PER ¾-CUP SERVING: Cal 230; Fat 1g; Sat fat 0g; Chol 0mg; Carb 53g; Protein 4g; Fiber 2g; Sodium 200mg

DRESSED-UP BROWN RICE

LET'S FACE IT: BROWN RICE HAS ISSUES. IT TAKES forever to cook and can be devilishly hard to get right. We can get over the long cooking time, but with such a long stay over the direct heat of the stovetop, there's always the risk that the bottom layer will turn dry and crusty, leaving you with far less edible rice than you expected. Sure, you can speed up the process by cooking it in the microwave, but that just creates new problems: One batch will be dry and brittle, another too sticky. And even if you address these shortcomings, there's the issue that, although healthy, brown rice served plain can be boring, even unappealing. This wholesome grain needed a fresh, more flavorful look.

Cooks who take the trouble know that rice cookers can deliver excellent results, but not everyone wants another appliance in the house. In the test kitchen, we've licked brown rice's cooking problems another way: We bake it in the oven, where the consistent, indirect heat actually simulates the environment of a rice cooker, eliminating scorching and creating perfect, evenly cooked rice every time. Armed with this method, we set out to win converts to this nutritious grain by bumping up its flavor and complementing its chewy texture with a few easy additions.

To get our bearings, we cooked a batch of oven-baked brown rice using our established method. We boiled

2⅓ cups water, stirred it into 1½ cups of brown rice in a glass baking dish, covered the dish tightly with foil, then slid it into the oven to bake for an hour. We knew that once we added other ingredients, the 8-inch square baking dish would get a little tight. Since we were sure that we would want to add at least a few sautéed vegetables, like onion and garlic, we would also be using a piece of cookware that could go on the stovetop. Why not streamline things by cooking everything in just one vessel? A roomy Dutch oven seemed like the best bet—plus its lid would mean we could eliminate the foil step. Putting the additions on hold until we perfected the cooking method, we prepped a new batch of brown rice, stirring the rice into water boiled in a Dutch oven, which we then covered and placed in the oven.

We were surprised, when we lifted the lid an hour later, that the rice looked brittle and bone-dry—the liquid had evaporated before the rice was cooked. The big culprit—literally—turned out to be the pot itself. Because the Dutch oven had a greater surface area than the 8-inch baking dish, more liquid was exposed to the heat of the oven, so more of it evaporated before the rice had a chance to cook. After some tinkering, we were able to achieve perfectly chewy brown rice in a Dutch oven by increasing the amount of liquid to 3¼ cups and the cooking time to 65 to 70 minutes. As we'd found with our Herbed Rice Pilaf (page 192), putting a towel under the lid after the rice had cooked absorbed condensation and kept water from dripping back into the pan. This gave us perfect, fluffy rice grains.

It was finally time to dress up our rice. Incorporating some chicken broth into the cooking liquid was an obvious first step toward bolstering flavor. Swapping out all the water for chicken broth, however, proved to be overkill; the subtle nutty flavor of the brown rice was overwhelmed. After a few tests, we found that replacing 1 cup of the water with broth enhanced the flavor of the rice without obscuring it.

Our next move was to determine when other additions should go into the pot: with the rice as it cooked, or after? It was a given that onions could go into the pot with the uncooked rice, and we decided to brown them in olive oil first for deeper flavor. We did the same with green peppers. Other ingredients, like peas and black beans, did best when gently warmed and stirred into the rice after it was removed from the oven. Just before

serving, we brightened the flavors of each variation with a sprinkle of fresh herbs and a squeeze of citrus.

These few ingredients transformed our plain grain into something so fresh and interesting, the naysayers would never believe it was still wholesome.

Brown Rice with Onions and Roasted Red Peppers
SERVES 5

Short-grain brown rice can also be used in this recipe. Serve with a sprinkling of grated Parmesan cheese, if desired.

- 2 onions, minced (about 2 cups)
- 1 teaspoon olive oil
- Salt
- 2¼ cups water
- 1 cup low-sodium chicken broth
- 1½ cups long-grain brown rice (see note), rinsed (see page 69)
- ¾ cup jarred roasted red peppers, drained, patted dry, and finely chopped
- ½ cup chopped fresh parsley
- ¼ teaspoon pepper
- 1 lemon, cut into wedges

1. Adjust an oven rack to the middle position and heat the oven to 375 degrees.

2. Combine the onions, oil, and ¼ teaspoon salt in a Dutch oven. Cover and cook over medium-low heat, stirring occasionally, until softened, 8 to 10 minutes. Uncover, increase the heat to medium-high, and continue to cook, stirring occasionally, until the onions are lightly browned, 4 to 6 minutes longer.

3. Add the water and broth, cover, and bring to a simmer. Remove the pot from the heat and stir in the rice. Cover and bake the rice until tender, 65 to 70 minutes.

4. Remove the pot from the oven, uncover, and fluff the rice with a fork. Stir in the roasted red peppers. Lay a clean, folded kitchen towel underneath the lid, cover, and let sit for 10 minutes. Stir in the parsley and pepper, and season with salt to taste. Serve with the lemon wedges.

PER ¾-CUP SERVING: Cal 200; Fat 1g; Sat fat 0g; Chol 0mg; Carb 45g; Protein 3g; Fiber 1g; Sodium 330mg

Brown Rice with Peas and Mint

Follow the recipe for Brown Rice with Onions and Roasted Red Peppers, omitting the oil and onions. Substitute 1 cup thawed frozen peas for the roasted red peppers, ¼ cup chopped fresh mint for the parsley, and ½ teaspoon grated lemon zest for the pepper. Sprinkle 1 ounce feta cheese, crumbled (¼ cup), over the rice before serving.

PER ¾-CUP SERVING: Cal 250; **Fat** 1g; **Sat fat** 5g; **Chol** 5mg; **Carb** 49g; **Protein** 7g; **Fiber** 4g; **Sodium** 320mg

Brown Rice with Black Beans and Cilantro

This variation makes a little extra rice and serves 6.

Follow the recipe for Brown Rice with Onions and Roasted Red Peppers, substituting 1 green bell pepper, stemmed, seeded, and chopped fine, for 1 of the onions. After the vegetables are lightly browned, stir in 3 garlic cloves, minced, and cook until fragrant, about 30 seconds. Substitute 1 (15-ounce) can black beans, drained and rinsed, for the roasted red peppers, ¼ cup chopped fresh cilantro for the parsley, and lime wedges for the lemon.

PER ¾-CUP SERVING: Cal 240; **Fat** 2.5g; **Sat fat** 0g; **Chol** 0mg; **Carb** 46g; **Protein** 7g; **Fiber** 5g; **Sodium** 350mg

NOTES FROM THE TEST KITCHEN

OUR FAVORITE ROASTED RED PEPPERS

You can certainly roast your own peppers at home, but jarred peppers are especially convenient. Since not all are created equal, we tasted eight supermarket brands, both straight out of the jar and in a soup. When they sampled the peppers plain, our tasters preferred firmer, smokier, sweeter-tasting peppers in strong yet simple brines of salt and water. Peppers packed in brines that contained garlic, vinegar, olive oil, and grape must—characteristic of most of the European peppers—rated second. The extra ingredients provided "interesting" and "lively" flavor profiles, but the vinegar often masked the authentic red pepper flavor and smoky notes that tasters preferred. The blandest peppers were also the slimiest ones, both of which rated dead last. Our winner? Tasters preferred the domestically produced **Dunbars Sweet Roasted Peppers,** which lists only red bell peppers, water, salt, and citric acid in its ingredient list.

CHEESY BROCCOLI AND RICE CASSEROLE

THE IDEA OF COMBINING BROCCOLI, RICE, AND cheese into a casserole sounds like it has the makings for a crowd-pleasing, easy weeknight supper. Unfortunately the popular, quick version of this casserole

TEST KITCHEN
MAKEOVER

is thrown together with gloppy condensed soup, lifeless frozen broccoli, and shelf-stable "cheese products," resulting in a stodgy mass of weak, muddled flavors—not to mention that this retro comfort food is basically a calorie bomb in a casserole dish, overloaded with greasy cheese and butter. We imagined a livelier, lighter casserole with tender rice, fresh broccoli flavor, and sharp cheddar bite.

We started with a half-dozen from-scratch recipes. They all worked similarly: Butter and flour are stirred together on the stovetop to make a roux; heavy cream is poured in and reduced; and cheese, fresh broccoli florets, and cooked rice are folded in before baking. These casseroles put the canned soup–frozen broccoli versions to shame, but in addition to being full of fat, they were still weak on flavor, the broccoli always came out too crunchy, and the rice was overcooked and blown out. Putting these issues of texture and flavor aside for the moment, we first wanted to see if we could make a credible light version of this dish.

We started with the sauce that binds everything together. First on the list was looking for an acceptable substitute for the heavy cream. We considered three lower-fat replacements: half-and-half, milk, and evaporated milk. Right off the bat, we dismissed the half-and-half because while it is lighter than cream, the quantity needed for this recipe would still contribute too much fat. The milk made a sauce that was a little too lean and thin, but the evaporated milk was a success, giving the sauce a velvety, smooth texture that tricked many of our tasters into thinking they were eating a full-fat casserole. Testing the difference between whole evaporated milk, 2 percent (low-fat) evaporated milk, and skim evaporated milk, we found that tasters preferred the low-fat version, since it had good flavor but was still low in fat. Cutting the evaporated milk with chicken broth added some needed depth to the sauce.

The sauce is usually thickened with a roux, and while a traditional butter-flour roux performed well when we tested it with our lighter sauce, it added back nearly as much fat as we had just worked to remove. Before testing low-fat thickening options, we wondered if using the rice itself to help thicken the sauce might allow us to cut back enough on the roux to get within a healthy range. We reasoned that adding the rice raw to the simmering sauce instead of stirring it in cooked just before baking would allow us to exploit the natural starch from the rice. To test our theory, we cooked up multiple casseroles, all made with raw rice added to the sauce and each with incrementally decreasing amounts of roux. We discovered in the end that the rice alone was all our casserole needed—we could eliminate the roux entirely. Adding the rice raw had another bonus: We got perfectly cooked, not blown-out, grains every time.

The cheese is obviously another one of the unhealthy culprits in the original recipe, and switching to low-fat cheese was an easy way to trim some calories and fat. Most of the recipes we found used at least 2 cups of cheddar; we found we could reduce this to 1½ cups of low-fat cheddar without affecting the texture. However, tasters began to complain that the casserole was bland. To get bolder cheese flavor without adding much fat, we supplemented the low-fat cheddar with some Parmesan, and its assertive, tangy flavor meant a little—just 6 tablespoons—could go a long way. Adding dry mustard and a hint of cayenne lent just the right boldness.

As for the broccoli, fresh was obviously better than frozen, but we knew we'd need some finesse to get the most out of it. In the test kitchen, we've learned that broccoli stalks have just as much flavor as the florets, but they take longer to cook. To ensure that everything was evenly cooked, we sautéed the chopped broccoli stalks with some onion for about 10 minutes before adding the liquids and rice to cook for about 20 minutes, and the broccoli florets went in right before we moved the casserole to the oven for a brief stint. Precooking the florets for just a few minutes in the microwave ensured that they were tender in the finished dish. With twice as much broccoli as in most recipes, our casserole now had plenty of fresh broccoli flavor.

In some recipes this style of casserole is simply topped with more cheese, and recipes closer to the back-of-the-can version sometimes opt for canned fried onions. Wanting something fresher and lighter, we made garlicky fresh bread crumbs enriched with more Parmesan. This topping baked up brown and crisp, adding a final layer of flavor and texture to our no-guilt casserole.

MAKEOVER SPOTLIGHT: BROCCOLI AND RICE CASSEROLE

	CALORIES	FAT	SAT FAT	CHOLESTEROL
BEFORE	350	20g	13g	55mg
AFTER	240	6g	3g	15mg

Cheesy Broccoli and Rice Casserole
SERVES 10

Don't be tempted to use either preshredded or nonfat cheddar cheese in this dish—the texture and flavor of the casserole will suffer substantially. For best results, choose a low-fat cheddar cheese that is sold in block form and has roughly 50 percent of the fat and calories of regular cheese (we like Cabot and Cracker Barrel brands).

  Vegetable oil spray
2 slices high-quality white sandwich bread, torn into pieces
2 teaspoons canola oil
  Salt and black pepper
1 ounce Parmesan cheese, grated (about ½ cup)
1 garlic clove, minced
2 bunches broccoli (about 3 pounds), florets cut into 1-inch pieces, stems trimmed and chopped medium
1 onion, minced (about 1 cup)
1¼ cups long-grain white rice
4 cups low-sodium chicken broth
1 (12-ounce) can low-fat evaporated milk
6 ounces 50 percent light cheddar cheese (see note), shredded (about 1½ cups)
¼ teaspoon dry mustard
⅛ teaspoon cayenne pepper

1. Adjust an oven rack to the middle position and heat the oven to 400 degrees. Lightly coat a 13 by 9-inch baking dish with vegetable oil spray and set aside.

2. Pulse the bread in a food processor to coarse crumbs, about 10 pulses. Transfer the crumbs to a bowl and stir in 1 teaspoon of the oil, ¼ teaspoon salt, and ¼ teaspoon black pepper. Spread the crumbs on a rimmed baking sheet and bake, stirring occasionally, until golden brown and dry, 8 to 10 minutes. Set aside to cool to room temperature, then stir in 2 tablespoons of the Parmesan and garlic.

3. Microwave the broccoli florets in a large bowl, covered, on high power, until bright green and tender,

CHEESY BROCCOLI AND RICE CASSEROLE

2 to 4 minutes; set aside. Combine the remaining 1 teaspoon oil, broccoli stems, onion, and ¼ teaspoon salt in a Dutch oven. Cover and cook over medium-low heat, stirring occasionally, until the vegetables are softened, 8 to 10 minutes.

4. Add the rice and cook, stirring constantly, until the ends of the rice kernels are transparent, 1 to 2 minutes. Stir in the broth and evaporated milk, and bring to a simmer over medium-high heat. Reduce the heat to medium-low and cook, stirring often, until the rice is tender, 20 to 25 minutes.

5. Off the heat, stir in the broccoli florets, remaining 6 tablespoons Parmesan, cheddar, dry mustard, and cayenne. Season with salt and black pepper to taste. Pour the mixture into the prepared baking dish and top with the bread-crumb mixture. Bake until the sauce is bubbling around the edges and the top is brown, about 15 minutes. Let cool for 5 minutes before serving.

PER ½-CUP SERVING: **Cal** 240; **Fat** 6g; **Sat fat** 3g; **Chol** 15mg; **Carb** 35g; **Protein** 15g; **Fiber** 4g; **Sodium** 610mg

NOTES FROM THE TEST KITCHEN

GETTING SERIOUS BROCCOLI AND CHEESE FLAVOR
Most back-of-the-box versions of this classic casserole are big on fat and calories and small on flavor. Our version is not only healthier, but it also has maximum broccoli and cheese flavor.

BROCCOLI STEMS
Using the stems in addition to the florets means big broccoli flavor in every bite.

DYNAMIC CHEESE DUO
Supplementing low-fat cheddar with a little bold Parmesan boosts the cheesy flavor without a jump in calories or fat.

BARLEY RISOTTO

THOUGH BARLEY HAS BEEN AROUND FOR THOUSANDS of years, today we probably come across it most often in beer, whiskey, or soups like our Mushroom-Barley Soup (page 40). Looking for other ways to incorporate this wholesome, hardy grain into our diet, we did a little research, and we turned up a number of barley recipes with a recurring theme: barley prepared using a risotto cooking method. This technique piqued our curiosity, and it seemed as if it had good possibility as an appealing side dish. We'd already perfected a method for making low-fat risotto (see page 149) with arborio rice, so we set out to see what we could do with the barley.

Barley is sold in numerous forms: hulled, pearl, Scotch, and flake, to name a few. We were most interested in the hulled and pearl, the two whole forms of the grain, since the others are crushed or flattened and wouldn't give us the consistency we were after. Hulled barley is the most nutritious form of barley on the market, but it's not that easy to find. When we did track it down, we quickly learned it had a long cooking time and unavoidable chewy texture, both of which result from the fact that though it has been hulled, the bran has been left intact. It didn't seem like a feasible option, so we turned our attention to the widely available pearl barley.

While not quite as nutritious as hulled barley, pearl barley is still fairly nutrient-rich and has a decent amount of fiber. Basically, pearl barley is hulled barley that has been polished until the bran is gone. With the bran removed, the cooking time is substantially reduced, and the texture of the grain becomes springy when cooked—a texture similar to that of perfectly cooked arborio rice. Also, because the bran is removed, the grain's starchy interior is exposed, which creates a supple, velvety sauce when simmered, again, much the same as the sauce in risotto.

With our choice of barley nailed down, we turned to testing our existing risotto method to cook the barley. We started by sautéing onion in olive oil until soft, and then we added the barley, which we sautéed until it was lightly browned and aromatic. Next, we added the wine and cooked the mixture until the wine had all been absorbed by the barley and the pan had turned dry. At this point we ladled a mixture of hot broth and water (we had found that a ratio of 4 cups of broth to 3 cups of water worked best) into the pot in stages until the grains were cooked al dente (meaning the grains were cooked through but still somewhat firm in the center). We finished the dish with a handful of grated Parmesan cheese and a small amount of butter (1 tablespoon) for richness. This method worked well, but we needed to make one minor adjustment because the barley wasn't completely cooked through. Pearl barley takes longer to cook than arborio rice, so we needed to use a bit more hot liquid. We tried again, this time upping the water amount by 1 cup, and it worked perfectly.

With the cooking technique under control, all we had to do now was boost the flavor of the barley risotto just a bit with the help of a few additional ingredients. We turned to simple flavors that would elevate and complement the barley's subtle earthy flavor. Chopped carrot, sautéed along with the onion, added a bit of welcome sweetness and depth, and a small amount of minced fresh thyme lent a woodsy flavor that tasters liked.

While no one will mistake barley risotto for traditional risotto, it is a unique and flavorful alternative and pairs well with dishes like roast chicken, beef tenderloin, and grilled vegetables.

Barley Risotto

SERVES 6

Pearl barley is crucial for this risotto and is widely available in supermarkets. You may not need to use all of the broth (we prefer to err on the side of having a little extra).

- 4 **cups low-sodium chicken broth (see note)**
- 4 **cups water**
- 1 **onion, minced (about 1 cup)**
- 1 **carrot, peeled and chopped fine**
- 1 **teaspoon olive oil**
  Salt
- 1½ **cups pearl barley, rinsed (see note)**
- 1 **cup dry white wine**
- 1 **teaspoon minced fresh thyme**
- 1½ **ounces Parmesan cheese, grated (about ¾ cup)**
- 1 **tablespoon unsalted butter**
  Pepper
- 2 **tablespoons chopped fresh parsley**
  Lemon wedges, for serving

1. Bring the broth and water to a simmer in a medium saucepan, reduce the heat to low, and cover to keep warm.

2. Meanwhile, combine the onion, carrot, oil, and ¼ teaspoon salt in a large saucepan. Cover and cook over medium-low heat, stirring occasionally, until the vegetables are softened, 8 to 10 minutes. Increase the heat to medium, add the barley, and cook, stirring frequently, until lightly browned and aromatic, about 4 minutes. Stir in the wine and cook until it has been completely absorbed, 2 to 3 minutes.

3. Stir in 3 cups of the hot broth and thyme, bring to a simmer, and cook, stirring every few minutes, until the liquid is absorbed and the bottom of the pan is almost dry, about 22 to 25 minutes. Stir in 2 cups more broth and continue to simmer, stirring occasionally, until the liquid is absorbed and the bottom of the pan is dry, 15 to 18 minutes longer.

4. Stir in ½ cup more broth every few minutes as needed to keep the pan bottom from drying out (you may not need all of the broth), and cook, stirring often, until the barley is al dente, 15 to 20 minutes.

5. Off the heat, vigorously stir in the Parmesan and butter. Season with salt and pepper to taste. Divide among 7 individual plates, sprinkle each portion with the parsley, and serve with the lemon wedges.

PER ¾-CUP SERVING: **Cal** 280; **Fat** 5g; **Sat fat** 2.5g; **Chol** 10mg; **Carb** 44g; **Protein** 8g; **Fiber** 9g; **Sodium** 600mg

BULGUR PILAF WITH MUSHROOMS

THROUGHOUT THE COUNTRIES OF THE EASTERN Mediterranean, including Turkey and Greece, bulgur is a staple grain. Produced from whole wheat kernels, it is vitamin-rich and a great way to add fiber to your diet. Bulgur is packed with an earthy, nutty flavor that is quite distinctive and is used in everything from *tabbouleh* (most famously) to meatballs (called *kibbe*) to—our top choice—pilaf.

An ideal canvas for any number of assertive flavors, bulgur teams up particularly well with mushrooms. The deep, complex essence and forest notes of the mushrooms match well with the earthy nuttiness of the bulgur. And because mushrooms are naturally low in calories and fat, they add a lot of intense flavor without adding too much around the waistline.

When bulgur is made, the whole wheat kernels are steamed, dried, and crushed into one of three grades—coarse, medium, or fine—each of which requires a different cooking method. Fine-grain bulgur, the variety most often seen in Middle Eastern dishes, must be rehydrated in hot liquid, not unlike couscous. Larger-grain bulgur, which we prefer for pilafs, must be simmered until tender, usually about 15 minutes.

Based on our work developing our Herbed Rice Pilaf (page 192), we already had a cooking method in mind. Using a large saucepan from start to finish, the aromatics would be sautéed, the mushrooms would be lightly browned, the bulgur would be added and toasted, and finally the cooking liquid would be added and the mixture simmered until the bulgur was tender. Testing, then, was a matter of developing the fullest mushroom flavor and discovering how long and at what temperature to simmer the bulgur for the best texture.

To get intense mushroom flavor without resorting to pricey exotics, we frequently combine standard cultivated mushrooms—creminis are among our favorites and they're easy to find—with dried porcini mushrooms. Dried mushrooms, which are relatively inexpensive and packed with flavor, impart an intensely earthy flavor and pungent aroma to the most mild-mannered fresh mushrooms. To further boost the mushroom flavor, we added both onion and garlic as well as soy sauce—odd in a Mediterranean dish but welcome nonetheless for the meaty flavor it brought out of the mushrooms and the rich color it added.

For the cooking liquid, we tried both chicken broth and water. Independently, chicken broth was too strong and muddied the dish's flavors, but using all water made the pilaf too lean-tasting. A combination of the two gave the pilaf body without calling attention to the chicken flavor. Equal parts of broth and water were just right. As we explored the best way to cook the bulgur, we tried every approach from a near boil to a quiet simmer. Rapid simmering cooked the bulgur unevenly and gave it an unpleasant chewiness. Very low heat cooked the bulgur more evenly, but at this point it was not perfect. Some of the bulgur grains were still a bit chewier, and overall the pilaf was too dense and moist. But as we had learned with our rice pilaf, allowing the bulgur pilaf to steam for 10 minutes after being removed from the heat ensured that the moisture was distributed throughout.

Almost all recipes for pilaf call for toasting the grain before adding liquid, but we found this step to be unnecessary with bulgur. However, we all agreed that herbs were a welcome addition, contributing depth as well as color. Thyme reinforced the pilaf's earthy edge but lacked visual presence. Parsley brightened both flavor and color, so we chose it over the thyme and opted for a fairly generous amount: ¼ cup. At this point, our pilaf was nearly there, but one taster felt that, while incredibly healthy, it was a little too lean and could use some added richness. Stirring a little bit of olive oil into the finished pilaf easily solved this issue; it helped bring together the flavors in the dish and added good body to the grains. By stirring in the oil at the end of cooking, we ensured maximum olive oil flavor. This pilaf was deeply flavored and rich, ready to win over new fans for a lesser known grain.

Bulgur Pilaf with Mushrooms
SERVES 6

Do not purchase "cracked wheat" in lieu of bulgur; while it looks like bulgur, the two are not the same. Cracked wheat is uncooked, whereas bulgur is parcooked, and the two require different cooking methods. We prefer moderately coarse bulgur, which has a texture like that of kosher salt, to finer, sandy bulgur. If cremini mushrooms are not available, an equal amount of white button mushrooms can be substituted.

- 8   ounces cremini mushrooms, halved if small, quartered if large (see note)
- 1   onion, minced (about 1 cup)
- 4   teaspoons olive oil
- ¼   ounce dried porcini mushrooms, rinsed and minced
     Salt
- 2   garlic cloves, minced
- 1   cup medium- to coarse-grain bulgur (see note)
- ¾   cup low-sodium chicken broth
- ¾   cup water
- 1   teaspoon low-sodium soy sauce
- ¼   cup chopped fresh parsley
     Pepper

1. Combine the cremini mushrooms, onion, 2 teaspoons of the oil, porcini mushrooms, and ¼ teaspoon salt in a large saucepan. Cover and cook over medium-low heat, stirring occasionally, until the vegetables are softened, 8 to 10 minutes. Uncover, increase the heat to medium-high, and continue to cook, stirring occasionally, until the vegetables are lightly browned, 4 to 6 minutes longer. Stir in the garlic and cook until fragrant, about 30 seconds.

2. Stir in the bulgur, broth, water, and soy sauce, and bring to a simmer over medium-high heat. Reduce the heat to low, cover, and cook until the liquid is absorbed and the bulgur is tender, 16 to 18 minutes.

3. Remove the pot from the heat and lay a clean, folded kitchen towel underneath the lid. Let sit for 10 minutes, then fluff the bulgur with a fork. Stir in the remaining 2 teaspoons oil and parsley, season with salt and pepper to taste, and serve.

PER ¾-CUP SERVING: Cal 130; Fat 3.5g; Sat fat 0g; Chol 0mg; Carb 22g; Protein 5g; Fiber 5g; Sodium 230mg

---

NOTES FROM THE TEST KITCHEN

CURLY VERSUS FLAT-LEAF PARSLEY

We use a fair amount of parsley in our bulgur pilaf, and you've probably noticed that your neighborhood grocer has two different varieties of this recognizable herb available (though there are actually more than 30 varieties out there)—curly-leaf and flat-leaf (also called Italian). Curly-leaf parsley is more popular, but in the test kitchen flat-leaf is by far the favorite. We find flat-leaf to have a sweet, bright flavor that's much preferable to the bitter, grassy tones of curly-leaf. Flat-leaf parsley is also much more fragrant than its curly cousin. While curly parsley might look nice alongside your steak, don't count on it to improve flavor if you use it in cooking. Reach for the flat variety in your supermarket, and your dinner guests will thank you. In a pinch, it's fine to substitute.

THE BEST LARGE SAUCEPAN

A large saucepan is an essential piece of cookware that no home cook can do without. To find out if brand matters, we tested eight models, all between 3.3 and 4 quarts in size. We tested the pans for sauté speed, ability to heat evenly, and user-friendliness. The most important quality turned out to be slow, even heating. The best pans for slow and steady cooking either were very heavy or had relatively thick bottoms, and an aluminum core also ensured even heating and minimal scorching. We also liked pans with long handles. Our favorite was the **All-Clad Stainless 4-Quart Saucepan,** $199.95, which

was the only pan to pass every test with flying colors. Testers liked the "solid," "restaurant-quality" feel and "perfectly proportioned" shape.

QUINOA PILAF

QUINOA, A STAPLE OF THE INCA CIVILIZATION AND still a staple of Peru, is generally treated as a grain even though it is actually a seed. It contains significantly more protein than most grains, and its protein is complete, which means it possesses all of the amino acids necessary for protein metabolism, unlike grains that have to be consumed in conjunction with other foodstuffs, such as beans, to unlock their nutritional benefits. But nutritional pluses aside, quinoa stands out because of its wholesome, hearty taste and addictive texture—the individual seeds pop when chewed, not unlike caviar. So, given all these pros, we expected the wonders of quinoa to be balanced with some significant cons, like intensive preparation or finicky cooking requirements.

We were wrong: Quinoa couldn't be easier to prepare. Almost every recipe we found employed the same method for cooking. Rinse the quinoa well to rid the grains of a mildly toxic protective layer (called saponin), which is unpleasantly bitter, bring it to a boil in stock or water, and simmer over low heat, covered, for 15 minutes. In the test kitchen we found that this basic method worked pretty well; however, it made for a wet, dense side dish, so we decided to focus our attention on making a pilaf that would be lighter, drier, and fluffier.

Using our rice pilaf method (see page 192), we sautéed an onion in a small amount of oil until it became soft and released its juice. Next, we added the quinoa to the pan, increased the heat, and toasted it. To ensure that the quinoa toasted properly, we found it was necessary to dry the grain on a kitchen towel after it had been rinsed, before it went in the pan. Tasters were surprised by the degree to which quinoa's flavor improved using this technique. Although toasting grains before adding liquid is standard pilaf procedure because it ensures plumped, individual grains, this step had an unexpectedly substantial impact on quinoa, whose otherwise subtle flavor undertones were greatly intensified.

Next we considered the cooking liquid. In previous tests we had learned that chicken broth can really boost the flavor of a grain. For some recipes we'd made, it was necessary to cut the broth with water (to keep the flavor of the grain unmuddied), but with quinoa, we found that straight chicken broth worked best, giving our pilaf excellent body and fortifying the other flavors in the dish. Finally, after the quinoa had simmered, we pulled the pan off the heat and let it sit, covered, for an extra 10 minutes. The grains steamed during this stage, soaking up extra moisture and ensuring that it was evenly distributed. We all agreed that quinoa takes very well to the pilaf method of cooking, giving us flawlessly and evenly cooked, slightly crunchy grains every time.

With the method down, it was time to fine-tune the flavoring. After myriad tests, we agreed the earthy nuttiness paired best with lighter ingredients. Tasters preferred the subtle sweetness of onion to the slight pungency of garlic, and lemon zest lent a nice hit of citrusy perfume. Stirring in a small amount of lemon juice at the end reinforced the brightness, and finally the earthiness of thyme balanced it all out. For a bolder variation, tasters thought corn, jalapeño, and cilantro worked well together, as the sweetness of the corn brought out the nuttiness of the quinoa, and the jalapeño added heat and paired well with the cilantro. Now we had another new spin on this healthy staple that also gave a nod to its South American roots.

Quinoa Pilaf

SERVES 6

If your market does not carry quinoa, you can almost always find it at natural foods stores. Make sure to thoroughly rinse the quinoa before cooking to remove its bitter exterior coating (the seeds are washed before packaging, but a bit of the compound may remain, so it is worth the precaution, as a small amount of saponin can ruin the dish). It's easy to tell when quinoa is done, as the brown seeds turn translucent.

- 1 **onion, minced (about 1 cup)**
- 1 **teaspoon olive oil**
  Salt
- 1½ **cups quinoa, rinsed (see note) and dried on a towel (see page 205)**
- 1¼ **cups low-sodium chicken broth**
- 1 **teaspoon grated lemon zest plus 2 teaspoons fresh lemon juice**
- 2 **tablespoons chopped fresh parsley**
- 1 **teaspoon minced fresh thyme**
  Pepper

1. Combine the onion, oil, and ¼ teaspoon salt in a large saucepan. Cover and cook over medium-low heat, stirring occasionally, until softened, 8 to 10 minutes. Increase the heat to medium, add the quinoa, and cook,

stirring frequently, until lightly browned and aromatic, about 4 minutes.

2. Stir in the broth and lemon zest, and bring to a simmer over medium-high heat. Reduce the heat to low, cover, and cook until the liquid is absorbed and the quinoa is transparent and tender, 16 to 18 minutes.

3. Remove the pot from the heat and lay a clean, folded kitchen towel underneath the lid. Let sit for 10 minutes, then fluff the quinoa with a fork. Stir in the lemon juice, parsley, and thyme, season with salt and pepper to taste, and serve.

PER ¾-CUP SERVING: Cal 170; Fat 3.5g; Sat fat 0g; Chol 0mg; Carb 30g; Protein 6g; Fiber 4g; Sodium 220mg

VARIATION

Quinoa Pilaf with Corn and Jalapeños
Fresh corn really makes this dish, but when it's not available, you can substitute 1½ cups of thawed, frozen corn. For more heat, include the jalapeño seeds and ribs when mincing.

- 2 **teaspoons olive oil**
- 2 **ears corn (see note), kernels removed from cobs (see page 205)**
- 1 **onion, minced (about 1 cup)**
  Salt
- 1½ **cups quinoa, rinsed and dried on a towel (see page 205)**
- 1¼ **cups low-sodium chicken broth**
- 2 **jalapeño chiles, stemmed, seeded, and minced (see note)**
- 1 **tomato, cored, seeded, and chopped fine**
- ¼ **cup chopped fresh cilantro**
- 2 **teaspoons fresh lime juice**
  Pepper

1. Heat 1 teaspoon of the oil in a large saucepan over medium-high heat until shimmering. Add the corn and cook, stirring frequently, until beginning to brown, about 5 minutes. Transfer the corn to a bowl and set aside.

2. Add the remaining 1 teaspoon oil, onion, and ¼ teaspoon salt to the saucepan. Cover and cook over medium-low heat, stirring occasionally, until softened, 8 to 10 minutes. Increase the heat to medium, add the quinoa, and cook, stirring frequently, until lightly browned and aromatic, about 4 minutes.

3. Stir in the broth and jalapeños, and bring to a simmer over medium-high heat. Reduce the heat to low, cover, and cook until the liquid is absorbed and the quinoa is transparent and tender, 16 to 18 minutes.

4. Remove the pot from the heat and lay a clean, folded kitchen towel underneath the lid. Let sit for 10 minutes, then fluff the quinoa with a fork. Stir in the corn, tomato, cilantro, and lime juice, season with salt and pepper to taste, and serve.

PER ¾-CUP SERVING: Cal 220; Fat 5g; Sat fat .5g; Chol 0mg; Carb 37g; Protein 8g; Fiber 5g; Sodium 220mg

NOTES FROM THE TEST KITCHEN

DRAINING AND DRYING QUINOA

1. Place the quinoa in a fine-mesh strainer and rinse under cool water until the water runs clear, occasionally stirring the quinoa around lightly with your hand. Let drain briefly.

2. Line a rimmed baking sheet with a clean kitchen towel and spread the drained quinoa out to dry, about 15 minutes.

3. To remove the quinoa from the towel, use the corners of the towel to shake the quinoa into the bowl.

CUTTING CORN OFF THE COB

Standing the corn upright inside a large bowl, carefully cut the kernels from the ear of corn using a paring knife.

INDIAN-STYLE CURRIED CHICKPEAS

BEANS ARE A GREAT LOW-FAT, PROTEIN-RICH STAPLE, but in recipes where beans are the star, there tends to be a reliance on pork fat for flavor and richness—not exactly a light approach to an otherwise incredibly healthy food. On top of that, preparing beans can be time-consuming; dried beans have to be presoaked for hours, then they take even longer to cook. Although we generally prefer the flavor and texture of dried beans to canned, sometimes you simply don't have the time (or the desire) to spend hours cooking dinner. We wanted to develop a flavorful, healthy side that used the convenience of canned beans and was doable any night of the week.

Our first step was determining which canned bean we liked best. After running through the options, we found tasters' favorite was chickpeas for their buttery flavor and the fact that, because they are so porous, they take on the flavors of a sauce without breaking down or getting mushy. Chickpeas also fare well during the canning process, emerging from the can as whole, evenly cooked beans with unbroken skins. Because chickpeas are common in Indian-style curries, a curried chickpea dish seemed like a logical choice for a meal that would be flavorful without being fatty or caloric, since the flavor would rely on a bold spice rather than rich ingredients.

Following the technique of most curry recipes, we began building a flavor base by sautéing onion in some oil. Once the onion was lightly browned, we stirred in garlic, ginger, and curry powder. This step of cooking the curry in oil before adding the liquid ingredients (called "blooming") greatly improved the flavor of the curry powder and prevented it from tasting raw in the finished dish. Next we stirred in some chicken broth to give the sauce some body. Along with the broth we added the chickpeas, as well as raisins, whose sweetness provided a pleasant counterpoint to the spices in the dish. We then covered the pan and lowered the heat, allowing the flavors to blend while the chickpeas softened and the raisins plumped. Once the chickpeas were softened, we uncovered the pan and increased the heat to drive off moisture and concentrate the flavors. After about three minutes of simmering, the sauce had reduced to a flavorful, thin coating that clung to the chickpeas.

Our curried chickpeas were almost there, but tasters wanted a little more richness and body in the sauce.

Stirring in ¼ cup of plain low-fat yogurt did the trick, and it also nicely tempered the flavors in the curry. We made sure to stir the yogurt in off the heat to prevent curdling. Chopped cilantro and fresh lime juice gave the curry some bright, fresh notes. Finally, we had a healthy, bean-focused light side dish that could be on the table in about 30 minutes.

Indian-Style Curried Chickpeas

SERVES 7

To turn this dish into a vegetarian entrée, substitute low-sodium vegetable broth for the chicken broth and serve with Herbed Rice Pilaf (page 192).

- 1 onion, minced (about 1 cup)
- 1 teaspoon canola oil
  Salt
- 4 garlic cloves, minced
- 2 teaspoons grated or minced fresh ginger
- 1 teaspoon curry powder
  Pepper
- 2 (15-ounce) cans chickpeas, drained and rinsed
- 1 cup low-sodium chicken broth (see note)
- ⅓ cup raisins
- ¼ cup plain low-fat yogurt
- 2 tablespoons minced fresh cilantro
- 2 teaspoons fresh lime juice

1. Combine the onion, oil, and ¼ teaspoon salt in a 12-inch skillet. Cover and cook over medium-low heat, stirring occasionally, until softened, 8 to 10 minutes. Uncover, increase the heat to medium-high, and continue to cook, stirring occasionally, until the onion is lightly browned, 4 to 6 minutes longer. Stir in the garlic, ginger, curry powder, and ¼ teaspoon pepper, and cook until fragrant, about 30 seconds.

2. Stir in the chickpeas, broth, and raisins, and bring to a simmer. Reduce the heat to medium-low, cover, and cook, stirring occasionally, until the chickpeas have softened and the flavors have blended, about 7 minutes. Uncover, increase the heat to high, and continue to cook until the liquid is reduced to a light coating on the bottom of the pan, about 3 minutes longer.

3. Off the heat, stir in the yogurt, cilantro, and lime juice. Season with salt and pepper to taste and serve.

PER ½-CUP SERVING: Cal 120; Fat 2g; Sat fat 0g; Chol 0mg; Carb 21g; Protein 5g; Fiber 4g; Sodium 420mg

---

NOTES FROM THE TEST KITCHEN

THE BEST CANNED CHICKPEAS

We sampled six brands of canned chickpeas, both plain (drained and rinsed) and pureed in a hummus recipe. None of our tasters could tolerate a bland bean, especially when eaten straight from the can. Low-sodium samples (with less than 250 milligrams of salt per ½ cup) were flavorless and dull, and others had a distinctly metallic, bitter flavor that couldn't be masked by the assertive ingredients in the hummus. Our favorite chickpeas were the ones from **Pastene;** tasters loved the creamy yet firm texture and their clean, slightly salty flavor.

SOUTHWESTERN BLACK BEAN SALAD

THESE DAYS IT SEEMS AS IF NO PICNIC IS COMPLETE without a bowl of summery black bean salad. Most recipes instruct the cook to open a couple of cans of black beans; add a combination of Southwestern-inspired ingredients like avocado, corn, tomatoes, bell peppers, onion, and chiles; and dress the mixture with some sort of vinaigrette. This sounds like a surefire winner, but too many recipes we tried lacked restraint, resulting in a mishmash of competing flavors and textures. The dressings were typically as dull as dishwater, with a copious amount of oil turning what should be a light, refreshing salad into a greasy dish. Clearly, for black bean salad, it was important to know what would fit—and when to quit.

We started with the beans. While we generally prefer dried beans to canned when it comes to both flavor and texture, we saw no reason convenient canned beans wouldn't work fine here, since we would have additional vegetables to boost the texture and a zesty vinaigrette. One 15-ounce can of black beans made a good base for serving a small group. From past tests we knew it was important to rinse the beans for the best consistency and flavor in the final salad. Next we tested all the usual suspects for add-ins. Although minced onion was in the majority of recipes we found in our research, tasters consistently found it too harsh, even when we used just a few tablespoons of relatively mild red onion. Scallions, however, were a crowd-pleaser, praised for both their mild onion flavor and their visual appeal. Bell pepper was also

SOUTHWESTERN BLACK BEAN SALAD

rejected for tasting too strong. Creamy avocado stayed— it gave the salad richness. Tasters liked the juicy freshness tomatoes lent, and corn added welcome sweetness and an appealing crunch that contrasted nicely with the creaminess of the beans and avocado. Curious whether we could simplify the recipe by using canned or frozen corn instead of fresh, we did a side-by-side tasting of salads made with each. The fresh corn was the clear winner; its superior taste and texture made it worth the small amount of additional preparation. To draw out its flavor and further improve its texture, we sautéed the corn in a skillet until it was toasty and just starting to brown.

Most black bean salad dressings are olive oil–lime juice vinaigrettes that use a ratio of 1 part acid (juice) to 3 parts oil. But this ratio made for a greasy, bland salad. After experimenting with gradually increasing ratios of juice to oil, we eventually turned that ratio upside down. We also found the somewhat unusual addition

of ½ teaspoon of honey balanced the punch from the citrus and added a welcome sweetness, and throwing the scallions into the dressing, rather than tossing them with the other ingredients at the end, mellowed them nicely. Tossing the cilantro with the vegetables and beans rather than stirring it into the dressing kept its leaves fresher and ensured that it was evenly distributed. Our salad now needed just a little kick. Rather than concoct a complicated mix of spices and chiles, we found that 1½ teaspoons of minced canned chipotle chiles whisked into the dressing did the job. All we had to do was combine it all. This black bean salad was guaranteed to disappear at our next picnic.

NOTES FROM THE TEST KITCHEN

WHY WE RINSE CANNED BEANS

Canned beans are made by pressure-cooking dried beans directly in the can with water, salt, and preservatives. As the beans cook, starches and proteins leach into the liquid, thickening it. To find out if rinsing the beans is really necessary, we used canned beans in two recipes: chickpeas for hummus and red kidney beans for chili. Tasters found no difference in the chili; there are so many bold flavors and contrasting textures in this dish that rinsing the beans didn't matter. However, we detected notable differences in the hummus. Most tasters thought the version with rinsed beans was brighter in flavor and less pasty than the version with unrinsed beans. So while rinsing the beans may not be necessary for a robust dish like chili, a thick, salty bean liquid does have the potential to throw a simpler recipe off-kilter. And rinsing beans takes only a few seconds, so there's no excuse not to do it.

ALL ABOUT CHIPOTLE CHILES

Chipotle chiles are jalapeño chiles that have been smoked over aromatic wood and dried. They are sold as is—wrinkly, reddish brown, and leathery—or canned in adobo, a tangy tomato-and-herb sauce. We recommend purchasing canned chipotles because they are already reconstituted by the adobo and, thus, are easier to use. Most recipes call for just a chile or two, as they are so potent, but the remaining chiles keep indefinitely if stored in an airtight container in the refrigerator, or they may be frozen. To freeze chipotles, spoon them out, each with a couple of teaspoons of adobo sauce, onto different areas of a baking sheet lined with wax paper, then place in the freezer. Once they are frozen, remove the chiles to a zipper-lock freezer bag, store in the freezer, and use as needed.

Southwestern Black Bean Salad
SERVES 5

Fresh corn is essential to this dish; don't be tempted to substitute frozen or canned corn here.

    3 tablespoons fresh lime juice (about 2 limes)
    4 teaspoons olive oil
    2 scallions, sliced thin
 1½ teaspoons minced canned chipotle chiles
       in adobo sauce
   ½ teaspoon honey
       Salt and pepper
    2 ears corn (see note), kernels removed from cobs
       (see page 205)
    1 (15-ounce) cans black beans, drained and rinsed
    1 large avocado, pitted, peeled, and cut into
       ½-inch pieces (see page 19)
    1 tomato, cored, seeded, and chopped medium
    3 tablespoons chopped fresh cilantro

1. Whisk the lime juice, 1 tablespoon of the oil, scallions, chiles, honey, ¼ teaspoon salt, and ¼ teaspoon pepper together in a large bowl and set aside.

2. Heat the remaining 1 teaspoon oil in a large saucepan over medium-high heat until shimmering. Add the corn and cook, stirring frequently, until beginning to brown, about 5 minutes. Transfer the corn to the bowl with the dressing and set aside.

3. Add the beans, avocado, tomato, and cilantro to the bowl with the corn, and gently toss to combine. Season with salt and pepper to taste and serve.

PER ¾-CUP SERVING: Cal 210; Fat 13g; Sat fat 1.5g; Chol 0mg; Carb 21g; Protein 6g; Fiber 7g; Sodium 300mg

LENTIL SALAD

LENTIL SALAD, A SIMPLE COMPOSITION OF TENDER, fiber-rich lentils and a bold but well-balanced vinaigrette, is great for eating light because it's rich in flavor and texture but not fat or calories. In its poorest form, lentil salad is bland and greasy with no interplay between the lentils and the dressing, an issue central to success when there are so few components. We wanted a recipe with harmony between the two.

We had tested five lentil varieties for our Lentil Soup (page 42)—brown, red, and green lentils, as well as black and small French green lentils, known as *lentilles du Puy*—so we did the same here, cooking up batches of each and tossing them in a bare-bones dressing. Just as in our soup tasting, the lentilles du Puy won out. They held their shape best and had an appealing earthy flavor.

Next we tackled seasonings. Since we were using French lentils, we looked through French cookbooks. Many recipes employed similar cooking methods and flavorings. Most simmered and drained the lentils, then tossed them, still warm, with vinaigrette. More often than not, the vinaigrette contained walnut oil, wine vinegar, Dijon, and aromatics. Generally, these salads were all good, but there was room for improvement.

Some tasters felt the vinaigrette lacked punch; others disliked the walnut oil. Figuring the vinegar (we liked sherry vinegar best) lost potency when mixed with the warm lentils, we decreased the ratio of oil to vinegar. Minimizing the oil to 2 tablespoons gave it the perfect body, but while this improved the brightness of the salad, it didn't improve it enough. Doubling the Dijon to 1 tablespoon gave the dressing the right bite.

Another change we made to the vinaigrette was to switch from walnut oil to extra-virgin olive oil. The walnut oil tended to overpower the salad; even in small amounts its slight bitterness muted the other flavors. The one positive attribute of the walnut oil that olive oil couldn't achieve was that it provided a necessary intensity. We needed to replace that dimension with another ingredient. Thinking of a pasta-cooking technique we often employ in the test kitchen, we added some reserved lentil cooking water to the salad. This worked well, and tasters liked that it gave the dish even more lentil-y richness. We moved to the final issue—texture.

The texture was rather one-dimensional. It needed crunch. Topping the salad with toasted walnuts improved the salad greatly, by adding texture and accentuating the earthiness of the lentils. We found that just ¼ cup of nuts did the trick. Scallions also improved the texture and provided pungency. The final ingredient, roasted red peppers, sweetened the salad and rounded out the other flavors. This healthy lentil salad hit all the marks with nice balance, deep flavor, and appealing texture.

Lentil Salad with Walnuts and Scallions
SERVES 6

Adding grilled chicken or turkey sausages turns this salad into a hearty entrée; with the addition of lettuce leaves or other greens, it also can be served as a light vegetarian meal.

- 1 cup (about 7 ounces) lentilles du Puy (French green lentils), rinsed and picked through
- ½ onion, root end left intact, halved
- 2 bay leaves
- 1 large sprig fresh thyme
- Salt
- 2 tablespoons sherry vinegar
- 2 tablespoons extra-virgin olive oil
- 1 tablespoon Dijon mustard
- Pepper
- ½ cup jarred roasted red peppers, drained, patted dry, and finely chopped
- ¼ cup walnuts, toasted (see page 16) and chopped coarse
- 2 scallions, sliced thin

1. Bring 4 cups water, lentils, onion, bay leaves, thyme, and ¼ teaspoon salt to a simmer in a medium saucepan over medium-high heat. Reduce the heat to medium-low and cook until the lentils are tender but still hold their shape, 25 to 30 minutes.

2. Meanwhile, whisk the vinegar, oil, mustard, and ¼ teaspoon pepper together in a small bowl and set aside.

3. Drain the lentils, reserving ½ cup of the cooking liquid, and discard the onion, bay leaves, and thyme. Transfer the lentils to a medium bowl. Toss the warm lentils with the vinaigrette and cool to room temperature.

4. Add the reserved cooking liquid, 1 tablespoon at a time as needed, until the lentils are well coated. Stir in the roasted red peppers, walnuts, and scallions, season with salt and pepper to taste, and serve.

PER ½-CUP SERVING: Cal 180; Fat 8g; Sat fat 1g; Chol 0mg; Carb 22g; Protein 67g; Fiber 5g; Sodium 210mg

SWEET-AND-SOUR BROCCOLI RABE

PERFECT VEGETABLES

M = TEST KITCHEN MAKEOVER

BROILED ASPARAGUS WITH MUSTARD VINAIGRETTE

WE LIKE TO THINK OF ASPARAGUS AS THE QUEEN of vegetables, but these elegant spears can easily go from crisp-tender and flavorful to mushy and drab if not properly cooked. While grilling is one of our favorite ways to prepare it, we wanted a technique that was easy and that we could rely on rain or shine. We wanted to find a simple cooking method that would deliver crisp, well-browned spears and deep flavor without having to fire up the grill. We also wanted to find a complementary light dressing for our spears that would add bright flavor without a lot of fat or calories.

To start, we tested three dry cooking methods—pan-roasting, sautéing, and broiling—and we settled on broiling as the best of the group. Pan-roasting and sautéing both proved adequate, but we felt we got better results from these techniques when we blanched or steamed the asparagus before browning it. That was too many steps for a simple recipe. Broiling required the least amount of work and gave us spears with good color and intensified flavor. Though broiling is similar to high-heat roasting, putting the asparagus just inches from the heating element guaranteed well-browned spears quickly. All we had to do was toss the spears with a little oil, then place them on a rimmed baking sheet and broil them until done.

But it wasn't all cut and dried. We had two big questions to settle: What is the ideal thickness for the spears, and how close to the broiler do they need to be? In our tests with thicker asparagus—spears around ¾ inch or more—the outer skin began to char before the center became fully tender. Another disadvantage of the thicker asparagus was that it often had to be peeled because the outer skin was too thick and tough to eat. Thinner asparagus—spears no thicker than ½ inch—not only let us skip the peeling step but also cooked more evenly.

So with our first issue settled, we moved on to the second. Working with thinner asparagus, we began testing how far to keep the spears from the heating element. At 4 inches the asparagus charred a bit; at 8 inches the spears took a little too long to cook, and, more important, tasters were disappointed in the mild browning when they were cooked this far from the heat. The middle ground, 6 inches, proved the best for cooking speed, control, and browning.

To complement the asparagus, tasters wanted a light vinaigrette with bold flavor. Mustard seemed like a natural pairing and had the intensity we were looking for. Tasters rejected brown mustard (the flavor was fleeting) and grainy mustard (they didn't like the texture), but bright Dijon was just right. A full tablespoon, combined with the same amount of white wine vinegar and 2 tablespoons of extra-virgin olive oil, gave us a dressing that packed a low-fat punch.

For additional flavor, we stirred in a teaspoon of chopped fresh tarragon, which was nice as far as it went, but tasters wanted something more. Garlic was an obvious choice, but when added to the vinaigrette raw, its flavor was harsh and overwhelming. Roasting the garlic would certainly tame its bite and encourage its sweet flavor; unfortunately, it also would take about an hour to accomplish using the oven. We needed a simpler approach to achieving the nutty flavor and buttery texture of roasted garlic. The microwave proved to be the ultimate tool. We found we could "roast" the garlic in the microwave to mellow its flavor in a minimum amount of time. We thinly sliced three cloves, sprinkled them with a little sugar to promote caramelization, and drizzled them with some olive oil. Five minutes in the microwave on low softened the cloves enough to let us mash them into a pulp, which we then added to our dressing. For even more garlic flavor, we reserved the

NOTES FROM THE TEST KITCHEN

TRIMMING ASPARAGUS SPEARS

1. Before cooking asparagus, it's important to remove the tough ends. Remove one asparagus spear from the bunch and snap off its tough end.

2. Using the broken asparagus as a guide, trim off the ends of the remaining spears using a chef's knife.

garlic-flavored oil from the microwave "roasting" step, tossing it with the asparagus before placing the spears under the broiler. This simple, flavorful recipe did justice to an all-time favorite vegetable.

Broiled Asparagus with Mustard Vinaigrette

SERVES 6

Look for asparagus spears that are no more than ½ inch thick. Any larger and the exterior may burn before they are cooked through.

- 2　tablespoons extra-virgin olive oil
- 3　garlic cloves, sliced thin
- ¼　teaspoon sugar
- 1　tablespoon white wine vinegar
- 1　tablespoon Dijon mustard
- 1　tablespoon water
- 1　teaspoon chopped fresh tarragon
- 　Salt and pepper
- 2　bunches thin (see note) asparagus (about 2 pounds), tough ends trimmed (see page 212)

1. Position an oven rack 6 inches from the heating element and heat the broiler. Combine 1 tablespoon of the oil, garlic, and sugar in a small microwave-safe bowl. Microwave on low, uncovered, until the garlic is softened and fragrant, about 5 minutes. Carefully transfer the softened garlic to a cutting board, reserving the oil. Mash the garlic to a fine paste using the side of a chef's knife.

2. Whisk the garlic paste, remaining 2 tablespoons oil, vinegar, mustard, tarragon, water, ⅛ teaspoon salt, and ⅛ teaspoon pepper together in a small bowl and set aside.

3. Place the asparagus in a single layer on a rimmed baking sheet and toss with the reserved garlic oil, ¼ teaspoon salt, and ⅛ teaspoon pepper. Broil the asparagus until tender and lightly browned, 6 to 10 minutes, shaking the pan halfway through to turn the spears. Transfer the asparagus to a platter, drizzle with the vinaigrette, and serve.

PER SERVING: Cal 90; Fat 4.5g; Sat fat 0.5g; Chol 0mg; Carb 8g; Protein 3g; Fiber 3g; Sodium 210mg

ROASTED BROCCOLI

WHILE WE ARE FIRM BELIEVERS IN THE CONCEN-trated flavor and speckled browning that can be obtained by roasting vegetables, we have always considered broccoli an exception to the rule. Its awkward shape, tough stems, and shrubby florets seem like a bad match for cooking with high, dry heat; moist cooking methods always seem like a better option for accommodating its idiosyncrasies. But plain steamed broccoli, healthy as it is, doesn't boast much in terms of flavor without some extra help. Roasting, however, has the appealing prospect of adding great flavor without requiring much fat. Since there are plenty of people who do consider broccoli fit for roasting and rave about the results, we set out to see what we were missing.

Though skeptical, we roasted a bunch following one of the recipes we had found. It tasted good—good enough to eat straight from the sizzling baking sheet. That said, this recipe and the others we tried still had their flaws. First of all, none clearly addressed how best to prepare the broccoli for roasting. How big, for example, should you cut florets from the crown, and what should be done with the stems to ensure that they cooked at the same rate? Second, aside from the broccoli in direct contact with the baking sheet, browning was sparse. And last, a fair number of the florets tended to char and taste bitter.

If contact with the baking sheet was the key to browning, it made sense that we should try to cut the broccoli in a way that maximized this contact. We tackled the crown first, lopping off the stem, flipping it on its base, and cutting it crosswise into slabs. Sadly, the cross sections fell apart into a jumble of odd-sized florets that cooked unevenly. Perhaps wedges would work. We sliced another crown in half, then cut each half into uniform wedges—much more promising; the florets now held together. Turning our attention to the stem, we sliced off the tough exterior, then cut the stem into ½-inch-thick chunks to help promote even cooking. These came out of the oven evenly cooked and with plenty of flavorful browning.

In the most successful recipes from our initial survey, the broccoli was dressed simply, with salt, pepper, and a splash of olive oil, so we followed suit. As for oven

ROASTED BROCCOLI

temperature, we tested everything from 350 degrees to 500 degrees. The upper end delivered the best browning (though it was still spotty), crispest texture, and most vibrant coloring; lower temperatures led to broccoli that was soft and a muddy, drab color. Yet while high heat delivered the best browning, it also increased the risk of charred florets. A couple of recipes suggested blanching or steaming the broccoli before roasting, but we found that these batches tasted bland, as if the flavor had been washed away. Eventually, we discovered that a preheated baking sheet cooked the broccoli in half the time and crisped the florets without any charring.

But despite the blazing heat and the fact that we had solved the problem of charred florets, the broccoli still wasn't as browned as we'd hoped. One of the more interesting recipes we found used a lemon juice–based vinaigrette to coat the broccoli before roasting, which resulted in remarkably even browning. We wondered if it was the fruit sugars in the lemon juice that generated such browning. Skipping the juice for now, we tossed a scant ½ teaspoon of sugar over the broccoli along with the salt and pepper, and the results were the best yet: blistered, bubbled, and browned stems that were sweet and full-flavored, along with crispy-tipped florets that tasted even better, especially when dressed with a spritz of lemon juice.

NOTES FROM THE TEST KITCHEN

PREPARING BROCCOLI CROWN FOR ROASTING

1. After cutting off the stalk and setting it aside (do not discard), place the head upside down, then cut it in half through the central stalk.

2. Lay each half on its cut side. For each half, if it is 3 to 4 inches in diameter, cut it into 3 or 4 wedges, or into 6 wedges if 4 to 5 inches in diameter.

Roasted Broccoli
SERVES 6

Be sure to trim away the outer peel from the broccoli stem, as it will turn tough when cooked.

- 1 **bunch broccoli (about 1½ pounds)**
- 4 **teaspoons olive oil**
- ½ **teaspoon sugar**
- ¼ **teaspoon salt**
- ¼ **teaspoon pepper**
-    **Lemon wedges, for serving**

1. Adjust an oven rack to the lowest position, place a foil-lined rimmed baking sheet on the rack, and heat the oven to 500 degrees. Cut off the broccoli stem, then remove its outer peel. Cut the stem into ½-inch-thick pieces. Following the photos, cut the crown in half, then into 4 wedges if 3 to 4 inches in diameter, or 6 wedges if 4 to 5 inches in diameter. Toss the broccoli pieces with the oil, sugar, salt, and pepper.

2. Carefully place the broccoli, flat sides down, on the preheated baking sheet and roast until the stem pieces are well browned and tender and the florets are lightly browned, 10 to 12 minutes. Transfer the broccoli to a platter and serve with the lemon wedges.

PER SERVING: Cal 70; Fat 3.5g; Sat fat 0g; Chol 0mg; Carb 8g; Protein 3g; Fiber 3g; Sodium 135mg

VARIATION

Roasted Broccoli with Olives and Garlic
Follow the recipe for Roasted Broccoli, omitting the pepper. While the broccoli roasts, cook 2 tablespoons olive oil, 5 garlic cloves, minced, and ¼ teaspoon red pepper flakes in an 8-inch skillet over medium-low heat, stirring occasionally, until fragrant and the garlic begins to brown, 5 to 7 minutes. Remove the skillet from the heat and stir in ¼ cup kalamata olives, pitted and chopped coarse, 2 teaspoons minced fresh oregano, and 2 teaspoons fresh lemon juice. Toss the roasted broccoli with the olive mixture before serving.

PER SERVING: Cal 120; Fat 9g; Sat fat 1.5g; Chol 0mg; Carb 9g; Protein 3g; Fiber 3g; Sodium 210mg

BROCCOLI RABE

BROCCOLI RABE, AN ITALIAN GREEN WITH POTENT broccoli flavor and a bitter, peppery bite, makes its presence known on the plate. The traditional method of sautéing it with a little olive oil and aromatics brings its big, bold flavors to the forefront, but we have always found that this preparation tends to be a little too one-dimensional and somewhat bitter. For us, the ideal plate of broccoli rabe should be intensely flavored, but we also want to be able to taste the other ingredients and flavors in the dish. So we set our sights on developing a dependable, light method of cooking this vegetable that would deliver less bitterness and a round, balanced flavor.

Some of the recipes we came across recommended parcooking the greens before sautéing to help draw out some of the bitter flavor. Hoping this technique would help take the edge off our broccoli rabe, we gave it a try. We tested both blanching and steaming, and we found that steaming produced little change—the bitterness was still intense. When we blanched the broccoli rabe in an ample amount of salted boiling water (4 quarts of water for about 1 pound of broccoli rabe), its flavor was exactly what we had hoped for: It was complex, mustardy, and peppery, with only a slight bitterness. However, we were now noticing a textural issue.

While testing our parcooking method, we found that the lower 2 inches or so of the stems were woody and tough. Even after peeling—a technique we often use for removing the tough outer layer of broccoli stems—they never softened properly, so we decided that they should be trimmed before cooking. The remaining upper portions of the stems, however, were tender enough to include in the recipe, and they didn't require any peeling. Cutting the stems into pieces about 1 inch long made them easier to eat and allowed them to cook in the same amount of time as the florets and the leaves.

Once blanched and drained in a colander, our broccoli rabe was ready to be sautéed with any number of seasonings, but we were particularly interested in using assertive flavors that could stand up to the punch of this vegetable. In southern Italy, broccoli rabe is often flavored with a vibrant sauce called agrodolce (which roughly translates as "sweet and sour"). Italians make this sauce by simmering vinegar with sugar and sometimes aromatics until the mixture is syrupy. This seemed like the perfect pairing.

In the empty pot that we had used to blanch the broccoli rabe, we began by sautéing onions and garlic in a little oil. Next we reached for red wine vinegar (we also tested the traditional balsamic vinegar, but we

---

NOTES FROM THE TEST KITCHEN

SOFTENING BROWN SUGAR
When brown sugar comes into contact with air, the moisture in the sugar evaporates, and the sugar turns rock-hard. This problem is almost inevitable if you use up your brown sugar slowly. There are two easy methods to soften it. For a quick fix, place the hardened brown sugar in a bowl with a slice of sandwich bread. Cover with plastic wrap and microwave for 10 to 20 seconds. For a long-term solution, invest in a terra-cotta Brown Sugar Bear, which will set you back only $3.25. Simply store brown sugar in a sealed container with your Brown Sugar Bear, which gets a brief soak in water before being added to the sugar.

OUR FAVORITE RED WINE VINEGAR
Red wine vinegar has a sharp but clean flavor that works perfectly in our Sweet-and-Sour Broccoli Rabe recipe. While acidity is the obvious key factor in vinegar, what appeals to the palate is actually the inherent sweetness of the grapes used to make this vinegar. Curious whether or not flavor is dependent on price, we pitted 10 supermarket brands against 4 high-end brands. **Spectrum Naturals Organic Red Wine Vinegar,** a slightly more expensive brand, won hands down for its peppery, sweet, and full-bodied flavors. However, if you can't find this brand, there is a supermarket deal to be had in our second-place winner, Pompeian Red Wine Vinegar, which is easier to find and boasted bright and fruity flavors.

VINEGAR SEDIMENT
Nearly all commercially made vinegar will last indefinitely in an unopened bottle. Once the bottle is opened and the vinegar exposed to air, however, harmless "vinegar bacteria" may start to grow. These bacteria cause the formation of a cloudy sediment that is nothing more than harmless cellulose, a complex carbohydrate that does not affect the quality of the vinegar or its flavor. We confirmed this with a side-by-side comparison of freshly opened bottles of vinegar and those with sediment (strained before tasting). Furthermore, the Vinegar Institute in Atlanta carried out storage studies of vinegar and determined that the shelf life of opened vinegar stored in a dark cabinet at room temperature is "almost indefinite." Though the sediment is harmless, you may not find it all that visually appealing. To rid your vinegar of sediment, simply strain the vinegar through a coffee filter set inside a fine-mesh strainer before using it.

found it became unpleasantly heavy when reduced). Most recipes we found called for granulated sugar, but we preferred brown sugar, which added warmth along with sweetness. Simmered alone, the mixture was certainly lively, but tasters wanted more complexity. Raisins and orange juice, both called for in some authentic agrodolce recipes, rounded out our sauce. When this mixture became syrupy, we tossed in the blanched broccoli rabe and in minutes turned an aggressive vegetable into a gentle giant.

Sweet-and-Sour Broccoli Rabe
SERVES 4

We prefer the additional sweetness of golden raisins in this dish; however, dark raisins can be substituted.

1 bunch broccoli rabe (about 1 pound), trimmed and cut into 1-inch pieces
   Salt
1 onion, minced (about 1 cup)
1 tablespoon extra-virgin olive oil
2 garlic cloves, minced
¼ cup golden raisins (see note)
¼ cup red wine vinegar
2 tablespoons orange juice
2 tablespoons brown sugar
   Pepper

1. Bring 4 quarts water to a boil in a large Dutch oven. Add the broccoli rabe and 1 tablespoon salt, and cook until just tender, about 2 minutes. Drain the broccoli rabe and set aside.

2. Combine the onion, 1 teaspoon of the oil, and ⅛ teaspoon salt in the pot. Cover and cook over medium-low heat, stirring occasionally, until softened, 8 to 10 minutes. Stir in the garlic and cook until fragrant, about 30 seconds.

3. Stir in the raisins, vinegar, orange juice, and brown sugar, and cook over medium heat until syrupy, 3 to 5 minutes. Add the broccoli rabe and cook, stirring occasionally, until well coated, about 2 minutes. Drizzle with the remaining 2 teaspoons oil, season with salt and pepper to taste, and serve.

PER SERVING: Cal 140; Fat 3.5g; Sat fat 0g; Chol 0mg; Carb 23g; Protein 5g; Fiber 1g; Sodium 260mg

STUFFED ZUCCHINI

IN OUR EXPERIENCE, STUFFED ZUCCHINI HAS BEEN either a healthy but bland vegetable side dish or an impressive attempt to mask the vegetable's flavor with rich, indulgent ingredients. Either way, the dish has never garnered any points with us. We prefer the delicate flavor of zucchini in basic preparations: sautéed with a little garlic, thrown on the grill, or lightly roasted in the oven. We wondered, however, if we had been premature in giving stuffed zucchini a bad name. After all, it sounds like a great way to jazz up a vegetable that seems to proliferate toward the end of summer, and the straightforward preparations we tend to rely on can grow old quickly. Realizing that this dish had the potential of being light and flavorful, we set out to create a stuffed zucchini recipe worth making.

We started with preparing the zucchini. We were surprised that most of the recipes we found didn't call for parcooking it. Because raw squash are extremely crisp, once halved, they were prone to snap as we hollowed them out in preparation for the filling. Additionally, we quickly learned that raw stuffed zucchini took up to an hour to cook through in the oven, and by that point, the filling was completely dried out. Parcooking the zucchini was a must.

We tried every method we could think of: blanching, steaming, broiling, roasting, and even microwaving. Moist parcooking methods were quickly dropped, as they only made the zucchini mushy and drained away valuable flavor. Broiling was also quickly dismissed, as it required close attention to avoid incineration. Roasting seemed like a more promising way to precook the squash, but in the end we decided that it took too long for our simple weeknight side dish. Ultimately, the microwave proved to be the best bet for parcooking. In about six minutes, the zucchini were crisp-tender and easy to scoop out. Slicing off the top third of the zucchini—instead of cutting them in half—gave us more room for filling and provided additional stability to the zucchini as we removed the seeds. It was time to turn our attention to the filling.

Right off the bat, we set up a few guidelines. We wanted to use light ingredients that we would likely have on hand, and we wanted to be able to prepare this filling quickly. Testing several bases, we found that bread cubes were a quick option, but their mushy texture made them not worth the time they saved.

STUFFED ZUCCHINI

Sautéed vegetables provided a much more appealing texture, but they were tedious to prepare. Cooked grains were a much more reliable route. They take minutes to prepare, can maintain their pleasant texture through cooking, and require very little fat. We eventually narrowed the options down to couscous, as it was the simplest and quickest to make. All we needed to do was boil some broth, stir in couscous and toast it for a few minutes for deeper flavor, turn off the heat, and cover the pan for a few minutes until the couscous was ready. For more flavor, we sautéed a shallot before adding the broth and stirred in ¾ cup of feta cheese and ¼ cup of kalamata olives, which gave us a nice Mediterranean-inspired combination. As a final touch, chopped fresh basil added a pungent, licorice-like note. This filling was firm enough to easily mound into the zucchini. We stuffed the zucchini and then baked them until the filling had heated through. Just 10 minutes in a very hot oven finished cooking the zucchini shell and warmed the filling.

Our stuffed zucchini seemed good to go, but some tasters felt that it needed to have a topping so that it looked and tasted like a finished dish. By taking out some of the crumbled feta that was in the filling and using it as a topping, we were able to achieve what we were after without additional kitchen time or fat. Once baked, the crumbled feta added great flavor and texture to the zucchini and turned a beautiful golden color, giving our stuffed zucchini the finished appearance we were searching for. Finally, we had a stuffed zucchini recipe we were proud to serve.

Stuffed Zucchini

SERVES 4

Purchase zucchini that are between 6 and 8 inches long. Any larger and they will be tough and seedy.

- 4 zucchini (see note)
- 1 shallot, minced (about 3 tablespoons)
- 1 teaspoon olive oil
- Salt
- ⅔ cup couscous
- ¾ cup low-sodium chicken broth
- 3 ounces feta cheese, crumbled (about ¾ cup)
- ¼ cup kalamata olives, pitted and chopped coarse
- 2 tablespoons chopped fresh basil
- Pepper

1. Adjust an oven rack to the upper-middle position and heat the oven to 475 degrees.

2. Slice off and discard the top third of each zucchini lengthwise and arrange the bottoms, cut-side down, in a microwave-safe baking dish. Microwave on high until the cut side of the zucchini is slightly translucent and easily pierced with the tip of a paring knife, 4 to 8 minutes.

3. Working with 1 zucchini at a time, carefully scoop out the seeds, following the photo, leaving a ¼-inch layer of flesh on the inside. Arrange the zucchini, cut-side up, in the baking dish and set aside.

4. Combine the shallot, oil, and ¼ teaspoon salt in a small saucepan. Cover and cook over medium-low heat, stirring occasionally, until softened, 4 to 6 minutes. Increase the heat to medium, add the couscous, and cook, stirring frequently, until lightly browned and aromatic, about 4 minutes.

5. Stir in the broth and bring to a brief simmer. Remove the saucepan from the heat, stir in ½ cup of the feta, olives, and basil, cover, and let sit for 5 minutes. Fluff the couscous with a fork and season with salt and pepper to taste.

NOTES FROM THE TEST KITCHEN

PREPPING ZUCCHINI FOR STUFFING

Raw zucchini are crisp and can snap when hollowed. We found that microwaving them for several minutes beforehand simplifies this task and shortens the cooking time, too.

After you've softened the zucchini in the microwave, use a small spoon to scrape out the seeds and pulp.

SHOPPING FOR FETA

Within the European Union, only cheese made in Greece from a mixture of sheep's and goat's milk can be legally called feta, but most of the feta in American supermarkets is made from pasteurized cow's milk that has been curdled, shaped into blocks, sliced, and steeped in brine. Feta can range from soft to semi-hard and has a tangy, salty flavor. It dries out quickly when removed from its brine, so always store feta in the brine in which it is packed (we do not recommend buying precrumbled "dry" feta).

6. Divide the couscous mixture evenly among the zucchini. Sprinkle with the remaining ¼ cup feta and bake until the cheese is slightly browned, about 10 minutes. Serve.

PER SERVING: Cal 240; Fat 8g; Sat fat 3.5g; Chol 20mg; Carb 32g; Protein 10g; Fiber 4g; Sodium 630mg

GLAZED BUTTERNUT SQUASH

WITH THE ARRIVAL OF THE COLDER MONTHS, OUR thoughts often turn to the warm and soul-satisfying flavors of glazed butternut squash. Coated in a little oil, sugar, and spice before roasting, butternut squash has flavors that intensify as the sweet coating caramelizes and browns. But while this dish may seem simple, that doesn't mean it's foolproof. All too often the recipes we tested produced sodden, sticky mashes of squash swimming in syrupy-sweet glazes, or worse, squash that barely cooked through before the glaze incinerated. We wanted to develop a recipe that featured tender squash lightly swathed in a sweet, savory, and caramelized glaze.

First we needed to find the perfect squash. We learned that all varieties of domestically grown butternut squash are in season from July through November. Squash purchased in the off-season is usually imported from Mexico and is likely to be more expensive, not to mention the fact that squash that has spent weeks in transit cooks up dry, fibrous, and pasty. Butternut squash should be hard and heavy for its size, an indication that it contains a lot of moisture and has not been sitting on the supermarket produce shelf for weeks. It should also be stored at cool room temperature, not in the refrigerator. When we stored squash for a few weeks in the refrigerator, chill damage set in, causing the flavor and texture to deteriorate.

Squash in hand, we got cooking. Past experiences with roasted squash had shown us that how we cut the squash greatly affected how it caramelized in the oven. After some experimentation with variously shaped cuts, from slender planks to half-moons, we settled on 1-inch cubes, which had enough surface area to become well covered with our coating (just some oil and granulated sugar at this point) and were small enough to cook to full tenderness by the time the sugar began to caramelize, a reasonable 45 minutes in a 425-degree oven.

Up until this point we had been tossing our squash in a moderate amount of oil to promote browning and reduce the risk of sticking. We knew some oil was essential, but mindful of every fat gram, we wanted to find out how little we could get away with. Cooking the squash on a foil-lined baking sheet that had been lightly coated with vegetable oil spray proved to be the best route. It enabled us to toss the squash with less oil and still achieve the desired browning without sticking, and there was no difficult cleanup to deal with.

Last, we moved on to finessing a glaze in which we would toss the squash before putting it into the oven. For the sweet element, tasters preferred the complexity and depth of dark brown sugar to granulated sugar, and we found a moderate ⅓ cup was all that was needed to adequately coat the squash. We tried adding shallots, garlic, thyme, parsley, and chives, but our tasters were emphatic that, in this case, less was more: A little salt, pepper, cinnamon, and cayenne provided a balanced seasoning without overwhelming the delicate flavor of the squash. Drizzled with a little cider vinegar at the end to keep the sweetness in check, this butternut squash was perfectly glazed, sweet, and satisfying but not cloying, just what we wanted on a cold winter's day.

Glazed Butternut Squash

SERVES 4

Light brown sugar can be substituted for the dark brown sugar.

Vegetable oil spray
1 medium butternut squash (about 2 pounds), peeled, halved lengthwise, seeded, and cut into 1-inch chunks
⅓ cup packed dark brown sugar (see note)
1 tablespoon canola oil
¼ teaspoon salt
¼ teaspoon black pepper
⅛ teaspoon ground cinnamon
Pinch cayenne pepper
1 teaspoon cider vinegar

1. Adjust an oven rack to the middle position and heat the oven to 425 degrees. Line a rimmed baking sheet with foil and lightly coat with vegetable oil spray.

2. Toss the squash, brown sugar, oil, salt, black pepper, cinnamon, and cayenne together in a large bowl until well coated. Transfer the squash to the prepared baking sheet and roast, stirring every 15 minutes, until well browned and tender, about 45 minutes. Transfer the squash to a platter, drizzle with the vinegar, and serve.

PER SERVING: Cal 170; Fat 4.5g; Sat fat 0g; Chol 0mg; Carb 34g; Protein 2g; Fiber 4g; Sodium 160mg

SKILLET-ROASTED CARROTS AND PARSNIPS

AS WE HAD LEARNED WITH OUR BUTTERNUT SQUASH recipe (see page 220), roasting is an ideal light method for cooking root vegetables because it concentrates their natural sugars and yields a rich, sweet taste and hearty texture without requiring much oil. Roasting also gives the vegetables a caramelized, golden skin that is a wonderful contrast to their soft, moist interior. But when you've got dinner cooking away in the oven, roasting a pan full of vegetables might not be an option. We wanted to find a way to create such a dish on the stovetop, using just a skillet. It was easy enough to find recipes for pan-roasted vegetables; the hard part started when we tried making them.

In many recipes carrots are cooked in combination with other root vegetables such as parsnips, rutabagas, and turnips in oil over medium or high heat, with the pan covered to simulate oven-roasting. These recipes produced vegetables with scorched exteriors and undercooked centers. Vegetables cooked this way over low heat never caramelized. In other recipes the vegetables are first steamed and then sautéed for color, but this required two pans, and the tender vegetables often overcooked and fell apart in the skillet. We had a lot of work to do.

Our first step was to whittle down our vegetable choices. We landed on carrots and parsnips for two reasons: Their similar shape made them easier to prep— both could easily be cut into the same shape—and their sweet, earthy flavors worked well together. We started out with 12 ounces of each, then peeled them and sliced them on the bias for an elegant presentation.

We knew that we'd have to cook these vegetables in oil to caramelize them, but as in all our light recipes, moderation was key. Starting with just 1 tablespoon of canola oil in a nonstick skillet, we browned the carrots and parsnips and then turned down the heat and covered the pan so they could cook through. This gave us evenly browned, tender vegetables, but they were dry and wrinkled by the time they were tender. To rectify the moisture loss, we tried adding ¾ cup water to the pan before covering to create a gentle steaming effect. Unfortunately, this step only washed away the caramelized coating on the vegetables. Could we avoid the loss by switching the cooking order and simmering the vegetables first, before sautéing them?

Back at the stovetop, we added the carrots, parsnips, and water to a cold skillet, covered it, and brought it to a simmer. Once the vegetables were almost cooked, we removed the lid and waited for the water to evaporate. Finally, we added the oil to the pan and sautéed the vegetables until they were well browned and tender. We were impressed with the caramelized color on the vegetables, but the softer-textured parsnips had become mushy in the time it took the heartier carrots to become tender. Waiting to add the parsnips until the carrots had softened, when we removed the lid and were ready to let the water evaporate, helped solve this problem. We also found that adding the oil at the outset of cooking along with the water prevented the vegetables from

SKILLET-ROASTED CARROTS AND PARSNIPS

sticking to the pan as the water evaporated. It also allowed us to stir the vegetables less toward the end of cooking, which helped maintain their shape.

We had achieved our goal of nicely browned, tender vegetables, but tasters felt the flavor was a little flat. Some recipes we found included sugar to enhance the natural sweetness of the vegetables, and we had the best success with just ¾ teaspoon of granulated sugar added along with the vegetables and water. A little salt added at the beginning, a few turns of the pepper mill, and a sprinkle of fresh parsley at the end of cooking rounded out the flavors. This simple and light stovetop recipe provided an easy opportunity to introduce new flavors to the duo of carrots and parsnips, so we developed one variation using orange juice, orange zest, and honey, and another with garlic and thyme.

Skillet-Roasted Carrots and Parsnips

SERVES 4

When shopping for parsnips, choose those that are no wider than 1 inch—larger parsnips are likely to have tough, fibrous cores.

- 12 **ounces carrots, peeled and sliced ½ inch thick on the bias**
- ¾ **cup warm water**
- 1 **tablespoon canola oil**
- ¾ **teaspoon sugar**
- ½ **teaspoon salt**
- 12 **ounces parsnips (see note), peeled and sliced ½ inch thick on the bias**
- 1 **tablespoon chopped fresh parsley**
  Pepper

1. Bring the carrots, water, oil, sugar, and salt to a simmer in a 12-inch nonstick skillet over medium heat. Cover and cook, stirring occasionally, until the carrots begin to soften, 7 to 9 minutes.

2. Uncover, increase the heat to high, and add the parsnips. Continue to cook, stirring occasionally, until the water has completely evaporated and the carrots and parsnips are tender and well browned, about 15 minutes longer.

3. Off the heat, stir in the parsley and season with salt and pepper to taste. Serve.

PER SERVING: **Cal** 130; **Fat** 4g; **Sat fat** 0g; **Chol** 0mg; **Carb** 24g; **Protein** 2g; **Fiber** 7g; **Sodium** 360mg

VARIATIONS

Skillet-Roasted Carrots and Parsnips with Honey and Orange

Follow the recipe for Skillet-Roasted Carrots and Parsnips, substituting 1½ teaspoons honey for the sugar. Stir ¼ teaspoon grated orange zest into the carrots and parsnips with the parsley.

PER SERVING: **Cal** 140; **Fat** 4g; **Sat fat** 0g; **Chol** 0mg; **Carb** 26g; **Protein** 2g; **Fiber** 7g; **Sodium** 360mg

Skillet-Roasted Carrots and Parsnips with Garlic and Thyme

Follow the recipe for Skillet-Roasted Carrots and Parsnips, stirring 2 garlic cloves, minced, and 1 teaspoon minced fresh thyme into the carrots and parsnips after they are tender and well browned; continue to cook until fragrant, about 30 seconds longer. Omit the parsley.

PER SERVING: **Cal** 140; **Fat** 4g; **Sat fat** 0g; **Chol** 0mg; **Carb** 25g; **Protein** 2g; **Fiber** 7g; **Sodium** 360mg

NOTES FROM THE TEST KITCHEN

CARROTS' PERFECT MATCH: PARSNIPS

Recipes for roasted carrots pair the vegetable with any one (or more) of a smattering of other root vegetables, from rutabagas to turnips, but we prefer matching carrots with parsnips. Because they are similar in shape to carrots, parsnips allow for evenly cooked vegetables, and their flavor is also the perfect match for its perhaps better-known cousin. Test cooks have described parsnips as "sugary and floral," like "a carrot doused in perfume," adding a distinct yet complementary flavor. Since older, larger parsnips can be tough and fibrous, look for parsnips that are no more than 1 inch in diameter.

SAUTÉED GREEN BEANS

THE STANDARD TECHNIQUE IN MOST RECIPES FOR sautéed green beans goes something like this: Parboil, shock in ice water, dry with towels, and finally, sauté. While the method has advantages—it allows you to do most of the prep work in advance—it simply takes too long and dirties too many dishes for a reasonable weeknight side dish. We wanted a streamlined technique that would be speedy enough for a last-minute supper, one that would yield tender, flavorful beans rich enough in taste and texture, without an excess of butter or oil, to warrant a place on the dinner table on a regular basis.

First, we tried simply sautéing the raw beans in a skillet with a little oil—big mistake. The dry heat took so long to penetrate the beans that their exteriors blackened before the interiors cooked through. Water was clearly going to be necessary. Our next thought was to work with a variation on parcooking that we had recently used on our Skillet-Roasted Carrots and Parsnips (see page 221). We threw the beans, a small amount of water, and some oil into a cold pan, covered it, and brought it to a simmer. Once the beans were almost cooked, we removed the lid and waited for the water to evaporate. We then simply added some minced garlic for a little bite and sautéed the beans until browned. While promising, the method wasn't the answer we had hoped for. The water took too long to evaporate, and the beans turned flaccid before they could brown. And even when we achieved lightly browned and properly cooked beans, the caramelized flavor seemed superficial.

Although our carrot and parsnip testing had demonstrated that sautéing the vegetables first, then adding water and steaming them until cooked through, led to a "washed-out" caramelized flavor, we felt as though this method might be workable for the smaller, quicker-cooking beans. So we briefly sautéed the beans until they were spotty brown but not yet cooked through, stirred in the garlic, then added ¼ cup water to the pan. As soon as the water hit the skillet, it turned to steam, and we quickly covered the pan. Once the beans were almost cooked (an efficient process in this steamy environment), we removed the lid and let the excess moisture evaporate. This produced the crisp-tender texture we were looking for, but now, just as predicted, tasters were commenting that our veggies tasted more like ordinary steamed beans.

The solution? We simply steamed the beans for about a minute less so they remained slightly undercooked, then blasted the heat once the lid was removed. This quickly evaporated what little water was left in the pan and allowed us to establish a second browning before the beans fully cooked through. As a final touch, a little lemon juice and parsley added to the skillet at the end of cooking brought a welcome vibrancy to our light dish.

For additional flavors, it was easy to come up with a few variations. We decided to limit extras to herbs, spices, and a few pantry items. Mixed into the skillet with the beans (or, in some cases, at the end once the beans were finished), combinations such as red onion and goat cheese and thyme, coriander, and sesame added complexity without tampering with the dish's one-pan simplicity.

Sautéed Green Beans with Garlic and Herbs
SERVES 4

We prefer cooking these green beans until crisp-tender; if you prefer them more done, increase the amount of water by 1 tablespoon and cook, covered, for an extra minute in step 2.

- 1 tablespoon olive oil
- 1 pound green beans, trimmed (see page 226) and cut into 2-inch lengths on the bias
- Salt and pepper
- 3 garlic cloves, minced
- ¼ cup water
- 1 tablespoon chopped fresh parsley
- 1 teaspoon fresh lemon juice

1. Heat the oil in a 12-inch nonstick skillet over medium heat until just smoking. Add the green beans, ¼ teaspoon salt, and ⅛ teaspoon pepper, and cook, stirring occasionally, until spotty brown, 4 to 6 minutes. Stir in the garlic and cook until fragrant, about 30 seconds.

2. Add the water, cover, and cook until the beans are bright green but still crisp, about 2 minutes. Uncover, increase the heat to high, and continue to cook until the water evaporates and the beans are crisp-tender and lightly browned, 3 to 5 minutes longer.

3. Off the heat, stir in the parsley and lemon juice, and season with salt and pepper to taste. Serve.

PER SERVING: Cal 70; Fat 3.5g; Sat fat 0g; Chol 0mg; Carb 9g; Protein 2g; Fiber 4g; Sodium 150mg

SAUTÉED GREEN BEANS

TRIMMING GREEN BEANS QUICKLY

Line up several green beans in a row on a cutting board. Trim about ½ inch from each end, then cut the beans as directed in the recipe.

VARIATIONS

Sautéed Green Beans with Red Onion and Goat Cheese

Follow the recipe for Sautéed Green Beans with Garlic and Herbs, adding 1 red onion, halved and sliced thin, with the water. Sprinkle with 1 ounce goat cheese, crumbled (about ¼ cup), before serving.

PER SERVING: **Cal** 100; **Fat** 5g; **Sat fat** 1.5g; **Chol** 5mg; **Carb** 12g; **Protein** 4g; **Fiber** 4g; **Sodium** 180mg

Sautéed Green Beans with Thyme, Coriander, and Sesame

Follow the recipe for Sautéed Green Beans with Garlic and Herbs, adding 1 teaspoon minced fresh thyme, ¼ teaspoon ground coriander, and ¼ teaspoon ground cumin with the garlic. Substitute 1 tablespoon toasted sesame seeds for the parsley.

PER SERVING: **Cal** 80; **Fat** 4.5g; **Sat fat** 0g; **Chol** 0mg; **Carb** 9g; **Protein** 3g; **Fiber** 4g; **Sodium** 160mg

BRAISED WINTER GREENS

WINTER GREENS ARE AN EXCELLENT, NUTRITIOUS dinnertime choice, but they can be a challenge to cook. The traditional approach to tackling meaty, assertively flavored greens like kale and collards is to do as Southerners do: Throw them into a pot of water with aromatics and literally cook the life out of them. Adding a little pork product at the end to add some flavor back to the dish is usually part of the deal as well. A lot of alternative methods call for first blanching and then sautéing the greens with the goal of retaining more of their deep color, fleshy texture, and earthy flavor. Neither of these methods has ever entirely satisfied us (the former certainly not from a nutritional standpoint). While the remaining cooking liquid (often called "liquor") from Southern-style braises tastes great, this method is an hours-long project, and many recipes produce soupy, limp greens. The blanching-then-sautéing route (which also entails draining and squeezing) is quicker and yields greens that still have chew, but it was too fussy for the quick vegetable side dish we were looking for. Plus, even a brief dip in boiling water can rob the greens of flavor that just gets poured down the drain. We wanted a one-pot recipe for kale or collards that highlighted the greens' pungent flavor and firm, meaty texture but wouldn't require parcooking or take hours to do.

Because the large, dense leaves of collards are more of a challenge to cook than kale, we began our testing with them. As is true of most greens, what looks like a mountain cooks down to a minuscule amount, so we prepped 2 pounds, removing the tough center ribs and chopping the leaves into rough pieces (for a whopping 24 cups!). Our first thought was to treat them as we do tender greens like spinach and chard—skip blanching and go directly to sautéing. Starting with a teaspoon of oil in a Dutch oven, we added onion and garlic (the usual companions to sautéed greens) and then began tossing in the collards.

We'd added only about half of the greens when it became clear that sautéing alone wasn't going to work: The collards took so long to soften that the leaves on the bottom of the pot started to scorch while the leaves on top remained virtually raw. Adding half a cup of liquid helped—but not enough. While we managed to wilt down the greens enough to fit all 24 cups into the pot, the water still evaporated well before they were tender.

There was no getting around the fact that if we weren't going to parcook the greens, we couldn't be stingy with the liquid we added to the pot. We didn't want to resort to a traditional braise in which liquid covers the greens—that would just produce the soupy greens we were trying to avoid—but what if we used just a couple of cups? That way, once the greens were softened, we could cook off any liquid that remained,

BRAISED WINTER GREENS

so that any flavor released from the greens would go right back in.

In our next test, we sautéed half of the collards with the onions and garlic, then poured in 2 cups of water and added the rest of the greens. After about 30 minutes, the greens had almost the tender-firm texture we wanted, so we removed the lid and allowed the liquid to cook off. When we tasted the greens, we knew we were almost there. The texture was perfect; we just needed to work on the flavor, which was a little one-dimensional. We added a dash of red pepper flakes to the pan when we sautéed the garlic and onions, and we replaced 1 cup of the water with chicken broth for the braising liquid. Tossing the cooked collards with lemon juice just before serving balanced the flavors, and a tablespoon of olive oil gave them a little extra richness.

With the collards successfully tamed, we tested our method using the more tender kale, and we were pleased to find that it translated almost seamlessly, only requiring slightly less time to braise. With our easier and faster-paced braising approach, we knew we'd be turning to these beneficial greens a lot more often.

NOTES FROM THE TEST KITCHEN

NO-TEARS ONION CHOPPING

When an onion is cut, the cells that are damaged in the process release sulfuric compounds as well as various enzymes, and those compounds and enzymes, which are separated when the onion's cell structure is intact, activate and mix to form a new compound that then evaporates in the air and irritates the eyes, causing us to cry. People over the years have suggested to us myriad ways to lessen this teary effect, but we've found the best options are to protect the eyes by covering them with goggles or contact lenses or to introduce a flame (from a candle or gas burner) near the cut onions. While the flame changes the activity of the compound that causes the tearing by completing its oxidization, contact lenses and goggles simply form a physical barrier that the compound cannot penetrate. So if you want to keep tears at bay when handling onions, light a candle or gas burner or put on some ski goggles.

Braised Winter Greens
SERVES 4

Don't dry the greens completely after washing; a little extra water clinging to the leaves will help them wilt when cooking in step 2.

- 1 onion, minced (about 1 cup)
- 4 teaspoons olive oil
  Salt
- 5 garlic cloves, minced
- ⅛ teaspoon red pepper flakes
- 2 pounds kale or collards (about 2 bunches), stemmed, leaves cut into 1-inch pieces
- 1 cup low-sodium chicken broth
- 1 cup water
- 2 teaspoons fresh lemon juice
  Pepper

1. Combine the onion, 1 teaspoon of the oil, and ⅛ teaspoon salt in a large Dutch oven. Cover and cook over medium-low heat, stirring occasionally, until softened, 8 to 10 minutes. Uncover, increase the heat to medium-high, and continue to cook, stirring occasionally, until the onion is well browned, 8 to 12 minutes longer. Stir in the garlic and pepper flakes, and cook until fragrant, about 30 seconds.

2. Add half of the kale and cook until wilted, about 1 minute. Add the remaining kale, broth, water, and ⅛ teaspoon salt, cover, reduce the heat to medium-low, and cook, stirring occasionally, until the greens are tender, about 30 minutes.

3. Uncover, increase the heat to medium-high, and continue to cook, stirring occasionally, until the liquid has completely evaporated, 8 to 12 minutes.

4. Off the heat, stir in the remaining 1 tablespoon oil and lemon juice and season with salt and pepper to taste. Serve.

PER SERVING: **Cal** 160; **Fat** 6g; **Sat fat** 1g; **Chol** 0mg; **Carb** 25g; **Protein** 7g; **Fiber** 5g; **Sodium** 380mg

MARINATED TOMATO SALAD

A GREAT SUMMER TOMATO IS BEST WHEN MODESTLY dressed—salt, pepper, a light drizzling of good-quality olive oil. However, sometimes we crave a little more complexity, and at times like these, a tomato salad is the sure answer. But creating a healthful and flavorful tomato salad can be a bit tricky—heavy vinaigrettes and additional ingredients can quickly lead to disaster. We didn't want to weigh down the flavor of our fresh tomatoes by piling on excessive components as a lot of recipes tend to do; instead we wanted to keep things light but interesting, using ingredients that would complement and build on our fresh, ripe tomatoes.

We started with the dressing. Tossing sliced tomatoes in a lively vinaigrette sounded like a great idea—until the salt in the dressing coaxed liquid out of the tomatoes and watered down the salad. (Not to mention that the texture of the tomatoes suffered.) We wanted a dressing that would enhance—not drown—the tomatoes.

Instead of experimenting this way and that with the dressing, we decided first we should try to rid the tomatoes of excess moisture. In the test kitchen, we often use salt to remove water from tomatoes: We slice the tomatoes, sprinkle them with salt, and allow them to drain to remove liquid and concentrate flavors (even in-season tomatoes benefit from this process). Following suit, we cut our tomatoes into ½-inch wedges, tossed them with ½ teaspoon of salt, and placed them on paper towels to drain. After 15 minutes the tomatoes had purged some of their liquid and were ready to absorb the dressing.

Returning to the vinaigrette, we wanted to keep it simple, so we limited our dressing ingredients to a modest 2 tablespoons of olive oil, a tablespoon of balsamic vinegar, some garlic and rosemary, and a little pepper. Sampling the tomatoes tossed in this dressing, tasters agreed that the texture of the tomatoes was no longer compromised by excess moisture, but they felt their flavor was a little detached from that of the dressing. Would a brief marinating period before serving solve the problem? Mixing up another batch, we let the tomatoes sit in the vinaigrette for 15 minutes before serving. This time there was full flavor in every bite.

Next we looked to the challenge of choosing additional ingredients that would add flavor and texture without overshadowing the mild, fresh tomatoes that were the star of the show. Small amounts of potent kalamata olives played off the tomatoes well, and cannellini

STORING TOMATOES

We've heard that storing a tomato with its stem end facing down can prolong shelf life, a helpful trick, we thought, since we inevitably buy tomatoes a few days, at least, before we end up using them. To test this theory, we placed one batch of tomatoes stem-end up and another stem-end down and stored them at room temperature. A week later, nearly all the stem-down tomatoes remained in perfect condition, but the stem-up tomatoes had shriveled and started to mold. Why the difference? We surmised that the scar left on the tomato skin where the stem once grew provides both an escape for moisture and an entry point for mold and bacteria. Placing a tomato stem-end down blocks air from entering and moisture from exiting the scar. To confirm this theory, we ran another test, this time comparing tomatoes stored stem-end down with another batch stored stem-end up, but with a piece of tape sealing off their scars. The taped, stem-end-up tomatoes survived just as well as the stem-end-down batch.

OUR FAVORITE CANNED WHITE BEANS

It is hard to beat the full flavor and firm texture of dried beans cooked from scratch, but it's much easier and speedier to substitute canned beans. Our light and simple marinated tomato salad doesn't miss out on the stronger flavor of the dried beans, and since the beans aren't cooked in this recipe, the softer canned beans won't turn mushy. But are all canned cannellini beans of equal caliber? We looked for multiple brands of nationally distributed cannellini beans to taste against one another and found so few that we decided to include both great Northern and navy beans in the tasting as well. From sweet to bland and chalky to mushy, the different brands ran the gamut in quality. Our favorite of the bunch was **Westbrae Organic Great Northern Beans** (left), which won accolades for their earthy flavor and creamy texture. In second place, tasters liked **Progresso Cannellini Beans** (right) for their "plump shape" and "sweet, slightly salty" flavor.

beans provided the perfect creamy counterpoint. As a final addition, toasted pine nuts brought a warm, rustic flavor and a touch of crunch to the salad. To allow all of the flavors to meld, we decided to marinate the ingredients together with the tomatoes (aside from the pine nuts, which we found were better served as a garnish on top of the salad). This salad was fresh and bright, a great way to enjoy the flavors of summer.

Marinated Tomato Salad with Olives and White Beans

SERVES 6

Great Northern beans or navy beans can be substituted for the cannellini beans.

1½ pounds tomatoes (3 large tomatoes), cored and cut into ½-inch wedges
½   teaspoon salt
1   (15-ounce) can cannellini beans (see note), drained and rinsed
¼   cup kalamata olives, pitted and chopped coarse
2   tablespoons extra-virgin olive oil
1   tablespoon balsamic vinegar
2   teaspoons minced fresh rosemary
1   garlic clove, minced
½   teaspoon pepper
4   teaspoons pine nuts, toasted (see page 16)

1. Toss the tomatoes with the salt in a large bowl. Spread the tomatoes on several layers of paper towels and let drain for 15 minutes; gently blot the tomatoes dry with more paper towels.

2. Transfer the tomatoes to a clean large bowl and toss with the beans, olives, oil, vinegar, rosemary, garlic, and pepper. Let the salad marinate for 15 minutes.

3. Season with salt and pepper to taste, sprinkle with the pine nuts, and serve.

PER SERVING: Cal 130; **Fat** 8g; **Sat fat** 1g; **Chol** 0mg; **Carb** 12g; **Protein** 4g; **Fiber** 3g; **Sodium** 290mg

CRUNCHY OVEN FRIES

JUST BECAUSE A DISH IS LOW-FAT, IT'S NO EXCUSE FOR lousy food, and oven fries should be no exception. Bland flavor and lackluster texture just aren't worth the savings in calories, especially when these "light" fries can taste like over-roasted potatoes with thick, leathery crusts and hollow interiors. We wanted oven fries worth eating.

An obvious key decision was picking the right potato. We tested russet, Yukon Gold, and boiling potatoes.

With milder flavors and sporting spotty crusts, both the Yukon Gold and boiling potatoes couldn't compare to the hearty flavor and even browning of the russets. We then looked at preparing the potatoes for the oven and found that tasters preferred the more distinct potato flavor of unpeeled potatoes cut into wedges, as opposed to the slightly milder-tasting (and fussier) option of peeling and trimming the potatoes into squared batons.

Next we baked the fries at temperatures ranging from 400 to 500 degrees. At lower temperatures, the fries didn't brown sufficiently, and the 500-degree oven was too hot and burned the fries at the edges. Baking the fries at 475 degrees was best, but they still needed a deeper golden color and a crisper texture. Adjusting the oven rack to the lowest position made for a significant improvement, as the intense heat from the bottom of the oven browned them quickly and evenly without causing the interiors to overcook, which results in the unsatisfactory hollow fry.

Up until now, we had been simply tossing the potatoes with some canola oil, salt, and pepper before spreading them on the baking sheet. When we focused our attention on the amount of oil, we found the differences between using incremental amounts from 1 to 5 tablespoons were astounding. Any fewer than 4 tablespoons left some of the fries uncoated and caused them to stick to the pan; 5 tablespoons made them disagreeably greasy. To guarantee even distribution of oil, we found it best to spread 4 tablespoons of oil on the baking sheet, toss the raw fries with just 1 teaspoon more oil, and spread them on the oiled sheet. That way, the oil in the pan cooked the fries without soaking them. We also sprinkled the seasonings over the oiled baking sheet instead of the potatoes. Like little ball bearings, the grains of salt and pepper kept the potatoes from sticking to the pan without getting in the way of browning.

Even though we had nailed down the basic cooking method, the fries were still beset with crusts that were too thick and interiors that were too mealy. Several recipes we had seen called for covering the fries for a portion of the baking time, so we tried wrapping the baking sheet with foil before placing it in the oven. This seemingly odd technique delivered just the thing we had been after: an oven fry with the creamy, smooth core of an authentic french fry. After a brief period of steaming the fries in this manner, we took off the foil cover so the crusts could crisp.

But the steaming process, though beneficial for the interior, was now turning our already thick crusts even tougher. To fix this we tried soaking, a method often employed when making french fries to ensure crisp crusts. We first tested soaking the raw potato wedges in cold tap water until the water turned cloudy, then proceeded with our recipe. These fries emerged from the oven with staggeringly crisp crusts. But perhaps the biggest surprise came when we tried soaking the fries in hot tap water. The cold water was taking almost an hour to turn cloudy, whereas the hot tap water took a convenient 10 minutes, which meant that we could prep the potatoes in roughly the same amount of time it took to heat up the oven.

These fries may have been low in fat and calories, but they had a crisp, golden brown exterior, a moist and creamy interior, and great potato flavor that meant we weren't craving those greasy deep-fried sticks one bit.

Crunchy Oven Fries
SERVES 4

We prefer the texture of unpeeled potatoes; however, feel free to peel the potatoes if desired. A traditional baking sheet will work in this recipe, but a nonstick baking sheet works particularly well. It not only keeps the fries from sticking, but because of its dark color, it encourages deep and even browning.

- 1½ **pounds russet potatoes (about 3 medium), scrubbed and cut lengthwise into 10 to 12 even wedges (see note)**
- ¼ **cup plus 1 teaspoon canola oil**
  Salt and pepper

1. Adjust an oven rack to the lowest position and heat the oven to 475 degrees. Place the potatoes in a large bowl, cover with hot tap water, and let sit for 10 minutes. Meanwhile, coat a large rimmed nonstick baking sheet with ¼ cup of the oil and sprinkle evenly with ¼ teaspoon salt and ¼ teaspoon pepper.

2. Drain the potatoes and pat dry thoroughly with paper towels. Toss the dried potatoes with the remaining 1 teaspoon oil, arrange in a single layer on the prepared baking sheet, and cover tightly with foil. Bake for 5 minutes, then remove the foil and continue to bake until the bottoms of the potatoes are golden brown, 15 to 20 minutes longer, rotating the baking sheet halfway through.

3. Scrape the potatoes loose from the pan with a metal spatula, then flip each wedge using tongs, keeping the potatoes in a single layer. Continue to bake until the potatoes are golden brown and crisp, 7 to 10 minutes longer, rotating the baking sheet halfway through. Drain the potatoes briefly on paper towels, season with salt and pepper to taste, and serve.

PER SERVING: **Cal** 240; **Fat** 12g; **Sat fat** 1g; **Chol** 0mg; **Carb** 31g; **Protein** 4g; **Fiber** 2g; **Sodium** 150mg

GREEK DINER–STYLE HOME FRIES

HOME FRIES ARE AS EASYGOING AS THEIR NAME implies, and they are a winning match with almost any meal, any time of day. We particularly like the style of home fries served at most modest Greek diners: lemony, garlicky, golden crisp potatoes, often paired with roast lamb or spinach pie. But while these tasty home fries might seem like easy work when being cooked on a well-seasoned, flat griddle, try re-creating the concept at home and you will quickly find yourself working incredibly hard, only to arrive at a disappointing result: a greasy mound of pale, undercooked potatoes. We wanted a straightforward way to make perfectly crisp and well-seasoned Greek diner–style potatoes in the home kitchen, and we wanted to keep them light and fresh-tasting so that we could feel good about eating them, too.

While the high heat of a professional griddle certainly seemed to us like the key to obtaining crisp and tender home fries, a fellow test cook with experience working in diners assured us that the real secret is parcooking the potatoes. After a bit of research, we discovered that most restaurants use leftover roasted or boiled potatoes (preferably medium-starch potatoes like Yukon Gold, which hold their shape well) to make their home fries. But who has precooked potatoes just sitting around at home? Being able to skip this step seemed like a long shot, which made us wonder why they were called home fries if they were so impractical to make at home.

Looking to see if we could avoid precooking, we began our testing with the simplest approach: Dice potatoes raw and cook them in a hot skillet with oil. But test after test, no matter how small we cut them, it proved challenging to cook raw potatoes all the way through and obtain a crisp brown crust at the same time. Low temperatures helped cook the inside, but the outside didn't get crisp. High temperatures crisped the outside, but the potatoes had to be taken off the heat so soon to prevent scorching that the insides were left raw. Precooking the potatoes was obviously a must.

Because we didn't want to spend an hour boiling or roasting potatoes, we turned to the best source for speed cooking in the kitchen: the microwave. In the test kitchen we often rely on the microwave to parcook potatoes quickly, so why wouldn't it work here? Tossing the diced potatoes in a little oil to prevent sticking, we popped the potatoes into the microwave. Success! After just five minutes, the potatoes were perfectly parcooked and ready for the skillet.

To cut back on the oil, this time we switched to a nonstick skillet to "home-fry" the potatoes. Tossing our parcooked potatoes into the pan with a tablespoon of oil over medium heat, we were quickly met with improved results—each individual piece of potato had a crisp exterior, and the inner flesh was tender, moist, and rich in potato flavor. However, tasters felt a thicker crust was still required. We tried turning the heat both up and down, but neither helped much. To replicate the heavy cast-iron tool used in many diners to press the potatoes flat against the griddle, we slid our heaviest pot (a Dutch oven) on top of the potatoes as they cooked. The weight of the Dutch oven kept the potatoes in constant contact with the hot skillet, producing a thick and even crust, but what a mess. Next we tried packing the potatoes down with a spatula to approximate the effect of the Dutch oven, letting the potatoes cook undisturbed. After five minutes, the potatoes were beginning to develop a thick golden brown crust, so we tossed them around, packed them down again, and waited some more. After we repeated this process a few more times, the potatoes were evenly browned and extra-crusty.

The last step was flavoring. Up until this point we had been sautéing our potatoes in canola oil, but tasters wanted some added richness. Swapping the oil in the pan for a tablespoon of butter did the trick. Sautéed onion was also a must, but when the onions were cooked with the potatoes, their moisture caused the home fries to lose their cherished crust. To keep the potatoes crispy, we browned the onions separately and added them to the pan just before the potatoes were finished. At the end, we tossed the potatoes with the classic additions of lemon juice, garlic, and oregano. Finally, we had hassle-free Greek diner–style home fries worthy of their name.

NOTES FROM THE TEST KITCHEN

THE GOLDEN STARCHES

High-starch/low-moisture potatoes, such as russets, may be great for baking and mashing, but when it comes to home fries, they are not the best choice. The fluffy flesh of these potatoes breaks down in the skillet, leaving nothing but a greasy pool of spuds. For tender tubers that retain their texture, we prefer medium-starch or waxy varieties, such as Yukon Gold, all-purpose, and red potatoes. They hold their shape in the skillet, develop a great crust, and fry up to a beautiful golden brown.

RUSSET POTATOES
A falling-apart mess

YUKON GOLD POTATOES
Intact, crisp, and browned

Greek Diner–Style Home Fries

SERVES 4

Although we prefer the sweetness of Yukon Gold potatoes, other medium-starch or waxy potatoes, such as all-purpose or red-skinned potatoes, can be substituted.

- 1½ pounds Yukon Gold potatoes (3 to 4 medium), scrubbed and cut into ¾-inch pieces (see note)
- 2 teaspoons canola oil
- 1 onion, minced (about 1 cup)
  Salt
- 1 tablespoon unsalted butter
- 2 tablespoons chopped fresh oregano
- 2 garlic cloves, minced
- 1 tablespoon fresh lemon juice
  Pepper

1. Toss the potatoes with 1 teaspoon of the oil in a large microwave-safe bowl. Cover and microwave on high until the potatoes are tender, 5 to 10 minutes, shaking the bowl halfway through.

2. Meanwhile, combine the remaining 1 teaspoon oil, onion, and ⅛ teaspoon salt in a 12-inch nonstick skillet. Cover and cook over medium-low heat, stirring occasionally, until softened, 8 to 10 minutes. Uncover, increase the heat to medium-high, and continue to cook, stirring occasionally, until the onion is well browned, 8 to 12 minutes longer. Transfer the onion to a small bowl.

3. Melt the butter in the skillet over medium heat. Add the potatoes and pack down with a spatula. Cook, without stirring, until browned on the first side, 5 to 7 minutes. Flip the potatoes, pack down again, and cook until browned on the second side, 5 to 7 minutes.

4. Reduce the heat to medium-low and continue to cook, stirring occasionally, until well browned and crisp, 9 to 12 minutes longer. Stir in the onion, oregano, garlic, and lemon juice, and cook for 1 minute. Season with salt and pepper to taste. Serve.

PER SERVING: Cal 200; Fat 5g; Sat fat 2g; Chol 10mg; Carb 35g; Protein 4g; Fiber 3g; Sodium 85mg

SCALLOPED POTATOES

SCALLOPED POTATOES ARE THE KIND OF COMFORTing dish that you could easily make into an entrée if fat and calories were no concern. But because it weighs in at 410 calories, 28 grams of fat (18 of them saturated), and 100 mg of cholesterol per serving even as a side dish, we were afraid that one of our perennial favorites was destined for extinction, appearing only on holidays, and even then with reservations. Our goal was to develop a recipe for scalloped potatoes that you would cook up more often than just on special occasions. We wanted it to be as rich as the original, but without all the guilt.

TEST KITCHEN
MAKEOVER

Most of the recipes we found for "low-fat" scalloped potatoes left a lot to be desired, and none came close to the real deal. In many of them high-fat dairy (like heavy cream and whole milk) was replaced with chicken broth—leaner, to be sure, but the potatoes took on an unpleasantly strong meaty flavor, not to mention that they lost a lot of their creamy, luxurious appeal. After testing combinations of chicken broth and other lower-fat dairy products, tasters came to the conclusion that they didn't care for any amount of chicken broth. They wanted honest, pure potato flavor, not chicken, in this dish.

Looking for another way to knock down the fat, we tried to find a dairy substitute for the heavy cream and whole milk combination. From evaporated milk to skim milk and everywhere in between, we tried them all. Evaporated milk was too sweet for our tastes; all whole milk with no heavy cream worked but did not fall within the range of fat grams that we had set as our goal (we were shooting for 5 grams or less if we could swing it). Skim milk broke into a nasty, curdled mess; 2 percent milk fared better but still curdled. The latter seemed like our best hope. If we could find a stabilizer that also worked to give body to the sauce, we might be able to stick with 2 percent milk.

Two teaspoons of cornstarch helped immensely in stabilizing and thickening our sauce, but it still lacked the creamy richness that tasters were hoping for. We then turned to an unlikely ingredient that we had used successfully to add creamy richness to our Linguine with Shrimp, Lemon, and Garlic (page 125): light cream cheese. Once again, the cream cheese saved the day. It added just the right amount of silkiness to the sauce, giving the illusion of creaminess without all of the calories or fat. For depth, we added onion and garlic, along with fresh thyme and a couple of bay leaves.

Up until this point, russets had been our potato of choice, but we were curious to see if other varieties might elevate our recipe even further. We tried making the gratin with all-purpose and Yukon Golds. Yukon Gold and all-purpose potatoes weren't bad, but tasters found them a bit waxy. The traditional russet, with its tender bite and earthy flavor, was the unanimous favorite. The russet also formed tighter, more cohesive layers owing to its higher starch content. The only thing that was missing now was that elusive brown, crispy cheese topping that many of us in the test kitchen consider the best part of scalloped potatoes.

Our first inclination was to use reduced-fat cheddar, an ingredient we had used successfully in our Cheesy Broccoli and Rice Casserole (page 197). Unfortunately, it added little flavor here and lacked the browning capabilities we were looking for in a topping. Next we turned to the potent flavor of Parmesan cheese, and just 2 ounces gave us the results we were after. Taking 2 tablespoons of the Parmesan from the topping and adding it to the potatoes with the cream cheese incorporated its flavor throughout. Now with just a mere 190 calories and 4 grams of fat per serving, we finally had everything the test kitchen expected from great scalloped potatoes, minus the guilt.

MAKEOVER SPOTLIGHT: SCALLOPED POTATOES

	CALORIES	FAT	SAT FAT	CHOLESTEROL
BEFORE	410	28g	18g	100mg
AFTER	190	4g	2g	10mg

Scalloped Potatoes

SERVES 8

Prepare and assemble all of your ingredients before slicing the potatoes or the potatoes will begin to turn brown (do not store the sliced potatoes in water). Slicing the potatoes ⅛ inch thick is crucial for the success of this dish; use a mandoline, a V-slicer, or a food processor fitted with a ⅛-inch-thick slicing blade to make the slicing work quick and easy.

- 1 onion, minced (about 1 cup)
- 1 teaspoon canola oil
- ½ teaspoon salt
- 1 garlic clove, minced
- 1 teaspoon minced fresh thyme
- ¼ teaspoon pepper
- 2½ pounds russet potatoes (5 medium), peeled and sliced ⅛ inch thick (see note)
- 2 cups 2 percent milk
- 2 bay leaves
- 1 tablespoon water
- 2 teaspoons cornstarch
- 2 ounces Parmesan cheese, grated (about 1 cup)
- 3 tablespoons light cream cheese

1. Adjust an oven rack to the middle position and heat the oven to 450 degrees.

2. Combine the onion, oil, and salt in a Dutch oven. Cover and cook over medium-low heat, stirring occasionally, until softened, 8 to 10 minutes. Stir in the garlic, thyme, and pepper, and cook until fragrant, about 30 seconds.

3. Add the potatoes, milk, and bay leaves, and bring to a simmer over medium heat. Reduce the heat to low, cover, and cook until the potatoes are almost tender and a paring knife can be slipped into a potato slice with some resistance, about 10 minutes. Remove and discard the bay leaves. Whisk the water and cornstarch together, then add to the pot and bring to a simmer. Off the heat, gently stir in 2 tablespoons of the Parmesan and the cream cheese, being careful not to break up the potatoes.

4. Transfer the mixture to an 8-inch square baking dish and sprinkle with the remaining 14 tablespoons Parmesan. Cover the dish with foil and bake for 20 minutes. Uncover and continue to bake until the potatoes are completely tender, a paring knife can be slipped into the center of the dish without resistance, and the top is golden brown, 10 to 15 minutes longer. Let cool for 10 minutes before serving.

PER SERVING: **Cal** 190; **Fat** 4g; **Sat fat** 2g; **Chol** 10mg; **Carb** 31g; **Protein** 8g; **Fiber** 2g; **Sodium** 310mg

ROASTED SWEET POTATOES

HOLIDAY SEASON INCARNATIONS OF SWEET POTATO casseroles are more of a heavy, dessert-like indulgence than a balanced side dish, more often than not suffering under heavy toppings and loaded with sweeteners. We've always found this a poor way to treat food that needs little fuss to taste great on its own, not to mention that it turns a food that is healthy into a caloric disaster. For a simply dressed version of sweet potatoes we could enjoy year-round, we liked the idea of using a method we employ with regular potatoes: Slice, toss with a little oil, then roast at a high temperature. If all went well, the sweet potatoes would emerge from the oven with a nicely caramelized exterior, smooth, creamy interior, and an earthy sweetness that would need little enhancement.

The trouble is, sweet potatoes don't always behave like their white- and yellow-fleshed relatives. Handled the same way, they can come out of the oven tasting starchy and dull. Returning them to the heat doesn't solve the problem, and it can even worsen things by burning the potatoes' edges. We set out to find a way to produce perfect roasted sweet potatoes every time.

The most common shape for roasted potatoes is the wedge, which is easy to cut and allows many pieces to fit on a rimmed baking sheet. But we found wedges unsuitable for our sweet potatoes. The thinner tips finished cooking long before the sides had softened. Cutting peeled potatoes into 1-inch chunks can help maintain more even dimensions with regular spuds, but the knobby shapes and tapered ends of the sweet potatoes made creating uniform cubes impossible. In the end, we took shape out of the equation and simply sliced peeled sweet potatoes into rounds. While the diameter varied, each round was the same height on the pan. We agreed that ¾ inch thick seemed just right.

It was time to move on to the cooking method. Roasted at 425 degrees (the temperature often recommended for regular spuds), the sweet potatoes browned nicely, but their interiors were starchy and fibrous and lacked sweetness. As we experimented with the oven temperature to get better results, we noticed a curious trend: the lower the temperature, the less browning but the sweeter the potatoes. After a little digging, we found an explanation: The starch in sweet potatoes, different from the starch in regular potatoes, is converted into sugars between 122 and 175 degrees. Once the internal temperature of the potato exceeds 175, no further conversion occurs. Thus, the lower the temperature, the longer the potatoes would stay within this range and the sweeter the spuds would be.

But dropping the temperature would also mean more time in the oven, and we didn't want a simple side dish to take all day. That's when we remembered a technique we'd come across for starting sweet potatoes in a cold (versus a preheated) oven—a different way to keep their internal temperature lower for longer. It was worth a try.

We put a batch of potato rounds on a baking sheet, placed them in a cold oven, then turned the heat to 425 degrees, using a digital thermometer to track their temperature. After 20 minutes, the thermometer registered 175. We cooked the potatoes for 25 minutes more until the bottom edges browned, then flipped them to let the other side brown. These potatoes tasted vastly better than the ones roasted in a preheated oven, but could we get them sweeter still?

We prepped a new batch, but to further delay heating, we covered them with foil before placing them in a cold oven. This time, the potatoes took 30 minutes to reach 175. We then removed the foil and continued to roast them as before. This 10-minute difference was small but significant. These potatoes were perfect: super-sweet and tender, with a slightly crisp caramelized exterior. The only problem was that they stuck to the pan, easily remedied in our next batch by covering the bottom of the pan with foil and coating it with vegetable oil spray.

As perfect as these potatoes were, tasters asked for some interesting variations. Adding a syrupy glaze would only take away from the natural sweetness we had worked hard to promote, so instead we created a few different spice mixtures, one that was barbecue-inspired, with spices like paprika and chili powder, and another that was Moroccan, with spices like turmeric, coriander, and cinnamon. Tossed with the potatoes and oil before roasting, these spice blends added balanced, bold flavor to the sweet potatoes that earned rave reviews.

Roasted Sweet Potatoes

SERVES 6

Note that this recipe calls for starting the sweet potatoes in a cold oven. Choose sweet potatoes that are as even in width as possible; trimming the small ends prevents them from burning. The sweet potatoes can be peeled if desired.

> Vegetable oil spray
> 3 pounds sweet potatoes (about 4 medium), scrubbed, ends trimmed (see note), sliced into ¾-inch-thick rounds
> 2 tablespoons canola oil
> Salt and pepper

1. Line a rimmed baking sheet with foil and lightly coat with vegetable oil spray. Toss the potatoes with the oil, ¼ teaspoon salt, and ¼ teaspoon pepper. Arrange the potatoes in a single layer on the prepared baking sheet and cover tightly with foil. Adjust an oven rack to the middle position and place the potatoes in the cold oven. Turn the oven to 425 degrees and cook for 30 minutes.

2. Uncover and continue to cook until the bottom edges of the potatoes are golden brown, 15 to 25 minutes.

3. Flip the slices and continue to cook until golden brown on both sides, 18 to 22 minutes longer. Season with salt and pepper to taste. Serve.

PER SERVING: Cal 220; Fat 5g; Sat fat 0g; Chol 0mg; Carb 40g; Protein 3g; Fiber 7g; Sodium 220mg

VARIATIONS

Roasted Sweet Potatoes with Barbecue Spices
Follow the recipe for Roasted Sweet Potatoes, adding 1½ teaspoons paprika, ½ teaspoon brown sugar, ½ teaspoon dried oregano, ¼ teaspoon chili powder, ¼ teaspoon ground cumin, and ⅛ teaspoon cayenne pepper with the oil.

PER SERVING: Cal 220; Fat 5g; Sat fat 0g; Chol 0mg; Carb 41g; Protein 4g; Fiber 7g; Sodium 220mg

Roasted Sweet Potatoes with Moroccan Spices
Follow the recipe for Roasted Sweet Potatoes, adding 1 teaspoon ground ginger, ¾ teaspoon ground coriander, ¾ teaspoon ground cumin, ¼ teaspoon ground cinnamon, and ¼ teaspoon ground turmeric with the oil.

PER SERVING: Cal 220; Fat 5g; Sat fat 0g; Chol 0mg; Carb 41g; Protein 4g; Fiber 7g; Sodium 220mg

NOTES FROM THE TEST KITCHEN

SWEET POTATOES VERSUS YAMS
The names "yam" and "sweet potato" have largely become synonymous in the United States, but they are actually two very distinct tubers. True yams belong to a completely different botanical family and are much scarcer in North America than sweet potatoes. Generally found in Asian or Latin markets, yams are often sold in chunks because they can grow to be several feet long. Because there are dozens of varieties of yams, the flesh color can range from white to light yellow to pink and the skin color from off-white to brown. All of them, though, have very starchy flesh.

Sweet potatoes are what we usually buy: longish, knobby tubers with dark, orangey-brown skin and vivid flesh within. The flesh cooks up moist, and the flavor is very sweet. These are actually a variety of sweet potato developed in Louisiana in the 1930s. The growers called them yams simply for marketing purposes to set them apart from other sweet potato varieties. In so doing, they have confused consumers to this day. The traditional varieties are Beauregard (usually sold as a conventional sweet potato), Jewel, and Red Garnet, with the buttery, sweet Beauregard being our favorite.

ROASTED SWEET POTATOES

CRUMB COFFEE CAKE

CHAPTER 11

BREAKFAST AND BAKED GOODS

M = TEST KITCHEN MAKEOVER

CINNAMON ROLLS

TEST KITCHEN
MAKEOVER

WITH THEIR BUTTERY YEAST DOUGH, SWIRL OF buttery cinnamon filling, and gooey coating of cream cheese frosting, it's no surprise cinnamon rolls disappear the minute they hit the table. So what's not to love? For starters, the hefty fat and calorie count—18 grams of fat and at least 400 calories typically in a roll. There's also the time commitment to making them, as cinnamon rolls can require a few hours of prep. Our goals were simple: Trim fat, and trim time.

Most "quick" cinnamon roll recipes replace the yeast dough with biscuit dough leavened with baking powder or baking soda. But when we tried to trim butter from this quick dough, the results were dry and crumbly. No matter how hard we tried, our lightened baking powder rolls just fell short. Switching gears, we returned to the more traditional yeasted rolls and tested several adventurous low-fat recipes. Tasters were not impressed by rolls made with odd butter substitutes, including applesauce, cottage cheese, and mashed potatoes.

We decided the best tactic was to return to the test kitchen's favorite high-fat, time-intensive recipe and looked for places to trim. The stick of butter in this rich dough was a good place to start. We tried dough made with just 2 tablespoons of melted butter, which we combined with skim milk in lieu of regular, and maple syrup in lieu of granulated sugar, since it would provide some moisture, which we had removed when taking out the butter. Eggs, traditional in a lot of sweet doughs, add richness, but we decided to see if we could get away without them. To our surprise, this dough made rolls that were soft and pillowy. True, the dough itself was not as flavorful or rich as the original, but we hoped that with a great filling and icing, it wouldn't matter.

Although the typical cinnamon-sugar filling contains up to 6 tablespoons of butter, we found we could get away with far less. As long as the filling was made with more brown sugar than white sugar—the former is more moist and helps ensure that the filling is plenty gooey when baked—just a tablespoon of melted butter was all that was needed to hold it together.

The creamy blanket of frosting is traditionally made with butter, cream cheese, and confectioners' sugar. The butter was easy enough to trim, but most recipes rely on an entire package of cream cheese. We tried replacing the cream cheese with buttermilk, but this glaze was thin and unsatisfying. When we tried nonfat cream cheese, tasters turned up their noses at the grainy texture. We eventually settled on light cream cheese, which offered much better texture and fuller flavor (almost as good as the full-fat), and we used far less than the typical recipe (just one-quarter of a package). To make the cream cheese go further, we were able to stretch it with skim milk with no complaints from tasters, and a little vanilla extract rounded out the flavor.

Most yeasted dough recipes require two lengthy rises, especially necessary with a heavy, butter-enriched dough. Our leaner dough was already rising relatively quickly, and we sped up the process further by putting it in a warm oven; the first rise took only 10 minutes. Once shaped and filled, the rolls doubled in size in about half an hour and then baked up in just 20 to 25 minutes. These cinnamon rolls were ready to eat about 90 minutes after we started—not bad for a recipe that usually takes three to four hours. Enjoyed warm from the oven, these rolls amazed tasters, who couldn't believe we had shaved almost 200 calories, nearly 15 grams of fat, and more than two hours of prep time from our traditional, full-fat cinnamon roll recipe.

MAKEOVER SPOTLIGHT: CINNAMON ROLLS

	CALORIES	FAT	SAT FAT	CHOLESTEROL
BEFORE	450	18g	11g	100mg
AFTER	260	3.5g	2.5g	10mg

Cinnamon Rolls

MAKES 12 ROLLS

Don't be afraid to use a little extra flour when shaping the rolls if the dough seems a little sticky. The rolls are best eaten as soon as they are iced, but they hold well at room temperature for up to 2 hours. You will need a standing mixer with a dough hook for this recipe.

DOUGH

    Vegetable oil spray

1⅓ cups skim milk, warmed (110 degrees)

  3 tablespoons maple syrup

  2 tablespoons unsalted butter, melted

3¾ cups (18¾ ounces) unbleached all-purpose flour

  1 packet instant or rapid-rise yeast (2¼ teaspoons)

  1 teaspoon salt

FILLING

- ½ cup packed (3½ ounces) dark brown sugar
- ¼ cup (1¼ ounces) granulated sugar
- 1 tablespoon unsalted butter, melted
- 2 teaspoons ground cinnamon
- ⅛ teaspoon salt

ICING

- 1 cup (4 ounces) confectioners' sugar
- ¼ cup light cream cheese
- 1 tablespoon skim milk
- ½ teaspoon vanilla extract

1. FOR THE DOUGH: Adjust an oven rack to the middle position and heat the oven to 200 degrees. When the oven reaches 200 degrees, turn it off. Lightly coat a large bowl and a 13 by 9-inch baking dish with vegetable oil spray and set aside.

2. Mix the milk, syrup, and melted butter together in a large measuring cup. Combine 3½ cups of the flour, yeast, and salt in the bowl of a standing mixer fitted with the dough hook. With the mixer on low speed, slowly add the milk mixture and mix until the dough comes together, about 2 minutes.

3. Increase the mixer speed to medium-low and knead until the dough is shiny and smooth, 4 to 6 minutes. (If, after 4 minutes, more flour is needed, add the remaining ¼ cup flour, 1 tablespoon at a time, until the dough clears the side of the bowl but sticks to the bottom.)

4. Turn out the dough onto a well-floured counter and knead to form a smooth, round ball. Place the dough in the greased bowl and cover tightly with plastic wrap. Let the dough rest in the warm oven for 10 minutes.

5. FOR THE FILLING: While the dough is resting, mix the brown sugar, granulated sugar, melted butter, cinnamon, and salt together in a medium bowl and set aside.

6. TO MAKE THE ROLLS: Roll the dough on a lightly floured counter into an 18 by 12-inch rectangle. With the long side facing you, sprinkle the sugar mixture over the dough, leaving a ½-inch border along the top edge. Following the photos, press on the filling so that it adheres to the dough. Starting at the edge nearest you, roll the dough into a tight log. Brush the border with water and pinch the seam closed. Roll the log, finishing with the seam-side down.

7. Slice the dough into 12 evenly sized rolls (about 1½ inches wide) using a chef's knife, then place in the prepared pan, cut-side up. Cover the pan with plastic wrap coated with vegetable oil spray and return to the warm oven until the rolls have nearly doubled in size, 30 to 40 minutes.

8. Remove the pan from the oven and heat the oven to 350 degrees.

9. Remove the plastic wrap and bake until the rolls are deep brown and the filling is melted, 20 to 25 minutes, rotating the pan halfway through.

10. FOR THE ICING: While the rolls are baking, whisk the confectioners' sugar, cream cheese, milk, and vanilla together in a small bowl until smooth. Remove the pan from the oven, turn the rolls out onto a wire rack, and flip them right-side up. Let the rolls cool for 10 minutes, then spread the icing over the top and serve.

PER ROLL: **Cal** 260; **Fat** 3.5g; **Sat fat** 2.5g; **Chol** 10mg; **Carb** 52g; **Protein** 5g; **Fiber** 1g; **Sodium** 260mg

---

NOTES FROM THE TEST KITCHEN

MAKING CINNAMON ROLLS

1. Pat the sugar mixture into the dough, leaving a ½-inch border along the top edge.

2. Carefully roll the dough into a cylinder, moistening the border with water to seal the dough.

3. Cut the cylinder in half, then in half again (making 4 pieces). Cut each piece into 3 pieces, yielding 12 rolls.

CRUMB COFFEE CAKE

TEST KITCHEN
MAKEOVER

THE BEST GREETING FOR SUNDAY BRUNCH GUESTS is a slice of warm coffee cake with a crunchy topping piled on top of rich, buttery cake. But if that greeting contains more than 20 grams of fat and 450 calories, it doesn't seem as friendly, does it? We wanted to develop a recipe for a lighter coffee cake, one that wouldn't fill up our guests before they sat down to a frittata and some fresh fruit, but we still wanted a cake that tasted rich and was crowned with an appealingly moist and flavorful topping.

A lot of crumb coffee cake recipes go so overboard on the topping that it drowns the cake, so our first step would be to reduce the total amount of topping—a mixture of white and brown sugars, flour, butter, and cinnamon. This move lightened our cake instantly. Typically there's also a fair amount of white sugar in the cake, but when we tried to reduce the sugar here, the cake turned horribly dry. The simple solution—an idea borrowed from the topping recipe (and a trick that was successful in the filling for our lighter Cinnamon Rolls, page 240)—was to use a combination of brown and white sugars. Brown sugar added plenty of moisture, making a big improvement in the cake's texture. In the end, we were able to trim ½ cup of white sugar from our recipe.

We had already determined that we needed at least 1 tablespoon of butter in the crumb topping; next we looked at reducing the amount of butter in the cake. Fat tenderizes baked goods, and not surprisingly our cake baked up tough when we cut back on the butter. We decided we could reduce the amount of butter slightly, but we needed to find another way to add back some moisture and tenderness. We tried all sorts of creative substitutes (buttermilk, yogurt, applesauce), but low-fat sour cream contributed the perfect richness as well as a tangy flavor.

Our cake was now very good—at least most of the time. The problem was that sometimes it still turned out tough. The reduced-fat batter was really thick, more like a sticky bread dough, and we were having trouble blending all the ingredients with a spoon or spatula. We suspected that when the cake baked up tough, it was probably because we were overworking the batter. We had to find a more reliable way to mix together our ingredients, even if it meant not keeping it as simple as mixing them by hand. An electric mixer didn't do much better, but the food processor proved to be the answer. The pulse button worked efficiently, making it easy to stop mixing the moment the batter was ready. All we had to do was pour it into the pan, sprinkle over the topping, and pop it into the oven. This coffee cake (and the many we made after) was perfectly tender.

With just one-half of the calories and one-quarter of the fat, our reduced-fat coffee cake was still tender and moist and nicely balanced by the crunchy crumbs on top.

MAKEOVER SPOTLIGHT: CRUMB COFFEE CAKE

	CALORIES	FAT	SAT FAT	CHOLESTEROL
BEFORE	470	24g	12g	105mg
AFTER	250	6g	3.5g	35mg

Crumb Coffee Cake

SERVES 10

It's best to serve this cake the same day you make it; the crunchy crumb topping will soften if covered or stored for more than a day. Low-fat cakes are prone to dryness, especially if overbaked, so pull the cake out of the oven just before you think it's done. Residual heat from the pan will finish the baking.

Vegetable oil spray
2   cups (10 ounces) unbleached all-purpose flour
¾   cup packed (5¼ ounces) light brown sugar
½   cup (3½ ounces) granulated sugar
½   teaspoon salt
½   teaspoon baking powder
¼   teaspoon baking soda
4   tablespoons (½ stick) unsalted butter, melted and cooled slightly
1   cup low-fat sour cream, at room temperature
1   large egg, at room temperature
1   teaspoon vanilla extract
1   teaspoon cinnamon

1. Adjust an oven rack to the middle position and heat the oven to 350 degrees. Lightly coat an 8-inch square baking pan with vegetable oil spray and set aside.

2. Pulse the flour, ½ cup of the brown sugar, granulated sugar, salt, baking powder, and baking soda together in a food processor to combine. With the food processor running, add 3 tablespoons of the melted butter and process until the flour mixture looks sandy.

3. Transfer ¼ cup of the flour mixture to a medium bowl and set aside. Add the sour cream, egg, and vanilla to the flour mixture in the food processor and pulse until the mixture just comes together, about 8 pulses. (Do not overmix.) Scrape the batter into the prepared pan and smooth the top.

4. Stir the remaining ¼ cup brown sugar and cinnamon into the bowl with the reserved flour mixture. Add the remaining 1 tablespoon butter and toss gently with a fork until the butter is evenly distributed, creating some larger pea-sized crumbs. Sprinkle the crumb mixture evenly over the batter.

5. Bake until the topping is golden brown and a toothpick inserted into the center of the cake comes out with a few crumbs attached, 30 to 35 minutes, rotating the pan halfway through.

6. Let the cake cool in the pan for 15 minutes and serve warm or at room temperature.

PER SERVING: **Cal** 250; **Fat** 6g; **Sat fat** 3.5g; **Chol** 35mg; **Carb** 41g; **Protein** 4g; **Fiber** 1g; **Sodium** 230mg

BLUEBERRY MUFFINS

COMPARED TO POPULAR BREAKFAST TREATS LIKE doughnuts or sausage biscuits, muffins certainly seem like a healthful option. Maybe it's because they often contain fruit, bran, or other good-for-you ingredients. But the truth is, one of those super-sized muffins from the coffee shop can contain up to 590 calories and 24 grams of fat. Homemade muffins are a much better choice, with an average of 11 grams of fat and 300 calories. But we knew we could do even better than that, so we set out to create a recipe for moist, flavorful muffins that were also light. We decided to focus on the classic blueberry muffin.

Traditional muffin recipes usually call for 8 to 10 tablespoons of butter; we wondered how much fat we could omit. Starting with some basic proportions—3 cups of flour, 1 cup of sugar, 2 eggs, and 1¼ cups of milk—we aimed to take the butter as low as possible without compromising texture or flavor. For our first tests, tasters sampled three batches of muffins with varying amounts of butter. All agreed that the muffins made

with 3 tablespoons were a bit tough and bland. It was a much closer contest between the other two contenders. Although tasters liked the delicate crumb and depth of flavor of the muffins made with 5 tablespoons of butter, the flavor of the muffins made with 4 tablespoons was just as good. It was the crumb of these muffins that left a little to be desired. We decided to work with the leaner 4 tablespoons of butter and focus on improving the crumb quality. We felt that the answer would be incorporating this modest amount of butter into the batter evenly.

Instead of using the typical method for making muffins (and quick breads) of measuring out wet and dry ingredients separately and then stirring the wet into the dry, we decided to employ the creaming method, which is typically used to make cake batters. The creaming method starts with creaming butter and sugar together until light and fluffy, beating in the eggs and flavoring, then adding dry and liquid ingredients alternately. This technique worked like a charm, giving us muffins that definitely had a more delicate crumb. To enhance the muffins' texture further, we also cut our all-purpose flour with some lower-protein cake flour. A ratio of 2 cups of all-purpose flour to 1 cup of cake flour was just right.

As for dairy, we needed something that would give our muffins a moist crumb and nice tang. Low-fat sour cream produced gummy muffins, so next we tried low-fat yogurt. These muffins were just what we were after. Since lemon is a natural partner with blueberries, we decided to add a bit of lemon juice and zest for brightness (some tasters didn't care for the lemon zest's perfume, so we agreed to make it optional). One teaspoon of vanilla contributed the right balancing depth.

With our batter down, we addressed the blueberries. For big berry flavor, we needed a full 2 cups of fresh blueberries. (We prefer small, fresh, wild blueberries; they are much sweeter than their bigger cultivated cousins.) When it came to incorporating the berries into the finished batter, we found that it works best to toss them with a little flour first. This helps the berries stay evenly suspended in the batter. In addition, the berries had to be gently folded into the batter; otherwise, they bled, giving the muffins an unappetizing blue-gray color.

This batter was good but somewhat heavy; it required a full tablespoon of baking powder for enough lift. This seemed like a lot, but tasters noted no off-flavors. We also included another leavener—baking soda. When baking soda is mixed with an acid, such as lemon juice and yogurt, it releases carbon dioxide, the gas that causes baked goods to rise.

With a great blueberry muffin recipe under our belts, we came up with a couple of variations—raspberry with almond and cranberry with orange—that produced perfect low-fat muffins every time.

Blueberry Muffins

MAKES 1 DOZEN MUFFINS

When fresh blueberries are not in season, frozen berries are a good alternative. To make sure that frozen berries do not bleed into the muffin batter (making the muffins an unappealing blue-gray color), rinse them under cool water in a mesh strainer until the water runs clear, then spread them on a paper towel–lined plate to dry.

> Vegetable oil spray
> 2 cups (10 ounces) plus 1 tablespoon unbleached all-purpose flour
> 1 cup (4 ounces) cake flour
> 1 tablespoon baking powder
> ½ teaspoon baking soda
> ½ teaspoon salt
> 1 cup (7 ounces) plus 1 tablespoon sugar
> 4 tablespoons (½ stick) unsalted butter, softened
> 2 large eggs
> 2 teaspoons fresh lemon juice plus 1 teaspoon grated lemon zest (optional)
> 1 teaspoon vanilla extract
> 1½ cups plain low-fat yogurt
> 2 cups fresh blueberries (see note)

1. Adjust an oven rack to the middle position and heat the oven to 375 degrees. Lightly coat a 12-cup muffin tin with vegetable oil spray and set aside.

2. Whisk 2 cups of the all-purpose flour, cake flour, baking powder, baking soda, salt, and ¼ cup of the sugar together in a medium bowl and set aside. In a large bowl, beat ¾ cup more sugar and butter together with an electric mixer on medium speed until light and fluffy, 3 to 6 minutes. Beat in the eggs, one at a time, until combined. Add the lemon juice, lemon zest (if using), and vanilla, and mix until incorporated, scraping down the bowl and beaters as needed.

3. Reduce the mixer speed to low. Beat in one-third of the flour mixture until just incorporated, followed by one-third of the yogurt, scraping down the bowl and beaters as needed. Repeat this process twice more, alternating between the remaining flour mixture and the remaining yogurt until the ingredients are just incorporated. (Do not overmix.)

4. Toss the blueberries with the remaining 1 tablespoon all-purpose flour, then gently fold them into the batter with a rubber spatula. Using a large ice-cream scoop or measuring cup, divide the batter evenly among the muffin cups and sprinkle the tops with the remaining 1 tablespoon sugar.

5. Bake until golden brown and a toothpick inserted into the center of a muffin comes out with just a few crumbs attached, 25 to 30 minutes, rotating the muffin tin halfway through. Let the muffins cool in the pan for 5 minutes, then flip them out onto a wire rack and

NOTES FROM THE TEST KITCHEN

NO MORE SINKING BERRIES

Blueberries are a classic stir-in for muffins, but all too often they sink to the bottom of the batter. We toss the berries with 1 tablespoon of flour; this keeps them evenly suspended, guaranteeing a little blueberry in every bite.

THE BEST MUFFIN TIN

With price tags ranging from $5 to a whopping $26, we wondered if there was a good reason for shelling out the big bucks for a simple muffin tin. It turns out there are differences in the way the tins perform. In our tests, the best tins browned the muffins evenly; the worst tins browned the muffins on top but left them pale on the bottom. Our tests proved that darker coated metals, which absorb heat, do the best job of browning baked goods, and heavy-duty (and higher-priced) models do not produce muffins that are any better than those baked in the lightweight models. **Wilton Ultra-Bake Muffin Tin,** $10.99, was the clear winner, in part because of its generous 2-inch lip that makes it easy to maneuver this tin in and out of the oven.

cool for 10 minutes before serving. (The muffins can be stored in an airtight container at room temperature for up to 3 days.)

PER MUFFIN: Cal 260; Fat 5g; Sat fat 3g; Chol 45mg; Carb 47g; Protein 6g; Fiber 1g; Sodium 320mg

VARIATIONS

Raspberry-Almond Muffins

It's important that you use fresh raspberries here, as frozen ones are too fragile and bleed too much even when rinsed.

Follow the recipe for Blueberry Muffins, substituting ½ teaspoon almond extract for the vanilla and 2 cups fresh raspberries for the blueberries. Omit the lemon juice and zest.

PER MUFFIN: Cal 250; Fat 5g; Sat fat 3g; Chol 45mg; Carb 45g; Protein 6g; Fiber 2g; Sodium 320mg

Cranberry-Orange Muffins

Combine 1½ cups dried cranberries, chopped fine, and ⅔ cup orange juice in a microwave-safe bowl. Cover and microwave on high until the juice is bubbling, about 1 minute. Let the cranberries sit, covered, until softened and plump, about 5 minutes. Strain the cranberries, discarding the juice. Meanwhile, process 1 cup plus 1 tablespoon sugar with 2 teaspoons grated orange zest in a food processor until pale orange, about 10 seconds. Follow the recipe for Blueberry Muffins, substituting the processed orange sugar for the sugar and the rehydrated cranberries for the blueberries. Omit the lemon juice and zest.

PER MUFFIN: Cal 290; Fat 5g; Sat fat 3g; Chol 45mg; Carb 56g; Protein 6g; Fiber 2g; Sodium 320mg

BANANA BREAD

GOOD BANANA BREAD IS SOFT, MOIST, AND FULL OF flavor. The traditional recipe is an easy one: Mashed overripe bananas are combined with vegetable oil and eggs, then mixed with flour, sugar, and leavener and baked. Seems like a nice, simple snack, but a single slice can contain up to 220 calories and 6 grams of fat. While these amounts are not terrible, we felt we could certainly find a leaner way to make moist,

full-flavored banana bread so that it could really count as a healthy snack.

During our research for existing low-fat banana bread recipes, we came across versions that called for baby food, applesauce, and even avocados to replace some of the sugar and oil. They all sounded a bit odd but worth a try at least. Not surprisingly, all of these breads failed to pass; they had dry or gummy textures and baked up with either weak or strange flavors. We would have to start from scratch and find another way to replace the sweetness, richness, and moisture of the sugar and oil.

We started by upping the amount of bananas, which boosted the flavor and sweetness of the bread, but we wanted even bolder banana flavor. We found one recipe that called for roasting unpeeled bananas, and we wondered if that might help the flavor. We roasted the bananas in the oven until their skins were totally black and their flesh was caramelized, which took about 20 minutes. We let the bananas cool, then peeled and mashed them. The roasted bananas were sweeter and more intensely flavored than raw bananas—we could now use less sugar in our batter.

Banana bread (like carrot cake) is normally made with oil, usually about ½ cup per loaf. We tried swapping out the oil for butter, and this gave our loaf a rich flavor that tasters actually preferred to the oil-based versions. But to keep the fat low for our light recipe, we had to drop down to such a small amount of oil that our bread became too spongy and dry. Looking for another way to add moisture and structure, we tried adding buttermilk, low-fat sour cream, and reduced-fat cream cheese in different test loaves. Buttermilk was distractingly tangy, and the low-fat sour cream made the bread too spongy. But the reduced-fat cream cheese (combined with just a tablespoon of canola oil) gave the bread good moisture and texture. Since tasters couldn't identify our secret ingredient as reduced-fat cream cheese, we made another banana bread with fat-free cream cheese to find out if they would notice a change in texture or flavor. Fortunately for us, they couldn't tell the difference between the bread made with the reduced-fat cream cheese and the one made with fat-free, so the fat-free cream cheese was in.

Finally, we had a moist, rich banana bread that was loaded with banana flavor—and tasters couldn't even tell it had a mere 150 calories and just 2.5 grams of fat per slice. Now it was truly a healthy snack.

BANANA BREAD

Banana Bread

MAKES ONE 8-INCH LOAF

Don't peel the bananas before roasting them. Adding more than 1½ cups of the roasted bananas to the batter will result in a dense, gummy loaf.

  Vegetable oil spray

4 large ripe bananas (see note)

2 large eggs

2 teaspoons vanilla extract

1¾ cups (8¾ ounces) unbleached all-purpose flour

½ cup (3½ ounces) sugar

2 teaspoons baking powder

¾ teaspoon baking soda

¼ teaspoon salt

1 tablespoon canola oil

2 ounces fat-free cream cheese, cut into 4 pieces and chilled

1. Adjust an oven rack to the middle position and heat the oven to 325 degrees. Lightly coat an 8½ by 4½-inch loaf pan with vegetable oil spray and set aside.

2. Bake the bananas on a rimmed baking sheet until the skins are completely black, about 20 minutes. (Do not turn off the oven.) Set the bananas aside to cool to room temperature.

3. Peel the bananas, then mash them with a potato masher in a small bowl until smooth. Measure out and reserve 1½ cups of the mashed bananas, discarding any excess.

4. Whisk the eggs and vanilla together in a small bowl and set aside. In a large bowl, mix the flour, sugar, baking powder, baking soda, and salt together with an electric mixer on medium-low speed until combined. Add the oil and cream cheese, one piece at a time, and mix until only pea-sized pieces of the cream cheese remain, about 1 minute. Slowly beat in the egg mixture, then add the mashed bananas and beat until incorporated, about 30 seconds.

5. Scrape the batter into the prepared pan and smooth the top. Bake until golden brown and a toothpick inserted into the center comes out with just a few crumbs attached, 50 to 60 minutes, rotating the pan halfway through.

6. Let the loaf cool in the pan for 10 minutes, then turn it out onto a wire rack and let cool for 1 hour before serving. (The bread can be wrapped tightly in plastic wrap and stored at room temperature for up to 3 days.)

PER ⅔-INCH SLICE: Cal 150; Fat 2.5g; Sat fat 0g; Chol 35mg; Carb 28g; Protein 4g; Fiber 1g; Sodium 260mg

CHEESE BREAD

TEST KITCHEN
MAKEOVER

THE ULTIMATE CHEESE BREAD IS ADDICTIVE. MOIST and hearty, a perfect slice is studded throughout with pockets of cheese and has a crunchy, cheesy crust. We love it simply toasted for a snack or served alongside a bowl of soup. But most recipes require so much cheese and butter that the amount of fat in a serving goes beyond what is OK for a healthy side or afternoon snack (usually a slice tallies about 11 grams of fat). We set out to make a cheese bread that had a moist crumb and boasted a good cheesy tang, but we wanted a recipe that was light enough that we could enjoy it without guilt.

We began by reviewing our full-fat recipe for cheese bread. The first test tried was cutting back on the cheese and using some low-fat dairy ingredients. Our original recipe called for 4 ounces each of shredded Parmesan and cheddar, 1¼ cups of whole milk, 3 tablespoons of butter, and to top it all off, ¾ cup of sour cream. That makes for one rich loaf. We reduced the Parmesan by half, changed to low-fat milk and low-fat sour cream, and switched the full-fat cheddar out in favor of the 50 percent reduced-fat variety. We weren't surprised when this bread turned out to be a flavorless doorstop. After all, we had cut out most of the richness and cheesiness. We needed to look deeper into our bag of baking tricks.

Thinking about other quick bread recipes, we realized buttermilk turns up in a lot of ingredient lists. It lends both tangy flavor and nice richness, and it's conveniently low in fat. So we decided to nix the milk, butter, and sour cream for the time being and see what happened when we used just buttermilk. We also went back to regular extra-sharp cheddar—we all agreed that even if we had to use less of the full-fat version, the reduced-fat cheddar wasn't working here. The full-fat cheese returned the great cheesy flavor to our loaf (3 ounces did the trick), and it was nicely complemented by the tang of the buttermilk. But without the butter, our cheese bread had a crumb that was on the spongy side. Clearly, some fat had to be added back into the mix. We found that by supplementing some of the buttermilk with just a tablespoon of canola oil, we were able to reclaim some of the richness and moisture of full-fat cheese bread. All along we had been adding one egg to the batter, which had worked in the original, and we saw no reason to mess with a good thing. We were definitely on the right track.

This was our best loaf yet, but the flavor still needed some finessing. To enhance the flavor of the cheese, we added ¼ teaspoon of dry mustard and a pinch of cayenne pepper. For a rich flavor and good color in the crust, we revisited the Parmesan cheese. At first, we just sprinkled some Parmesan on top of the batter before putting our loaf pan into the oven. This was fine, but not outstanding. Then we hit on the idea of coating the pan bottom with cheese as well, guaranteeing a cheesy, crispy exterior all the way around. But how little cheese could we get away with? After some trial and error, we decided that a few tablespoons for the pan, a few tablespoons for the top, and about ¼ cup mixed into the batter provided a good nuttiness and saltiness without adding too much fat.

After 45 minutes in the oven, our cheese bread had a moist crumb and full cheesy flavor—and with almost half the fat of the original (and only 170 calories) per slice, this was one light indulgence we could definitely get addicted to.

MAKEOVER SPOTLIGHT: CHEESE BREAD

	CALORIES	FAT	SAT FAT	CHOLESTEROL
BEFORE	240	11g	7g	50mg
AFTER	170	6g	2.5g	30mg

Cheese Bread

MAKES ONE 8-INCH LOAF

Shredding the Parmesan on the large holes of a box grater and sprinkling it over the top of this bread adds a nice texture and helps prevent the cheese from burning; do not grate it fine or use pre-grated Parmesan. The texture of this bread improves as it cools, so resist the urge to slice the loaf while it is piping hot.

      Vegetable oil spray
  2   ounces Parmesan cheese, shredded
      on the large holes of a box grater
      (about ⅔ cup; see note)
2½   cups (12½ ounces) unbleached all-purpose flour
  1   tablespoon baking powder
  1   teaspoon salt
  ¼   teaspoon dry mustard
  ⅛   teaspoon cayenne pepper
  ⅛   teaspoon black pepper
  3   ounces extra-sharp cheddar cheese, cut into
      ¼-inch cubes (about ¾ cup)
1¼   cups low-fat buttermilk
  1   tablespoon canola oil
  1   large egg

1. Adjust an oven rack to the middle position and heat the oven to 350 degrees. Lightly coat an 8½ by 4½-inch loaf pan with vegetable oil spray, sprinkle 3 tablespoons of the Parmesan evenly over the bottom of the pan, and set aside.

2. Whisk the flour, baking powder, salt, mustard, cayenne, and black pepper together in a large bowl. Stir in 3 tablespoons more Parmesan and the cheddar, breaking up any clumps. In a medium bowl, whisk the buttermilk, oil, and egg together until smooth. Gently fold the buttermilk mixture into the flour mixture with a rubber spatula. (Do not overmix.) The batter will be heavy and thick.

3. Scrape the batter into the prepared pan and smooth the top. Sprinkle the remaining Parmesan evenly over the top. Bake until golden brown and a toothpick inserted into the center comes out clean, 45 to 50 minutes, rotating the pan halfway through.

4. Let the loaf cool in the pan for 5 minutes, then turn it out onto a wire rack and let cool for 1 hour before serving. (The bread can be wrapped tightly in plastic wrap and stored at room temperature for up to 3 days.)

PER ⅔-INCH SLICE: Cal 170; Fat 6g; Sat fat 2.5g; Chol 30mg; Carb 19g; Protein 7g; Fiber 1g; Sodium 490mg

Roasted Red Pepper and Scallion Cheese Bread

Be sure to pat the roasted red peppers dry before adding them to the buttermilk.

Follow the recipe for Cheese Bread, adding ½ cup jarred roasted red peppers, drained, patted dry, and chopped, and 2 scallions, minced, to the buttermilk mixture.

PER ⅔-INCH SLICE: Cal 170; Fat 6g; Sat fat 2.5g; Chol 30mg; Carb 20g; Protein 7g; Fiber 1g; Sodium 490mg

Chipotle Cheese Bread

Follow the recipe for Cheese Bread, omitting the cayenne pepper and adding 2 teaspoons minced chipotle chiles in adobo sauce to the buttermilk mixture.

PER ⅔-INCH SLICE: Cal 170; Fat 6g; Sat fat 2.5g; Chol 30mg; Carb 20g; Protein 7g; Fiber 1g; Sodium 490mg

Sun-Dried Tomato and Garlic Cheese Bread

Follow the recipe for Cheese Bread, adding ¼ cup chopped sun-dried tomatoes and 2 medium garlic cloves, minced, to the buttermilk mixture.

PER ⅔-INCH SLICE: Cal 170; Fat 6g; Sat fat 2.5g; Chol 30mg; Carb 20g; Protein 8g; Fiber 1g; Sodium 500mg

BUTTERMILK BISCUITS

A TENDER, GOLDEN BUTTERMILK BISCUIT FRESH from the oven is its own advertisement. But even without a slather of butter or jam, one average-sized biscuit has upward of 200 calories and, worse, 12 grams of fat. We wanted to make a lower-calorie, lower-fat version, but we worried that the straightforward ingredient list would be limiting, giving us little room for a successful recipe makeover.

TEST KITCHEN MAKEOVER

A favorite test kitchen recipe for full-fat buttermilk biscuits calls for pulsing vegetable shortening (for tenderness) and butter (for flavor) together in a food processor with flour, salt, sugar, and leaveners until the fat is evenly dispersed. The mixture is transferred to a bowl and buttermilk is stirred in, then the dough is briefly kneaded, patted into a circle, cut into rounds, and baked.

NOTES FROM THE TEST KITCHEN

THE SECRET TO LIGHTER BISCUITS
While regular buttermilk biscuits rely on a combination of shortening and butter, we found we could trim fat and calories by cutting out the shortening altogether and using neufchatel, a type of cream cheese with one-third less fat (and slightly more moisture) than the regular variety, in place of some of the butter, saving 60 calories and 7.5 grams of fat per biscuit, without sacrificing flavor or texture. Freezing the neufchatel makes it behave like chilled butter in regular biscuits, creating pockets of steam that give the biscuits their fluffy, flaky charm. You can find it at the supermarket next to the regular cream cheese; sometimes it's just labeled "⅓ less fat" cream cheese.

We wondered how this full-fat recipe would compare with a handful of low-fat buttermilk biscuit recipes from "healthy" cookbooks and the Web, and we were pleasantly surprised that a few of these recipes produced biscuits with decent buttermilk flavor. Their texture was another story, though: Some were crumbly and dry, one was oddly springy, and others were crusty like hard dinner rolls. Biscuits made with substitutes like fat-free mayonnaise or low-fat margarine had a slightly chemical taste and were gummy and unnaturally pale. We decided our best bet was to work backward, slimming the full-fat biscuit recipe where we could.

Almost 75 percent of our original recipe's calories came from only 4 tablespoons of shortening and 8 tablespoons of butter. To make these biscuits less weighty, we would need to eliminate a substantial portion of the fat. There was a danger in doing so, as we had learned with nearly all our earlier baked good makeovers, because fat adds flavor and improves texture. Removing the shortening from the recipe seemed like a logical starting point, because while it improves the tenderness of baked goods, it contributes little flavor. Tasters didn't mind the texture of a batch made without shortening, but this move trimmed the calories by only a fraction. Some of the butter would have to come out, too.

We already knew that the way fat is incorporated can influence texture just as much as the amount (consider our Blueberry Muffins, page 243). Perhaps we could get away with using less butter if we found a clever way to combine it with the other ingredients. We tried folding, massaging, and layering butter into the dough in order to achieve flaky layers, but no matter what we did, fewer than 8 tablespoons of butter made for tough, unpleasantly lean biscuits. We returned to the laundry list of fat substitutes we had already tested and one by one replaced some of the butter with each. Ultimately, a combination of 4 tablespoons of butter and 3 tablespoons of neufchatel (cream cheese with one-third less fat) provided enough buttery flavor and tenderness to distinguish these biscuits from dinner rolls while reducing the fat of each biscuit by almost two-thirds.

The biscuits now tasted similar to a full-fat version, but the texture had gone from appealingly fluffy to somewhat gluey and tacky. The problem? Chilled butter breaks into pieces resembling coarse meal after a few pulses with flour in the food processor; in the oven, these bits of fat melt and create pockets of steam that contribute to a biscuit's fluffy, flaky charm. Chilled cream cheese, we found, smears and clumps, making our biscuits heavy. Would freezing the cream cheese make it hold together like butter? We gave it a try, at the same time putting the butter in the freezer for good measure. One hour later, the cream cheese was hard enough to pulse into small pieces along with the butter. These biscuits had a texture that mimicked that of an all-butter biscuit.

With just a few changes here and there, we were able to cut fat and calories from our full-fat biscuits, but, to the joy of all our tasters, the fluffy, buttery appeal of the original had definitely stayed intact.

MAKEOVER SPOTLIGHT: BUTTERMILK BISCUITS

	CALORIES	FAT	SAT FAT	CHOLESTEROL
BEFORE	220	12g	7g	20mg
AFTER	160	4.5g	3.5g	15mg

Buttermilk Biscuits

MAKES 12 BISCUITS

Do not underbake these biscuits, as they will taste slightly gummy. Check for doneness by picking up a biscuit and looking at the bottom of it after 17 minutes of baking. If the underside is still pale, bake up to 3 minutes longer until golden brown on the top and bottom.

- 3 **cups (15 ounces) unbleached all-purpose flour**
- 1 **tablespoon sugar**
- 1 **tablespoon baking powder**
- ¾ **teaspoon salt**
- ½ **teaspoon baking soda**
- 4 **tablespoons (½ stick) unsalted butter, cut into ½-inch pieces and frozen for 1 hour**
- 3 **tablespoons neufchatel (⅓ less fat) cream cheese, cut into ½-inch pieces and frozen for 1 hour**
- 1¼ **cups low-fat buttermilk**

1. Adjust an oven rack to the middle position and heat the oven to 450 degrees. Line a baking sheet with parchment paper and set aside.

2. Pulse the flour, sugar, baking powder, salt, and baking soda together in a food processor to combine. Scatter the butter and neufchatel over the top and continue to pulse until the mixture resembles coarse meal, about 15 pulses. Transfer the mixture to a large bowl. Stir in the buttermilk with a rubber spatula until the dough comes together.

3. Turn out the dough onto a lightly floured counter. Knead the dough gently until smooth, 8 to 10 times. Pat the dough into a 9-inch circle, about ¾ inch thick.

4. Using a floured 2½-inch biscuit cutter, stamp out 6 biscuits and arrange upside down on the prepared baking sheet, spaced 1½ inches apart. Gather the remaining dough, pat into a ¾-inch-thick circle, and stamp out the remaining 6 biscuits.

5. Bake until the biscuits begin to rise, about 5 minutes, then rotate the baking sheet and reduce the oven temperature to 400 degrees. Continue to bake until golden brown, 12 to 15 minutes longer. Transfer the biscuits to a wire rack and let cool for 10 minutes before serving. (The biscuits can be stored in an airtight container at room temperature for up to 3 days.)

PER BISCUIT: **Cal** 160; **Fat** 4.5g; **Sat fat** 3.5g; **Chol** 15mg; **Carb** 23g; **Protein** 3g; **Fiber** 1g; **Sodium** 350mg

BUTTERMILK BISCUITS

VEGETABLE FRITTATA

WHEN YOU WANT TO TAKE BREAKFAST BEYOND scrambled eggs or basic omelets, frittatas are the perfect solution. They incorporate more filling than an omelet, making them more substantial, and they're only slightly more involved than scrambling eggs, resulting in an impressive yet easy dish. As easy as they are, though, they are not without challenges. Often they end up rubbery and dry, not to mention that most frittata recipes call for a number of eggs that's double (or close to double) the number of servings. If we used 12 whole eggs in a recipe to serve 6, the fat count per person would be roughly 10 grams and the cholesterol would be 420 milligrams, and that wouldn't even include any oil for the pan or other ingredients like cheese. We wanted to build a light frittata, one that tasted moist and hearty, with fillings that had a lot of appeal but didn't spike the fat and calorie count any further.

We started with the obvious: the eggs. We needed to find a way to cut back, but we knew that with less fat we'd be faced with less moisture and richness—we'd have to really work to keep our frittata firm yet moist. To see how low we could go with the number of whole eggs, swapping them out in favor of egg whites, we decided to run a few tests. We made three separate frittatas using the standard method of sautéing aromatics and vegetables, adding the eggs to the pan to cook for a few minutes, then finishing the frittata in the oven. We offered our tasters these frittatas but didn't tell them that one was made with 6 eggs and 6 whites, one with 4 eggs and 8 whites, and the third with 2 eggs and 10 whites. There was no shock when it came to opinions on the last frittata—tasters found it to be tough and rubbery. As for the other two frittatas, the one with an equal number of whole eggs and egg whites was rated just slightly better in terms of flavor and texture than the frittata with 4 eggs and 8 whites.

We had the optimum number of eggs determined, but our frittata was lacking when it came to appearance; it looked flat and thin—not exactly the picture of a hearty, filling breakfast. To amp up the volume of our frittata, we decided to whip the whites separately before combining them with the whole eggs and adding them to our pan. Coming out of a 350-degree oven, this frittata looked perfect—it had more volume and was puffed up, but it was a bit dry. We decided to make another frittata, but instead of finishing it in a heated oven, we finished it under the broiler, a common method for cooking frittatas. The resulting frittata was evenly cooked and nicely puffed without being too dry, exactly what we had been looking for. One more trial with lightly beaten—not whipped—eggs and egg whites told us the broiler was doing the same thing the whipping had been doing: puffing the frittata. While whipping our eggs wasn't exactly a tedious step, it was, nevertheless, an extra step we could now cut.

At this point, we focused on the frittata's flavor and fillings. Sliced red bell pepper and a few handfuls of baby spinach would be our additions for a colorful and light frittata. We began our tests using a small amount of olive oil to sauté the onion, garlic, and pepper. Adding a few tablespoons of whole milk with our eggs added some appealing richness, but tasters thought the resulting frittata could use even more richness and flavor. We agreed some grated Parmesan would do the trick, and we balanced this addition of fat by switching to low-fat milk. We also added some chopped basil for a nice herbal note. Now we had a moist and flavorful frittata that didn't taste low-fat at all.

Frittata with Spinach, Bell Pepper, and Basil
SERVES 6

Do not substitute skim milk here. You will need a 10-inch ovensafe nonstick skillet for this recipe.

- 6 large eggs
- 6 large egg whites
- 1 ounce Parmesan cheese, grated (about ½ cup)
- 3 tablespoons 1 percent low-fat milk (see note)
- 2 tablespoons chopped fresh basil
  Salt
- ¼ teaspoon pepper
- 1 small onion, minced (about ½ cup)
- 1 red bell pepper, stemmed, seeded, and sliced thin
- 1 teaspoon olive oil
- 1 garlic clove, minced
- 3 ounces baby spinach (about 3 cups)

1. Position an oven rack 6 inches from the broiler element and heat the broiler. Whisk the eggs, egg whites, cheese, milk, basil, ¼ teaspoon salt, and pepper together in a medium bowl.

2. Combine the onion, bell pepper, oil, and ¼ teaspoon salt in a 10-inch ovensafe nonstick skillet. Cover and cook over medium-low heat, stirring occasionally, until the vegetables are softened, 8 to 10 minutes. Stir in the garlic and cook until fragrant, about 30 seconds. Stir in the spinach, one handful at a time, and cook until wilted, about 1 minute.

3. Increase the heat to medium, add the egg mixture to the skillet, and cook, gently pushing, lifting, and folding it from one side of the pan to the other, until large, very wet curds form, 1 to 2 minutes. Shake the skillet to distribute the eggs evenly and continue to cook, without stirring, until the bottom is lightly browned, 1 to 2 minutes longer. Transfer the skillet to the oven and broil until the frittata has risen and the surface is puffed and spotty brown, 3 to 4 minutes.

4. Being careful of the hot skillet handle, remove the skillet from the oven and let sit until the eggs in the very center are cooked and moist but not runny, 1 to 3 minutes. Run a spatula around the edge of the skillet to loosen the frittata, then gently slide it out onto a platter. Serve warm or at room temperature.

PER SERVING: **Cal** 130; **Fat** 7g; **Sat fat** 2.5g; **Chol** 215mg; **Carb** 5g; **Protein** 13g; **Fiber** 1g; **Sodium** 430mg

Frittata with Asparagus, Mushrooms, and Goat Cheese

SERVES 6

Do not substitute skim milk here. You will need a 10-inch ovensafe nonstick skillet for this recipe.

- **6 large eggs**
- **6 large egg whites**
- **2 ounces goat cheese, crumbled (about ½ cup)**
- **3 tablespoons 1 percent low-fat milk (see note)**
- **2 tablespoons chopped fresh parsley**
- **2 teaspoons grated lemon zest**
- **Salt**
- **¼ teaspoon pepper**
- **4 ounces white mushrooms, trimmed and sliced thin**
- **1 small onion, minced (about ½ cup)**
- **1 teaspoon olive oil**
- **4 spears asparagus, tough ends trimmed, cut into ¼-inch lengths**
- **1 garlic clove, minced**

1. Position an oven rack 6 inches from the broiler element and heat the broiler. Whisk the eggs, egg whites, cheese, milk, parsley, lemon zest, ¼ teaspoon salt, and pepper together in a medium bowl.

2. Combine the mushrooms, onion, oil, and ¼ teaspoon salt in a 10-inch ovensafe nonstick skillet. Cover and cook over medium-low heat, stirring occasionally, until the vegetables are softened, 8 to 10 minutes. Add the asparagus, increase the heat to medium, and continue to cook, stirring occasionally, until the vegetables are crisp-tender, about 2 minutes longer. Stir in the garlic and cook until fragrant, about 30 seconds.

3. Add the egg mixture and cook, gently pushing, lifting, and folding it from one side of the pan to the other, until large, very wet curds form, 1 to 2 minutes. Shake the skillet to distribute the eggs evenly and continue to cook, without stirring, until the bottom is lightly browned, 1 to 2 minutes longer. Transfer the skillet to the oven and broil until the frittata has risen and the surface is puffed and spotty brown, 3 to 4 minutes.

4. Being careful of the hot skillet handle, remove the skillet from the oven and let sit until the eggs in the very center are cooked and moist but not runny, 1 to 3 minutes. Run a spatula around the edge of the skillet to loosen the frittata, then gently slide it out onto a platter. Serve warm or at room temperature.

PER SERVING: **Cal** 140; **Fat** 8g; **Sat fat** 3g; **Chol** 215mg; **Carb** 4g; **Protein** 13g; **Fiber** 1g; **Sodium** 360mg

BREAKFAST STRATA

STRATA IS A LAYERED CASSEROLE MADE UP OF SIMPLE ingredients—bread, eggs, cheese, and cream—that come together in the oven to form a golden brown, puffed, hearty, savory bread pudding. While strata is easy enough to prepare and even easier to assemble the night before (a big bonus), it's not the simplest dish to lighten up. Between the cream, cheese, a generous number of eggs, and butter for sautéing aromatics, strata isn't exactly diet food. It is one of the most indulgent breakfast treats there is, but we didn't want to feel racked with guilt every time we wanted to enjoy it. Our goal was to find the middle ground and develop a recipe for a rich and moist strata that was lighter and healthier than the original version.

TEST KITCHEN
MAKEOVER

Looking at the test kitchen's previously developed full-fat strata, we decided to start by examining more closely the foundation of the strata—the bread. In the past, we've toasted slices of supermarket French or Italian bread (artisan loaves were too crusty and dry)—the perfect neutral sponge to absorb the egg-and-cream custard—and then spread a few tablespoons of butter over the toasted bread to add some richness before placing the slices in the baking dish and covering it with the custard. Thinking this was an easy place to cut some fat, we opted to leave the butter out. We also tried toasting cubed bread rather than whole slices, and our tasters preferred the extra crunchiness and texture of the cubed bread.

It was time to look at the tender custard that binds the pieces of bread together; our full-fat strata relies on six whole eggs, so we set out to determine if we could use fewer than that. We tried various tests using a mix of whole eggs and egg whites, but these custards just didn't have enough fat to hold together. We decided we would have to stick with the original recipe's six whole eggs. However, there was another place to cut fat in the custard, as strata recipes commonly call for half-and-half or heavy cream (our version used half-and-half). We thought a good way to scale back on fat would be to use skim or low-fat milk instead. Unfortunately these versions were sorely lacking in richness. We turned next to whole milk, which did the trick and turned out a creamy strata.

Our light strata was good at this point, but its flavors really needed to be amped up. Sautéed onions and garlic provided a big hit of flavor. We had a surprise in store when we tested another flavoring common to strata recipes: white wine. To cut out some of the booziness imparted by the wine, we reduced the wine to cook off the alcohol and concentrate the flavor, and we found the reduced wine brightened the flavor of the whole dish considerably.

For a healthy boost, we decided to add some spinach, sautéing it in the pan with the onion and garlic to remove excess moisture that would otherwise end up waterlogging our strata. As for the cheese, we turned to feta since it is lower in fat than most cheeses used in strata, and its tangy bite is a great match for spinach. With all the flavor in our strata, no one missed fattier add-ins like sausage.

One of strata's charms is that it can be assembled well ahead of time. We tested stratas that had been assembled and rested overnight, for four hours, and for one hour, as well as another that had not been rested at all. Only the just-made strata, which was noticeably less cohesive than the rested versions, failed to make the cut. Otherwise, there wasn't much difference among them in texture, so you can give it the rest that fits your schedule best, anywhere from one hour to overnight.

In our full-fat recipe, we weighted the assembled strata during its rest, a step that helped produce perfectly even, custardy texture throughout. We ran tests with and without this step and (not surprisingly) decided to keep it in place, as it helped our layers stay unified. After almost an hour in the oven, this healthier strata was rich, custardy, and full-flavored.

MAKEOVER SPOTLIGHT: BREAKFAST STRATA

	CALORIES	FAT	SAT FAT	CHOLESTEROL
BEFORE	440	29g	16g	270mg
AFTER	340	18g	10g	255mg

Breakfast Strata

SERVES 6

Do not substitute low-fat or skim milk in this recipe.

     Vegetable oil spray
½   loaf supermarket French or Italian bread
     (about 6 ounces), cut into ½-inch cubes
     (about 4 cups)
2   tablespoons unsalted butter
1   onion, minced (about 1 cup)
1   garlic clove, minced
10   ounces frozen spinach, thawed, squeezed dry,
     and chopped coarse
½   cup dry white wine
6   large eggs
1¾ cups whole milk (see note)
1   teaspoon salt
¼   teaspoon pepper
6   ounces feta cheese, crumbled (about 1½ cups)

1. Adjust an oven rack to the middle position and heat the oven to 275 degrees. Lightly coat an 8-inch square baking dish with vegetable oil spray.

2. Spread the bread cubes on a rimmed baking sheet and bake until thoroughly dry and crisp, 30 to 40 minutes.

3. Melt the butter in a 10-inch nonstick skillet over medium heat. Add the onion and cook, stirring occasionally, until softened, 5 to 7 minutes. Stir in the garlic and cook until fragrant, about 30 seconds. Stir in the spinach and cook until the spinach is heated through, about 2 minutes. Transfer the spinach mixture to a medium bowl. Add the wine to the skillet and simmer over medium-high heat until reduced to ¼ cup, about 3 minutes; set aside to cool separately.

4. Whisk the reduced wine, eggs, milk, salt, and pepper together in a large bowl. Stir in the spinach mixture, 1 cup of the cheese, and the dried bread cubes until well combined. Pour the mixture into the prepared baking dish and cover with plastic wrap. Following the photo, weight the strata down with a large zipper-lock bag filled with sugar. Refrigerate the weighted strata for at least 1 hour or up to 24 hours.

5. When ready to bake, adjust an oven rack to the middle position and heat the oven to 325 degrees. Meanwhile, remove the weight from the strata and let sit at room temperature for 20 minutes.

6. Sprinkle the remaining ½ cup cheese over the strata and bake until the surface is puffed and the edges pull away slightly from the dish, 50 to 55 minutes, rotating the baking dish halfway through. Let the strata cool for 10 minutes before serving.

PER SERVING: **Cal** 340; **Fat** 18g; **Sat fat** 10g; **Chol** 255mg; **Carb** 23g; **Protein** 16g; **Fiber** 2g; **Sodium** 1050mg

VARIATION

Breakfast Strata with Spinach, Sun-Dried Tomatoes, and Goat Cheese

Follow the recipe for Breakfast Strata, adding ½ cup sun-dried tomatoes, minced, to the cooked spinach in step 3 and cooking until fragrant, about 30 seconds, and substituting goat cheese for the feta cheese.

PER SERVING: **Cal** 360; **Fat** 19g; **Sat fat** 10g; **Chol** 240mg; **Carb** 25g; **Protein** 18g; **Fiber** 2g; **Sodium** 870mg

---

NOTES FROM THE TEST KITCHEN

WEIGHTING THE STRATA

Pressing the strata and letting it sit for at least an hour gives the bread time to absorb the custard.

Place a large zipper-lock bag full of sugar or dried beans on top of the prepared strata. The weighted strata can be refrigerated for up to 24 hours before baking.

MULTIGRAIN PANCAKES

A TALL STACK OF FLUFFY, COMPLEXLY FLAVORED multigrain pancakes is a breakfast we can enjoy eating and feel good about, too. In reality, of course, that's a pretty tall order. Heavy grains like whole wheat, oats, barley, and buckwheat, while healthy, often make for dense, leaden pancakes, so coming up with a recipe for airy, healthy pancakes is a challenge. Sure, there are a lot of multigrain pancake recipes out there, but for the most part the results are dense, heavy, and utterly unappealing. The few recipes that do make both fluffy and flavorful pancakes do it by skimping on the grains, an easy—but to us unsatisfactory—solution. We decided to start with a basic buttermilk pancake recipe and see how we could incorporate our grains to give us the healthy morning meal we were after.

After some trial and error, we found a mix of whole wheat flour and all-purpose flour punctuated with a variety of grains—oats, rye flakes, wheat germ, and more—produced pretty good pancakes that weren't horribly dense. The mixing method couldn't have been easier: Blend the wet and dry ingredients independently, then whisk the two together just before cooking. We seemed to be on the right track, but while these pancakes were truly multigrain, the ingredient list was becoming far too long. There had to be a simpler way.

We found several grain mixes at the grocery store and thought they might be the answer. But the hard grains in these mixes (like coarse cornmeal and chewy barley) made pancakes that were too gritty. We tried soaking them in the recipe's liquid components for a lengthy period of time, but even then they didn't sufficiently hydrate. Then someone suggested trying a multigrain cold cereal. Hard, crunchy cereals, like Grape-Nuts and granola, made pancakes that were far too textured for our tasters. But muesli, made from raw whole oats (rather than the toasted oats of granola), wheat germ, rye flakes, and barley, along with some toasted nuts and dried fruit, had a variety of grains and flavorful add-ins in one convenient package. The first batch of pancakes we made with muesli had great flavor, but used right out of the package, it made pancakes that were too chewy and gummy. Soaking the muesli in the liquid components of the batter remedied the chewiness, but to counteract the gumminess, we had to grind some in the food processor to make a homemade "flour," which we used to replace some of the all-purpose

MULTIGRAIN PANCAKES

flour. These pancakes had good texture and were much lighter, but they needed a little more help in the form of leavening.

Pancakes can be leavened naturally, with whipped egg whites, or chemically, typically with a combination of baking powder and baking soda. Whipping egg whites was a bit more effort than we wanted to exert early in the morning, so we opted to use the chemical leaveners. After experimenting with the proportions, we found that a full 2¼ teaspoons of baking powder and ½ teaspoon of baking soda did the trick.

The texture and lightness were now spot-on and the flavor more than decent, but we couldn't help but think we could improve the flavor even more with some tweaking. A splash of vanilla added depth, and a couple of tablespoons of brown sugar went far in emphasizing the earthiness of the grains and added a welcome touch of sweetness. At this point, a few tasters thought the buttermilk, held over from our original buttermilk pancake recipe, was a bit too sour, impinging on the flavor of the grains. We nixed the buttermilk in favor of a less acidic-tasting blend of milk and lemon juice. This mixture made for a surprisingly cleaner, richer-tasting pancake with the bonus of an even lighter texture.

These multigrain pancakes were airy and had an appealing complex flavor with good texture—an ideal healthy start to the day, any day of the week.

NOTES FROM THE TEST KITCHEN

MULTIGRAIN MAKEOVER
Some multigrain pancake recipes load up on unprocessed grains—great for flavor but bad for texture. To avoid gummy, chewy pancakes (but still keep them truly multigrain), we made our own multigrain "flour" by processing store-bought muesli cereal in a food processor. To give our pancakes a subtle hint of that hearty whole grain texture, we added a few tablespoons of unprocessed muesli to the batter.

TOO MUCH CHEW
Pancakes made with muesli right out of the box have great flavor but are a bit too chewy.

PERFECT COMBO
Processing some muesli into "flour" and leaving some whole provides great texture.

Multigrain Pancakes
MAKES 15 (4-INCH) PANCAKES

We found that Familia brand no-sugar-added muesli is the best choice for this recipe. (If you can't find Familia, look for Alpen or any other no-sugar-added muesli.) Do not substitute low-fat or skim milk in this recipe or the pancakes will be too dry. Letting the pancake batter sit for 5 minutes before cooking is crucial; if the batter doesn't rest, the pancakes will cook up flat and run together in the pan. Serve with maple syrup or fresh fruit if desired. You can keep the pancakes warm in a 200-degree oven on a wire rack set over a baking sheet if you prefer to serve them all at once.

2 **cups whole milk (see note)**
4 **teaspoons fresh lemon juice**
1½ **cups (7 ounces) no-sugar-added muesli (see note)**
¾ **cup (3¾ ounces) all-purpose flour**
½ **cup (2¾ ounces) whole wheat flour**
2 **tablespoons brown sugar**
2¼ **teaspoons baking powder**
½ **teaspoon baking soda**
½ **teaspoon salt**
2 **large eggs**
5 **teaspoons canola oil**
¾ **teaspoon vanilla extract**

1. Whisk the milk and lemon juice together in a medium bowl and set aside until thickened, 5 to 10 minutes. Meanwhile, process 1¼ cups of the muesli in a food processor until finely ground, 2 to 2½ minutes. Transfer the processed muesli to a large bowl and whisk in the remaining ¼ cup muesli, all-purpose flour, whole wheat flour, brown sugar, baking powder, baking soda, and salt.

2. Whisk the eggs, 1 tablespoon of the canola oil, and the vanilla into the thickened milk mixture until combined. Make a well in the center of the muesli mixture, pour the thickened milk mixture into the well, and whisk very gently until just incorporated (a few lumps should remain). Let the batter rest for 5 minutes. (The pancake batter can be made up to this point and refrigerated in an airtight container for up to 24 hours. Whisk the batter to recombine and adjust its consistency as needed with water before cooking.)

3. While the batter rests, heat a 12-inch nonstick skillet over medium heat for 3 to 5 minutes. Brush the pan bottom with a thin layer of the remaining 2 teaspoons oil. Using ¼ cup of the batter per pancake, add the batter to the skillet (2 or 3 pancakes will fit at a time) and cook until large bubbles begin to appear, about 2 minutes.

4. Flip the pancakes and continue to cook until golden brown, about 1½ minutes longer. Transfer the pancakes to a plate and serve. Repeat with the remaining batter, brushing the skillet with oil as needed between batches.

PER SERVING (3 PANCAKES): Cal 390; Fat 12g; Sat fat 3g; Chol 95mg; Carb 58g; Protein 13g; Fiber 4g; Sodium 670mg

VARIATIONS

Multigrain Blueberry Pancakes

For a full batch of pancakes, you will need about 1 cup blueberries. Frozen blueberries, thawed and patted dry, can be substituted here.

Follow the recipe for Multigrain Pancakes, sprinkling 1 tablespoon blueberries over each pancake after adding the batter to the skillet.

PER SERVING (3 PANCAKES): Cal 410; Fat 12g; Sat fat 3g; Chol 95mg; Carb 63g; Protein 13g; Fiber 5g; Sodium 670mg

Multigrain Banana Pancakes

For a full batch of pancakes, you will need 2 bananas.

Follow the recipe for Multigrain Pancakes, gently pressing 4 or 5 thin slices of ripe banana into each pancake after adding the batter to the skillet.

PER SERVING (3 PANCAKES): Cal 440; Fat 12g; Sat fat 3g; Chol 95mg; Carb 70g; Protein 13g; Fiber 6g; Sodium 670mg

GRANOLA

NUTS, GRAINS, AND DRIED FRUIT SOUND VIRTUOUS enough, but when they're combined to make granola, they turn into something that is often anything but innocent. Most granolas contain so much sugar and butter or oil that they seem better fitted to the cookie aisle than the cereal or health food section at the grocery store. We wanted to redeem this popular cereal, snack, and yogurt topping to bring it back to its healthy origins. But could we do this without sacrificing flavor and texture? We set out to create a recipe with big crunchy clusters of granola, with just the right amount of sweetness and a ratio of grains to nuts that didn't tip the scale.

We quickly learned the key to making great granola is choosing the right ingredients and combining them in the right proportions. Grain flakes are the foundation of granola. We found recipes that used oats, wheat, and rye, but oats were our out-and-out favorite—wheat left a bitter aftertaste and rye had too distinct a flavor. In the world of oats, we tested old-fashioned rolled oats (the typical choice), as well as instant oats and quick-cooking oats. Not surprisingly, old-fashioned oats were favored because they added good texture. The other two baked up sandy.

Next we focused on add-ins. Coarsely chopped nuts worked best, and tasters favored almonds and cashews. Since we wanted our granola to be super-healthy and not super-fatty, we kept the amount of nuts low—⅓ cup of each to 3 cups of oats—and supplemented them with nutritious sesame and sunflower seeds. With these small seeds, we found a little goes a long way. Adding heart-healthy ground flaxseeds gave the granola an extra healthy punch. (Tasters didn't even notice that we'd sneaked them in!) Our last addition was dried fruit, and we settled on raisins for their general appeal.

To both bind and sweeten the granola, we tested honey, maple syrup, and molasses, all of which were common in the recipes we found. We all preferred the idea of a granola with big clusters (rather than a loose, crumbly one), so the binder would play a big role. We made three test batches, each using ¾ cup of one of the options. Maple syrup made a crumbly granola, and its flavor wasn't discernible over the nuts and seeds. Molasses was a great binder, but it imparted an unwelcome bitterness. Honey, however, worked perfectly. In the slow, even heat of the oven, its moisture evaporated and the granola mixture was bound firmly together. Testing amounts, we found that ½ cup of honey was all it took to bind and lightly sweeten our granola.

With the main ingredients and proportions in place, we focused on fine-tuning the cooking method. Up to this point we had been mixing all our ingredients together raw, spreading them out on a baking sheet, and baking for 45 minutes in a 325-degree oven. In many recipes the nuts and oats are pre-toasted in the oven, so we gave it a try. We had to toast in batches, since each ingredient required a different amount of time; though the granola definitely had a deeper, nuttier flavor and crunchier texture after 30 minutes of toasting, we wanted to find a quicker method. By toasting our ingredients in a skillet, and adding them in stages, we were able to speed up the process and achieve the intense, toasted flavor we were after much more quickly.

The addition of a few tablespoons of heart-healthy canola oil helped the dry, lean oats turn a perfect nutty brown. (Compared to other granola recipes, which use as much as a stick of butter, ours was still low in fat.) To keep the raisins from burning, we found it necessary to add them when the granola came out of the oven.

Once the mixture was toasted, we tossed it with our honey, flaxseeds, and a touch of salt and slid it into the oven. Now our granola needed only 15 minutes of oven time to turn a rich golden brown and release a heady aroma of warm oats and toasted nuts. And finally, to ensure big clusters, after the granola came out of the oven we pushed it to one side of the baking sheet to make it compact. Once the granola cooled, it was easy to break the mixture into large chunks, perfect for topping our yogurt or just eating as is.

Toasted Granola
MAKES ABOUT 6 CUPS

Do not substitute quick-cooking or instant rolled oats in this recipe, or the granola will taste sandy rather than crunchy.

- ⅓ cup slivered almonds
- ⅓ cup cashews, chopped coarse
- 3 cups old-fashioned rolled oats (see note)
- 3 tablespoons canola oil
- ¼ cup sunflower seeds
- 2 tablespoons sesame seeds
- ½ cup honey
- 2 tablespoons ground flaxseeds
- ¼ teaspoon salt
- ½ cup raisins

1. Adjust an oven rack to the middle position and heat the oven to 325 degrees. Toast the almonds and cashews in a 12-inch skillet over medium heat, stirring often, until fragrant and beginning to darken, about 3 minutes. Stir in the oats and oil and toast until the oats begin to turn golden, about 2 minutes. Stir in the sunflower seeds and sesame seeds, and continue to toast until the mixture turns golden, about 2 minutes longer.

2. Off the heat, stir in the honey, flaxseeds, and salt until well coated. Spread the granola evenly on a large rimmed baking sheet. Bake, stirring every few minutes, until the granola is light golden brown, about 15 minutes.

3. Remove the baking sheet from the oven and stir in the raisins. With a spatula, push the granola onto one half of the baking sheet and press gently into a ½-inch-thick slab. Let the granola cool to room temperature, about 30 minutes. Loosen the dried granola with a spatula, break into small clusters, and serve. (The granola can be stored at room temperature in an airtight container for up to 1 week.)

PER ½-CUP SERVING: Cal 240; Fat 11g; Sat fat 1g; Chol 0mg; Carb 33g; Protein 5g; Fiber 3g; Sodium 55mg

VARIATIONS
Tropical Fruit Granola

Follow the recipe for Toasted Granola, substituting 1 cup chopped dried tropical fruit (such as pineapple, papaya, and/or mango) and ¼ cup unsweetened shredded coconut for the raisins.

PER ½-CUP SERVING: Cal 280; Fat 12g; Sat fat 2.5g; Chol 0mg; Carb 39g; Protein 5g; Fiber 4g; Sodium 70mg

Cranberry-Ginger Granola

Follow the recipe for Toasted Granola, substituting ¾ cup dried cranberries and ¼ cup finely chopped crystallized ginger for the raisins.

PER ½-CUP SERVING: Cal 250; Fat 11g; Sat fat 1g; Chol 0mg; Carb 36g; Protein 5g; Fiber 4g; Sodium 55mg

NOTES FROM THE TEST KITCHEN

OUR FAVORITE ROLLED OATS
Old-fashioned rolled oats are the go-to type for baking, including our granola recipe. We recently held a tasting of five brands to find the best oat for the job. Our tasters gave top marks to **Bob's Red Mill Organic Extra Thick Rolled Oats** (left) that had "nice and plump" flakes with a "decent chew." And while the winner took time to cook—about 10 minutes for chewy oatmeal, 20 minutes for softer cereal—our second-ranked brand, **Quaker Old-Fashioned Oats** (right), took just five minutes. Quaker also aced our baking tests, so if you want to buy only one brand for both breakfast and baking, it's your best choice.

CARROT CAKE

M = TEST KITCHEN MAKEOVER

CHOCOLATE CHIP COOKIES

TEST KITCHEN **MAKEOVER**

IT'S NO WONDER THAT BIG AND CHEWY CHOCOLATE chip cookies from the corner bakery taste so good. With huge amounts of chocolate chips, butter, and sugar, they easily tally more than 300 calories and 15 grams of fat per cookie. But when you take a bite of a typical "healthy" version of this all-time favorite, dry and anything but chocolaty, it's pretty easy to understand why the bakeries don't have a lot of competition. We made five different recipes we found for low-fat cookies, and the best of the lot were merely tasteless; the worst ones had unpleasant flavors, were tiny, or both. Could we make a low-fat chocolate chip cookie that didn't look or taste like a diet cookie?

Our first inclination was to simply reduce the quantities of all the high-fat ingredients in the test kitchen's regular thick and chewy chocolate chip cookie recipe. After many tests in which we reduced butter, sugar, and eggs by varying amounts, we succeeded in creating what we felt was a great-tasting low-fat chocolate chip cookie. But this feeling was short-lived: Since most of the butter, which acts as a tenderizer, had been taken out, within an hour of coming out of the oven our chewy cookies turned into rocks.

So we began searching for a low-fat ingredient that could replicate butter's tenderizing power without changing the flavor profile of the cookie. Applesauce, a common ingredient in "healthy" baked goods, seemed like a good place to start. Unfortunately, tasters complained not only of a strange aftertaste but also that the cookies looked more like corrugated cardboard than dessert. Molasses kept the cookies moist and tender, but they were a strange brown color and tasted too strongly of molasses. The only thing that raised our spirits was watching tasters cringe when they bit into the banana-puree cookies, which one taster described as "insulting to cookies everywhere."

With our frustration mounting, we tried one last "healthy" ingredient to make sure we had exhausted our options before moving on—homemade date puree, made from cooking and mashing dried dates. We replaced three-quarters of the butter in our favorite full-fat recipe with date puree and held our breath as tasters gave these cookies a try. We were pleasantly surprised when tasters said they had a rich, sweet flavor with only a slight, almost unidentifiable hint of "fruitiness." Thanks to our new "butter substitute," we had flavorful and tender cookies that stayed moist for days, not hours. Now we just needed to fine-tune the flavor.

While the slight hint of fruitiness from the dates wasn't unpleasant, we didn't want even a trace of an "unusual" taste in these cookies. Unfortunately, as soon as we reduced the amount of fruit puree, the cookies turned back into rocks. Pressing the cooked dates through a strainer helped eliminate any date chunks, but the fruit flavor was still present. Rather than taming the fruit flavor, one taster suggested trying to pump up the butter flavor (we had held on to 3 tablespoons of the original 12) by melting and browning it. Sure enough, the nutty, concentrated flavor of the browned butter boosted the buttery flavor of the cookies, adding just enough richness to mask any remaining hint of date. And since this batter was so flavorful, we could now cut the full cup of chocolate chips (many recipes call for even more) back to just half a cup, and the cookies still tasted chocolaty.

These cookies tasted every bit as good as regular chocolate chip cookies, but they did have one attribute we weren't crazy about: shiny, smooth tops instead of the craggy tops we expected. We found we could get the craggy tops we wanted by separating each ball of cookie dough in half, then pressing the two pieces together with the jagged torn edge facing up.

Although we were originally pessimistic about using a "healthy" fat substitute in our low-fat chocolate chip cookies, we were happy to be wrong. The combination of date puree and browned butter makes a tender cookie that can stand up to any bakery cookie in flavor, size, and staying power.

MAKEOVER SPOTLIGHT: CHOCOLATE CHIP COOKIES

	CALORIES	FAT	SAT FAT	CHOLESTEROL
BEFORE	310	15g	10g	45mg
AFTER	170	4g	2.5g	15mg

Big and Chewy Chocolate Chip Cookies

MAKES 18 COOKIES

Dried dates can be found in the nut and dried fruit section of the supermarket. Be sure to buy dates that are still supple.

    1   cup water
    ¼   cup finely chopped dates (see note)
    3   tablespoons unsalted butter
    2   cups (10 ounces) unbleached all-purpose flour
    ½   teaspoon baking soda
    ½   teaspoon salt
    1¼ cups packed (8¾ ounces) light brown sugar
    1   large egg
    2   teaspoons vanilla extract
    ½   cup semisweet chocolate chips

1. Adjust an oven rack to the middle position and heat the oven to 325 degrees. Line 2 baking sheets with parchment paper and set aside.

2. Bring the water to a boil in a small saucepan over medium-high heat. Add the dates and simmer until tender and most of the water has evaporated, about 20 minutes. Using a rubber spatula, press the dates through a fine-mesh strainer into a medium bowl. Scrape the dates remaining in the strainer into the bowl (you should have ¼ cup puree).

3. Melt the butter in a small saucepan over medium heat and cook until nutty brown, about 4 minutes. Set aside off the heat and cool to room temperature.

4. Whisk the flour, baking soda, and salt together in a medium bowl. In a large bowl, beat the date puree, browned butter, and brown sugar together with an

---

NOTES FROM THE TEST KITCHEN

SHAPING CHOCOLATE CHIP COOKIES

Our revamped cookies tasted great, but they didn't have the craggy tops we expected. Here's how we got the look we were after.

1. Roll 2 tablespoons of dough into a ball. Hold the dough ball with the fingertips of both hands and pull it into two equal halves, creating jagged edges.

2. Rotate the cookie halves so that the jagged surfaces are facing up. Press the two halves together at their base so that they form a single ball.

3. Space the balls of dough, jagged-side up, 2 inches apart on the prepared baking sheets.

THE KEYS TO LIGHTER COOKIES

We cut fat and calories from the typical chocolate chip cookie—without sacrificing flavor or chew—thanks to the addition of a few ingredients:

DATES
Cooked, pureed dates add moisture and chew to the cookies.

BROWNED BUTTER
Browning the butter intensifies its flavor, so a little butter can taste like a lot.

TIPS FOR BROWNING BUTTER

When making browned butter, it helps to use a saucepan or skillet with a light-colored interior since the dark color of nonstick or anodized aluminum cookware makes it difficult to judge the color of the butter as it browns. Use medium to medium-high heat, and stir or swirl the butter occasionally so that the milk solids brown evenly. Finally, if you aren't using the browned butter immediately, transfer it to a bowl; if left in the saucepan or skillet, residual heat can cause it to continue cooking, and before you know it, your perfectly browned butter will be black.

electric mixer on medium speed until blended. Beat in the egg and vanilla until combined. Reduce the mixer speed to low and beat in the flour mixture until just incorporated. Reserve 2 tablespoons of the chocolate chips, then stir in the remaining chips by hand.

5. Working with 2 tablespoons of dough at a time, roll the dough into balls. Following the photos, tear the balls in half and press back together with the torn side up. Lay the cookies jagged-side up on the prepared baking sheets, spaced about 2 inches apart. Press the reserved 2 tablespoons chips evenly over the cookies.

6. Bake the cookies, one sheet at a time, until the edges are light golden brown and the centers are soft and puffy, 15 to 18 minutes, rotating the baking sheet halfway through.

7. Let the cookies cool on the baking sheet for 10 minutes, then serve warm or transfer to a wire rack and let cool completely.

PER COOKIE: **Cal** 170; **Fat** 4g; **Sat fat** 2.5g; **Chol** 15mg; **Carb** 31g; **Protein** 2g; **Fiber** 1g; **Sodium** 110mg

OATMEAL-RAISIN COOKIES

TEST KITCHEN **MAKEOVER**

HERE IN THE TEST KITCHEN, MANY OF US ADMIT that we used to give ourselves a pat on the back for choosing an oatmeal-raisin cookie over other sweets, figuring the oatmeal and raisins made it a "healthy" choice. That was before learning that some of these cookies weigh in at close to 270 calories and 10 grams of fat. Many supermarkets sell "low-cal" versions, but when they replace real butter and sugar with engineered fat and artificial sugar, the chewy texture and natural oat flavor have a habit of disappearing, too.

The recipes for homemade low-fat oatmeal cookies we tried were equally disappointing. One recipe used nonfat sour cream instead of butter, producing pale cookies with a lingering chemical aftertaste. In another, fat and sugar were replaced with applesauce for a gruesome, cottony cookie. Batch after batch of cookies sat uneaten in the test kitchen. Clearly, for good color, flavor, and texture, some fat was necessary. Just as we had done with several other baked goods recipes we had successfully lightened up, we decided to bake a batch of the test kitchen's favorite full-fat cookies and then see where we could trim and whittle.

Reducing the amount of butter from 16 tablespoons to 6 and using a single egg instead of two substantially cut the amount of fat, but compared to the full-fat version, these cookies were nothing to brag about. While they didn't have the cloying artificial taste of other diet oatmeal cookies, they didn't have the seductive butter flavor or chew of full-fat, either. Taking a cue from our Big and Chewy Chocolate Chip Cookies (page 262), we tried browning the butter to intensify its nuttiness and add more richness. Tasters loved the pronounced buttery taste in this batch.

But reducing the fat in the original recipe had done more than affect flavor; it had changed the texture. The oats that were pleasantly chewy yet tender in the full-fat version had turned tough, as if they barely cooked during baking. We wondered if precooking them before proceeding with the recipe would solve the problem. We tried dry-toasting the oats in the oven, in the microwave, and in a stovetop skillet before admitting defeat. In every case the finished cookies were leathery. Then a taster suggested that the oats might benefit from sautéing with the butter as it browned. That did the trick. As the oats cooked, they lost toughness and gained a welcome butter-toasted flavor.

To cut even more calories, we tried reducing the amount of sugar, but with that the cookies became brittle. We should have known: Sugar adds moisture as well as sweetness. To compensate, we tried adding water to a reduced-sugar batter, but even a drizzle made the cookies damp and fragile. Again, we thought of our low-fat chocolate chip cookies, in which a puree of softened dried dates added moisture. Since these were oatmeal-raisin cookies, we reached for the box of raisins instead. After a few tries, we found that the best results came from simmering chopped raisins on the stovetop with ¾ cup of water until the fruit was plump and the pan almost dry. We then stirred the raisin "pulp" into the dough with the whole raisins and proceeded as usual. These cookies baked up supple and chewy, with a caramel-y backdrop of raisin flavor, and we'd managed to cut the fat per cookie by 6 grams and the calories by nearly 100.

MAKEOVER SPOTLIGHT: OATMEAL-RAISIN COOKIES

	CALORIES	FAT	SAT FAT	CHOLESTEROL
BEFORE	270	10g	7g	45mg
AFTER	180	4g	2.5g	20mg

OATMEAL-RAISIN COOKIES

Oatmeal-Raisin Cookies

MAKES 20 COOKIES

Quick-cooking rolled oats can be substituted for the old-fashioned oats here; however, the cookies will have a little less flavor. Instant oats will adversely affect the texture of the cookies and should not be used.

- ¾ cup water
- 1 cup raisins, ½ cup chopped fine, ½ cup left whole
- 6 tablespoons (¾ stick) unsalted butter
- 1¾ cups (5¼ ounces) old-fashioned rolled oats (see note)
- 1½ teaspoons ground cinnamon
- 1 cup (5 ounces) unbleached all-purpose flour
- ½ teaspoon salt
- ¼ teaspoon baking powder
- ¼ teaspoon baking soda
- 1½ cups packed (10½ ounces) light brown sugar
- 1 large egg
- 2 teaspoons vanilla extract

1. Adjust an oven rack to the middle position and heat the oven to 350 degrees. Line 2 baking sheets with parchment paper and set aside.

2. Bring the water to a boil in a small saucepan over medium-high heat. Add the chopped raisins and simmer until plump and most of the water has evaporated, about 15 minutes. Transfer the raisins to a small bowl and cool to room temperature.

3. Melt the butter in a 12-inch skillet over medium heat. Add the oats and cook, stirring constantly, until just golden, about 5 minutes. Stir in the cinnamon and cook until fragrant, about 30 seconds. Set aside off the heat and cool to room temperature.

4. Whisk the flour, salt, baking powder, and baking soda together in a medium bowl. Whisk the brown sugar, egg, and vanilla together in a large bowl until smooth. Stir in the plumped and whole raisins, oat mixture, and flour mixture until just combined.

5. Working with 2 tablespoons of dough at a time, roll the dough into balls. Lay the cookies on the prepared baking sheets, spaced about 2 inches apart. Flatten the cookies to a ½-inch thickness with the bottom of a drinking glass.

6. Bake the cookies, one sheet at a time, until the edges are light golden brown and the centers are just set, 13 to 16 minutes, rotating the baking sheet halfway through.

7. Let the cookies cool on the baking sheet for 10 minutes, then serve warm or transfer to a wire rack and let cool completely.

PER COOKIE: Cal 180; Fat 4g; Sat fat 2.5g; Chol 20mg; Carb 33g; Protein 2g; Fiber 2g; Sodium 90mg

---

NOTES FROM THE TEST KITCHEN

SAME OLD INGREDIENTS, BRAND-NEW TECHNIQUES
Simply reducing the amounts of butter and sugar in oatmeal cookies will leave you with tough, flavorless cookies. While some recipes rely on strange stir-ins like applesauce or fat-free sour cream, we found a better approach.

RAISINS
To keep the cookies moist and chewy, we add a raisin paste, made by stewing chopped raisins and water, to the dough.

BUTTERY TOASTED OATS
To enhance the flavor of the cookies, we toast the oats in butter until they turn golden brown and fragrant.

OUR FAVORITE COOKIE SHEET
For such a simple-looking piece of equipment, the cookie sheet is rife with problems. Warping, sticking, overbrowning, underbrowning—it's a miracle that edible, attractive cookies get made at all on these temperamental squares of metal. We tested more than a dozen brands, and what did we learn? All of the dark-colored, nonstick cookie sheets we tested consistently overbrowned the bottoms of cookies. Light-colored sheets, on the other hand, were prone to sticking, but because we always bake cookies on parchment paper, we chose the (much) lesser of two evils. Lightweight sheets failed to make the cut because they warped. Sheets with only one handle proved difficult to rotate during baking, and those with four sides made it difficult to transfer cookie-loaded parchment paper from sheet to a wire rack to cool. The **Vollrath Cookie Sheet,** $24.95, turned out to be the one we'd been waiting for. It is roomy and sturdy, with handles on the short sides (where we like them) and minimal sticking, even when unlined.

FUDGY BROWNIES

IT TURNED OUT TO BE A FAMILIAR LOW-FAT BAKED goods story: When we tasted batch after batch of "healthy" brownies, it took just one bite every time for us to regret the effort. Either the texture was dry or the chocolate flavor was anemic. The best of the lot were cakey and spongy, which is OK if what you want is a flat piece of chocolate cake. But it's not acceptable if you want a real brownie, which should be moist, fudgy, and packed with chocolate flavor. It was time for the test kitchen to see what it could do. Full-fat fudgy brownies tend to rely on a generous amount of butter (usually an entire stick) and unsweetened chocolate (at least 2 ounces, often more). Could we cut down on the caloric and fatty ingredients but still create something that had all the original appeal?

Many low-fat brownie recipes call for "alternative" ingredients such as applesauce, prune puree, or even yogurt, but the test kitchen's opinion of these stand-ins for a low-fat brownie was unanimously negative. Applesauce masked the chocolate flavor and gave the brownies a texture that reminded us of an oily sponge. Prune puree yielded flavorless hockey pucks. Yogurt produced a pleasing texture, but tasters turned up their noses at the tart flavor. We agreed to stick with the test kitchen's favorite recipe for fudgy brownies and see where we might cut things back.

Cocoa powder, which is unsweetened chocolate with most of the fat removed, is a common ingredient in many low-fat chocolate recipes. We quickly learned that replacing all of the chocolate with cocoa powder was a mistake. The result was brownies with an unbearably dry texture. Replacing all but 2 ounces was vastly better. We also found that Dutch-processed brands contributed more flavor than "natural" cocoas. And we were better off using bittersweet chocolate than unsweetened, as it has less fat per ounce (by about 5 grams); tasters couldn't tell much difference when we made the switch.

Next we had to confront another familiar problem with cutting fat in baked goods: the butter issue. Leave it out of brownies entirely and you might as well throw them in the trash. But to make a significant dent in the calorie and fat, we couldn't add more than 2 tablespoons, and that meant dry, cakey brownies. We would have to find another source of moisture to make our brownies gooey. A squirt of chocolate syrup (such as Hershey's),

which contains no fat and plenty of chocolate flavor, helped things along, but it wasn't enough. In our research, we ran across several low-fat chocolate cake recipes that called for nonfat sour cream. Could it help our brownies? After our first test, we would have said no. The brownies were still too dry. But deciding not to give up the tactic so fast, we gave low-fat sour cream a try—it has only about one-third the fat of the regular stuff. These brownies were much better than those made with nonfat, and they were not only moist and fudgy but also tender (the acidity in sour cream has a tenderizing effect on baked goods). We also managed to cut out one of the egg yolks without compromising the texture of the brownies.

With just a few tweaks here and there, we had trimmed nearly half the calories and two-thirds of the fat from our favorite fudgy brownie recipe, and these low-fat brownies were good enough to merit a second, even a third bite—with no regrets.

MAKEOVER SPOTLIGHT: FUDGY BROWNIES

	CALORIES	FAT	SAT FAT	CHOLESTEROL
BEFORE	210	11g	7g	40mg
AFTER	110	4g	1.5g	15mg

Fudgy Brownies
MAKES 16 BROWNIES

For a truly fudgy consistency, don't overbake the brownies; as soon as a toothpick inserted into the center comes out with a few sticky crumbs attached, the brownies are done. If the toothpick emerges with no crumbs, the brownies will be cakey. To keep the brownies moist, do not cut until ready to serve.

 Vegetable oil spray
¾ cup (3¾ ounces) unbleached all-purpose flour
⅓ cup (1 ounce) Dutch-processed cocoa powder
½ teaspoon baking powder
¼ teaspoon salt
2 ounces bittersweet chocolate, chopped
2 tablespoons unsalted butter
1 cup (7 ounces) sugar
2 tablespoons low-fat sour cream
1 tablespoon chocolate syrup
1 large egg plus 1 large egg white
2 teaspoons vanilla extract

1. Adjust an oven rack to the middle position and heat the oven to 350 degrees. Following the photos on page 268, line an 8-inch square baking pan with a foil sling, lightly coat the foil with vegetable oil spray, and set aside.

2. Whisk the flour, cocoa, baking powder, and salt together in a medium bowl. Melt the bittersweet chocolate and butter together in a large bowl in the microwave, stirring often, 1 to 3 minutes. Let the mixture cool slightly.

3. Whisk the sugar, sour cream, chocolate syrup, egg, egg white, and vanilla into the chocolate mixture. Fold in the flour mixture with a rubber spatula, in 3 additions, until just incorporated.

4. Scrape the batter into the prepared pan and smooth the top. Tap the pan against the counter several times to settle the batter. Bake the brownies until a toothpick inserted into the center comes out with a few crumbs attached, 20 to 25 minutes, rotating the pan halfway through.

5. Let the brownies cool completely in the pan, set on a wire rack, about 2 hours. Remove the brownies from the pan using the foil, cut into 2-inch squares, and serve.

PER BROWNIE: **Cal** 110; **Fat** 4g; **Sat fat** 1.5g; **Chol** 15mg; **Carb** 20g; **Protein** 2g; **Fiber** 1g; **Sodium** 65mg

NOTES FROM THE TEST KITCHEN

MAKING A FOIL SLING

Brownies can be nearly impossible to remove from their baking pans, no matter how well the pan is greased. After baking countless batches, we finally found a method that works every time. Lining the pan with an aluminum foil "sling" before baking prevents any casualties. Once cooled, the brownies may be lifted easily from the pan, transferred to a cutting board, and cut into tidy squares.

1. Fold two long sheets of aluminum foil so that they are as wide as the baking pan. Lay the sheets of foil in the pan, perpendicular to one another, with the extra foil hanging over the edges of the pan.

2. Push the foil into the corners and up the sides of the pan. Try to iron out any wrinkles in the foil, smoothing it flush to the pan. Spray the sides and bottom with vegetable oil spray, then scrape the batter into the pan.

3. After the brownies have baked and cooled, use the foil sling to lift and transfer them to a cutting board before cutting them into squares. The foil should easily peel away.

SOUR CREAM IN BROWNIES?

We found that an unlikely ingredient—low-fat sour cream—helps keep our low-fat brownies fudgy like the real thing.

PEACH SHORTCAKES

FRUIT SHORTCAKES MAY SEEM LIKE THE PERFECT light summertime dessert, involving little more than fruit tossed with sugar, sandwiched between a split biscuit, and topped with a dollop of whipped cream. But lo and behold, the buttery shortcakes, saccharine fruit, and overload (let's admit that it's always more than a dollop) of whipped cream all add up quickly. Our goal was to develop a foolproof recipe for fruit shortcakes with tender biscuits, juicy fruit, and fluffy whipped cream that also kept the fat and calories to a minimum.

Since the test kitchen is all too familiar with berry shortcakes, we decided to branch out and try another fruit. Peaches are one of our summertime favorites, so we headed in that direction. We started by scanning cookbooks for recipes, and most of what we found were tacked-on modifications of berry shortcakes that simply called for replacing the berries with peaches. We tried this approach, only to find that the peaches turned out bone dry, nothing like what we were after in a shortcake. We wanted our peaches to be as appealing as the berries in shortcakes usually are, swathed in a sweet juice that soaks into the shortcake, lending an indulgent appeal and bringing the whole dessert together.

The problem is that peaches don't react to macerating (soaking in sugar, a process that not only sweetens

PEACH SHORTCAKE

PEELING PEACHES

1. With a paring knife, score a small X at the base of each peach. Then lower the peaches into boiling water and simmer until the skins loosen, 30 to 60 seconds.

2. Transfer the peaches immediately to ice water and let cool for about 1 minute.

3. Use a paring knife to remove strips of loosened peel, starting at the X on the base of each peach.

BOOSTING JUICE AND FLAVOR

Macerating fruit in sugar is the traditional method for releasing its juice, but for peaches, this step alone is not enough. Here's how we supplement maceration to get a juicy peach filling for our shortcakes.

1. Microwaving some of the peaches with sugar and orange juice softens their cell walls, making the cells more susceptible to rupturing (and thus releasing juice).

2. Mashing the microwaved peaches completely breaks down their cell walls, increasing the amount of juice they release.

the fruit but extracts juice from it) the same way that berries do. Berries release more liquid than peaches during maceration since their cell walls are weaker and more permeable, and because their nubby exterior allows for more exposed surface area than a smooth peach.

So to even the playing field, we first sliced the peaches thin to maximize their surface area. We then macerated most of them as usual, but we also pulled one-quarter of the peaches aside and instead microwaved these with some sugar and orange juice (a nice complementary, bright flavor) until they were completely tender. We then mashed these cooked peaches with a potato masher, and finally we mixed the peachy jam with the macerated peaches. Shortcakes made with these peaches gave us the juicy filling we were after. All that was left to do for the filling was fine-tune the sugar amount. Most shortcake recipes call for tossing the fruit with ½ cup of sugar or more, but we found that 6 tablespoons were sufficient to draw out the juice and lightly sweeten the fruit.

It was time to focus on the biscuits. Simple, straightforward drop biscuits held the most promise. All the work can be done directly in a bowl, and the craggy results are perfect for catching liquid. Starting with the test kitchen's existing full-fat recipe, we cut the amount of butter in half and used a combination of 1 percent milk and low-fat yogurt in place of the usual heavy cream. These biscuits looked good and tasted fine on their own, but when topped with peaches, they proved a little too airy for a shortcake. To give them a little more heft so that they would hold up better under the weight of the fruit, we added an egg to the batter. These biscuits were hearty enough to support the fruit and juice.

Last, we turned to the whipped topping. Lightly sweetened whipped cream is typical, but our light peach shortcakes couldn't afford all the fat and calories. Tasters shunned store-bought whipped topping for its artificial flavor, foamy texture, and odd greasy aftertaste. Looking for light ingredients that we could use to cut the heavy cream, we played around with reduced-fat cream cheese, plain yogurt, and even gelatin, but we finally settled on low-fat sour cream. We whipped the heavy cream to soft peaks with a little sugar and vanilla extract, then folded in the sour cream. With its thick, creamy texture and tangy flavor, sour cream helped to create a topping that was not so different from the real deal in texture and flavor. And by swapping in ¼ cup of the sour cream for ¼ cup of the heavy cream, we were able to cut 2 grams of fat per serving from the topping.

With that, our hopes (and hard work) were finally rewarded. We had a juicy peach filling, tender biscuits that could absorb the juice but were firm enough to stand up to the filling, and silky and rich whipped topping.

Peach Shortcakes

SERVES 8

If your peaches are firm, you should be able to peel them with a sharp vegetable peeler. If they are too soft to withstand the pressure of a peeler, peel them following the photos on page 270.

FRUIT

- 2 **pounds ripe but firm peaches (4 to 5 medium), peeled (see note), pitted, and cut into ¼-inch-thick wedges**
- 6 **tablespoons sugar**
- 2 **tablespoons orange juice**

BISCUITS

- 2 **cups (10 ounces) unbleached all-purpose flour**
- 2 **tablespoons sugar**
- 2 **teaspoons baking powder**
- ¾ **teaspoon salt**
- ½ **cup plain low-fat yogurt**
- 6 **tablespoons 1 percent milk**
- 1 **large egg**
- 4 **tablespoons (½ stick) unsalted butter, melted and cooled slightly**
  Vegetable oil spray

WHIPPED TOPPING

- ¼ **cup heavy cream**
- 1 **tablespoon sugar**
- ½ **teaspoon vanilla extract**
- ¼ **cup low-fat sour cream**

1. FOR THE FRUIT: Toss three-quarters of the peaches with ¼ cup of the sugar in a large bowl and let sit, tossing occasionally, for 30 minutes.

2. Meanwhile, toss the remaining peaches with the remaining 2 tablespoons sugar and orange juice in a medium microwave-safe bowl. Microwave on high until the peaches are bubbling, 1 to 2 minutes, stirring twice during cooking. Using a potato masher, crush the peaches into a coarse pulp and let sit for 30 minutes.

3. FOR THE BISCUITS: While the peaches sit, adjust an oven rack to the middle position and heat the oven to 475 degrees. Line a large baking sheet with parchment paper and set aside.

4. Whisk the flour, 4 teaspoons of the sugar, baking powder, and salt together in a large bowl. Whisk the yogurt, milk, and egg together in a medium bowl, then stir in the melted butter until small clumps form.

5. Stir the yogurt mixture into the flour mixture until the dough comes together and no dry flour remains. Lightly coat a ¼-cup dry measuring cup with vegetable oil spray and use the measuring cup to drop eight mounds of dough onto the prepared baking sheet, spaced 1½ inches apart (if the dough sticks to the cup, use a small spoon to pull it free).

6. Sprinkle the remaining 2 teaspoons sugar evenly over the biscuits and bake until the tops are golden brown and crisp, about 13 minutes, rotating the baking sheet halfway through. Transfer the biscuits to a wire rack and let cool for 15 minutes before assembling.

7. FOR THE WHIPPED TOPPING: Whip the cream, sugar, and vanilla in a large bowl with an electric mixer on medium-low speed until frothy, about 1 minute. Increase the mixer speed to high and continue to whip until the cream forms soft peaks, 1 to 3 minutes longer. Gently fold in the sour cream.

8. TO ASSEMBLE: Split each biscuit in half and place the bottoms on 8 individual serving plates. Spoon a portion of the crushed peach mixture over each biscuit bottom, followed by the peach slices and any exuded juice. Top the peaches with a heaping 1 tablespoon of the whipped topping, cap with the biscuit top, and serve.

PER SERVING: Cal 320; Fat 10g; Sat fat 6g; Chol 55mg; Carb 49g; Protein 6g; Fiber 2g; Sodium 390mg

BLUEBERRY GRUNT

WHILE WE WERE LOOKING FOR AN INTERESTING fruit dessert other than the old standbys like cobblers and crisps, we came across blueberry grunt. Berries are stewed in water, sugar, and cinnamon, then the mixture is topped with dollops of drop-biscuit dough, covered, and cooked on the stovetop until the dumplings are cooked through. The simplicity had us hooked, as did the unusual idea of a fluffy steamed dumpling topping. And because this dessert was already naturally lean, it wouldn't require a lightened makeover. Though a grunt can be made with any manner of fruit, blueberry grunt is especially popular in New England and Nova Scotia and sounded like a great addition to our repertoire of light fruit desserts.

Dense fruit fillings for cobblers and pies are usually thickened with cornstarch or tapioca, but grunt filling is traditionally looser—it uses no thickeners (up to ½ cup of water is actually added), creating a soupy filling that soaks into the dumplings. In the test kitchen, however, we felt the need to break with tradition and thicken the filling; it was too bland in our minds and made the dumplings too soggy. We started by cooking down the berries (with sugar, cinnamon, lemon zest, and just 2 tablespoons of water) to a jam-like consistency. This concentrated the flavor, but tasters missed the texture of whole berries. As a compromise, we cooked down half the berries until jammy, then stirred in the remaining berries before topping the mixture with the dumplings. We found that just a little cornstarch (1 teaspoon) further tightened the filling without making it too thick.

The dumplings (drop biscuits made from flour, milk, melted butter, sugar, baking powder, and salt) were less soggy without the watery filling beneath them, but they were still a little bland and dense. Replacing the milk with buttermilk added a nice tang, and the buttermilk also reacted with the baking soda, making the dumplings much lighter. Tasters noticed another problem, however: The tops of the cooked dumplings were strangely soggy. The cause, we realized, was condensation dripping from the inside of the pot lid onto our otherwise perfect dumplings. The solution was as easy as placing a clean kitchen towel under the lid to absorb the condensation. For a final burst of flavor and texture, we sprinkled cinnamon sugar on the cooked dumplings before serving. This grunt was so good we were sure it would soon be known for more than just its funny name.

Blueberry Grunt

SERVES 12

Do not use frozen blueberries here, as they will make the filling watery.

FILLING

- 8 cups (2½ pounds) fresh blueberries
- ½ cup (3½ ounces) sugar
- 2 tablespoons water
- 1 teaspoon grated lemon zest plus 1 tablespoon fresh lemon juice
- ½ teaspoon ground cinnamon
- 1 teaspoon cornstarch

DUMPLINGS

- 2¼ cups (11¼ ounces) unbleached all-purpose flour
- ½ cup (3½ ounces) sugar
- 1½ teaspoons baking powder
- ½ teaspoon baking soda
- ½ teaspoon salt
- ¾ cup low-fat buttermilk
- 6 tablespoons (¾ stick) unsalted butter, melted and cooled slightly
- 1 teaspoon vanilla extract
  Vegetable oil spray
- ½ teaspoon ground cinnamon

1. FOR THE FILLING: Cook 4 cups of the blueberries, sugar, water, lemon zest, and cinnamon together in a Dutch oven over medium-high heat, stirring occasionally, until the mixture is thick and jam-like, 10 to 12 minutes.

2. Whisk the lemon juice and cornstarch together in a small bowl, then stir into the blueberry mixture. Add the remaining 4 cups blueberries and cook until heated through, about 1 minute. Set the pot aside off the heat and cover to keep warm.

3. FOR THE DUMPLINGS: Whisk the flour, 6 tablespoons of the sugar, baking powder, baking soda, and salt together in a large bowl. Whisk the buttermilk, melted butter, and vanilla together in a medium bowl. Stir the buttermilk mixture into the flour mixture until the dough comes together and no dry flour remains.

4. Lightly coat a ¼-cup dry measuring cup with vegetable oil spray and use the measuring cup to drop 12 mounds of dough on top of the warm berry mixture (if the dough sticks to the cup, use a small spoon to pull it free).

5. Wrap the lid of the Dutch oven with a clean kitchen towel (keeping the towel away from the heat source) and cover the pot. Bring to a simmer over medium-low heat and cook until the dumplings have doubled in size and a toothpick inserted into the center comes out clean, 18 to 24 minutes.

6. Combine the remaining 2 tablespoons sugar and cinnamon in a small bowl. Uncover the pot, sprinkle the dumplings with the cinnamon sugar, and serve.

PER SERVING: **Cal** 270; **Fat** 6g; **Sat fat** 4g; **Chol** 15mg; **Carb** 52g; **Protein** 4g; **Fiber** 3g; **Sodium** 240mg

---

NOTES FROM THE TEST KITCHEN

MAKING BLUEBERRY GRUNT

1. After the filling is ready and you have made the dumpling dough, use a ¼-cup measuring cup lightly coated with vegetable oil spray to drop evenly sized balls of dough over the warm filling.

2. Wrap the lid of the Dutch oven with a kitchen towel before covering the grunt to absorb condensation during cooking. This will keep the dumplings light and fluffy.

3. Before serving, sprinkle cinnamon sugar over the steamed dumplings to add a crunchy contrast.

BETTER BERRY TREATMENT

We have discovered that cleaning berries with a mild vinegar solution and carefully drying them destroys bacteria and mold spores, extending a berry's life. Wash the berries in a bowl with 3 cups water and 1 cup white vinegar, then drain them in a colander and rinse under running water. Place the berries in a salad spinner lined with paper towels, and spin them for 15 seconds or until they are completely dry. Store the berries in a loosely covered paper towel–lined container.

PAN-ROASTED PEACHES

WHEN PEACHES ARE SOFT AND RIPE, THEY ARE BEST enjoyed as is, eaten out of hand, but peaches that are not quite ripe and still a bit firm are better suited to roasting, where the heat of the oven can work its magic, caramelizing the exterior of the peaches and rendering them soft (but not mushy) and incredibly sweet and juicy. Prepared this way, they also make an easy and healthy dessert.

But as with roasting any vegetable or fruit, it isn't as simple as throwing the fruit on a pan, cooking with high heat, and calling it a day. You have to get the technique and method just right, or you will end up with fruit that has been cooked unevenly, that is charred on the outside but undercooked inside, or that is simply a mushy, shapeless pile that doesn't even slightly resemble its original appearance. We started our testing by halving and pitting the peaches, then sprinkled the cut sides with sugar. We then roasted them on a baking sheet in a 400-degree oven, which seemed like a reasonable place to start for a straightforward roasting recipe. However, just as we had expected, it wasn't quite so simple. Right from the start, our tasters said they wanted more caramelization, and we realized this simply wouldn't be possible in the oven because the peaches would become tender before they had a chance to brown properly. Worse, any browning that did occur stuck to the pan, not the peaches. We needed to subject the cut sides of the peaches to high heat so that the exposed flesh could caramelize quickly before the interior cooked too much; once that was accomplished, we could finish cooking the peaches through. Perhaps we would have better luck if we started cooking the peaches on the stovetop in a nonstick skillet.

We melted a little butter in the skillet, then added the sugar-sprinkled peaches, cut-side down. After just two minutes on the stovetop, the peaches were beginning to caramelize, so we transferred them to the oven to roast until tender. We tested various times and temperatures and found that about 30 minutes in a 400-degree oven gave us the ideal results. The peaches benefited from the richness of the butter, which also helped glaze them nicely and promoted browning.

We briefly considered adding more butter and sugar to the pan to make a caramel sauce to pour over the peaches, but we realized this was an unnecessary addition of fat and calories when the peaches had plenty

PAN-ROASTED PEACHES

of flavor on their own. They make a wonderfully light dessert as is, or they can be served with just a small scoop of vanilla frozen yogurt. Roasted peaches are also an excellent and unexpected side dish when drizzled with balsamic vinegar and served alongside roasted chicken or pork. Simple and elegant, they make a refreshing summertime dish, no matter how you choose to serve them.

Pan-Roasted Peaches
SERVES 4

Do not use either rock-hard or overly ripe peaches when making this recipe. These peaches can be served savory or sweet. They are great drizzled with balsamic vinegar and served with chicken or pork, or serve as is for dessert or with vanilla frozen yogurt. You will need an ovensafe nonstick skillet for this recipe.

- 4 ripe but firm peaches (7 to 8 ounces each), halved and pitted (see note)
- 1 tablespoon sugar
- 2 tablespoons unsalted butter

1. Adjust an oven rack to the middle position and heat the oven to 400 degrees.

2. Sprinkle the cut sides of each peach with the sugar. Melt the butter in a 12-inch ovensafe nonstick skillet over medium heat. Add the peaches, cut-side down, and cook until beginning to brown, about 2 minutes.

3. Transfer the skillet to the oven and roast the peaches until tender when pierced with a paring knife or skewer and the cut sides are caramelized, 25 to 35 minutes. Using potholders (the skillet handle will be hot), remove the skillet from the oven. Remove the peaches from the skillet and serve.

PER SERVING: Cal 130; Fat 6g; Sat fat 4g; Chol 15mg; Carb 20g; Protein 2g; Fiber 3g; Sodium 0mg

VARIATION
Pan-Roasted Plums
Follow the recipe for Pan-Roasted Peaches, substituting 4 ripe but firm plums (6 to 7 ounces each), halved and pitted, for the peaches and reducing the cooking time in step 3 to 15 to 25 minutes.

PER SERVING: Cal 100; Fat 6g; Sat fat 4g; Chol 15mg; Carb 13g; Protein 1g; Fiber 1g; Sodium 0mg

BAKED APPLES

THOUGH THEY HAVE FOR THE MOST PART BEEN forgotten over the years, baked apples are a naturally light dessert that is appealingly simple, homey, and comforting. We soon found, however, that despite their simplicity, there were some pitfalls to overcome on our way to finding the best recipe.

The most common problem in existing recipes we tested was that the apples split or became too mushy when baked. The ideal baked apple should soften yet hold its shape and remain moist without becoming mushy. The key would be choosing the right apple. We tested nine varieties, and among common ones, McIntoshes were mushy, and Red Delicious and Granny Smith apples were too dry. Only Golden Delicious apples rated well. Several lesser-known varieties also baked up nicely, including Baldwin and Cortland.

With the apple chosen, we moved on to the issue of the splitting skin. After further testing, we surmised that steam was causing the apple skin to split open. To allow the steam to escape, we found it helpful to remove a strip of skin around the stem with a vegetable peeler.

When it came to baking, we found that the apples required a moderate 350-degree oven; higher temperatures caused the apples to split. To keep the apples moist, we found it best to bake them surrounded by a pool of cider, which reinforced the apples' flavor without adding too many calories. However, there was one drawback: The sauce was always too watery. Many recipes we found rectify this by including cream or butter to finish the sauce, but in our case that wasn't an option. Our solution was to take the liquid remaining in the pan after the apples had finished cooking and reduce it on the stovetop. After a brief simmer, we had a super-concentrated sauce that clung to the apples.

Now that we had perfected the technique, we directed our attention to the filling and flavoring. A quarter-cup of sugar sprinkled over the apples helped to tame their inherent tartness, and a dash of cinnamon helped bring forth the apples' flavor. Dried fruit (we liked both cranberries and cherries) provided a contrasting tang to the apples while adding no fat and just a few calories. To fill the apples we hollowed out the core without puncturing the blossom ends. We found the easiest and most thorough way to core a whole apple is with a melon baller, starting at the stem and moving down to scoop out and remove the core. We filled our apples with the dried fruit, sprinkled on the sugar and cinnamon, and popped them into the oven to bake. Scattering some toasted walnuts over the apples right before serving lent good texture and flavor and really made this dish stand out. We think baked apples are ready for a revival.

Cider-Baked Apples with Dried Cranberries

SERVES 4

Use Golden Delicious, Cortland, or Baldwin apples here. Take care not to puncture the blossom end (opposite the stem end) of the apples when coring them. The walnuts add great flavor and texture to the finished apples; however, they do add calories and fat to the dish. Feel free to substitute dried cherries for the cranberries. For a special treat, serve the baked apples with a dollop of low-fat ice cream or frozen yogurt.

> 4   large apples (about 8 ounces each; see note)
> ½   cup dried cranberries (see note)
> ¼   cup (1¾ ounces) sugar
> ¼   teaspoon ground cinnamon
> 1½   cups apple cider
> 2   cinnamon sticks
> ¼   cup walnuts, toasted (see page 16) and chopped fine (see note; optional)

1. Adjust an oven rack to the middle position and heat the oven to 350 degrees. Using a vegetable peeler, remove a strip of apple peel from the top of each apple. Following the photo, use a melon baller to remove the stem and core of the apple, being careful not to cut all the way through the blossom end.

2. Place the apples in an 8-inch square baking dish. Divide ¼ cup of the dried cranberries evenly among the apple cavities. Mix the sugar and ground cinnamon together in a small bowl, then sprinkle the mixture in and around the apples. Add the remaining ¼ cup dried cranberries, cider, and cinnamon sticks to the baking dish.

3. Bake the apples until tender when pierced with a paring knife or skewer, 45 to 55 minutes, brushing the apples with the cider several times during baking. (Be careful not to overbake the apples or the skins will split.)

4. Transfer the apples to individual bowls and tent loosely with foil while making the sauce. Pour the cooking liquid with the dried cranberries and cinnamon sticks into a small saucepan, bring to a simmer over medium-high heat, and cook until the liquid has reduced to 1 cup, 7 to 10 minutes. Remove and discard the cinnamon sticks. Spoon some of the sauce over each apple, sprinkle with the walnuts (if using), and serve, passing the remaining sauce separately.

PER SERVING (WITHOUT WALNUTS): **Cal** 200; **Fat** 0g; **Sat fat** 0g; **Chol** 0mg; **Carb** 53g; **Protein** 0g; **Fiber** 3g; **Sodium** 10mg

PER SERVING (WITH WALNUTS): **Cal** 250; **Fat** 5g; **Sat fat** 0g; **Chol** 0mg; **Carb** 54g; **Protein** 2g; **Fiber** 4g; **Sodium** 10mg

VARIATIONS

Cider-Baked Apples with Rum and Golden Raisins

Follow the recipe for Cider-Baked Apples with Dried Cranberries, substituting ½ cup golden raisins for the dried cranberries. Add ¼ cup dark rum to the dish with the cider in step 2. Before serving, stir 2 tablespoons more rum into the sauce.

PER SERVING (WITHOUT WALNUTS): **Cal** 260; **Fat** 0g; **Sat fat** 0g; **Chol** 0mg; **Carb** 56g; **Protein** 1g; **Fiber** 4g; **Sodium** 15mg

PER SERVING (WITH WALNUTS): **Cal** 310; **Fat** 5g; **Sat fat** 0g; **Chol** 0mg; **Carb** 57g; **Protein** 2g; **Fiber** 4g; **Sodium** 15mg

Cider-Baked Apples with Fresh Ginger and Orange

Follow the recipe for Cider-Baked Apples with Dried Cranberries, substituting a 3-inch-long strip of orange peel and a 1-inch piece of fresh ginger, peeled and cut into coins, for the cinnamon sticks in step 2. Before serving, remove and discard the orange peel and ginger coins from the sauce.

PER SERVING (WITHOUT WALNUTS): **Cal** 200; **Fat** 0g; **Sat fat** 0g; **Chol** 0mg; **Carb** 53g; **Protein** 0g; **Fiber** 3g; **Sodium** 10mg

PER SERVING (WITH WALNUTS): **Cal** 250; **Fat** 5g; **Sat fat** 0g; **Chol** 0mg; **Carb** 54g; **Protein** 2g; **Fiber** 4g; **Sodium** 10mg

---

NOTES FROM THE TEST KITCHEN

PREPARING APPLES FOR BAKING

After removing a strip of peel from the stem end of the apple with a vegetable peeler, use a melon baller to scoop out the core, being careful not to puncture the blossom end.

MARBLE CHEESECAKE

TEST KITCHEN
MAKEOVER

OF ALL THE DESSERTS, CHEESECAKE—RICH, CREAMY, and with its trademark tang—may seem like one of the most indulgent. It's hard to imagine that a low-fat version resembling the original could even be possible. It shouldn't be shocking that most recipes for low-fat cheesecake we've come across produce a rubbery, gummy mess, chock-full of artificial and off-flavors. Despite that discouraging precedent, the test kitchen spent months developing a recipe for low-fat New York–style cheesecake that tasted so good we can honestly say we will never go back to a full-fat version. Made with cottage cheese, light cream cheese, and drained yogurt, this lightened cheesecake is rich and creamy and contains half the calories and just one-third the fat of the original.

Now we wanted to build on that success. We wondered if there was a way to incorporate chocolate into that recipe to make a marble cheesecake. With the addition of chocolate, a slice of traditional marble cheesecake, not surprisingly, logs even more calories and fat than a slice of the regular stuff, at 670 calories and 49 grams of fat per serving. We had a long way to go to make a guilt-free version that packed genuine rich, chocolaty flavor.

Using the existing recipe as a jumping-off point, we melted semisweet chocolate and swirled it into the cheesecake batter. The results weren't promising. The chocolate had a grainy texture and was so poorly integrated into the cake that as it cooled, huge cracks appeared all over the top where the chocolate came together with the plain batter. Next we tried chocolate syrup, but it added too much moisture to the batter and made the cheesecake runny. Cocoa was an obvious test to run, but we knew we couldn't just mix in the powder as is; we needed to dissolve it first. So we mixed ¼ cup of cocoa powder with ¼ cup of batter and swirled this chocolate batter back into the plain batter. We slid the cake into the oven and baked it with the preferred standard New York method that we had used successfully for our plain low-fat cheesecake, starting off at 500 degrees for about 10 minutes, then 200 degrees for about an hour and a half. But what we ended up with were pockets of bitter, pasty cocoa and more unappealing cracks on the top of the cheesecake. Could we dilute the intense bitterness of the cocoa and solve the appearance issues at the same time?

Our plain low-fat recipe called for 1 tablespoon of vanilla extract. We decided to double this amount, using half to make a paste by mixing it with the cocoa, and we added an extra 2 tablespoons of sugar to this mixture to counteract the bitterness issue. Then we added batter to the paste until it reached the same consistency as the plain batter. In the end, it took 1 cup of the batter to get the result we were after. Hopeful that this was the answer to our cake's problems, we swirled the plain batter and chocolaty batter together, baked the cake, and waited patiently for it to cool. The results were well worth the wait. This was a creamy, crack-free cheesecake with deep chocolate flavor, and at 360 calories and a mere 14 grams of fat, it was one we could really enjoy.

MAKEOVER SPOTLIGHT: MARBLE CHEESECAKE

	CALORIES	FAT	SAT FAT	CHOLESTEROL
BEFORE	660	49g	30g	270mg
AFTER	350	14g	8g	85mg

Chocolate Marble Cheesecake

SERVES 12

Be sure to use light cream cheese for this recipe, not ⅓ less fat cream cheese.

CRUST

- 9 whole graham crackers, broken into rough pieces
- 4 tablespoons (½ stick) unsalted butter, melted
- 1 tablespoon sugar
  Vegetable oil spray

FILLING

- 1 pound 1 percent cottage cheese, drained 10 to 24 hours
- 1 pound plain low-fat yogurt, drained 10 to 24 hours
- 1 pound light cream cheese, at room temperature (see note)
- 1½ cups plus 2 tablespoons sugar
- 2 tablespoons vanilla extract
- ¼ teaspoon salt
- 3 large eggs, at room temperature
- 2 tablespoons Dutch-processed cocoa

1. FOR THE CRUST: Adjust an oven rack to the middle position and heat the oven to 325 degrees. Process the graham crackers in a food processor to fine crumbs. Combine the crumbs with the butter and sugar in a small bowl. Transfer the crust mixture to a 9-inch springform pan and press it evenly into the pan bottom. Bake the crust until fragrant and beginning to brown, 10 to 15 minutes. Cool on a wire rack. Taking care not to disturb the crust, coat the inside of the springform pan with vegetable oil spray, set the pan on a rimmed baking sheet, and set aside.

2. FOR THE FILLING: Increase the oven temperature to 500 degrees. Process the drained cottage cheese in the food processor until no visible lumps remain, about 1 minute, scraping down the sides of the bowl as needed. Add the drained yogurt and cream cheese, and process until smooth, 1 to 2 minutes, scraping down the sides of the bowl as needed. Add 1½ cups of the sugar, 1 tablespoon of the vanilla, and salt, and process until smooth, about 1 minute, scraping down the sides of the bowl as needed. With the processor running, add the eggs, one at a time, and process until smooth.

3. Combine the remaining 2 tablespoons sugar and cocoa in a bowl. Stir 1 cup of the cheesecake batter and the remaining 1 tablespoon vanilla into the sugar-cocoa mixture until smooth.

4. Pour the plain cheesecake batter into the prepared pan. Following the photos, spoon and swirl the chocolate batter into the plain batter. Bake for 10 minutes. Reduce the oven temperature to 200 degrees (hold the oven door open until an oven thermometer reads 200 degrees) and bake until the center of the cheesecake registers 150 degrees on an instant-read thermometer, about 1 hour.

5. Transfer the cake to a wire rack and run a paring knife around the edge of the cake to loosen. Cool completely, about 3 hours, then wrap the pan tightly with plastic wrap and refrigerate until cold, at least 3 hours.

6. To unmold the cheesecake, remove the sides of the pan and blot any excess moisture from the top of the cheesecake with paper towels. Let the cheesecake stand at room temperature for 30 minutes before serving.

PER SERVING: **Cal** 350; **Fat** 14g; **Sat fat** 8g; **Chol** 85mg; **Carb** 44g; **Protein** 13g; **Fiber** 0g; **Sodium** 520mg

PUTTING THE MARBLE IN CHEESECAKE

1. Using a tablespoon, gently spoon the chocolate batter onto the plain batter around the edge and in the center, leaving about ½ inch between each spoonful. (If there's extra chocolate batter, add it to previous drops.)

2. Using the handle end of a wooden spoon or spatula, drag the handle back and forth through the batter to make a marbled pattern.

DRAINING YOGURT AND COTTAGE CHEESE

Draining away the excess liquid from both the cottage cheese and the yogurt is an essential step when preparing our Chocolate Marble Cheesecake. Don't be tempted to drain both in the same strainer—the drained cottage cheese needs to be pureed in a food processor until smooth. Be sure to use a brand of yogurt that doesn't contain modified food starch, gelatin, or gums—each prevents the yogurt from draining properly.

1. For the cottage cheese, line a bowl with several layers of paper towels, spoon the cottage cheese into the bowl, cover with plastic wrap, and refrigerate at least 10 hours and up to 24 hours.

2. For the yogurt, place a fine-mesh strainer over a bowl lined with 3 or 4 coffee filters or a double layer of cheesecloth. Spoon the yogurt into the strainer, cover with plastic wrap, and refrigerate at least 10 hours or up to 24 hours.

CHOCOLATE BUNDT CAKE

TEST KITCHEN
MAKEOVER

WITH THEIR DECORATIVE SHAPE, BUNDT CAKES DON'T require frosting or fussy finishing techniques, and this is especially true of a chocolate Bundt cake, which should taste every bit as good as it looks, with a fine crumb, moist texture, and rich chocolate flavor. But unfortunately when it comes to low-fat chocolate Bundt cakes, typically all bets are off. Despite their tantalizing looks, most of these cakes deliver a minimum of chocolate flavor, and many are dry, rubbery, and devoid of any flavor whatsoever. We were determined to improve upon these low-fat disasters and create a chocolate Bundt cake that would taste as good as it looked.

A traditional chocolate Bundt cake calls for 6 to 8 ounces of bittersweet chocolate (plus cocoa powder), but this amount of chocolate was far too much for a cake we were trying to lighten. Our first thought was to remove the melted chocolate altogether and replace it with cocoa powder, which is much lower in fat. But the cake resulting from this idea tasted bitter, and its texture was dry and chalky, reminiscent of third-rate brownies. We decided to add the melted chocolate back, but only an ounce at a time. With 3 ounces of chocolate and ¾ cup of cocoa, we found a good balance. The cake had a robust chocolate flavor and a lot less fat. But we wanted to see if we could get even more chocolate flavor. Several recipes we had seen called for mixing hot water with the cocoa powder before adding it to the cake batter. So we poured boiling water over the cocoa and chocolate to dissolve them before combining them with the rest of the ingredients, and we found that this step not only dispersed the cocoa particles throughout the batter but also helped to bloom the flavor. In addition, we dissolved a small amount of espresso powder along with the chocolate and cocoa and added a healthy tablespoon of vanilla extract. Both flavors complemented the floral nuances of the chocolate. This cake had the best chocolate flavor possible.

The next fatty culprit we turned our attention to was the butter, since most Bundt cakes have 12 tablespoons or more. We found that using oil in place of butter, and just ½ cup, not only cut out a fair amount of the saturated fat but also yielded a cake that had a much more intense chocolate flavor, which the butter had masked. Another source of fat in the cake was the eggs. In order to achieve a solid, dense structure that will hold its shape, most Bundt cakes include four or five eggs. After some tinkering, we found that we could reduce the number of eggs to two and increase the amount of leavener slightly and still achieve a statuesque cake.

Now that we had a great, complex chocolate flavor and had eliminated a significant portion of the fat, we could focus on the texture. Although our cake had great flavor and a nice crumb, it still lacked moistness. We tried decreasing the amount of flour, but this compromised the structure of the cake. We considered adding more oil or another egg, but these alternatives seemed counterproductive to our core mission of developing a lower-fat cake. Finally, we switched from granulated to light brown sugar, which not only added moistness but also improved the flavor. But even after making this change to the recipe, we were still falling short of our goal of a really moist cake. In our initial tests we had used buttermilk as the liquid base for the cake. We liked the tangy flavor the buttermilk added, but we began to wonder if the thickness of the buttermilk was causing the cake to seem dry. So we tried making the cake using low-fat milk instead. This cake was an improvement, but we felt we could do even better, and in the back of our minds we were wondering if the dairy was also masking the chocolate flavor. So we made the cake again, but this time we omitted the dairy and used water. It gave us the results we wanted: The batter was looser, the finished cake was much more moist, and the chocolate flavor was intensified. And we had cut out 100 calories per serving and 7 grams of fat, not to mention cutting the amount of saturated fat significantly. This indulgent, chocolaty dessert was as guilt-free as we could have hoped.

MAKEOVER SPOTLIGHT: CHOCOLATE BUNDT CAKE

	CALORIES	FAT	SAT FAT	CHOLESTEROL
BEFORE	420	18g	10g	100mg
AFTER	320	11g	2g	25mg

Chocolate Bundt Cake

SERVES 16

Although you can substitute natural cocoa for Dutch-processed, the cake won't rise as high. If you don't have baking spray with flour, mix 1 tablespoon butter with 1 tablespoon flour into a paste and brush inside the pan.

  Baking spray with flour
- 3 **ounces bittersweet chocolate, chopped fine**
- ¾ **cup Dutch-processed cocoa powder (see note)**
- 1 **teaspoon espresso powder**
- 1 **cup boiling water**
- 1¾ **cups (8¾ ounces) unbleached all-purpose flour**
- 1 **teaspoon salt**
- 1 **teaspoon baking soda**
- 2 **cups packed (14 ounces) light brown sugar**
- ½ **cup vegetable oil**
- 2 **large eggs**
- 1 **tablespoon vanilla extract**

1. Adjust an oven rack to the lower-middle position and heat the oven to 350 degrees. Lightly coat a standard 12-cup Bundt pan with baking spray and set aside.

2. Combine the chocolate, cocoa, and espresso powder in a large bowl. Pour the boiling water over the chocolate mixture, cover, and let sit for 5 minutes to melt the chocolate. Whisk the chocolate mixture until smooth, then set aside to cool slightly, about 2 minutes. In a separate bowl, whisk the flour, salt, and baking soda together.

3. Process the melted chocolate mixture, brown sugar, oil, eggs, and vanilla together in a food processor until smooth, about 1 minute. Transfer the batter to a large bowl. Sift half of the flour mixture over the batter and gently whisk in. Repeat with the remaining flour mixture and continue to whisk the batter gently until most of the lumps are gone. (Do not overmix.)

4. Scrape the batter into the prepared pan and smooth the top. Tap the pan against the counter several times to settle the batter. Wipe any drops of batter off the sides of the pan. Bake the cake until a toothpick inserted into the center comes out with a few moist crumbs attached, 50 to 55 minutes, rotating the pan halfway through.

5. Let the cake cool in the pan for 10 minutes, then flip the cake onto a wire rack and let cool completely, about 1½ hours. Serve.

PER SERVING: Cal 320; **Fat** 11g; **Sat fat** 2g; **Chol** 25mg; **Carb** 51g; **Protein** 6g; **Fiber** 5g; **Sodium** 170mg

NOTES FROM THE TEST KITCHEN

THE BEST BUNDT PANS

The fluted, turban-shaped baking pans introduced by Nordic Ware as Bundt pans in the 1950s eventually gained widespread popularity, largely thanks to a slew of Bundt cake mixes marketed by Pillsbury. Today there are a number of brands available. We wondered which was best, so we tested eight so-called nonstick pans, each with a simple ridged design and a minimum capacity of 12 cups. We prepared our chocolate Bundt cake in each, as well vanilla cakes to test for evenness and depth of browning. The best performer overall was the **Nordic Ware Platinum Series 12-Cup Bundt Pan** (left), which was also the most expensive of the test group at $27.99. It had the best shape, with the most clearly defined ridges, and it browned the cake evenly and deeply and released it easily. Although the runner-up, **Baker's Secret Nonstick Fluted Tube Pan** (right), was made of lightweight material, it passed all of our tests with above-average results, and better yet, we picked it up at our local supermarket for $11.99.

ARE NONSTICK BAKING SPRAYS WORTHWHILE?

There's nothing worse than turning a loaf or cake pan over and seeing half a cake drop out. A coating of butter and flour does the trick, but we aren't wild about the crusty white "frost" it sometimes leaves behind on the cake. Could nonstick sprays do a better job? We tested two nonstick cooking sprays (vegetable or canola oil under aerosol pressure) and two baking sprays (nonstick cooking sprays with a flour component) for making a Bundt cake and a classic genoise cake. The cooking sprays—Pam and Everbake—worked fairly well, but they weren't perfect. The baking sprays, **Pam for Baking No-Stick Cooking Spray** (left) and **Baker's Joy** (right), worked well—every cake came out of the pan with nary a blemish. The uniformly blended flour-oil mixture made it easy to achieve an even coating, and the more solid texture of the baking sprays kept grease from pooling in the crevices, which can dull the ridges of a Bundt cake.

ANGEL FOOD CAKE

ANGEL FOOD CAKE HAS A VERY SHORT INGREDIENT list—mostly egg whites, sugar, and flour. But as with so many simple recipes, the devil is in the details. To name a few, if you don't sift the flour, separate the egg whites with tremendous care, and fold with a gentle touch, the majestic, snowy-white cake turns out depressingly dense, squat, and wet. Over seven weeks in the kitchen, we baked more than 100 angel food cakes to discover, once and for all, what matters, what doesn't, and how to achieve perfection. That's a tall order, but we rose to the challenge.

Unlike most other cakes, angel food cake contains no butter or oil—you don't even grease the cake pan. It doesn't require baking soda or baking powder, either, relying solely on beaten egg whites for its dramatic height. To make angel food cake, you whip egg whites with sugar and cream of tartar until white peaks form, fold in flour and flavorings, and bake.

Given the brevity of the recipe and the constancy of ingredients and basic method, it's puzzling how widely the outcomes can vary. Several experienced test cooks recently baked angel food cakes from nearly identical recipes on the same day in the same kitchen with the same equipment. Some of the cakes were tender and statuesque with a delicate crumb; others were misshapen and heavy. Why?

Reviewing all the various recipes, we grew intimidated by the many dire warnings. But we discovered several steps that made no difference or could be streamlined. We tested whipping both cold eggs whites and room-temperature egg whites and found that both will whip to the same volume (the room-temperature eggs will just take a few minutes longer). We also learned there is no need to panic if the whites are slightly under- or overbeaten. We tried making cakes with eggs in both conditions, several times, and all our cakes turned out respectably. And while your cake is baking, it doesn't matter one speck if you jump up and down in front of the oven or open the door to take a peek. Several times. Your cake won't fall.

As for the flour, some recipes call for sifting it up to eight times. We tried making a cake with flour at the opposite extreme, skipping sifting entirely, but the resulting cake was squat. After a multitude of tests, we came up with a creative solution that maximized the results. We put the flour in the food processor to aerate it quickly and then sifted it just once. We also found that cake flour was far superior to all-purpose. Whereas the latter produced cakes that tasters said had a texture resembling Wonder Bread, cake flour, which is finer than all-purpose, produced a delicate, tender crumb and was easier to incorporate into the whites. The exact amount of flour used was also critical. No matter what we tried, the cake was slightly wet and spongy when we used 1 cup of flour. But when we added just 2 tablespoons additional flour, our cake had flawlessly tender texture, test after test.

But the real key to angel food cake lies in voluminous, stable egg whites. We learned the hard way that the merest speck of yolk precludes whipping them to peaks; even just ½ teaspoon of yolk in 12 whites prevented peaks from forming. Adding cream of tartar to foamy whites is a step we found in many recipes, and one worth keeping since it offered insurance against deflated whites. It is acidic, which helps stabilize egg whites, as would lemon juice or vinegar, but we tested the latter two and, not surprisingly, the flavor was distractingly affected.

For the sugar, we tested cakes made with both plain granulated sugar and confectioners' sugar, and both were acceptable, but somewhat heavy. Simply putting the granulated sugar in the food processor gave us a happy medium: fine, light, and clump-free sugar that wouldn't deflate the egg whites.

After almost two months of baking a half-dozen cakes every day, we finally had what we thought was the perfect recipe. The true test came when we gave it to several inexperienced bakers. Without fail, each produced identical tall, sweet stunners. When asked if they'd run into any problems, their answer was better than angels singing: "Piece of cake!"

ANGEL FOOD CAKE

Angel Food Cake

SERVES 12

Cake flour is key in this recipe; do not use all-purpose flour. If your angel food cake pan does not have a removable bottom, line the bottom of the pan with parchment paper. In either case, do not grease the pan (or the paper).

- 1 cup plus 2 tablespoons (4½ ounces) cake flour (see note)
- ¼ teaspoon salt
- 1¾ cups (12¼ ounces) granulated sugar
- 12 large egg whites
- 1½ teaspoons cream of tartar
- 1 teaspoon vanilla extract

1. Adjust an oven rack to the lower-middle position and heat the oven to 325 degrees. Whisk the flour and salt together in a bowl. Process the sugar in a food processor until fine and powdery, about 1 minute. Reserve half of the sugar in a small bowl. Add the flour mixture to the food processor with the remaining sugar and process until aerated, about 1 minute.

2. In a large bowl, whip the egg whites and cream of tartar together with an electric mixer on medium-low speed until frothy, about 1 minute. Increase the mixer speed to medium-high. With the mixer running, slowly add the reserved sugar and beat until soft peaks form, about 6 minutes. Add the vanilla and mix until incorporated.

3. Sift the flour mixture over the egg whites in 3 additions, folding gently with a rubber spatula after each addition until incorporated. Scrape the batter into a 12-cup tube pan.

4. Bake the cake until a toothpick inserted into the center comes out clean and cracks in the cake appear dry, 40 to 45 minutes. Cool, inverted, to room temperature, about 3 hours. To unmold, run a knife along the interior of the pan. Turn the cake out onto a platter. Serve.

PER SERVING: Cal 170; Fat 0g; Sat fat 0g; Chol 0mg; Carb 38g; Protein 4g; Fiber 0g; Sodium 105mg

NOTES FROM THE TEST KITCHEN

SEPARATION ANXIETY

Most of the time when we're separating eggs, if a stray bit of yolk finds its way into the whites, we scoop it out with the eggshell. However, our Angel Food Cake depends entirely on whipped egg whites for lift, and even the barest trace of yolk spells ruin, so for this situation we are extra-careful. When we make this cake (or meringues), we separate the eggs with a three-bowl method. Should a yolk break, it won't spoil the entire bowl of whites.

1. Crack the egg over the first bowl and let the white fall into the bowl.

2. Drop the yolk into the second bowl.

3. Pour the white from the first bowl into the third bowl, then repeat the process with the remaining eggs.

OUR FAVORITE TUBE PAN

Tube pans are not just for looks—the tube helps these very tall cakes bake faster and more evenly. After testing six brands, baking angel food and yellow sponge cakes in each, we learned that what matters most is heft, finish (dark is better), and a removable bottom. Our favorite pan, the **Chicago Metallic Professional Nonstick Angel Food Cake Pan with Feet,** $19.95, also had feet on its rim, handy for elevating the upturned pan as the cake cooled.

VARIATIONS

Lemon-Poppy Seed Angel Food Cake

Follow the recipe for Angel Food Cake, adding 2 tablespoons grated zest and 2 tablespoons juice from 2 to 3 lemons along with the vanilla extract in step 2. Fold 1 tablespoon poppy seeds into the batter along with the flour in step 3.

PER SERVING: **Cal** 170; **Fat** 0g; **Sat fat** 0g; **Chol** 0mg; **Carb** 38g; **Protein** 5g; **Fiber** 0g; **Sodium** 105mg

Chocolate-Almond Angel Food Cake

Follow the recipe for Angel Food Cake, replacing ½ teaspoon of the vanilla extract with ½ teaspoon almond extract in step 2. Fold 2 ounces finely grated bittersweet chocolate into the batter along with the flour in step 3.

PER SERVING: **Cal** 190; **Fat** 1.5g; **Sat fat** 1g; **Chol** 0mg; **Carb** 41g; **Protein** 5g; **Fiber** 1g; **Sodium** 105mg

CARROT CAKE

MANY PEOPLE ARE UNDER THE ILLUSION THAT because its principal ingredient is a vegetable and it

TEST KITCHEN
MAKEOVER

uses oil (which has less saturated fat than butter), carrot cake must be a healthy dessert. What they forget is that a single serving can tip the scales at more than 500 calories and 31 grams of fat.

We gathered half a dozen so-called healthy recipes. The worst recipe of the bunch contained a predictable overabundance of ingredients like soy flour, flax seed meal, and tofu, and it produced a sodden cake with wobbly tofu icing. Recipes that incorporated fat-free dairy ingredients (sour cream, cream cheese, and mayonnaise) tasted artificial, and those that used fruit purees in place of fat made for cakes with the texture of damp sponges.

We decided to go with our tried-and-true method of starting with our winning high-fat carrot cake and then putting it on a diet. Right off the bat, we nixed the nuts and raisins—tasty, yes, but they weren't essential to the recipe and they added fat and calories. We started by halving the number of eggs (from four to two) used in our favorite carrot cake recipe, and we cut the amount of oil from 1½ cups to just ½ cup. To no one's surprise, this cake was dry and chalky. Since carrots contribute

much of the moisture, we decided to gradually increase their quantity in the hope of solving the problem without adding back fat. But in cake after cake, extra carrots made a batter that was difficult to spread and a cake that was too heavy. Ultimately, we realized that 1 pound of shredded carrots (what was used in the original recipe) was all we would be able to pack into our cake.

A recipe we'd tested early on used strained prunes in place of all the oil. It had made the cake unpleasantly bouncy, but on the upside that cake had been exceptionally moist. Maybe the prunes working in tandem with ½ cup of oil could produce a moist, tender cake. They did. Unfortunately, the prunes' dark color was all wrong, and this cake tasted like a cross between spice cake and fruitcake. Test cakes in which we combined oil with apple and pear purees didn't taste like carrot cakes, either. But pureed carrots—yes, baby food—contributed moisture and the right flavor.

The cake was now good enough to eat on its own, but no way would tasters pass up adding frosting. In most carrot cake icing recipes, cream cheese, butter, and confectioners' sugar are beaten together. Tasters rejected the batch we made with fat-free cream cheese as "unnatural" and gummy. The flavor of light cream cheese (less than half the fat of full-fat cream cheese) was better, but this frosting was runny. Neufchatel (cream cheese with one-third less fat) contributed just the right amount of heft and tang.

Replacing the butter in the icing was trickier. We needed something light and fluffy, like creamed butter. We rejected making our own meringue (too fussy) but figured marshmallow creme—which is made with egg whites, corn syrup, and sugar and is fat free—might work. Sure enough, the creme blended easily with the neufchatel, giving us just the right icing to top our lightened-up carrot cake. And with cake that had a whopping 30 grams less fat and 350 fewer calories than that original version, we all agreed: Mission accomplished.

MAKEOVER SPOTLIGHT: CARROT CAKE

	CALORIES	FAT	SAT FAT	CHOLESTEROL
BEFORE	500	31g	7g	80mg
AFTER	290	12g	3g	40mg

Carrot Cake

SERVES 15

Shred the carrots on the large holes of a box grater or with the shredding disk of a food processor. To ensure thick frosting, use marshmallow creme (such as Fluff or Kraft Jet-Puffed), not marshmallow sauce.

CAKE

Vegetable oil spray

2½ cups (12½ ounces) unbleached all-purpose flour

2 teaspoons baking powder

1½ teaspoons ground cinnamon

1 teaspoon baking soda

½ teaspoon freshly grated nutmeg

½ teaspoon salt

⅛ teaspoon ground cloves

2 large eggs

1 (4-ounce) jar carrot baby food

1 cup packed (7 ounces) dark brown sugar

½ cup canola oil

1 pound carrots, peeled and shredded (see note)

FROSTING

1 (8-ounce) package neufchatel cream cheese, softened (see note)

1 cup marshmallow creme (see note)

1½ teaspoons vanilla extract

¼ cup (1 ounce) confectioners' sugar

1. FOR THE CAKE: Adjust an oven rack to the middle position and heat the oven to 350 degrees. Lightly coat a 13 by 9-inch baking pan with vegetable oil spray, line the bottom of the pan with parchment paper, and set aside.

2. Whisk the flour, baking powder, cinnamon, baking soda, nutmeg, salt, and cloves together in a medium bowl. In a large bowl, beat the eggs, baby food, and sugar together with an electric mixer on medium speed until smooth and creamy, 1 to 2 minutes. With the mixer still running, slowly add the oil and mix until thoroughly incorporated, about 1 minute. Reduce the mixer speed to low. Add the flour mixture in two additions, scraping down the bowl and beaters as needed, and mix until the batter is nearly smooth. Fold in the carrots by hand.

3. Scrape the batter into the prepared pan and smooth the top. Tap the pan against the counter several times to settle the batter. Bake the cake until a toothpick inserted into the center comes out with a few moist crumbs attached, 24 to 28 minutes, rotating the pan halfway through.

4. Let the cake cool in the pan for 10 minutes. Run a paring knife around the edge of the cake and flip the cake onto a wire rack. Peel off the parchment paper, flip the cake right-side up, and let the cake cool completely, about 1½ hours.

5. FOR THE FROSTING: In a medium bowl, beat the cream cheese, marshmallow creme, and vanilla together with an electric mixer on medium-high speed until combined. Sift the confectioners' sugar over the cream cheese mixture and beat on low speed until the mixture is smooth, about 1 minute.

6. Spread the frosting evenly over the top and sides of the cake and serve.

PER SERVING: **Cal** 290; **Fat** 12g; **Sat fat** 3g; **Chol** 40mg; **Carb** 41g; **Protein** 5g; **Fiber** 2g; **Sodium** 340mg

NOTES FROM THE TEST KITCHEN

SECRETS TO A LIGHTER CARROT CAKE

To give our reduced-fat, reduced-calorie carrot cake the flavor and texture of a full-fat cake, we had to get a little creative.

CARROT BABY FOOD
Just one tub of carrot baby food adds moisture and a mild carroty sweetness. (Look for brands that contain only carrots and water.)

MARSHMALLOW CREME
Using marshmallow creme in place of some of the butter and sugar yields a thick, rich frosting with no additional fat.

OUR FAVORITE VEGETABLE PEELER

When peeling carrots (or any vegetable) in bulk, a lightweight vegetable peeler is a nice bonus. Hoping to find a relatively light, sharp peeler, we tested four models. The Kyocera Ceramic Perfect Peeler, $17.95, and **Messermeister Pro-Touch Swivel Peeler,** $5.95, passed every peeling test with flying colors, including the toughest of all: tomatoes. Although we like the adjustable blade on the Kyocera (which weighs just 2.2 ounces), testers preferred the slightly smoother motion of the 1.5-ounce Messermeister peeler, which they found comfortable even after peeling piles of apples and potatoes. It's our favorite.

Conversions and Equivalencies

SOME SAY COOKING IS A SCIENCE AND AN ART. We would say that geography has a hand in it, too. Flour milled in the United Kingdom and elsewhere will feel and taste different from flour milled in the United States. So, while we cannot promise that the loaf of bread you bake in Canada or England will taste the same as a loaf baked in the States, we can offer guidelines for converting weights and measures. We also recommend that you rely on your instincts when making our recipes. Refer to the visual cues provided. If the bread dough hasn't "come together in a ball," as described, you may need to add more flour—even if the recipe doesn't tell you so. You be the judge.

The recipes in this book were developed using standard U.S. measures following U.S. government guidelines. The charts below offer equivalents for U.S., metric, and Imperial (U.K.) measures. All conversions are approximate and have been rounded up or down to the nearest whole number. For example:

1 teaspoon = 4.929 milliliters, rounded up to 5 milliliters
1 ounce = 28.349 grams, rounded down to 28 grams

VOLUME CONVERSIONS

U.S.	METRIC
1 teaspoon	5 milliliters
2 teaspoons	10 milliliters
1 tablespoon	15 milliliters
2 tablespoons	30 milliliters
¼ cup	59 milliliters
⅓ cup	79 milliliters
½ cup	118 milliliters
¾ cup	177 milliliters
1 cup	237 milliliters
1¼ cups	296 milliliters
1½ cups	355 milliliters
2 cups	473 milliliters
2½ cups	592 milliliters
3 cups	710 milliliters
4 cups (1 quart)	0.946 liter
1.06 quarts	1 liter
4 quarts (1 gallon)	3.8 liters

WEIGHT CONVERSIONS

OUNCES	GRAMS
½	14
¾	21
1	28
1½	43
2	57
2½	71
3	85
3½	99
4	113
4½	128
5	142
6	170
7	198
8	227
9	255
10	283
12	340
16 (1 pound)	454

CONVERSIONS FOR INGREDIENTS COMMONLY USED IN BAKING

Baking is an exacting science. Because measuring by weight is far more accurate than measuring by volume, and thus more likely to achieve reliable results, in our recipes we provide ounce measures in addition to cup measures for many ingredients. Refer to the chart below to convert these measures into grams.

INGREDIENT	OUNCES	GRAMS
Flour		
1 cup all-purpose flour*	5	142
1 cup cake flour	4	113
1 cup whole wheat flour	5½	156
Sugar		
1 cup granulated (white) sugar	7	198
1 cup packed brown sugar (light or dark)	7	198
1 cup confectioners' sugar	4	113
Cocoa Powder		
1 cup cocoa powder	3	85
Butter†		
4 tablespoons (½ stick, or ¼ cup)	2	57
8 tablespoons (1 stick, or ½ cup)	4	113
16 tablespoons (2 sticks, or 1 cup)	8	227

* U.S. all-purpose flour, the most frequently used flour in this book, does not contain leaveners, as some European flours do. These leavened flours are called self-rising or self-raising. If you are using self-rising flour, take this into consideration before adding leavening to a recipe.
† In the United States, butter is sold both salted and unsalted. We generally recommend unsalted butter. If you are using salted butter, take this into consideration before adding salt to a recipe.

OVEN TEMPERATURES

FAHRENHEIT	CELSIUS	GAS MARK (imperial)
225	105	¼
250	120	½
275	130	1
300	150	2
325	165	3
350	180	4
375	190	5
400	200	6
425	220	7
450	230	8
475	245	9

CONVERTING TEMPERATURES FROM AN INSTANT-READ THERMOMETER

We include doneness temperatures in many of our recipes, such as those for poultry, meat, and bread. We recommend an instant-read thermometer for the job. Refer to the table above to convert Fahrenheit degrees to Celsius. Or, for temperatures not represented in the chart, use this simple formula:

Subtract 32 degrees from the Fahrenheit reading, then divide the result by 1.8 to find the Celsius reading.

EXAMPLE:

"Roast until the thickest part of a chicken thigh registers 175 degrees on an instant-read thermometer." To convert:

175° F − 32 = 143°
143° ÷ 1.8 = 79° C (rounded down from 79.44)

Index

D

Desserts

  Cakes

    Angel Food, 281–83, *282*

    Angel Food, Chocolate-Almond, 284

    Angel Food, Lemon–Poppy Seed, 284

    Carrot, *260,* 284–85

    Chocolate Bundt, 279–80

  Chocolate Marble Cheesecake, 277–78

  Cookies and bars

    Big and Chewy Chocolate Chip Cookies, 262–64

    Fudgy Brownies, 267–68

    Oatmeal-Raisin Cookies, 264–66, *265*

  see also Fruit desserts

Dutch ovens, ratings of, 64

E

Easy Roast Turkey Breast, 73–75

Eggplant

  and Beef, Stir-Fried, in Oyster Sauce, 89–90

  Mushrooms, and Goat Cheese,

    Vegetable Pizza with, 138–39

  Parmesan, 142–44

  Sweet Potatoes, Green Beans,

    and Chickpeas, Vegetable Curry with, 157

Eggs

  Frittata with Asparagus, Mushrooms,

    and Goat Cheese, 253

  Frittata with Spinach, Bell Pepper, and Basil, 252–53

  separating yolks and whites, 283

  Spaghetti Carbonara, 121–22

Equipment, ratings of

  Bundt pans, 280

  cookie sheets, 266

  Dutch ovens, inexpensive, 64

  fish spatulas, 148

  food processors, 97

  garlic presses, 28

  juicers, inexpensive, 12

  knives, carving, 93

  ladles, 29

  mandolines, 234

  muffin tins, 244

  pizza cutters, 138

  saucepans, 203

  skillets, nonstick inexpensive, 90

  tart pans, 158

  thermometers, instant-read, 81

  tube pans, 283

  vegetable peelers, 285

F

Fennel

  Leeks, and Saffron, Hearty Chicken Stew with, 43–45

  preparing, 44

Feta

  Breakfast Strata, 253–55

  and Broccoli, Roasted Vegetable Pizza with, 135–37, *136*

  Cherry Tomatoes, Olives, and Mint,

    Sautéed Chicken Breasts with, *52,* 54–55

  Greek Grilled Stuffed Chicken Breasts, 166

  shopping for, 219

  Stuffed Zucchini, 217–20, *218*

Fish

  Baked Cod Provençal, 106–7

  Grilled, Tacos, 180–81

  Halibut en Papillote with

    Zucchini and Tomatoes, *98,* 100–101

  Oven-Fried, *108,* 109–11

  Salmon

    Apricot-Orange Glazed, 103

    Balsamic Glazed, 101–2

    fillets, skinning, 105

    Poached, Salad with Potatoes and Green Beans, 17–18

    Poached, with Herb-Caper Vinaigrette, 103–6, *104*

    Poached, with Herb-Dijon Vinaigrette, 106

    primer on, 105

    Wood-Grilled, 177–78, *179*

    Wood-Grilled, Barbecued, 178

    Wood-Grilled, Chinese, 178

    Wood-Grilled, Lemon-Thyme, 178

  storing, 103

Fish sauce, taste tests on, 69

Fish spatulas, ratings of, 148

Five-spice powder, taste tests on, 130

Flame tamer (heat diffuser), makeshift, 152

Foil sling, for brownies, 268

Fontina cheese

  Grilled Herb-Stuffed Chicken Breasts, 164–65

  Spinach Lasagna, 131–34, *132*

Food processors, ratings of, 97

Fries, Crunchy Oven, 230–31

Fries, Home, Greek Diner-Style, 231–33

Frittata with Asparagus,

  Mushrooms, and Goat Cheese, 253

Frittata with Spinach, Bell Pepper, and Basil, 252–53

Fruit

  citrus, segmenting, 16

  Tropical, Granola, 259

  see also Fruit desserts; *specific fruits*

Fruit desserts

  Blueberry Grunt, 272–73

  Cider-Baked Apples with Dried Cranberries, 275–76

  Cider-Baked Apples with Fresh Ginger and Orange, 276

  Cider-Baked Apples with Rum and Golden Raisins, 276

  Pan-Roasted Peaches, 273–75, *274*

  Pan-Roasted Plums, 275

  Peach Shortcakes, 268–71, *270*

Fudgy Brownies, 267–68

G

Garam masala, taste tests on, 157
Garden Minestrone, *22,* 24–25
Garlic
  and Chiles, Grilled Marinated Flank Steak with, 173
  and Herbs, Sautéed Green Beans with, 224, *225*
  and Olives, Roasted Broccoli with, 215
  prepeeled, about, 101
  and Rosemary, Grilled Marinated
    Flank Steak with, 172–73
  and Sun-Dried Tomato Cheese Bread, 249
Garlic presses, ratings of, 28
Ginger
  -Apple Chutney, Quick, 79
  and Chiles, Grilled Shrimp with, 184
  -Cranberry Granola, 259
  Curried Rice Salad, 193–95, *194*
  Fresh, and Orange, Cider-Baked Apples with, 276
  grating, tip for, 195
Glazed Butternut Squash, 220–21
Goat Cheese
  Asparagus, and Mushrooms, Frittata with, 253
  Eggplant, and Mushrooms,
    Vegetable Pizza with, 138–39
  Grilled Vegetable and Bread Salad, 187–89, *188*
  and Red Onion, Sautéed Green Beans with, 226
  Spinach, and Sun-Dried Tomatoes,
    Breakfast Strata with, 255
  Stuffed Portobello Mushrooms, 145–48, *146*
Grains
  Barley Risotto, 200–201
  Bulgur Pilaf with Mushrooms, 201–3
  Creamy Polenta with
    Wild Mushrooms, Spinach, and Tomatoes, 152–53
  Multigrain Banana Pancakes, 258
  Multigrain Blueberry Pancakes, 258
  Multigrain Pancakes, 255–58, *256*
  Mushroom-Barley Soup, 40–42
  quinoa, draining and drying, 205
  Quinoa Pilaf, 203–4
  Quinoa Pilaf with Corn and Jalapeños, 204–5
  Wheat Berry and Arugula Salad, 19–21, *20*
  see also Oats; Rice
Granola, Toasted, 258–59
  Cranberry-Ginger, 259
  Tropical Fruit, 259
Grapefruit
  and Avocado, Poached Shrimp Salad with, *1,* 18–19
  segmenting, 16
  -Tarragon Sauce, Pan-Roasted
    Chicken Breasts with, 62–63
Greek Diner-Style Home Fries, 231–33
Greek Grilled Stuffed Chicken Breasts, 166

Green Beans
  Garden Minestrone, *22,* 24–25
  and Potatoes, Poached Salmon Salad with, 17–18
  Sautéed
    with Garlic and Herbs, 224, *225*
    with Red Onion and Goat Cheese, 226
    with Thyme, Coriander, and Sesame, 226
  Sweet Potatoes, Eggplant,
    and Chickpeas, Vegetable Curry with, 157
  trimming, tip for, 226
Greens
  Asian Chicken Noodle Soup, 29–30
  kale, preparing, 49
  Rustic White Bean Stew, 48–49
  Wheat Berry and Arugula Salad, 19–21, *20*
  Winter, Braised, 226–28, *227*
  see also Cabbage; Lettuce; Spinach
Gremolata, 150
Grilled dishes
  Barbecued Pulled Chicken, 167
  Grilled Chicken Breasts
    with Apricot-Mustard Glaze, 162–63
    with Barbecue Glaze, 163
    with Hoisin-Sesame Glaze, 163
  Grilled Fish Tacos, 180–81
  Grilled Glazed Tofu, 186–87
  Grilled Marinated Flank Steak
    with Garlic and Chiles, 173
    with Garlic and Rosemary, 172–73
  Grilled Pork Chops and Peaches, 175–77
  Grilled Scallops with Orange-Chili Vinaigrette, 184–85
  Grilled Shrimp
    with Chiles and Ginger, 184
    Lemon, 181–83, *182*
    New Orleans, 184
  Grilled Stuffed Chicken Breasts
    Greek, 166
    Herb-Stuffed, 164–65
    Tex-Mex, 165
  Grilled Turkey Burgers, *168,* 169–70
  Grilled Vegetable and Bread Salad, 187–89, *188*
  Smoked Pork Loin, *160,* 173–75
  Smoked Turkey Breast, 170–71
  Wood-Grilled Salmon, 177–78, *179*
    Barbecued, 178
    Chinese, 178
    Lemon-Thyme, 178
Grills
  adding wood chips to, 166
  checking propane level for, 169
  gauging heat level, 162
Ground Turkey Tacos, 72–73
Grunt, Blueberry, 272–73

H

Halibut en Papillote with
    Zucchini and Tomatoes, *98*, 100–101
Hearty Chicken Stew
    with Leeks, Fennel, and Saffron, 43–45
Heat diffuser (flame tamer), makeshift, 152
Herb(s)
    -Caper Vinaigrette, Poached Salmon with, 103–6, *104*
    -Dijon Vinaigrette, Poached Salmon with, 106
    Herbed Rice Pilaf, *190*, 192–93
    -Lemon Sauce, Creamy, 115
    -Stuffed Chicken Breasts, Grilled, 164–65
    wilted, refreshing, 32
    see also specific herbs
Hoisin (sauce)
    Chinese Chicken Salad, 6–7
    -Sesame Glaze, Grilled Chicken Breasts with, 163
    taste tests on, 7
Honey-Mustard Glazed Tofu, 155
Horseradish Sauce, Slow-Roasted Beef with, 92–93
Hot sauce, taste tests on, 5

I

Indian Curried Chickpeas, 205–6
Ingredients, tastings of
    balsamic vinegar, 103
    blue cheese, 5
    butternut squash, precut vs. whole, 38
    capers, 57
    chicken breasts, boneless, skinless, 54
    chicken broth, 29
    chickpeas, canned, 206
    chipotle chiles, 208
    corn tortillas, 32
    curry powder, 157
    Dijon mustard, 115
    feta cheese, 219
    fish sauce, 69
    five-spice powder, 130
    garam masala, 157
    hoisin sauce, 7
    hot sauce, 5
    lasagna noodles, no-boil, 133
    mayonnaise, 3
    molasses, 84
    nonstick baking sprays, 280
    oats, rolled, 259
    Old Bay Seasoning, 115
    olive oil, extra-virgin, 21
    olives, kalamata, 54
    orange juice, 70
    Parmesan, supermarket, 143
    parsley, 203

Ingredients, tastings of *(cont.)*
    pickles, 166
    rice, Arborio, 150
    rice, basmati, 66
    roasted red peppers, 197
    salmon, 105
    sandwich bread, 110
    soba noodles, 10
    sweet potatoes, 236
    tempeh, 51
    tomatoes, canned diced, 143
    vinegar, cider, 220
    vinegar, red wine, 216
    white beans, canned, 229
    white wines, for cooking, 107

J

Juicers, inexpensive, ratings of, 12

K

Kale
    preparing, 49
    Rustic White Bean Stew, 48–49
Knives, carving, ratings of, 93

L

Ladles, ratings of, 29
Lasagna
    noodles, no-boil, taste tests on, 133
    Spinach, 131–34, *132*
Leeks
    Fennel, and Saffron, Hearty Chicken Stew with, 43–45
    Spring Vegetable Risotto, 149–50, *151*
    Spring Vegetable Soup, 25–27
Lemon(s)
    Chicken Piccata, 55–58, *56*
    Gremolata, 150
    -Herb Sauce, Creamy, 115
    Linguine with Fresh Clam Sauce, 127
    –Poppy Seed Angel Food Cake, 284
    Shrimp, and Garlic, Linguine with, 125–27
    Shrimp, Grilled, 181–83, *182*
    -Thyme Wood-Grilled Salmon, 178
Lentil(s)
    Salad with Walnuts and Scallions, 209
    Soup, 42–43
    sweating, effect of, 42
Lettuce
    Buffalo Chicken Salad, 4–5
    Chicken Caesar Salad, 2–4

N

New Orleans Grilled Shrimp, 184
No-Cook Pizza Sauce, 139
Nonstick baking sprays, taste tests on, 280
Noodle(s)
    Asian Chicken Noodle Soup, 29–30
    lasagna, no-boil, taste tests on, 133
    Pork Lo Mein, 127–31, *129*
    soba, about, 10
    Soba, Cold, Salad with Chicken, 7–9
    Soba, Cold, Salad with Tofu, *8,* 9–10
Nuts
    Lentil Salad with Walnuts and Scallions, 209
    Toasted Granola, 258–59
        Cranberry-Ginger, 259
        Tropical Fruit, 259
    toasting, 16
    see also Almond(s)

O

Oatmeal-Raisin Cookies, 264–66, *265*
Oats
    Oatmeal-Raisin Cookies, 264–66, *265*
    rolled, taste tests on, 259
    Toasted Granola, 258–59
        Cranberry-Ginger, 259
        Tropical Fruit, 259
Old Bay Seasoning, about, 115
Olive oil, extra-virgin, taste tests on, 21
Olives
    Cherry Tomatoes, Feta, and Mint, Sautéed Chicken
        Breasts with, *52,* 54–55
    and Garlic, Roasted Broccoli with, 215
    kalamata, taste tests on, 54
    Roasted Vegetable Pizza
        with Broccoli and Feta, 135–37, *136*
    Stuffed Zucchini, 217–20, *218*
    and White Beans, Marinated Tomato Salad with, 229–30
Onion(s)
    Caramelized, Spice-Rubbed
        Pork Roast en Cocotte with, 81–82
    Chicken Biryani, 65–67
    chopping, and eye protection, 228
    Red, and Goat Cheese, Sautéed Green Beans with, 226
    and Roasted Red Peppers, Brown Rice with, 195–96
Orange(s)
    -Chili Vinaigrette, Grilled Scallops with, 184–85
    -Cranberry Muffins, 245
    -Cranberry Sauce, Simple, 75
    orange juice, taste tests on, 70
    and Pan-Seared Scallops,
        Wilted Spinach Salad with, 13–16, *14*
    segmenting, 16
Oven-Fried Fish, *108,* 109–11

P

Pancakes, Multigrain, 255–58, *256*
Pancakes, Multigrain Banana, 258
Pancakes, Multigrain Blueberry, 258
Pan-Roasted Chicken Breasts
    with Grapefruit-Tarragon Sauce, 62–63
    with Lemon-Herb Sauce, 60–61
    with Spicy Thai Sauce, 62
Pan-Roasted Peaches, 273–75, *274*
Pan-Roasted Plums, 275
Pan-Seared Inexpensive Steak
    with Hearty Mushroom Sauce, 85–86
Pan-Seared Scallops, 111–12
Parmesan
    Barley Risotto, 200–201
    Cheese Bread, 247–48
        Chipotle, 249
        Roasted Red Pepper and Scallion, 249
        Sun-Dried Tomato and Garlic, 249
    Cheesy Broccoli and Rice Casserole, 197–200, *199*
    Chicken Caesar Salad, 2–4
    Eggplant, 142–44
    Frittata with Spinach, Bell Pepper, and Basil, 252–53
    Scalloped Potatoes, 233–35
    Skillet Baked Ziti, 134–35
    Spinach Lasagna, 131–34, *132*
    taste tests on, 143
    Vegetable Tart, *140,* 158–59
Parsley
    curly versus flat-leaf, taste tests on, 203
    Greek Grilled Stuffed Chicken Breasts, 166
    Gremolata, 150
    wilted, refreshing, 32
Parsnips
    about, 223
    and Carrots, Skillet-Roasted, 221–23, *222*
        with Garlic and Thyme, 223
        with Honey and Orange, 223
Pasta
    with Butternut Squash and Sage, *116,* 118–19
    lasagna noodles, no-boil, taste tests on, 133
    Linguine with Fresh Clam Sauce, 127
    Linguine with Shrimp, Lemon, and Garlic, 125–27
    Penne with Chicken and Summer Vegetables, 119–20
    Pesto Salad with Chicken and Vegetables, 10–12
    Pork Lo Mein, 127–31, *129*
    Skillet Baked Ziti, 134–35
    Spaghetti and Meatballs, 122–25, *123*
    Spaghetti Carbonara, 121–22
    Spinach Lasagna, 131–34, *132*
    Tortellini and Vegetable Soup, 27–28
    see also Couscous; Noodle(s)
Peach(es)
    Pan-Roasted, 273–75, *274*
    peeling, 270
    and Pork Chops, Grilled, 175–77
    Shortcakes, 268–71, *270*
    storing, 176